AF477029

CORNISH RAILWAYS

IMAGES OF
CORNISH RAILWAYS

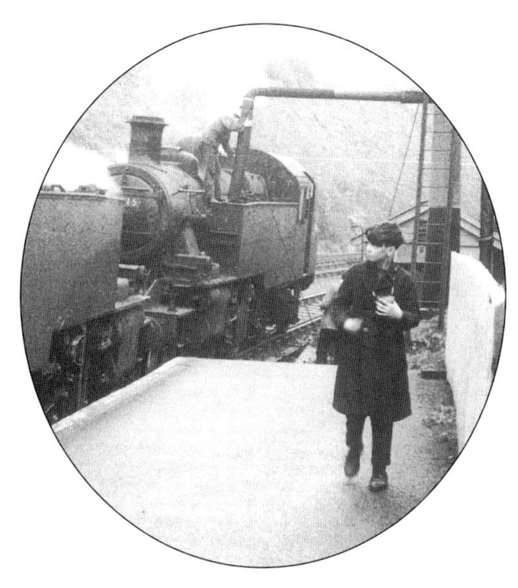

CLASSIC PHOTOGRAPHS FROM
THE MAURICE DART RAILWAY COLLECTION

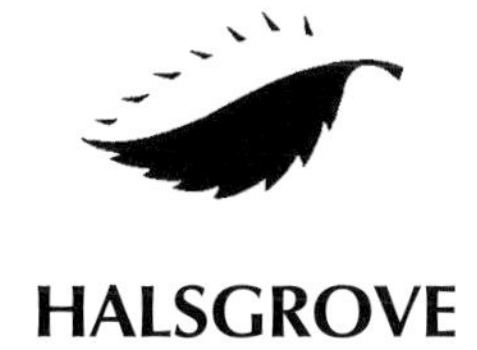

HALSGROVE

British Library Cataloguing-in-Publication Data
A CIP record for this title is available from the British Library

ISBN 978 1 84114 587 7

HALSGROVE
Halsgrove House,
Ryelands Industrial Estate,
Bagley Road, Wellington, Somerset TA21 9PZ
Tel: 01823 653777   Fax: 01823 216796
email: sales@halsgrove.com

Part of the Halsgrove group of companies
Information on all Halsgrove titles is available at: www.halsgrove.com

Printed and bound in Great Britain by CPI Antony Rowe Ltd., Wiltshire

CONTENTS

INTRODUCTION

Most Saturday afternoons my parents would take me with them to either Devonport, reached by tram, or Plymouth, to which we caught a motor train to Millbay. So my interest in railways steadily developed. During the summers of 1937, 1938 and 1939, the three of us spent a week travelling by train to Torquay, Paignton or Goodrington, with sometimes a venture to Kingswear and across to Dartmouth on the 'MEW', or to Dawlish Warren. We used a family holiday runabout ticket for the week and set out from St Budeaux on an excursion train that ran daily from Saltash to Paignton and which, from memory, was usually hauled by a Castle class locomotive to Newton Abbot. From our front downstairs and bedroom windows at Higher St Budeaux I was able to watch trains in the distance as they ran around the curves west of Saltash station. I asked my father on one occasion why we did not go to Cornwall instead of to Paignton and he replied that it was better to go up the line. This was probably because there was a daily excursion train from Saltash to Paignton, although we frequently had to change trains at Newton Abbot and cross over the footbridge. So, apart from going over on the ferry from Saltash Passage to Saltash one Sunday morning in 1938 to see 'KING GEORGE VI' (yes, I was taken to see a King class locomotive in Cornwall) which was viewed from the gate at the entrance to the goods yard, I had to wait for the war years to enter Cornwall by train.

My father would also bring home books about railways. They had been loaned to him for me to look at and they contained many photographs of railway subjects. During the Second World War I was evacuated to Bude by train from Friary. I stood in the corridor for most of the way to 'see where I was going' much to the consternation of the WVS ladies who were accompanying us. This was followed by a period at St Austell using trains to and from North Road. Whilst there, at the evacuated Grammar school, I met many older boys who were railway enthusiasts and my 'railway education' commenced properly.

My father had been transferred from Devonport to the Dockyard at Gibraltar during 1944, and in the summer of 1947 I went there by sea for a holiday for several weeks. My father was an amateur photographer and whilst there he taught me to use a box camera. I immediately started taking photographs of Gibraltar Dockyard locomotives from a balcony!

On returning to St Budeaux I found my father's two old cameras and managed to obtain a film for each. A large folding Kodak that used A-122 film turned out to have a pin hole in the bellows, only discovered when the results of the first film were seen. This made it unusable. The other was an old Box Brownie which had a push-over lever shutter release and had one good and one faulty viewfinder that showed two images, one above the other. I persevered with this but did not know enough to achieve much success. I tried to record trains passing through St Budeaux and went to Laira shed late in September and took photos, some against the low evening sun. Still, we all had to learn by experience. With those which I had taken at Gibraltar, this was the start of my collection of railway photographs. Later, my employment brought me to lodge at St Austell where I finally took up permanent residence.

As time progressed I was able to buy better cameras and commenced longer railway trips to places further afield. My railway interest widened from purely collecting engine names and numbers to encompass signalling and railway history. This was progressed by meeting more very knowledgeable older railway enthusiasts and railwaymen, many of whom became lifelong friends of mine. I developed a desire to obtain photographs of some of the locomotives that I had seen in my early years, so the process of searching for and purchasing photos commenced. As my interest and knowledge grew, so likewise did the quest for more photos. This now encompassed all of Devon and Cornwall and large sections of Wales, along with various classes of locomotives from all over the country. An interest in narrow gauge and industrial railways developed. So the 'Archive' steadily grew from filling an expanding suitcase to occupying a considerable expanse of shelf space in two rooms.

When it was suggested that I compile some books making use of some of these images I thought that it would be a great idea as many of them, to the best of my knowledge, had not previously been used in publications. The first book covers Plymouth and South Devon, and this, the second volume, covers all of Cornwall. With so many photos available the choice has been difficult but constraints such as copyright and previous use have been considered. I have tried not to include many frequently photographed locations. Some older historic images are included but I have attempted to give a good overall coverage of the area from around 1900 to the present day. I have included a representative selection of diesels and also some industrial scenes to attempt to cater for all interests. So many photographs of the preservation era have been published that I have avoided this period with a couple of exceptions. I have also included some items which are not photographically perfect but are worthy of insertion because of their content. Some of the period scenes include infrastructure. These images may be of great interest to modellers of historic locomotives with period layouts. The variety of different locomotive types recorded has rendered it impossible to include sections portraying stations, sidings, signal boxes, tunnels and viaducts.

As this, and hopefully subsequent books, will feature images from my personal collection, the layout follows the order in which the collection is arranged. This follows locomotive wheel arrangement and types from the largest downwards in decreasing order of size, with a few exceptions. This is a system that was used in the past by several notable authors. It presents a markedly different layout to the now standard practice of following routes geographically. However, with my Cornish photos, as I am heavily involved with the Bodmin & Wenford Railway, in my collection I have a separate section for any photos taken of lines and locomotives in that area. Readers seeking photos at specific locations should refer to the index of locations at the end of the book.

I have attempted to make the captions detailed without delving too deeply into railway history or becoming too technical. Any errors that are discovered are purely attributable to myself. I trust that within the contents there is material to cater for most railway interests and that memories of a bygone age of railways will be recalled.

ACKNOWLEDGEMENTS

I express special thanks to my friend of many years, Mike Daly, and also to Kenneth Brown for permission to reproduce photos taken by them. Likewise I express thanks for permission to use photos which I have purchased from the collections of the Stephenson Locomotive Society, The Locomotive Club of Great Britain (Ken Nunn collection) and Rail Archive Stephenson (Photomatic). Also my thanks and apologies are proffered to other photographers whose work has been used and not credited. Where no credit is given the photographer is unknown. I also extend my thanks to Steve Jenkins for advice when describing some of the carriage and wagon stock and to Gillian Searle for checking the proofs and for suggesting amendments. I am also indebted to Simon Butler of Halsgrove for suggesting the idea of this series of books.

REFERENCE SOURCES

A Detailed History of British Railways Standard Steam Locomotives. RCTS.
A Regional History of the Railways of Great Britain. Vol.1. The West Country.
David St.John Thomas. David & Charles.
British Railways Locomotive Stock Changes and Withdrawal Dates. 1948 –1968. Michael McManus.
British Railways Steam Locomotives 1948 – 1968. Hugh Longworth. OPC.
GWR Locomotive Allocations. J.W.P.Rowledge. David & Charles.
Locomotives of the Great Western Railway. RCTS.
Locomotives of the LSWR. D.L.Bradley. RCTS.
Locomotives of the Southern Railway. D.L.Bradley. RCTS.
The Allocation History of BR Diesels & Electrics. Roger Harris.
Track Layout Diagrams of the GWR/BRWR. R.A.Cooke.
My personal notebooks dating from 1945.

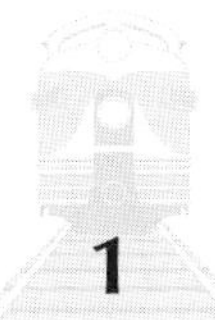

EIGHT COUPLED ENGINES

This section includes the well respected GWR 2800 and 2884 class 2-8-0s, which were capable of hauling trains of one hundred loaded coal wagons. It has often been stated that these locomotives rarely entered Cornwall but that is a fallacy. During the Second World War and for several years afterwards, they were frequent visitors to the Duchy. In the run up to and for several weeks following D-Day, there was an almost continuous stream of these engines working trains of munitions bound for Falmouth. Also included are the GWR eight coupled tanks, several different members being based at St Blazey to work trains over the steeply graded lines via Pinnock tunnel to Fowey and to St Dennis Junction via Luxulyan bank. For around eighteen months during 1951-52, one of the GWR 7200 class 2-8-2Ts, 7209, was based at St Blazey. Also, in 1951 several other members of the class spent a few weeks at St Blazey. Unfortunately no photos of these locos working in Cornwall have come to light, the nearest being a shot of one of them working a down goods past St Budeaux West which does not qualify for inclusion in this volume. Also, despite LMS 8F 8435 being based at Penzance and other members of the type from Laira working into Cornwall during 1944-45, no photos of these have been located. One WD 2–8-0 is reported as having been under repair at St Blazey in the 1940s but no photos have been found. The reasons for this lack of photos were the wartime restrictions on photography as well as the non-availability of film.

2800 class 2-8-0 2810 from Aberdare shed keeps company with the Breakdown train in the shed yard at Truro in 1947. An engine from that Welsh shed would have been a rare visitor to Cornwall. Truro West Signal Box is behind the breakdown train. Kenneth Brown collection.

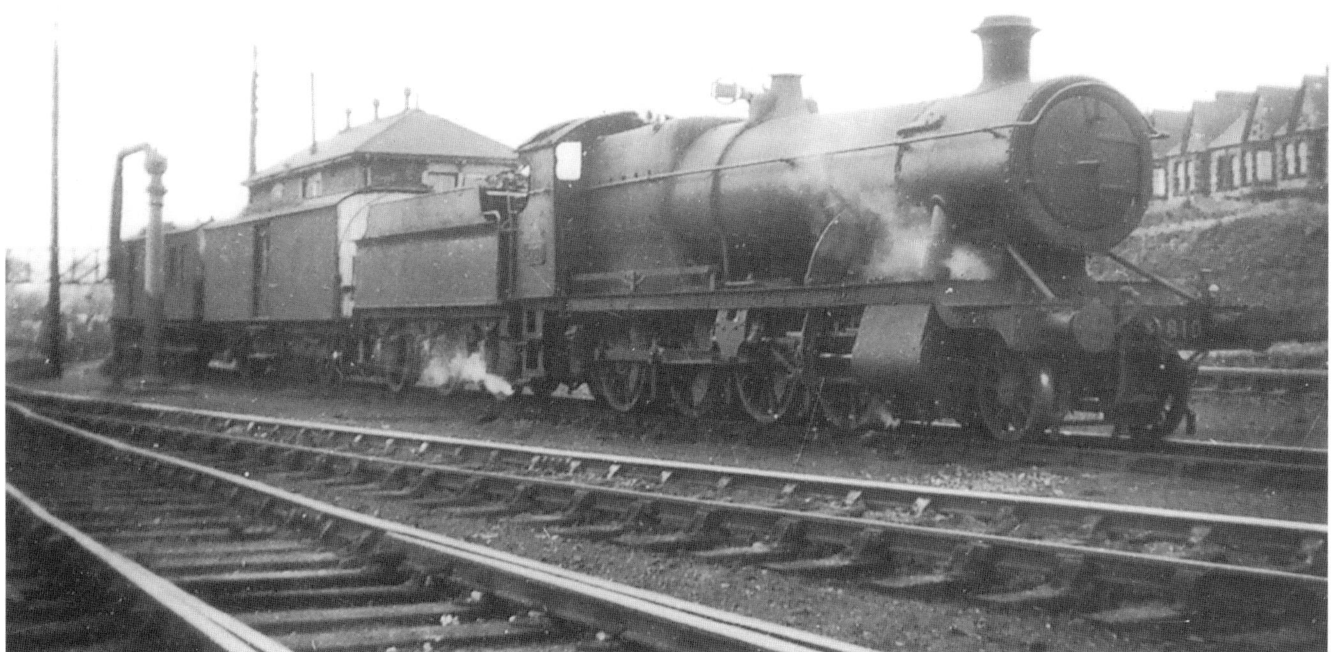

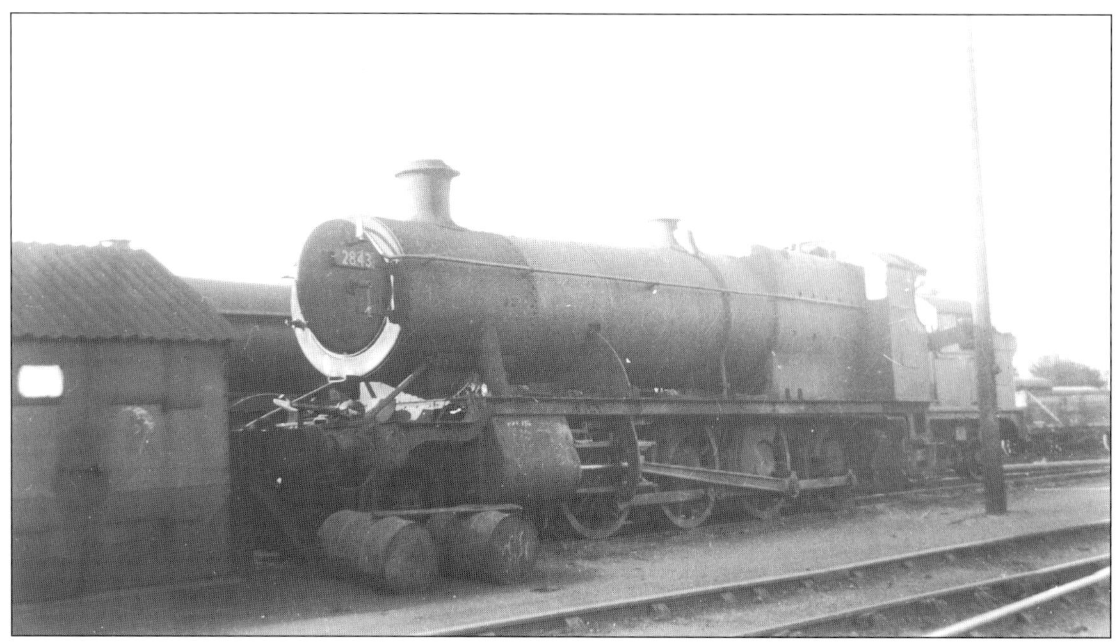

It was very unusual to find a 2-8-0 under repair in Cornwall but on 24 May 1956, 2800 class 2843 from Laira shed was in the yard at Truro shed with its smokebox door open. It was waiting to be re-united with its tender which was in the one road Works receiving attention for a 'Hot Box'. 4575 class 2-6-2T 4587 is behind the 2-8-0. Maurice Dart

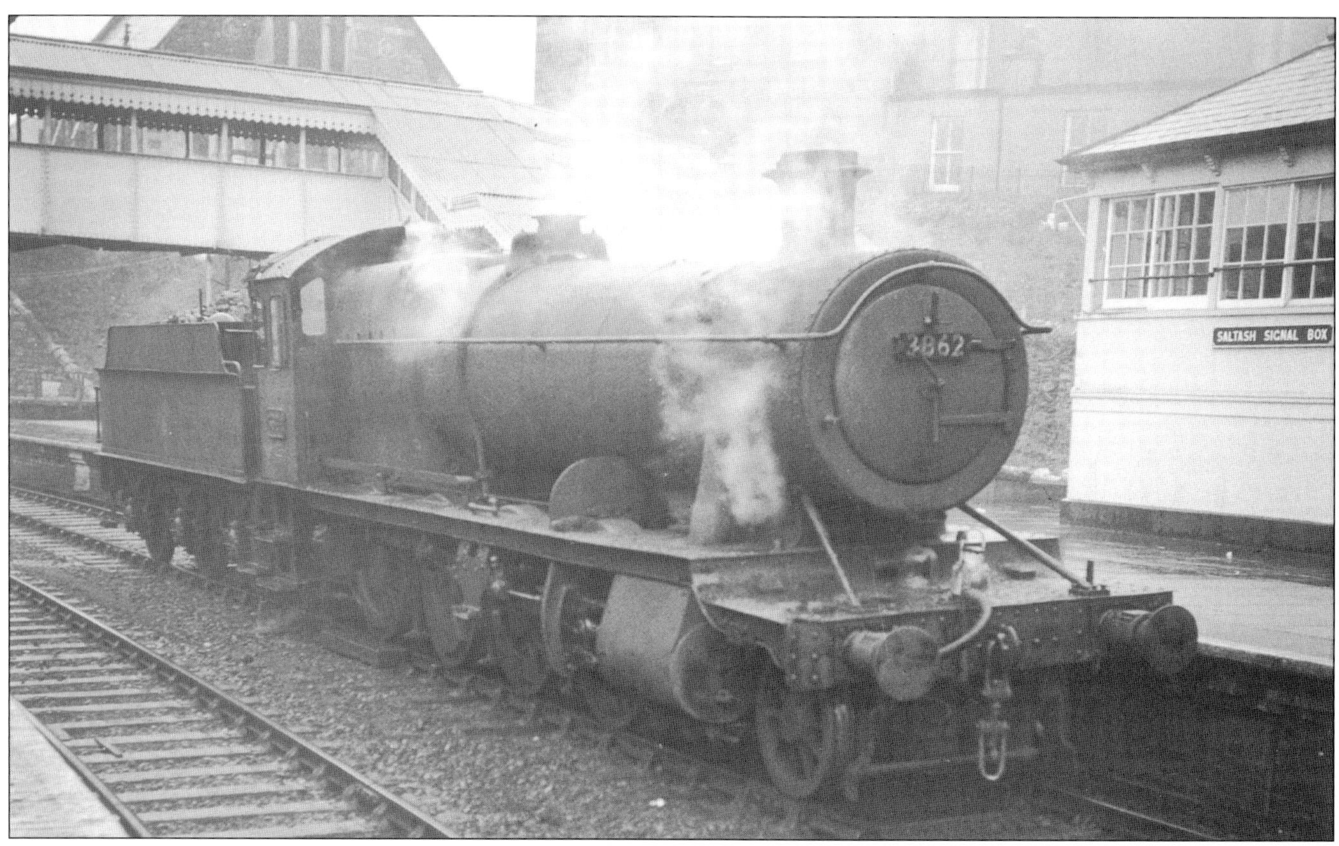

One of the later design of 2-8-0s, Laira's 2884 class 3862, pauses by the signalbox at Saltash at 7 o'clock in the morning on a wet 16 March 1960. Maurice Dart.

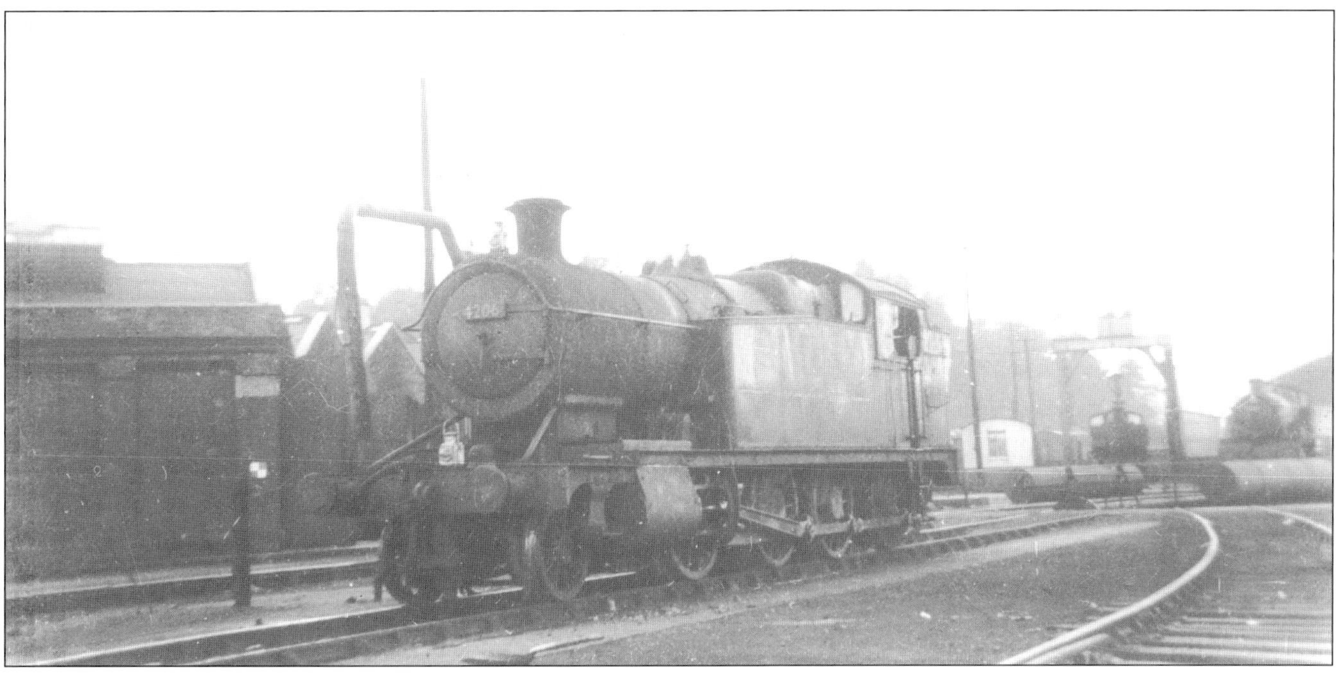

4200 class 2-8-0T 4206 has come off the turntable at St Blazey shed during the evening of 23 April 1956. In the background under the hoist is 1600 class 0-6-0PT 1624 beside which is Grange class 4-6-0 6826 'NANNERTH GRANGE'. Maurice Dart.

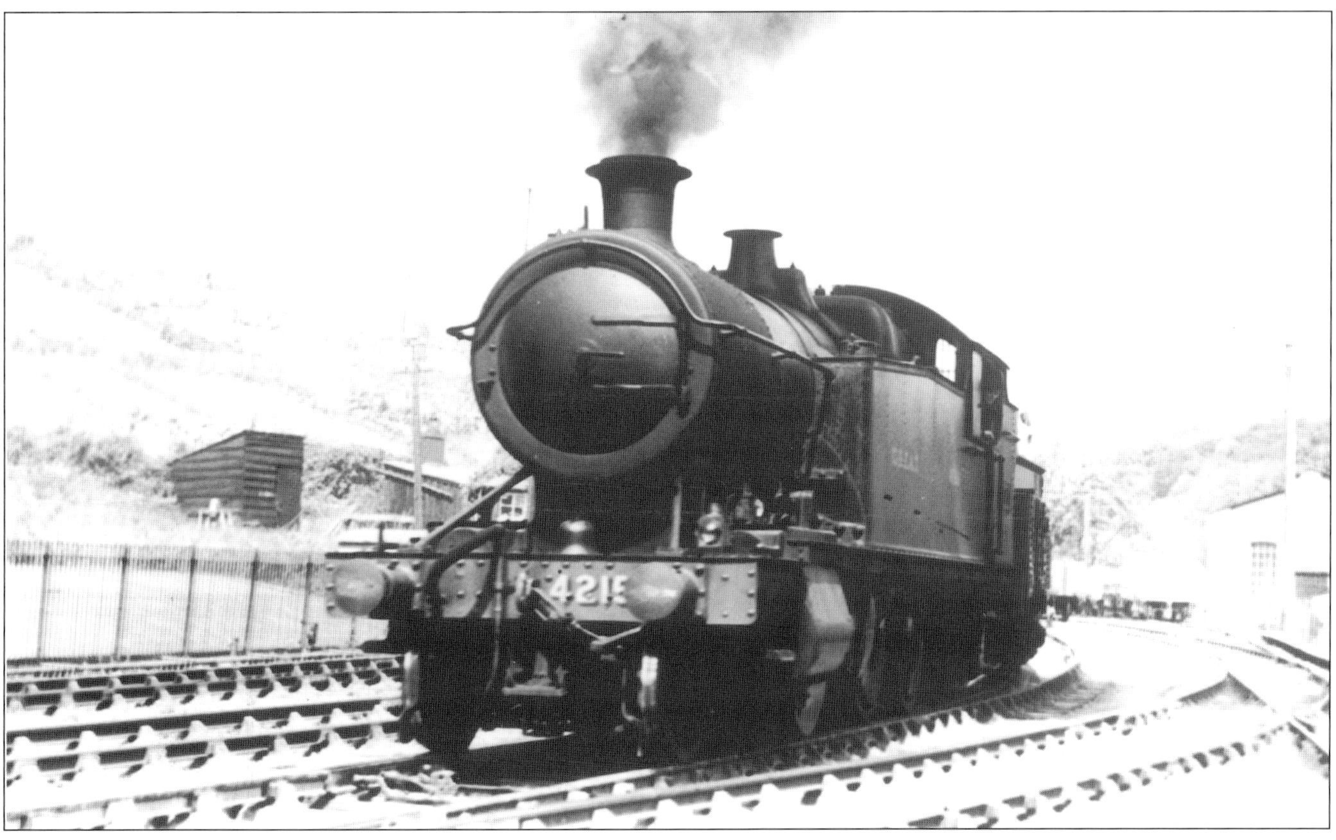

Another member of the same class, 4215, pulls away from the jetties at Fowey and approaches the station with goods' empties 22 May 1935. H.C.Casserley.

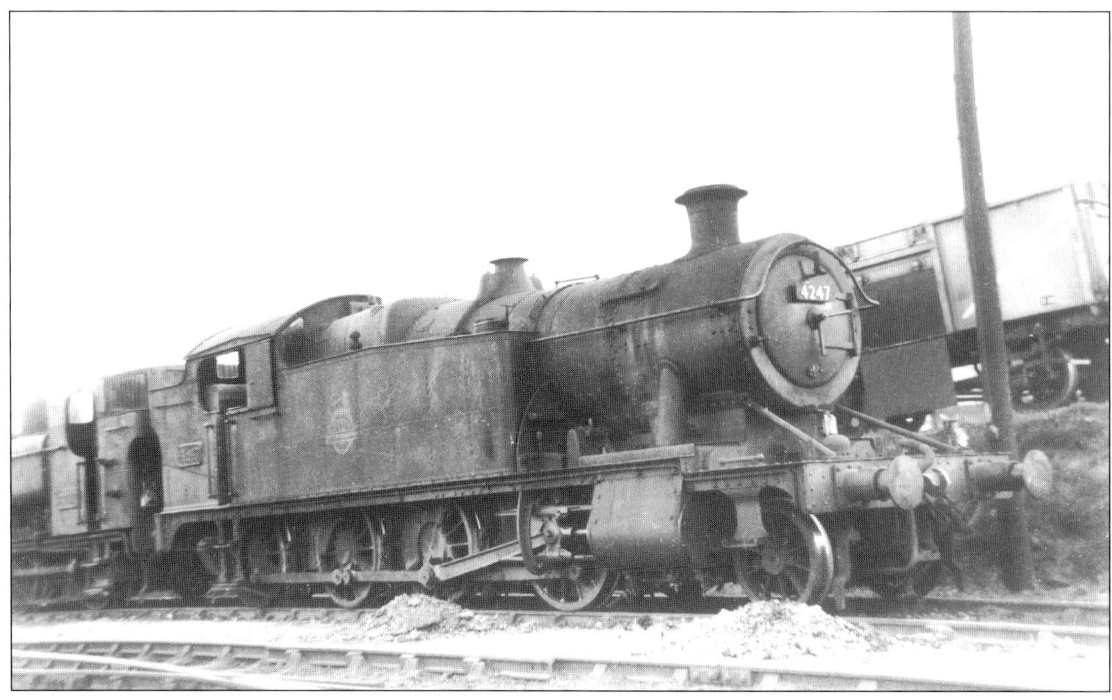

A further member of the class, 4247 from St Blazey awaits coaling at the shed in the evening of 23 April 1956. Standing behind is 8750 class 0-6-0PT 3787 which was 'on loan' from Laira.
Maurice Dart.

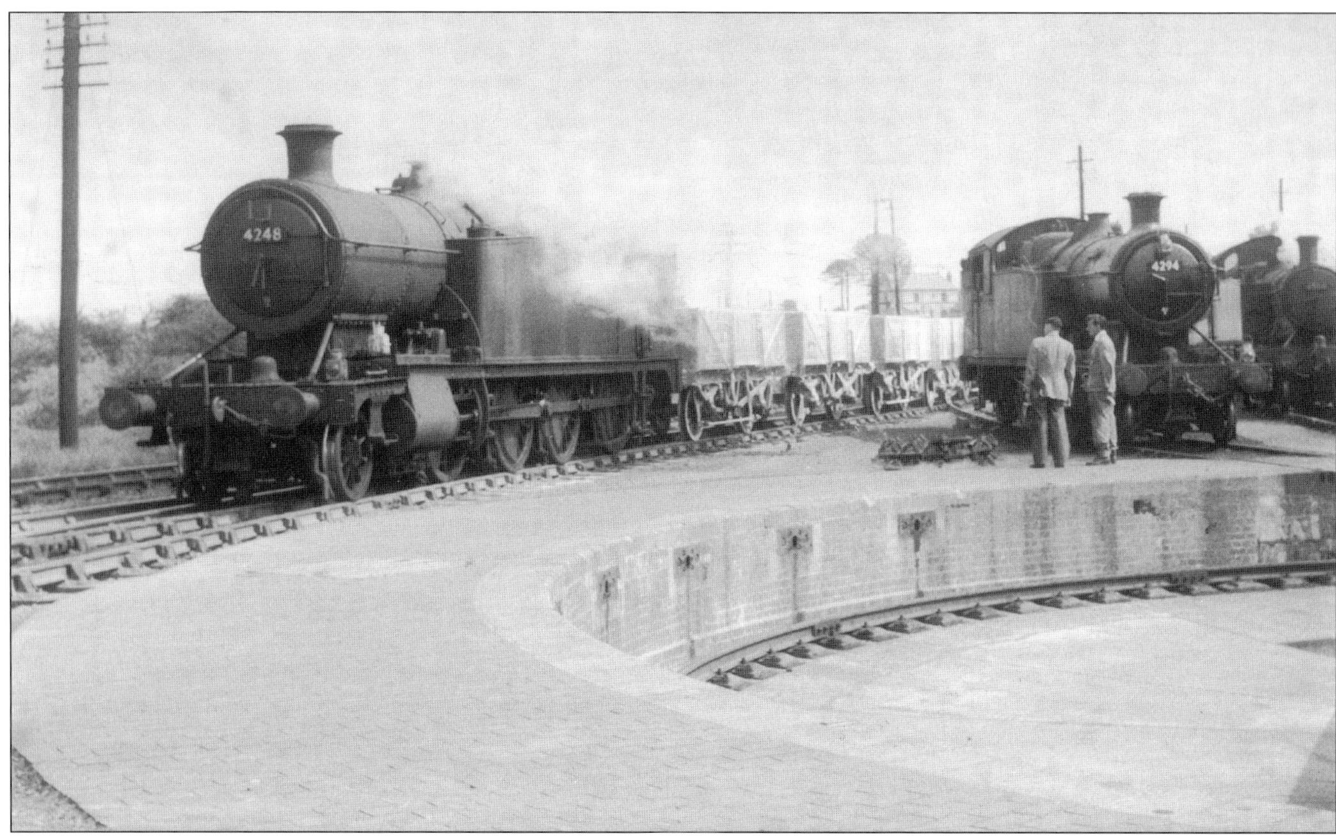

Here we have two members of the class at St Blazey in 1958. 4248, which was 'on loan' from Ebbw Junction shed, Newport, passes 4294 which is standing by the turntable. The train of empty clay wagons from Fowey is heading past the shed for St Blazey yard. On the right can be seen 4575 class 2-6-2T 4584. Norman Simmons/Hugh Davies Photos.

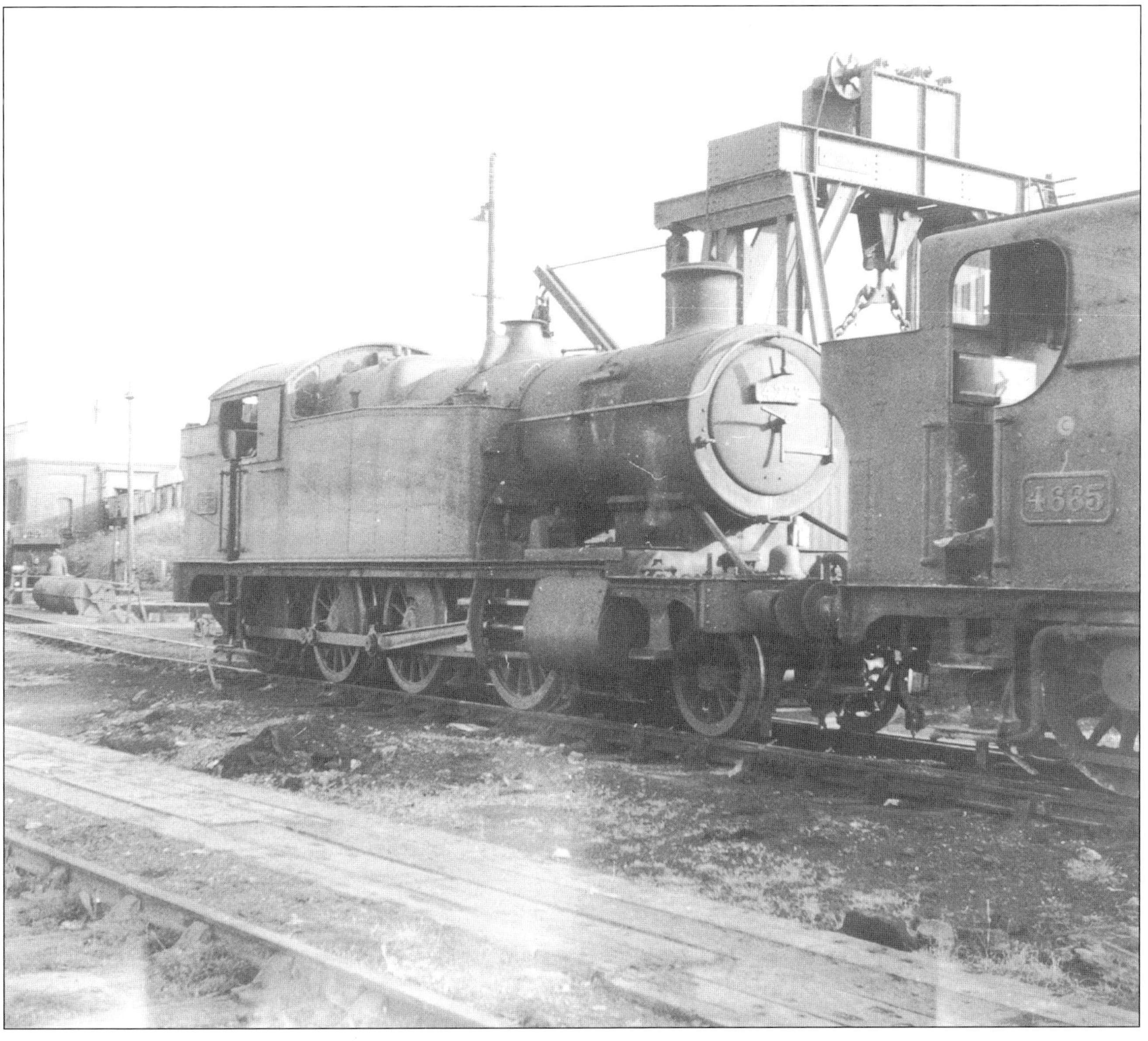

On the evening of 5 June 1961 4273 stands by the hoist in the yard at St Blazey shed behind 8750 class 0-6-0PT 4665. Other pannier tanks await coaling in the background. Maurice Dart.

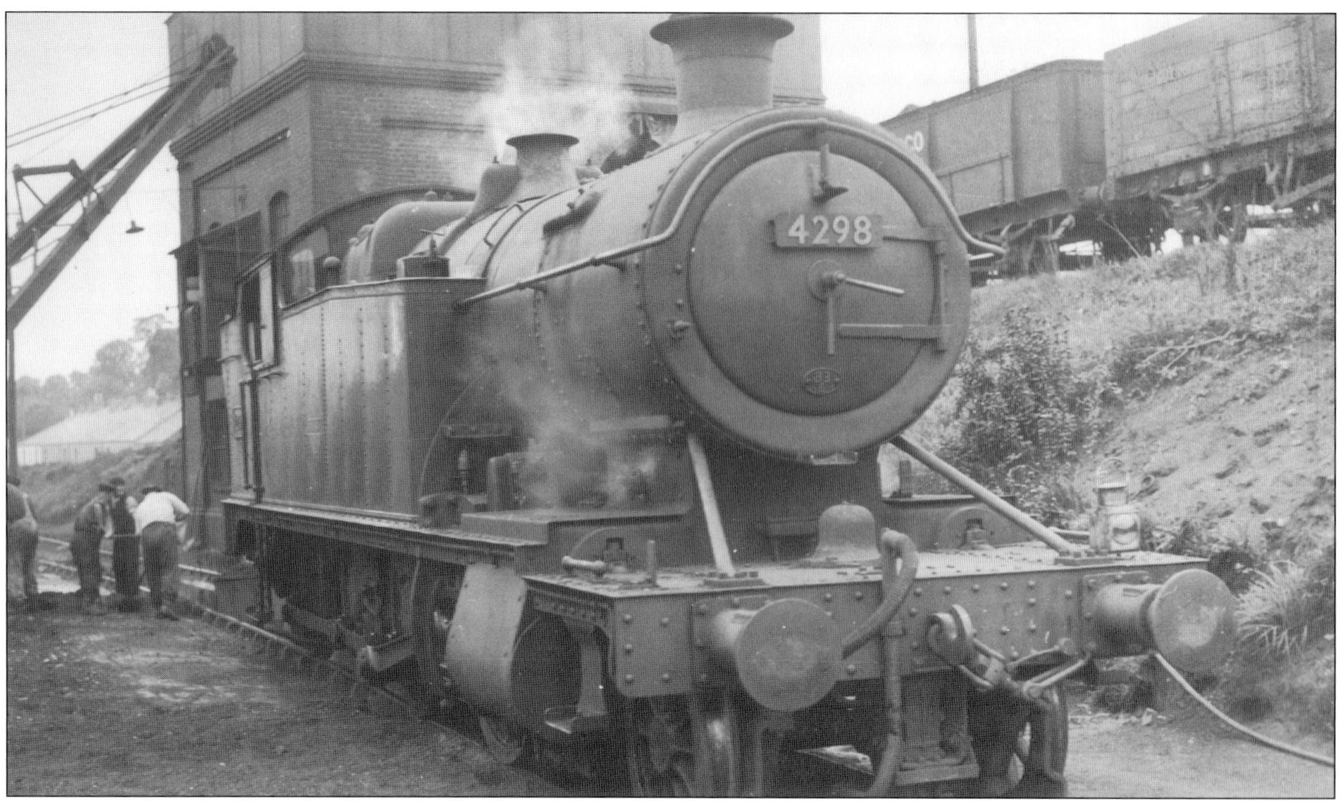

In September 1952, 4298 has just been coaled at St Blazey shed.

With the shed buildings at St Blazey partly visible in the left background, one of the later 5205 class locos stands near a building which is in use by Wagon Repairs Ltd. of Par Harbour. This is a very rare photo of straight framed 5274 which was shedded at St Blazey for a period. This was one of the batch of engines that were rebuilt as 7200 class 2-8-2Ts and it emerged from Swindon Works in February 1936 as 7239.

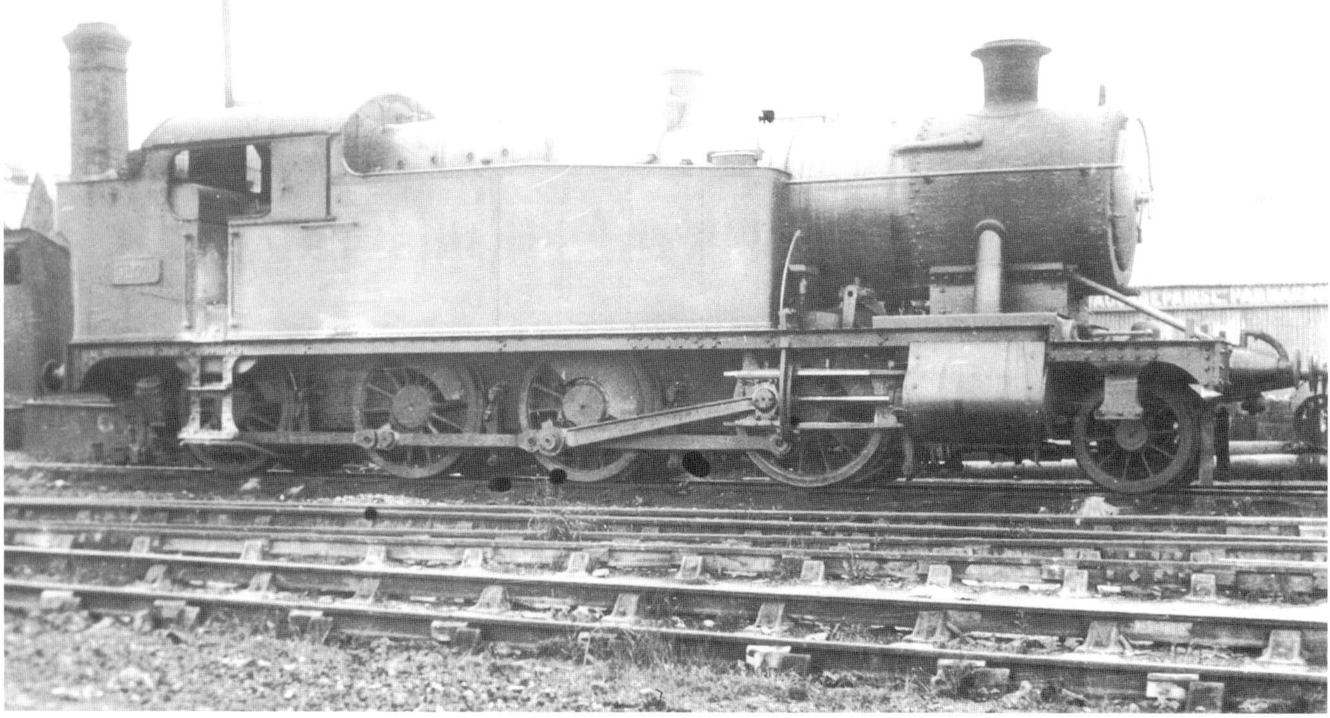

2

PACIFIC 4-6-2s

This type of engine was virtually unknown on the GWR system in Cornwall until Laira gained an allocation of British Railways Standard 4-6-2s of the 'Britannia' class in August 1951 from when they regularly worked to Penzance until they moved away at the end of 1956 and early 1957. The SR introduced their Lightweight 'West Country' class Pacifics during June 1945 and they started to appear on North Cornwall services to Padstow. However, examples of these ventured into Cornwall on special workings over the GWR line in 1949, 1951 and 1961, but, alas, no photos have come to light of these rare events. As there is a separate section in the book devoted to the area between Bodmin Road and Padstow, photos of this type are included in that section.

In May 1964 a Special train arranged by Plymouth Railway Circle was hauled by one of the SR locos between Plymouth and Penzance and this is included here.

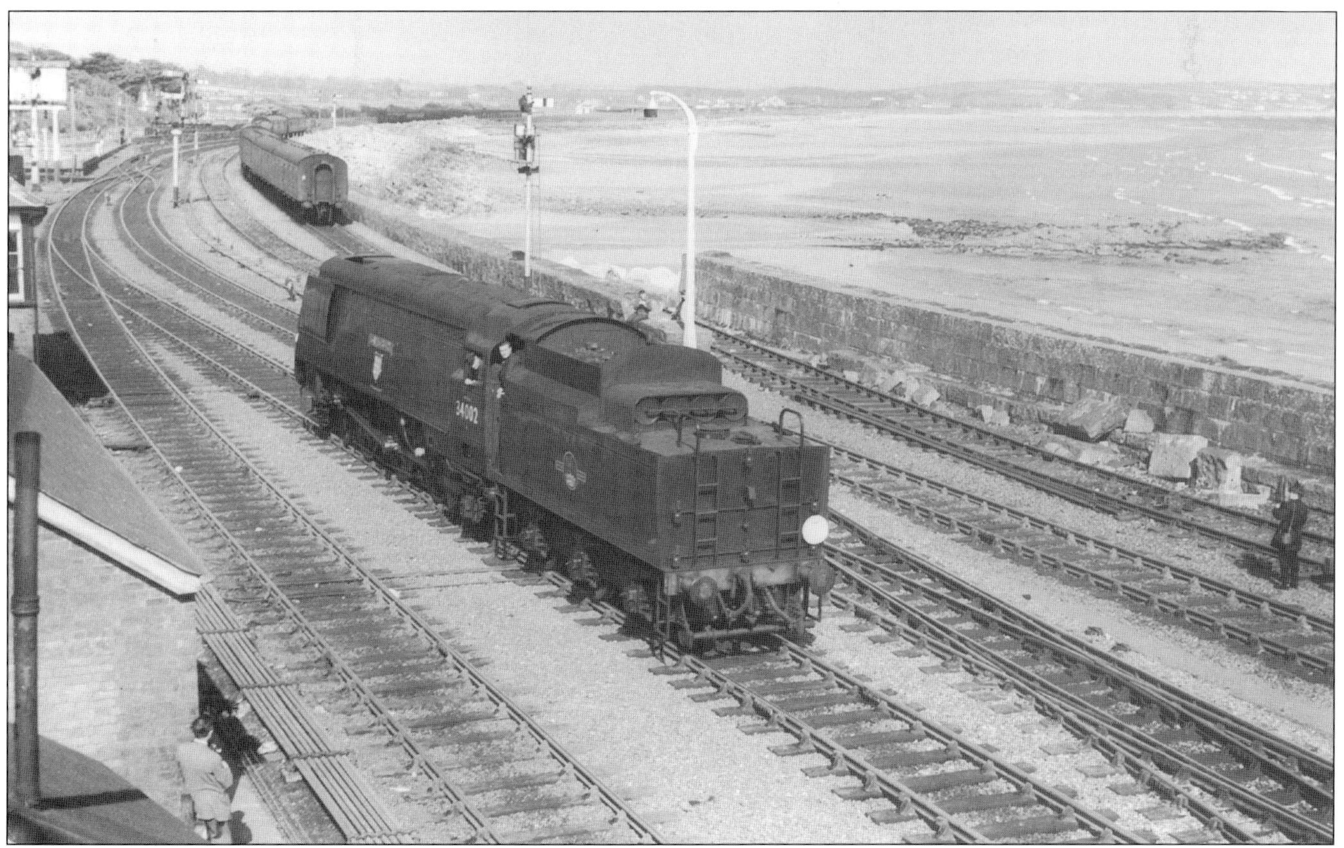

'West Country' class 34002 'SALISBURY' worked the Plymouth Railway Circle special train to Penzance on 3 May 1964 and is backing on to the train after returning from servicing at Long Rock shed. This engine from Exmouth Junction shed was the first member of the type to work west of Truro and the first to work a passenger train on the ex GWR main line into Cornwall. The water tank seen on the left, marks the site of Penzance's second engine shed. S.C.Nash.

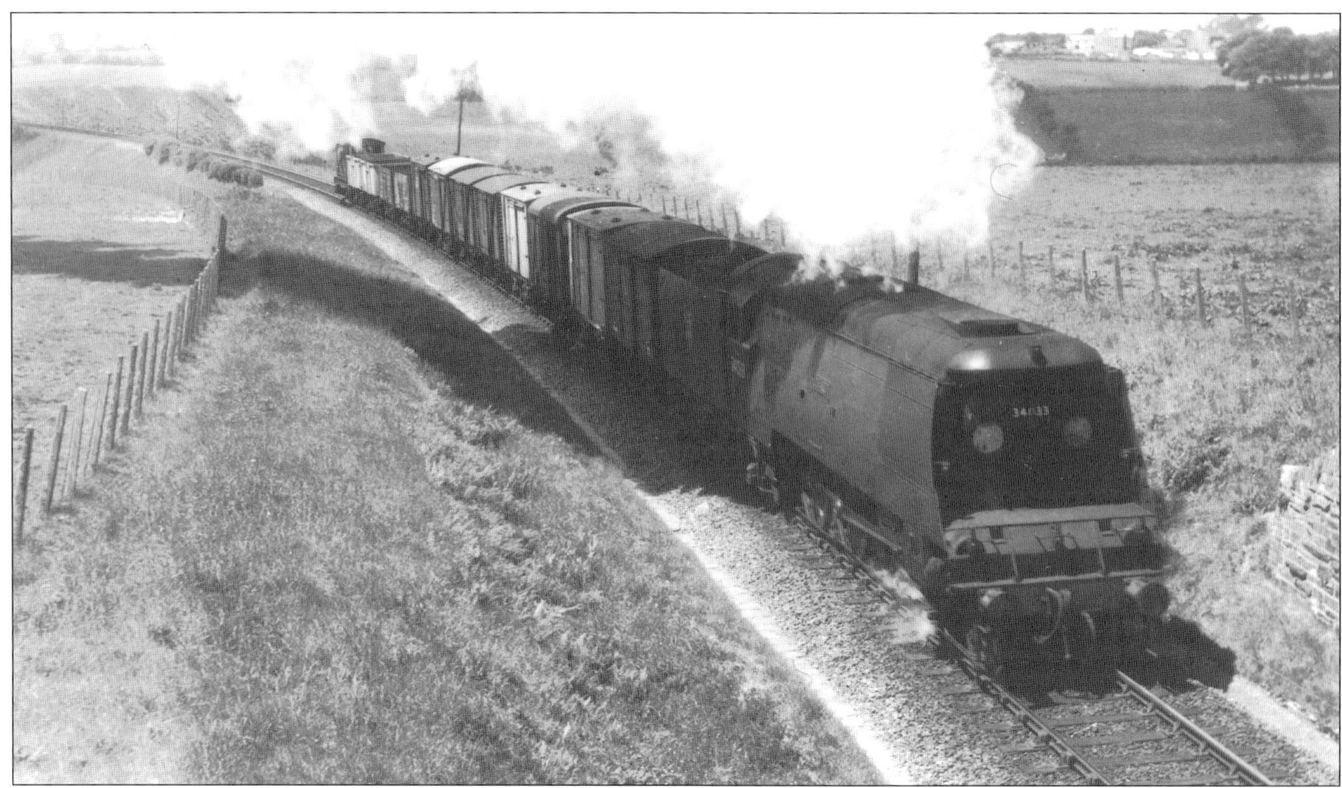

Another Exmouth Junction 'West Country' class, 34033 'CHARD', heads an up goods east of Delabole in June 1957. Rail Archive Stephenson(Photomatic).

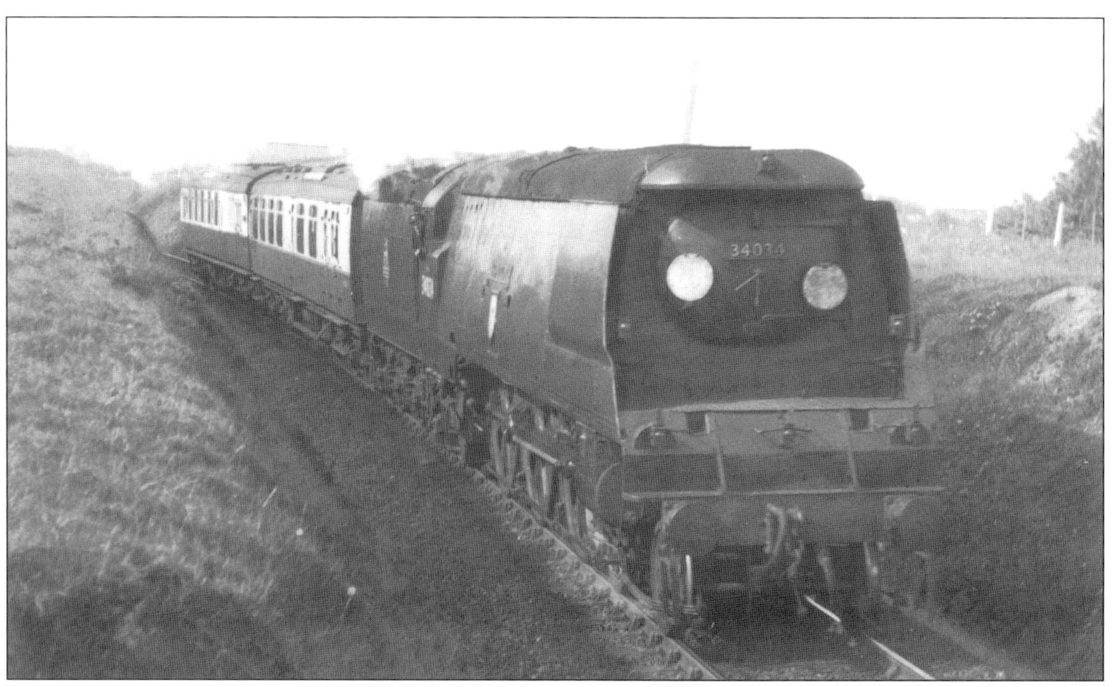

'West Country' class 34034 'HONITON', also from Exmouth Junction shed, is near Port Isaac Road in May 1956 with the two coach portion of the Atlantic Coast Express from Padstow. The leading coach is a Bulleid brake and the second is a Maunsell brake. Rail Archive Stephenson(Photomatic).

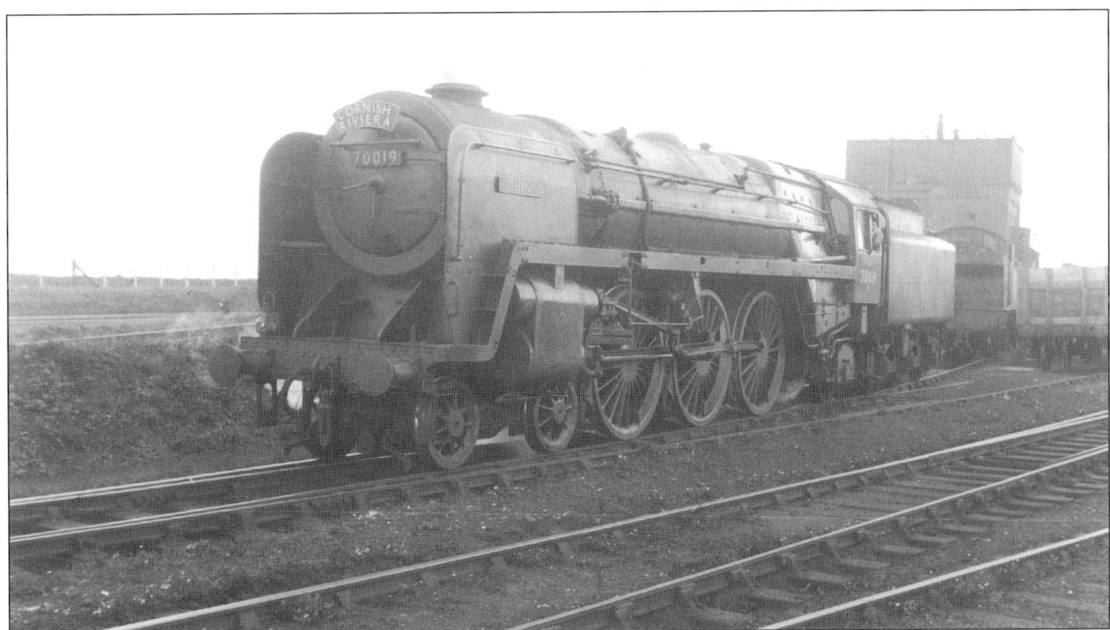

Laira's 'Britannia' class 70019 'LIGHTNING' has worked the down 'Cornish Riviera Express' to Penzance and has come on to Long Rock shed for servicing. As was the usual practice with tender engines, it was turned on arrival and is backing up to a 4500 class 2-6-2T on the coaling line on 2 September 1952.

'Battle of Britain' class 34061 '73 SQUADRON' was another resident of Exmouth Junction shed. It is seen at St Kew Highway on a down passenger working in the mid 1950s composed of Mark I stock. The typical LSWR signal box is prominent with the goods siding diverging behind it. The station house is in the background. David Lawrence/Hugh Davies Photos.

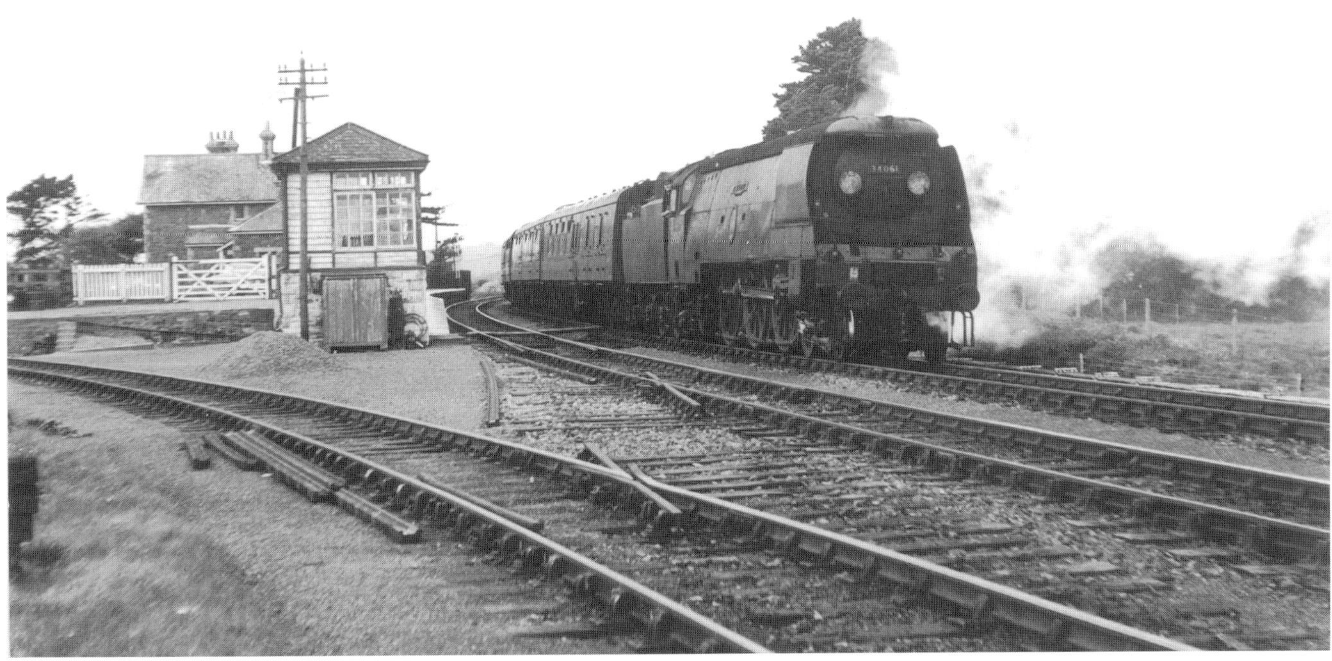

3

CASTLE CLASS 4-6-0s

These fine engines worked most of the express passenger trains in Cornwall where they replaced the Star class 4-6-0s. They were also, at times, to be found working perishables trains. The larger and more powerful King class 4-6-0s were not officially permitted to enter Cornwall. But two trials were carried out in 1938 to test their performance over some of the curves. The first ran to Liskeard and the next reached west of Doublebois but did not cross St Pinnock viaduct. Also, during the war when Plymouth was subjected to Blitz raids, some of the Kings on Laira shed were driven to Cornwall and placed inside Shillingham tunnel for safety until the raid ceased. There have been other instances of Kings entering the Duchy, with 'KING GEORGE V' reported as reaching Penzance on a special train in 1935, and 'KING JOHN' reaching Truro in the late 1950s after three diesels failed. However once again, unfortunately, none of these visits have turned up recorded on film. All of the Castles depicted here were familiar to the author before the outbreak of war.

A few of the early Castles were rebuilt from Star class engines. But 111 'VISCOUNT CHURCHILL' seen when based at Laira was reconstructed in September 1924 from the GWR's only Pacific loco 111 'THE GREAT BEAR'. The train has left Penzance and is passing Ponsondane carriage sidings. The engine was withdrawn in July 1953. P.J.Kelley.

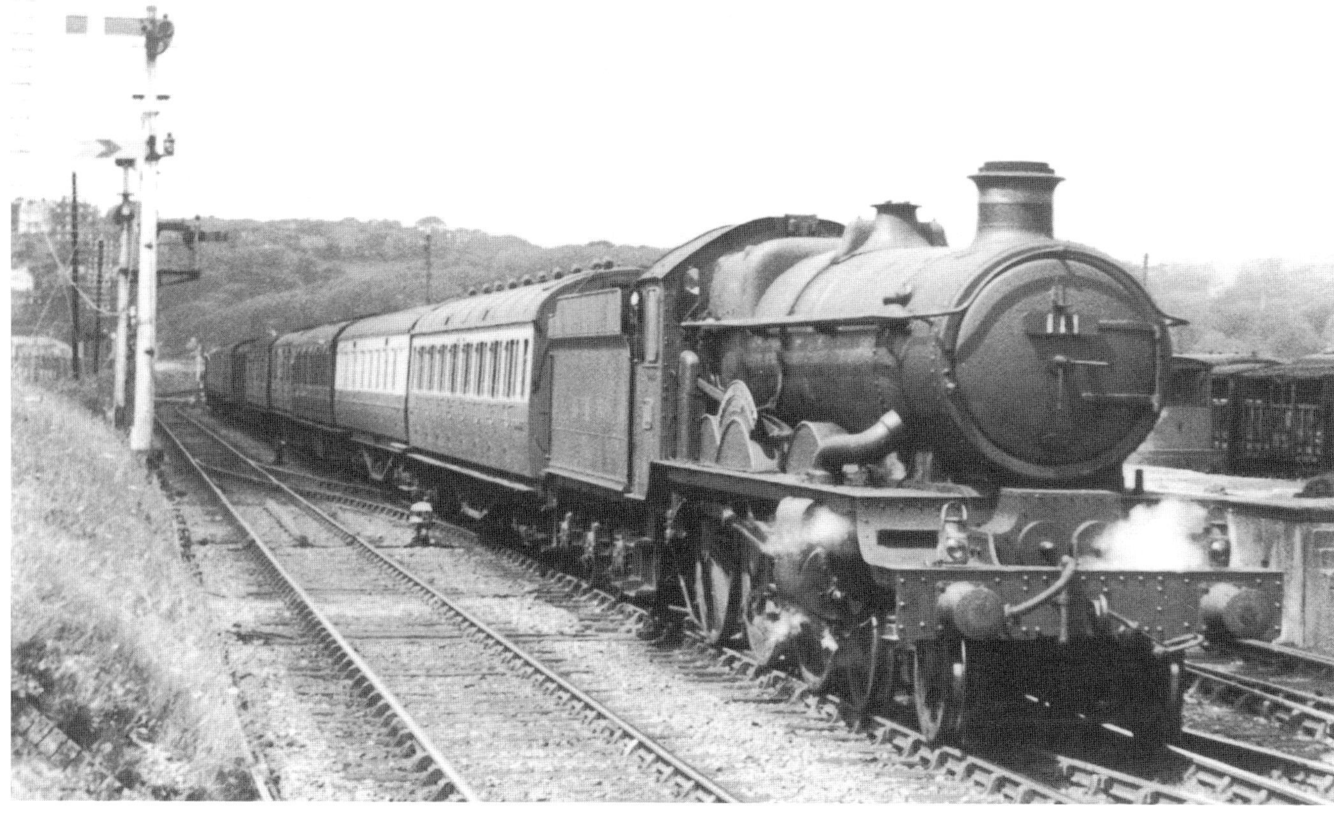

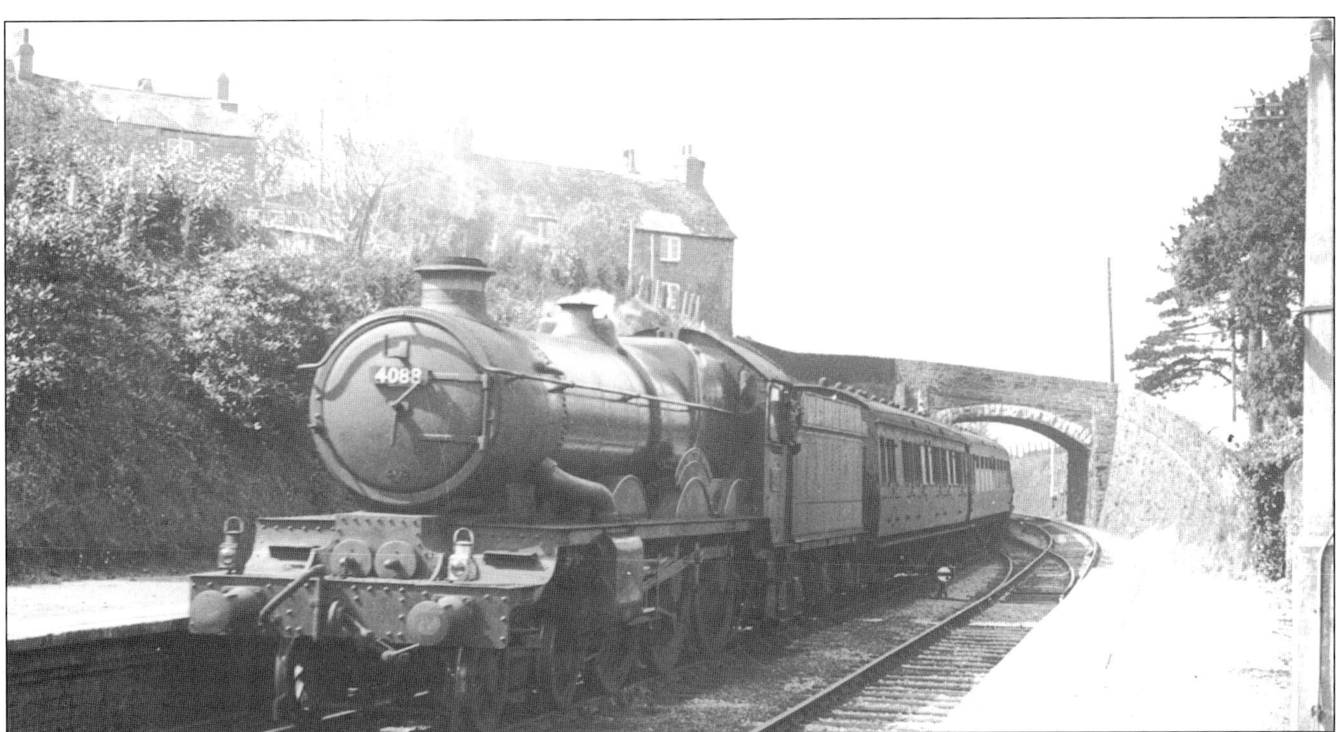

'Wrong line working' is in operation as 4088 'DARTMOUTH CASTLE' brings an up express through St Germans in 1950. This engine was mainly based at Laira during this period but must have had a short stint at Penzance shed as it is carrying a 83G shedplate. C.M. & J.M Bentley.

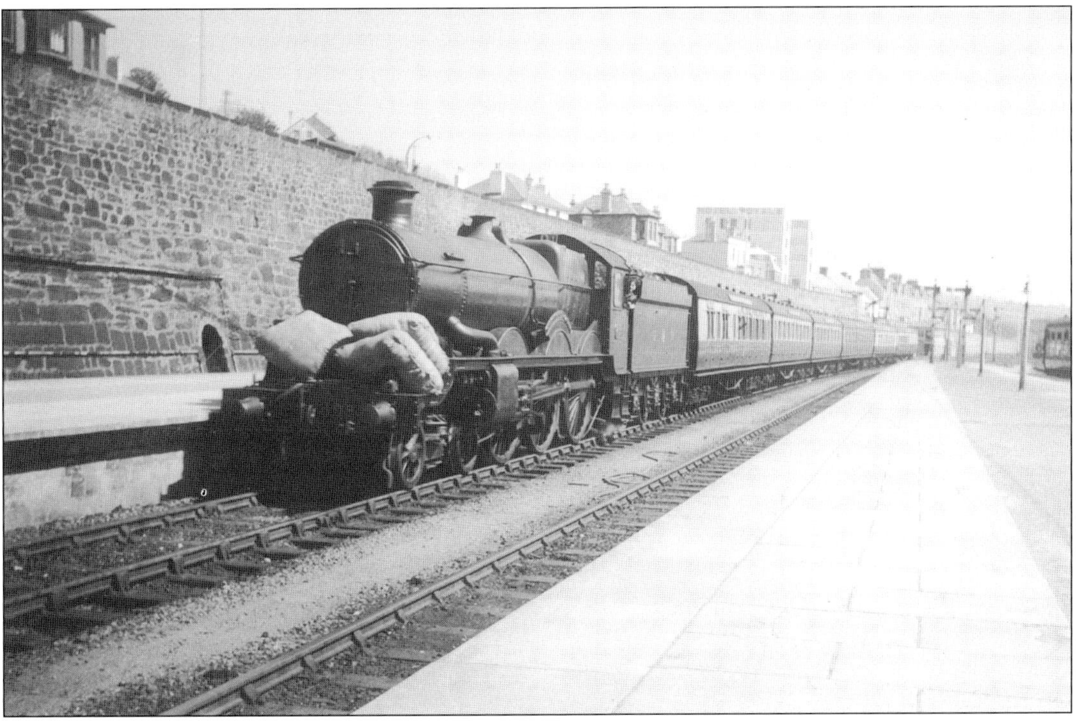

Showing no signs of BR ownership, 4090 'DORCHESTER CASTLE' from Penzance shed is backing its train out from the terminus on 19 May 1948. This most unusual photo shows what appears to be several mattresses piled onto the buffer beam of the engine. Doubtless these had been removed from a Sleeping carriage and were deemed to be worn out so were destined for use at Long Rock shed!

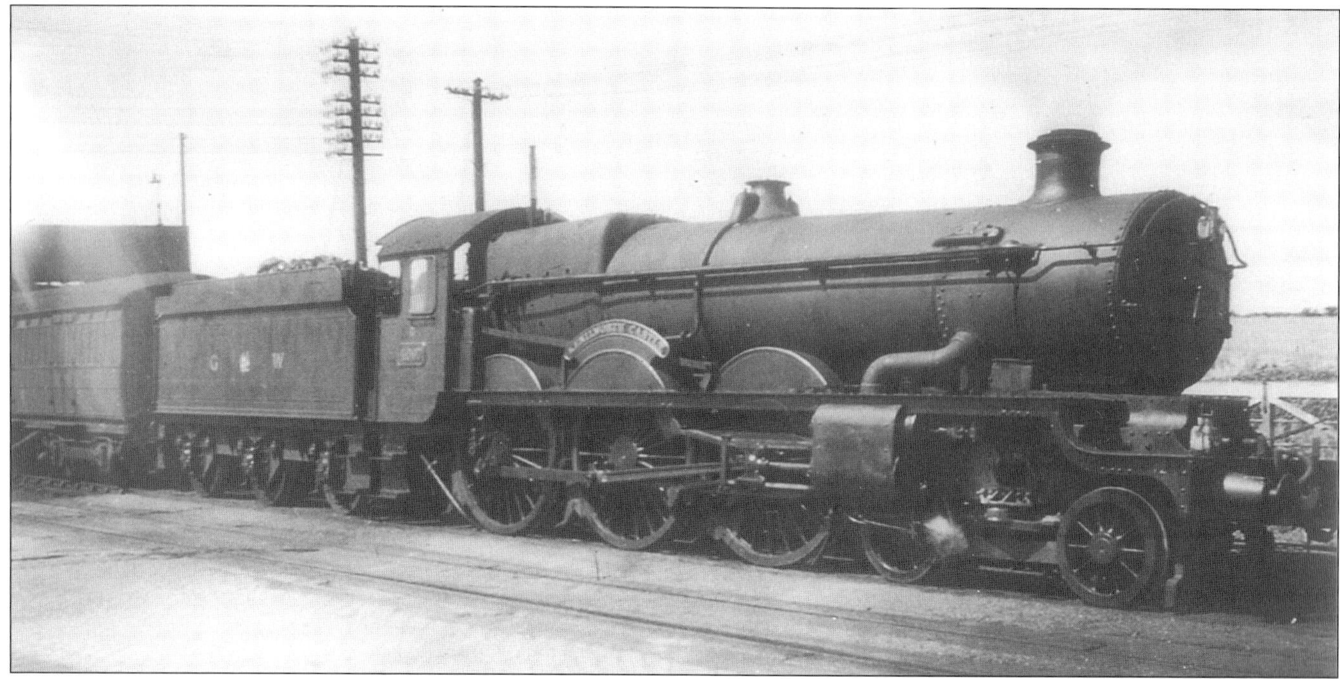

4097 'KENILWORTH CASTLE' is carrying a PZ(Penzance) shed stencil on the front side of the frame as it stands blocking the wide level crossing at Gwinear Road with an up parcels train in 1948. The leading carriage is a Gresley brake. Kenneth Brown collection.

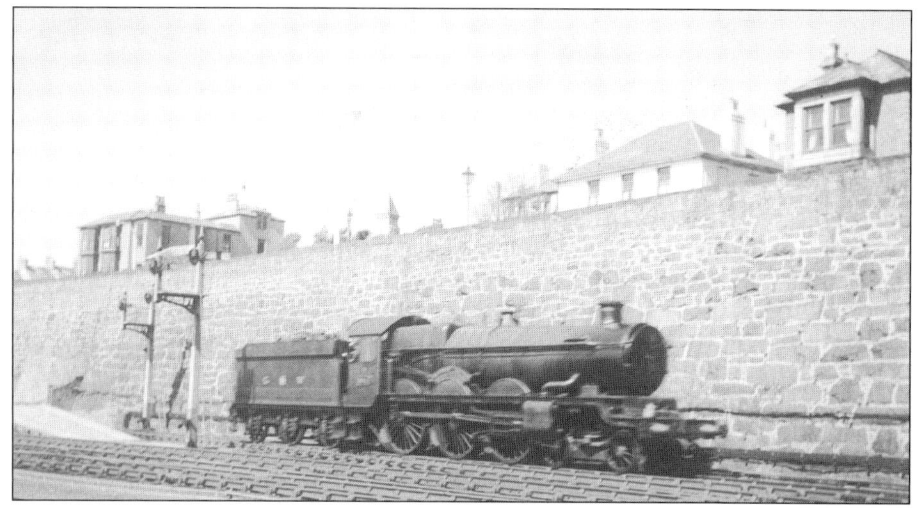

At Penzance station on 20 May 1948 Newton Abbot shed's 5041 'TIVERTON CASTLE' is backing on to a train ready to depart. The wall alongside the station made an ideal vantage point for enthusiasts and still does so!

During 1939 a train bound for Newquay is negotiating the diverted line near Ruthvoes, which avoided Toldish tunnel, between St Dennis Junction and St Columb Road. The train is double headed. A 2-6-2T is hidden behind the pilot loco which is 5012 'BERRY POMEROY CASTLE' which had recently been transferred from Cardiff Canton to either Laira or Newton Abbot.

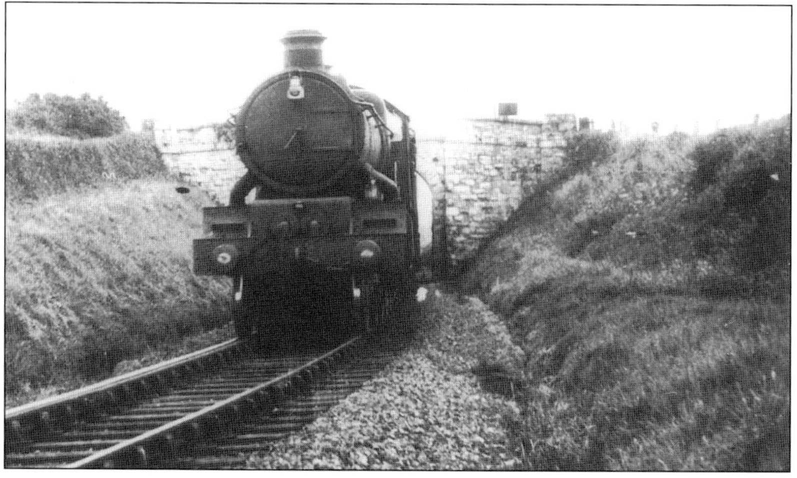

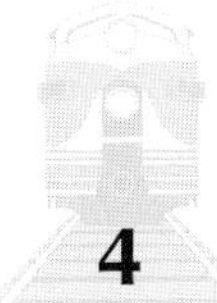

4

HALL, GRANGE AND MANOR CLASS 4-6-0s

The Halls displaced the Mogul 2-6-0s on most of the stopping passenger trains and some of the expresses in Cornwall. They were equally at home working goods and perishables trains. In fact a batch of the early Halls was shedded at Penzance from new for a period. When the Granges arrived, with their driving wheels of 5ft 8in diameter, they soon showed what excellent engines they were with their acceleration and climbing ability. The lightweight Manors were rare visitors to Cornwall before the 1950s. In fact the author well recalls everyone's surprise when filthy dirty 7811 'DUNLEY MANOR' appeared working passenger trains through St Austell for a couple of weeks during 1945. Later they became familiar when the three Cornish sheds gained some on allocation.

Having climbed the bank through the valley, the 5.8pm train from Par to Newquay passes through Luxulyan headed by 4906 'BRADFIELD HALL' from Truro shed on 16 August 1959. One of the arms for collecting the single line token can be seen to the right of the first carriage. The small arm on the signal post was to permit access to the stub end of Treffry's Tramway which was retained as a refuge siding. Peter Hay.

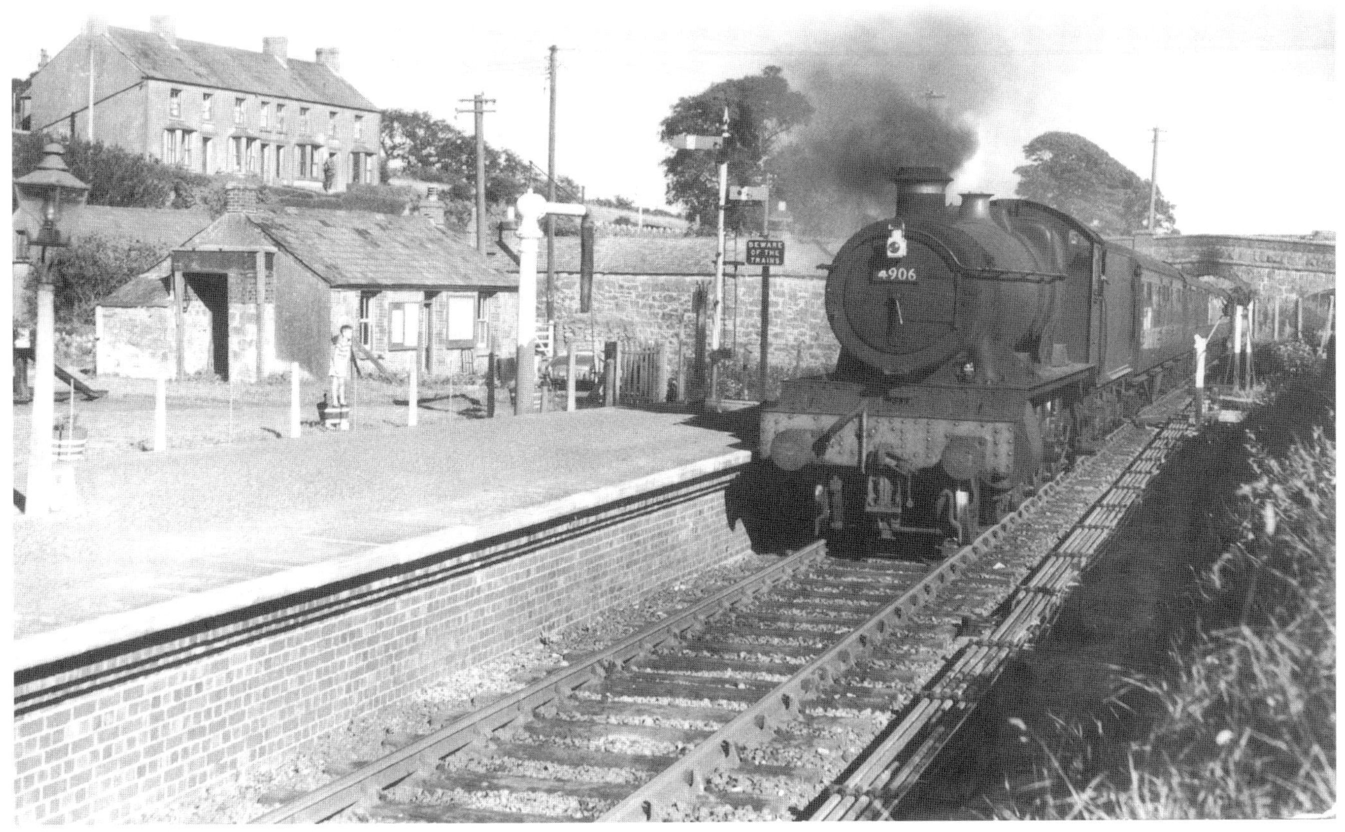

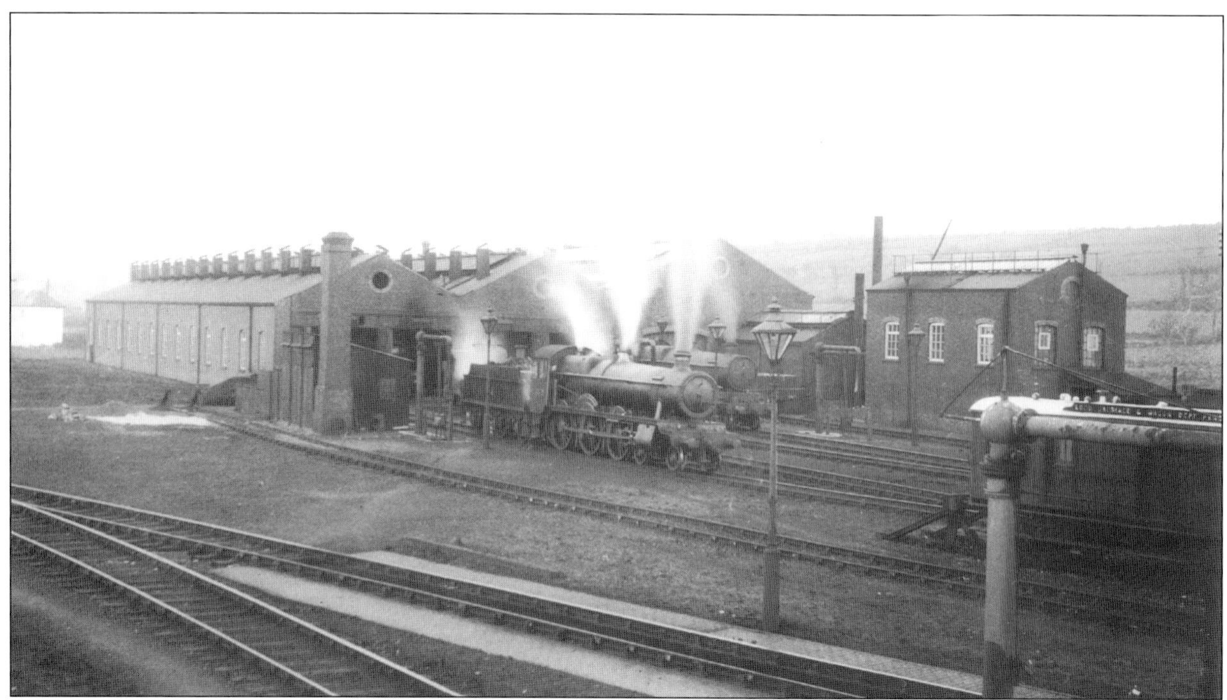

This overview of Long Rock shed, Penzance was taken on 16 January 1934. A Castle class loco is in the background but this is one of the rarest photos in this book. The nearest engine is Penzance based 4911 'BOWDEN HALL' which was badly damaged at Keyham in one of the Blitz raids on Plymouth/Devonport early on 29 April 1941. The engine was condemned on 10 June and was cut up at Swindon Works. Luckily, the photographer also took a close up of the engine. T.Corin.

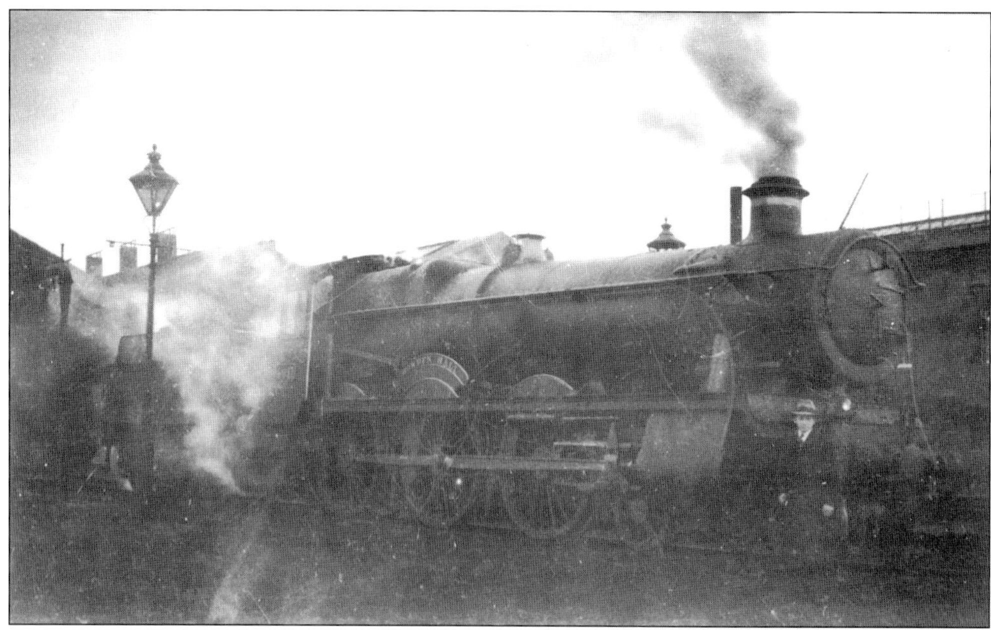

The close up just mentioned was not of such good quality as the photographer was 'learning to use a camera' (he later became a commercial photographer). However, due to the scarcity of views of this engine I considered that it merited inclusion. A young Shed Foreman Harold Luscombe, who was later shedmaster at Laira, is posed by the engine. He is wearing an overcoat to protect him from the January weather! T.Corin.

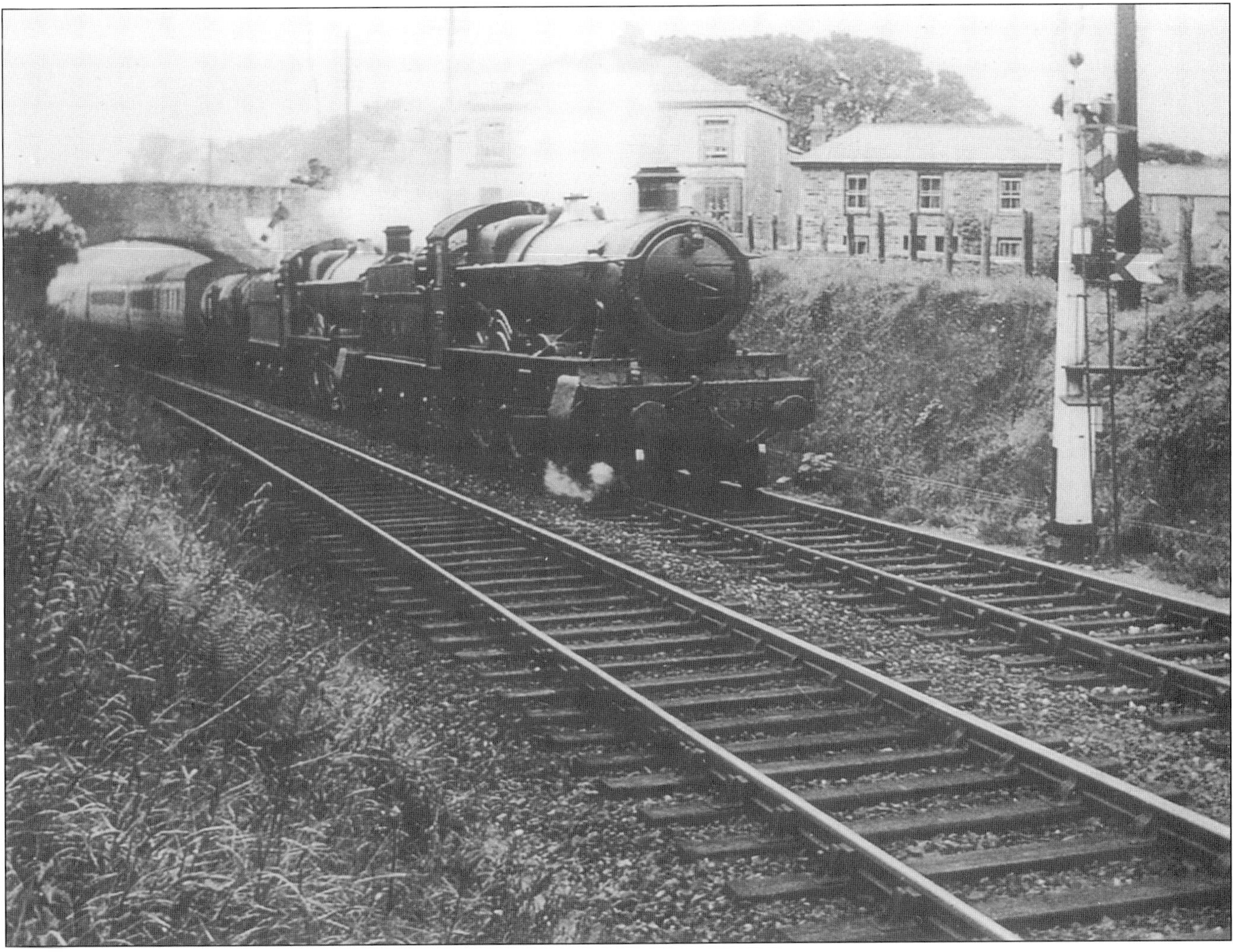

An up mixed parcels train passing Pool, near Redruth is hauled by an unidentified Grange which is piloted by 4936 'KINLET HALL'. This loco has been preserved and restored to traffic and visited Cornwall on 7 April 2001.

Kenneth Brown collection.

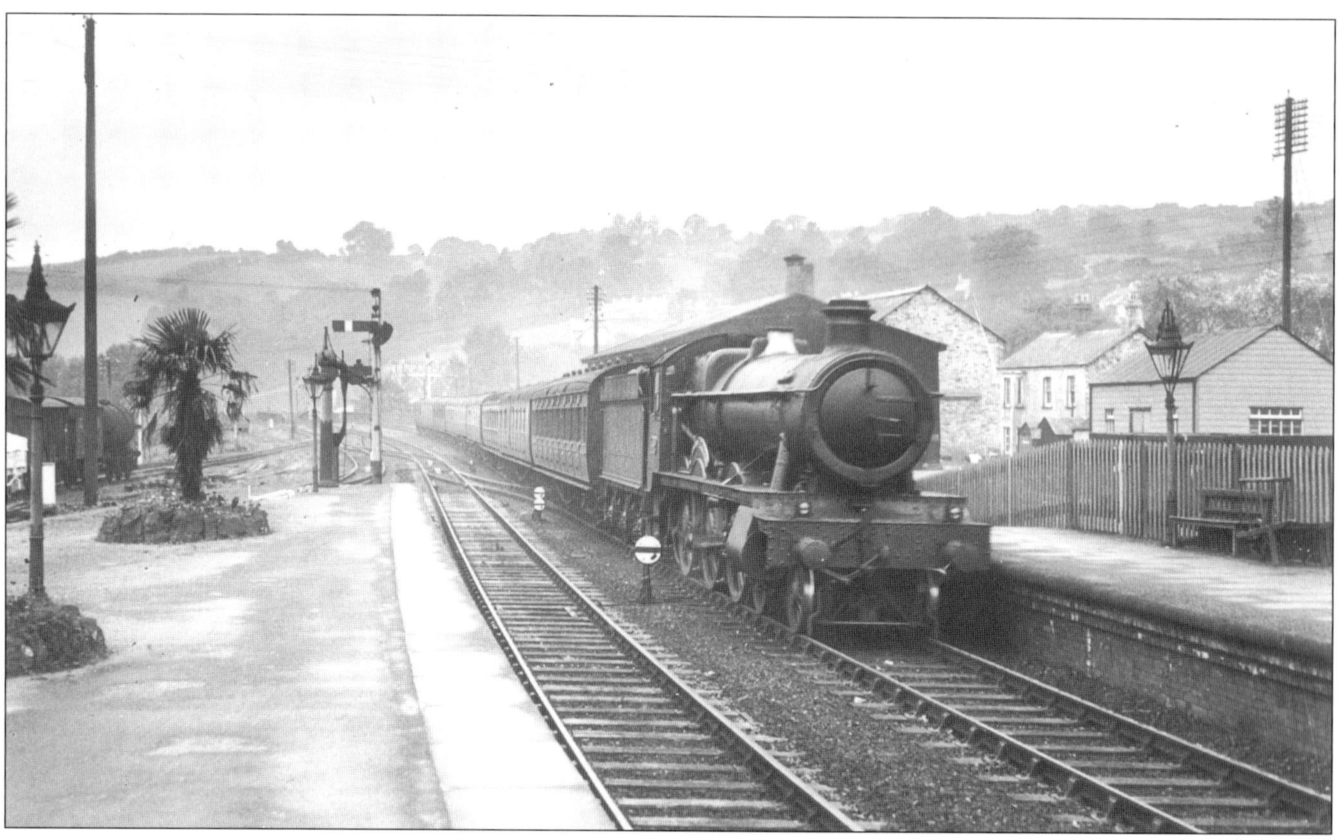

An up express enters Lostwithiel in charge of 4978 'WESTWOOD HALL', which has a very shiny safety valve bonnet, during September 1933. The goods shed is behind the engine. Dr.Ian.C.Allen.

A very short goods train is being shunted into sidings at Long Rock in 1937 by Laira's 4982 'ACTON HALL'. The wagon behind the engine is a GWR fruit van.

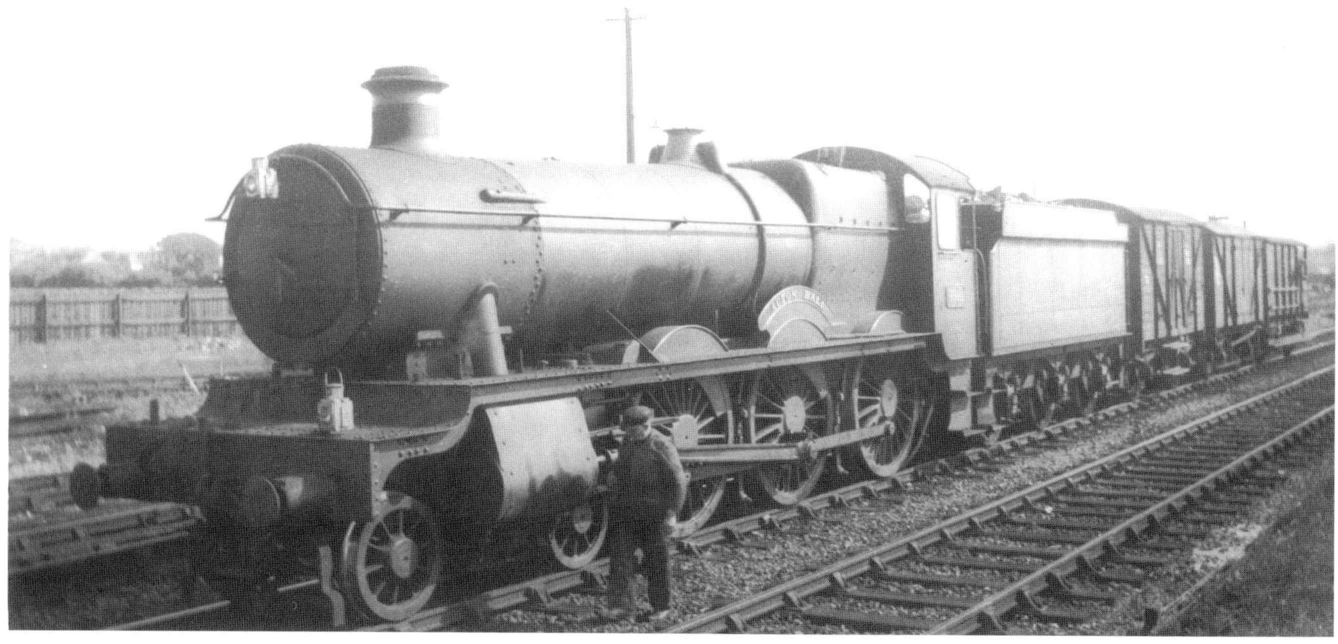

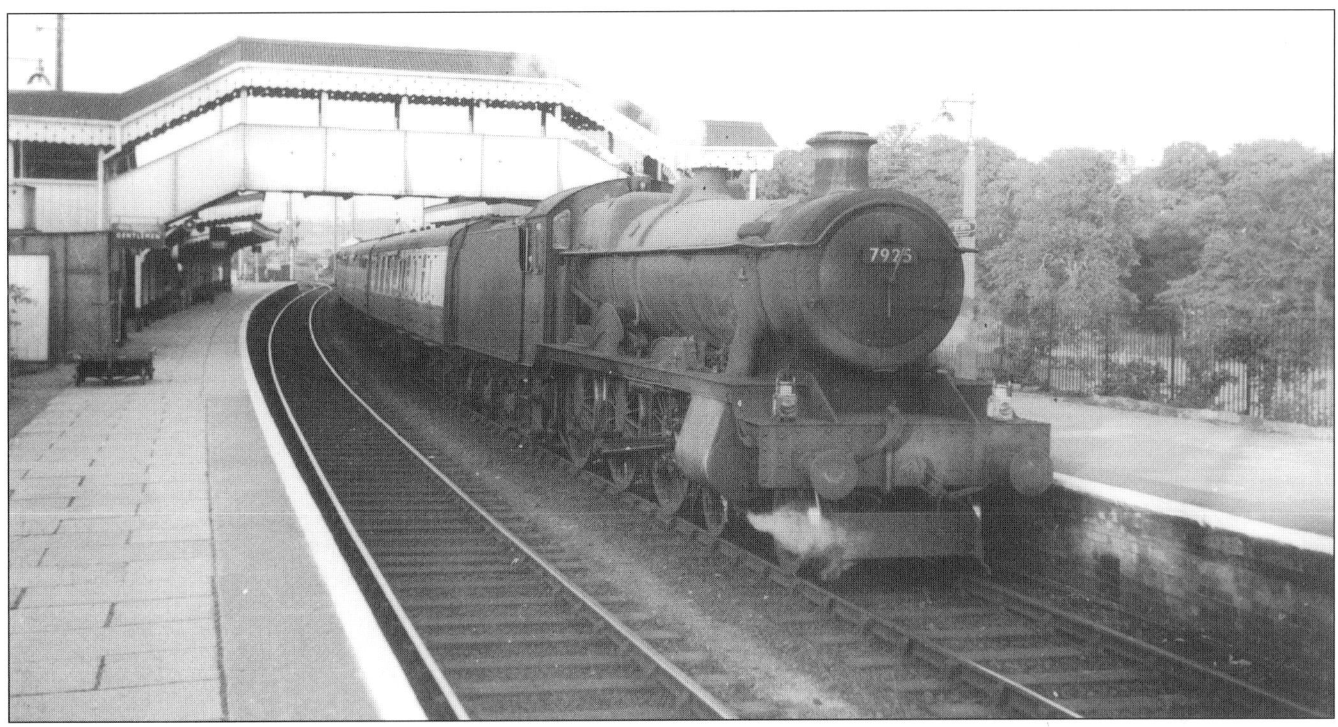

Hall class engines numbered from 6959 onwards were built to a improved design that incorporated 'Plate Frames'. They were known as 'Modified Halls' and one of these was Penzance based 7925 'WESTOL HALL' which is stopping at St Erth on a down passenger train composed of Mark I stock, in the mid 1950s.

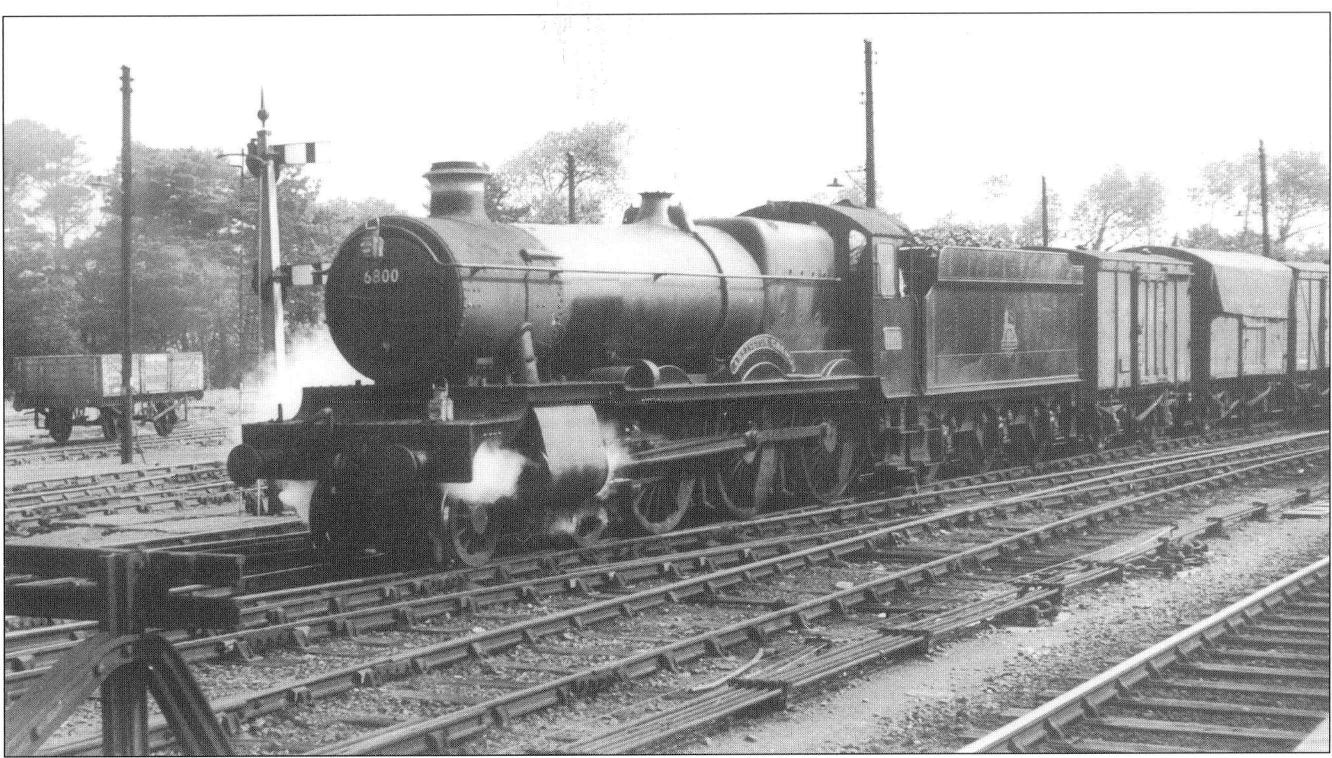

The first Grange 6800 'ARLINGTON GRANGE' was shedded at Penzance for the first seventeen years of its life. It is waiting in the yard at Truro on a down goods on 21 August 1956. This engine was a common sight at Plymouth pre-war. The leading vehicle is a LMS plywood van. A.R.Goult.

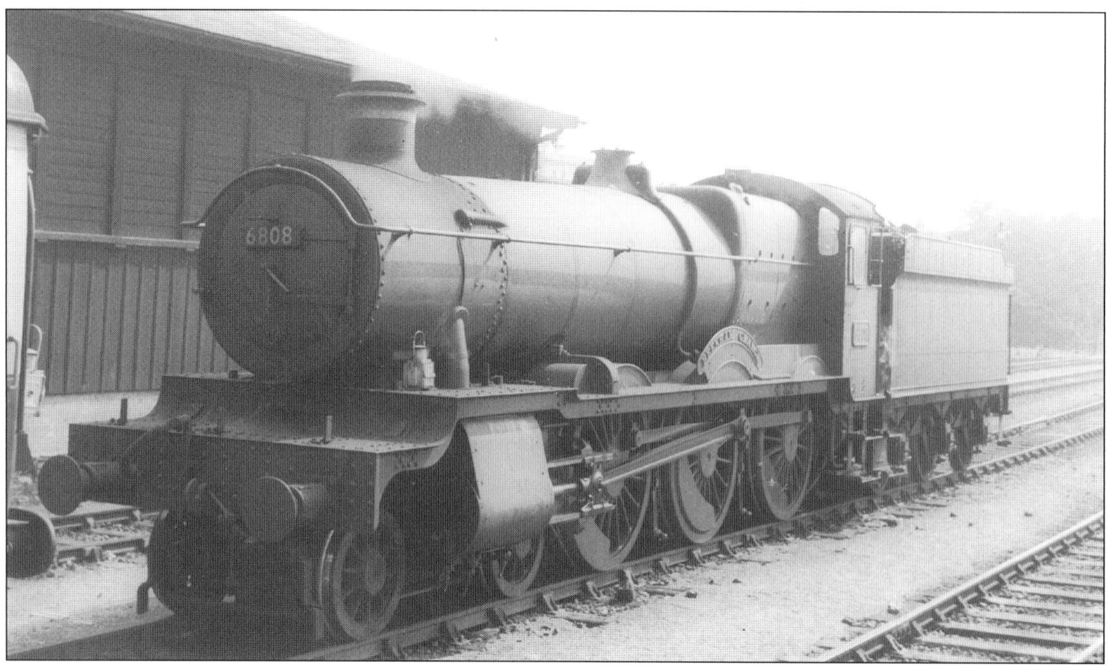

This is a rare photo of Penzance shed's 6808 'BEENHAM GRANGE' running round a train from London which it had worked into the terminus at Falmouth on 17 July 1956.

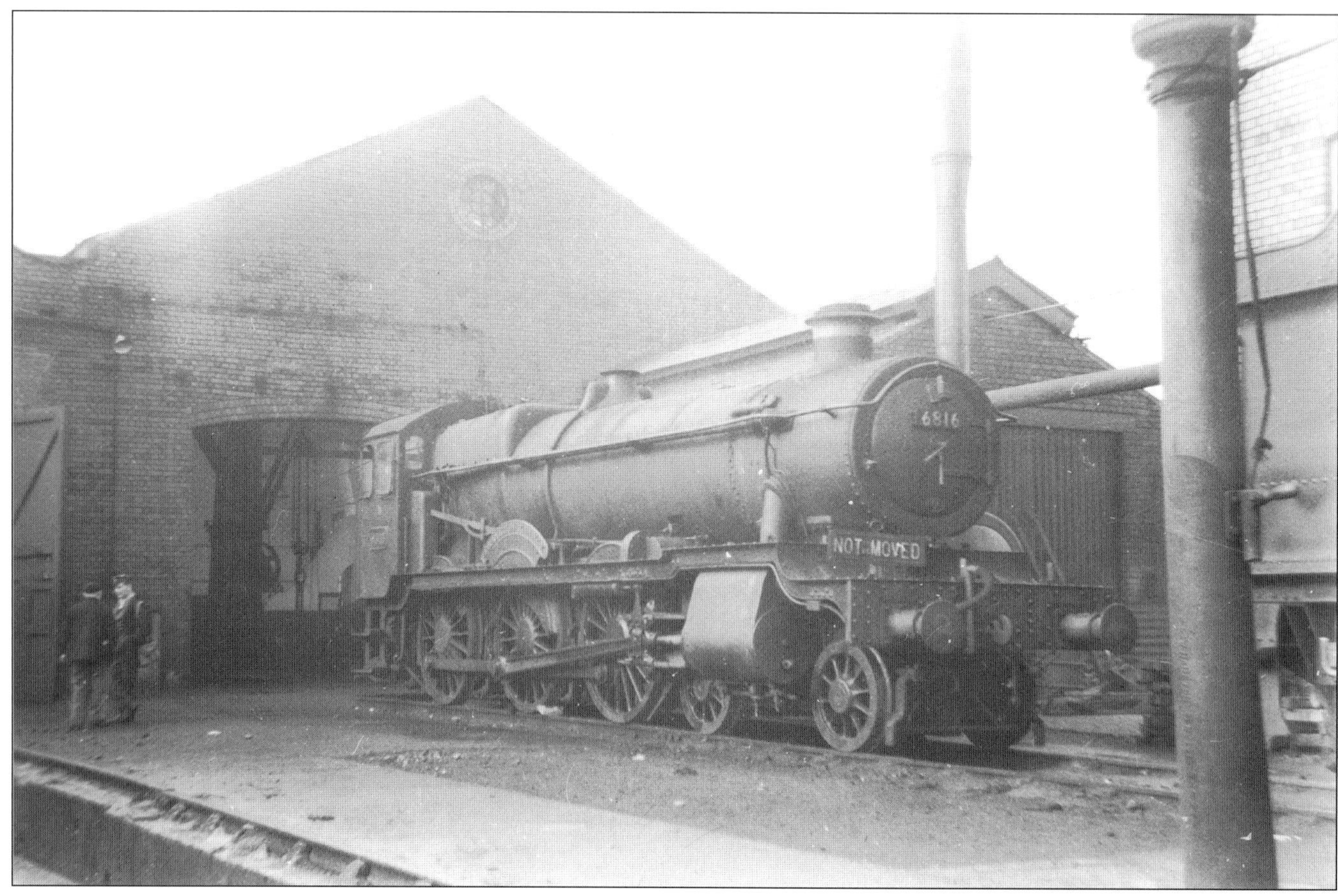

Two railwaymen have a chat alongside locally shedded 6816 'FRANKTON GRANGE' which has been separated from its tender and is standing outside the one road 'Factory' or Works at Long Rock on 16 February 1958. Maurice Dart.

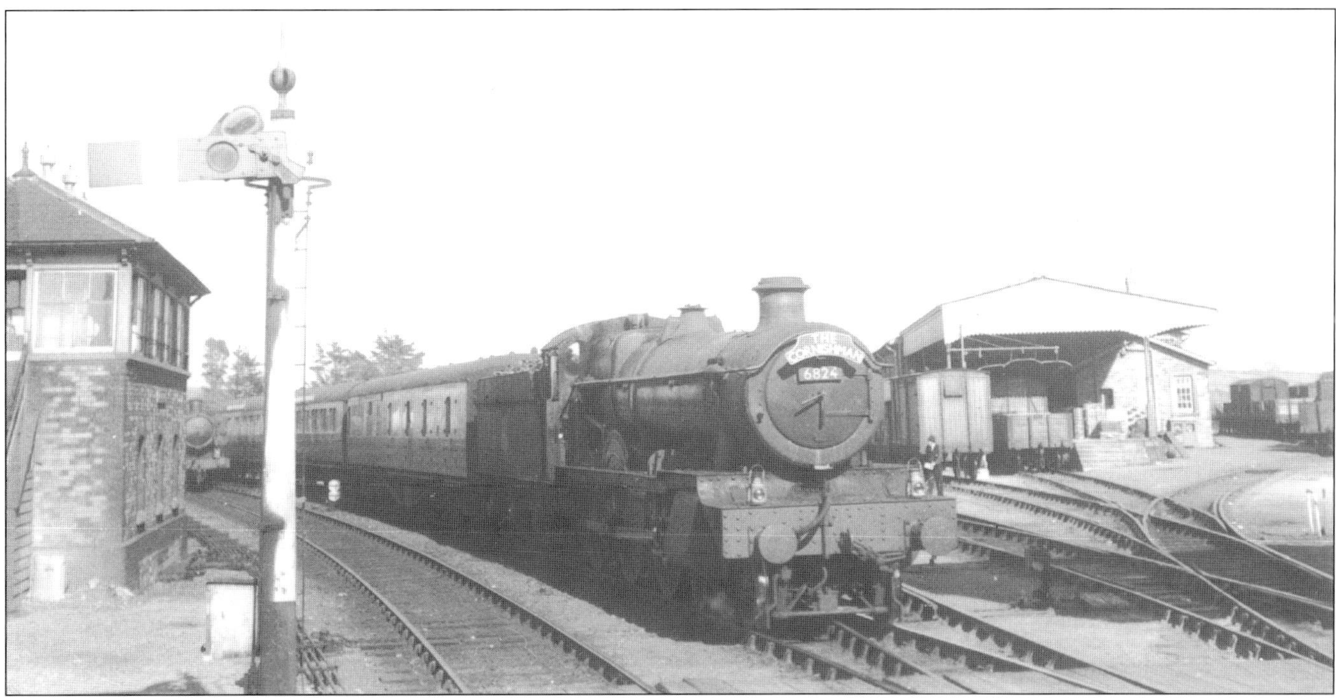

The down 'Cornishman' runs past the goods shed and East signal box to enter Truro in 1953. It is hauled by Penzance shed's 6824 'ASHLEY GRANGE'. A Hawksworth carriage is the leading vehicle. 9400 class 0-6-0PT 9434 is visible between the train and the signal box. The signal is the Truro Up Starter and is fitted with off-set spectacles which enhanced viewing in difficult locations. C.M & J.M.Bentley.

Probus & Ladock was a rarely photographed location. So this is a rather scarce shot of Penzance's 6838 'GOODMOOR GRANGE' passing the timber constructed platforms with an up milk train on 17 July 1951.

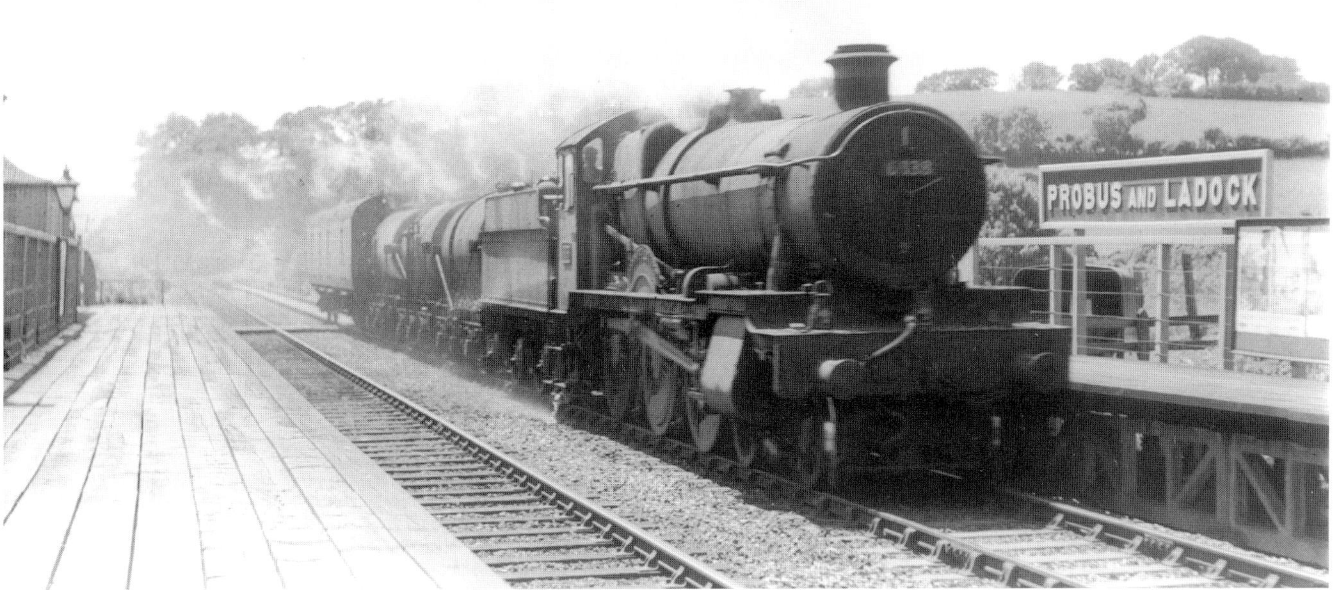

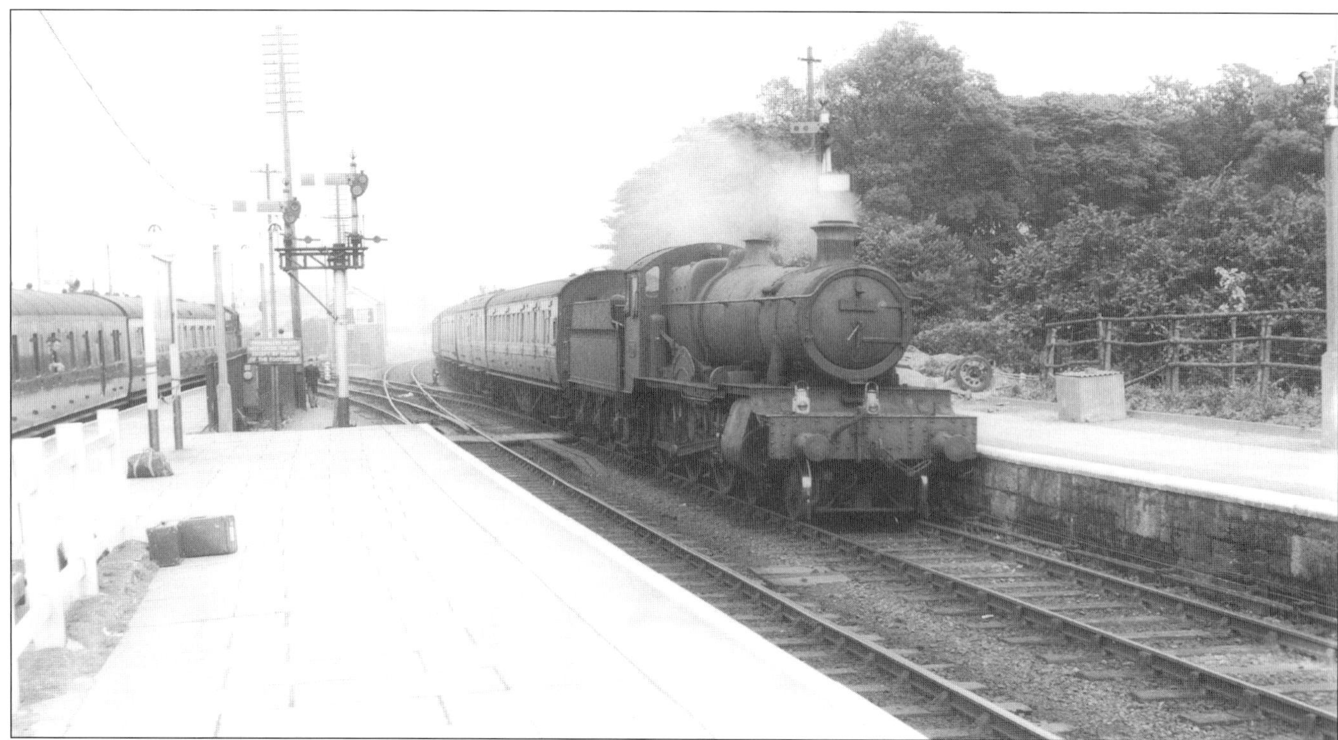

A down parcels train passes through St Erth hauled by 7809 'CHILDREY MANOR' from Laira shed in July 1957. Two LMS carriages are at the front of the train. To the left, a 4500 class 2-6-2T awaits departure with a train for St Ives.

Laira's 7820 'DINMORE MANOR' comes off Blackwater viaduct to pass through Chacewater on a down goods on 15 June 1956. The leading wagon is a Banana van. R.Cogger.

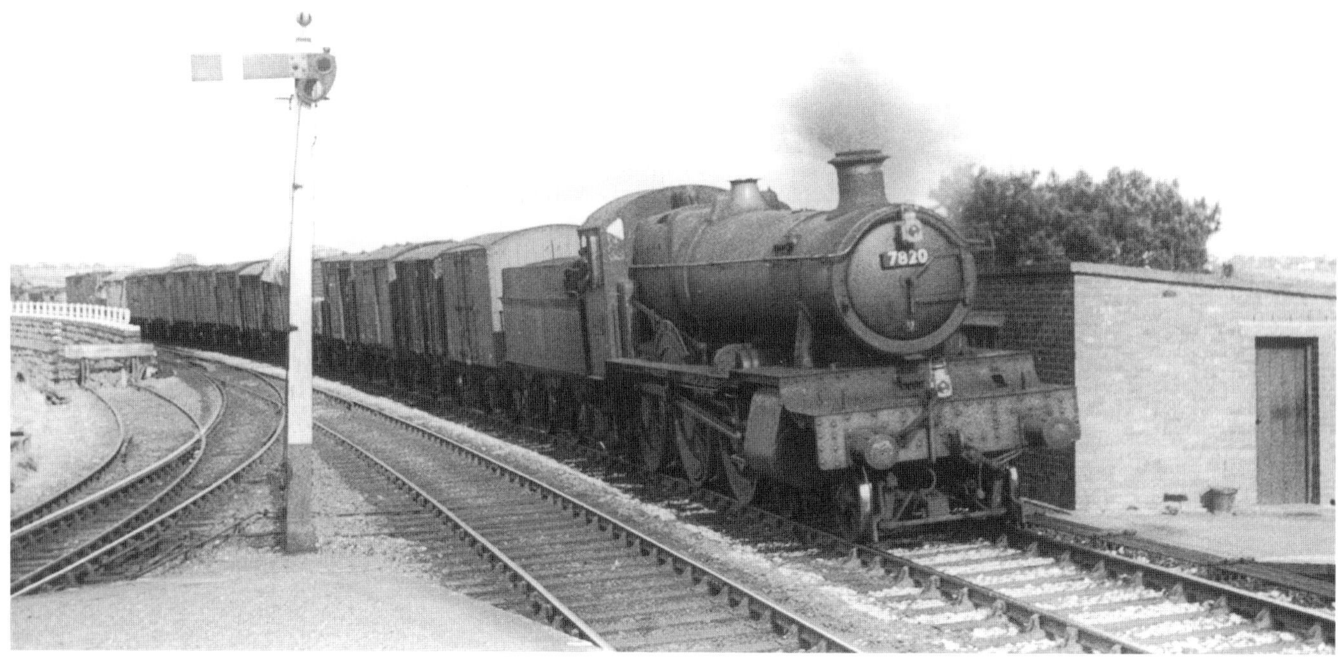

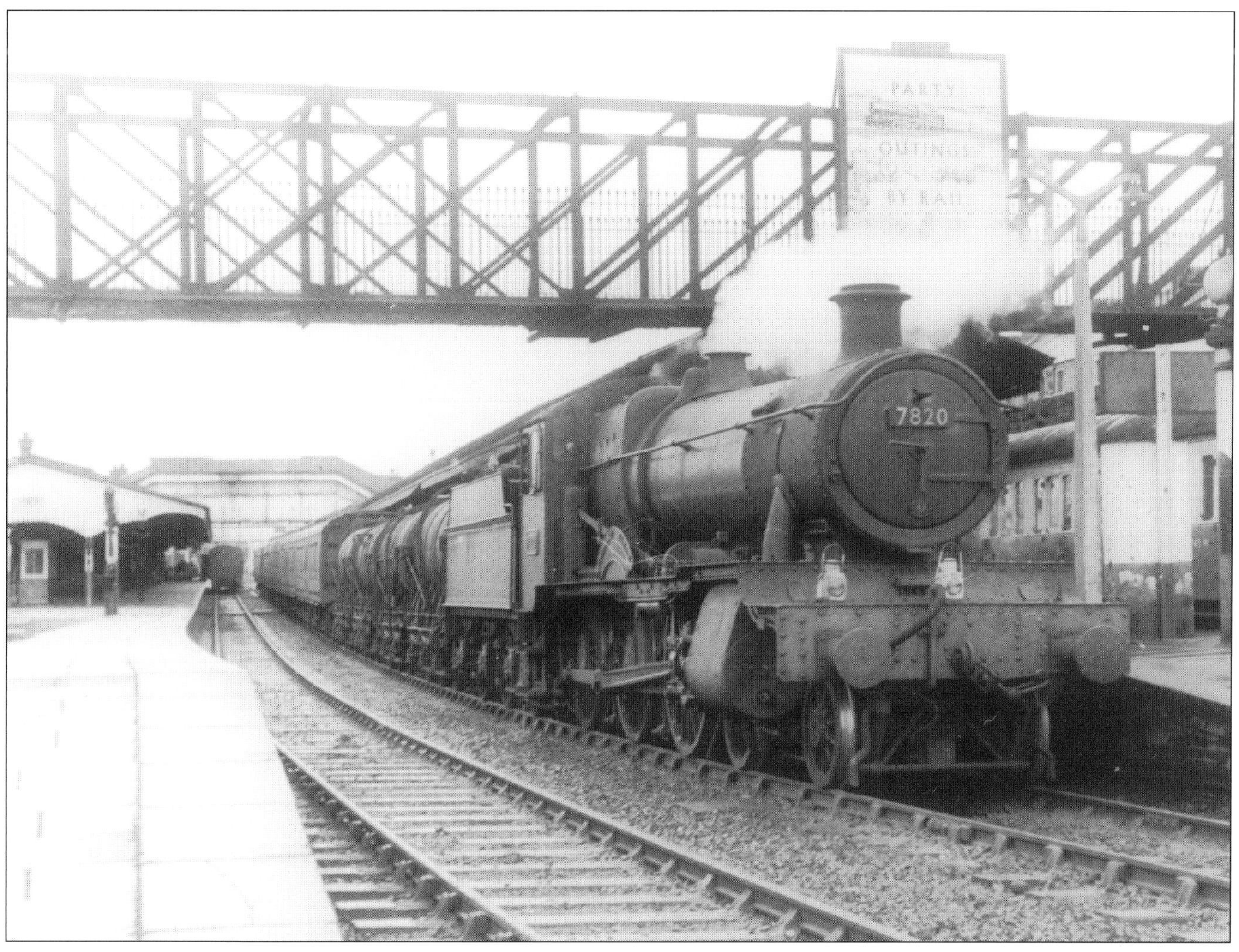

The same loco 7820 'DINMORE MANOR' stands at Truro on a down milk and parcels train. As the engine is carrying a 83F (Truro) shedplate, the photo was taken between 28 November 1959 and 17 June 1960. D.I.D.Loveday.

5

STAR CLASS 4-6-0s

These locomotives replaced the smaller Bulldog and Duke class 4-4-0s on main trains in the county and worked them until they themselves were superseded by the more modern Castles and Halls. Concurrent with the Stars were the two cylinder Saints, but I have been unable to locate any photos of those engines in Cornwall. Indeed, I only ever saw one of the class in the county and that was in June 1945, when a very dirty 2987 'BRIDE OF LAMMERMOOR' hauled a long down passenger train up St Austell bank one Saturday afternoon.

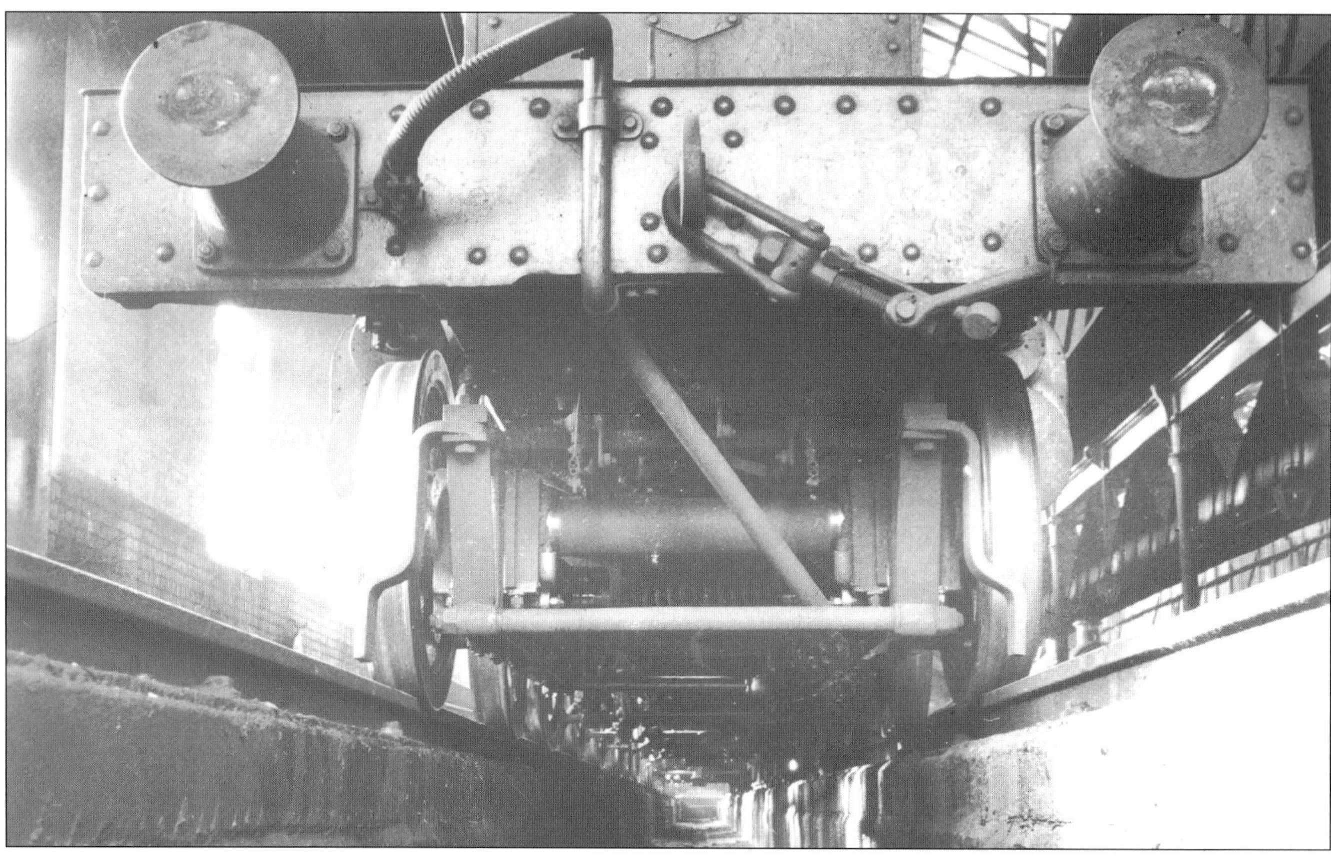

We start this section with a most unusual view of part of the front of 4007 'RISING STAR'. The shot was taken from an inspection pit when the engine was inside Long Rock shed during 1934. It shows the problem associated with attempting to record on film the yellow figures of the number that were painted on a red background. This engine was re-named 'SWALLOWFIELD PARK' in May 1937 and was withdrawn in September 1951. It was shedded at Exeter during 1934. T.Corin.

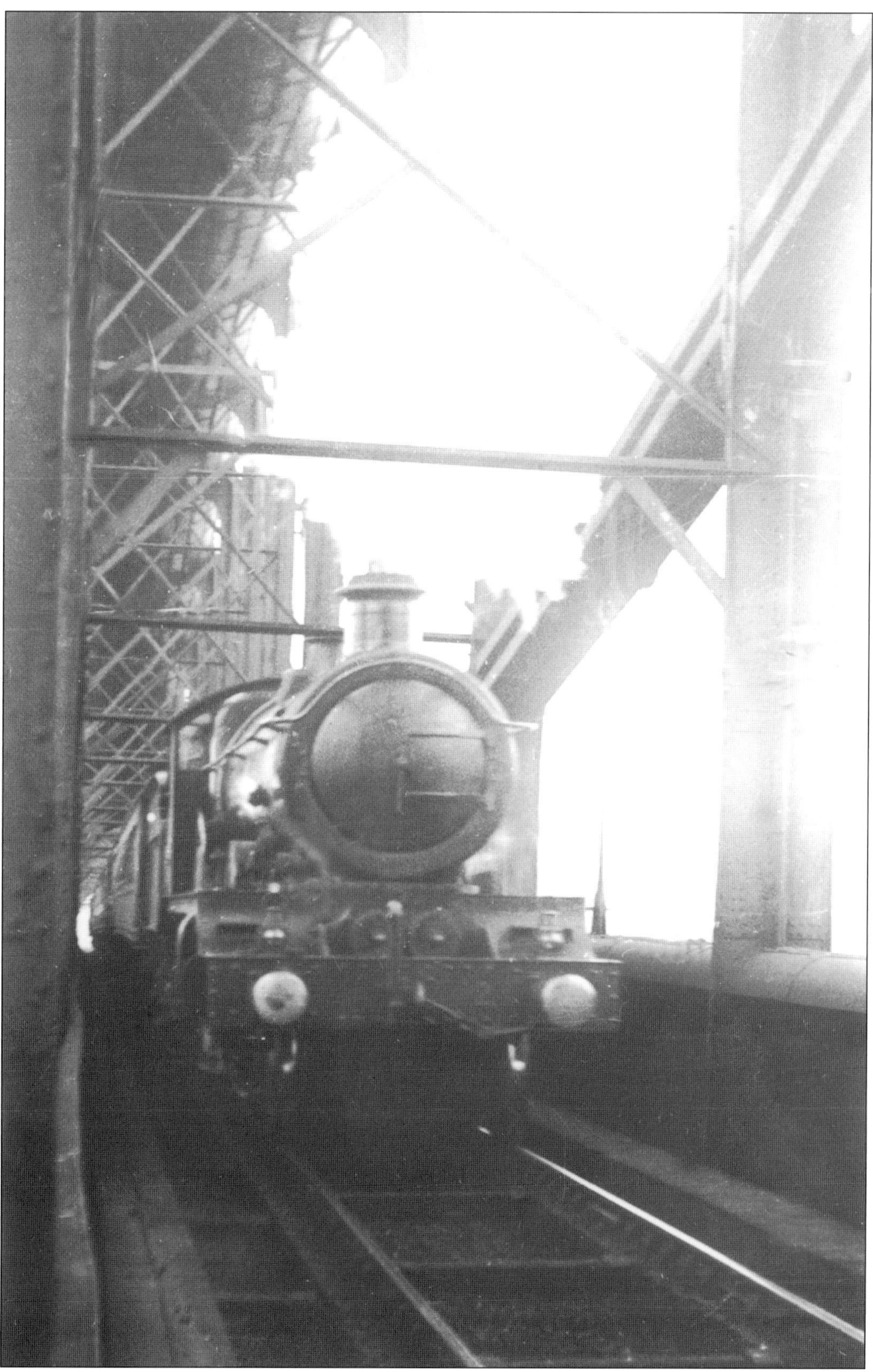

Seen from an unusual vantage point on the Royal Albert Bridge is 4024 'KING JAMES' working the 11am Penzance to Paddington express on 6 April 1919. In September 1927 this engine was re-named 'THE DUTCH MONARCH' and was again re-named 'DUTCH MONARCH' during October or November of the same year. The engine was withdrawn in February 1935.
Locomotive Club of Great Britain/Ken Nunn collection.

Laira had a Star allocated quite late on in the class's life. It was 4054 'PRINCESS CHARLOTTE' which is backing an empty milk tank and parcels train out of Penzance station on 11 October 1950. An SR van is behind the engine. The engine was withdrawn on 29 February 1952.

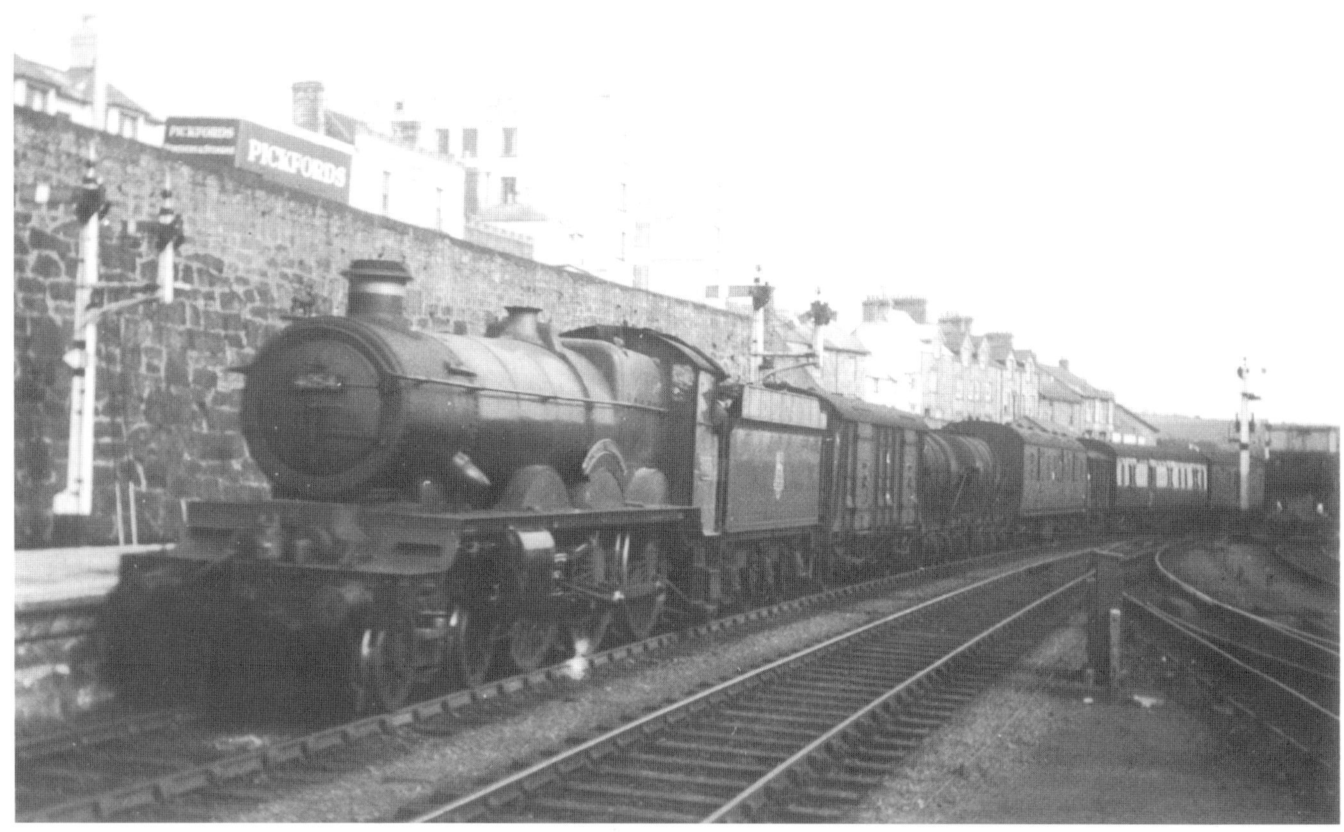

6

COUNTY CLASS 4-6-0S

The County class first appeared in 1945 and were more powerful than the Castles as they had a boiler pressure of 280 lb/sq.in. This gave them a distinct advantage on the hilly main line route in Cornwall so they soon appeared on main passenger trains and maintained a presence until almost the end of steam. Laira also possessed a few BR Standard class 4MT 4-6-0s of the 75XXX series and although these worked into Cornwall no photos of them in the county have been found.

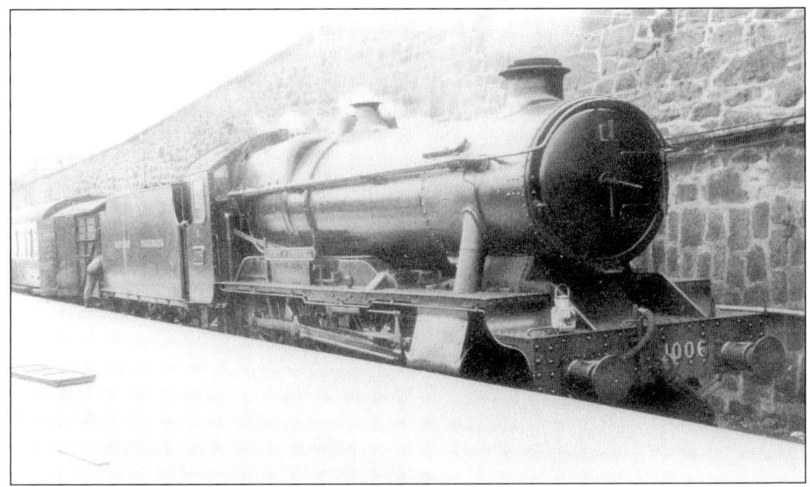

With its tender lettered 'BRITISH RAIL-WAYS', 1006 'COUNTY OF CORNWALL' from Laira shed stands at Penzance station at the head of a passenger train during 1948. The vehicle immediately behind the engine was originally a GWR cattle wagon which had been converted to a fruit van during the 1930s. Kenneth Brown.

Just coming off the coaling line at its home shed, Long Rock, on 24 June 1962 having had it's tender refilled is 1001 'COUNTY OF BUCKS'. The loco has been fitted with a double blast-pipe. L.R.Peters.

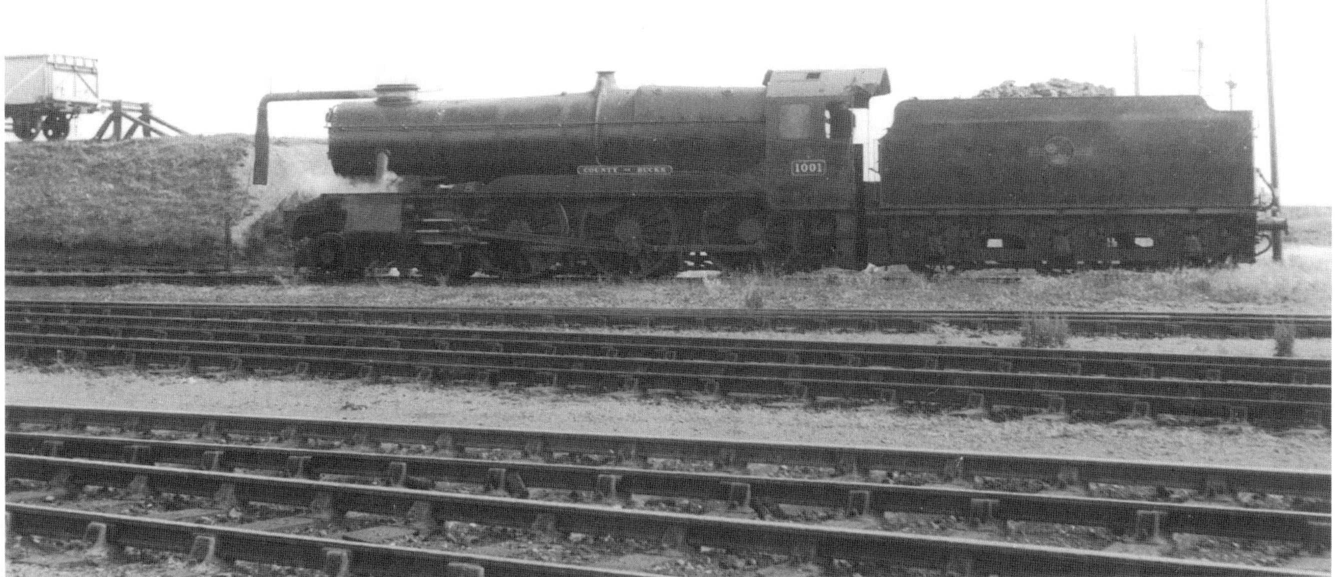

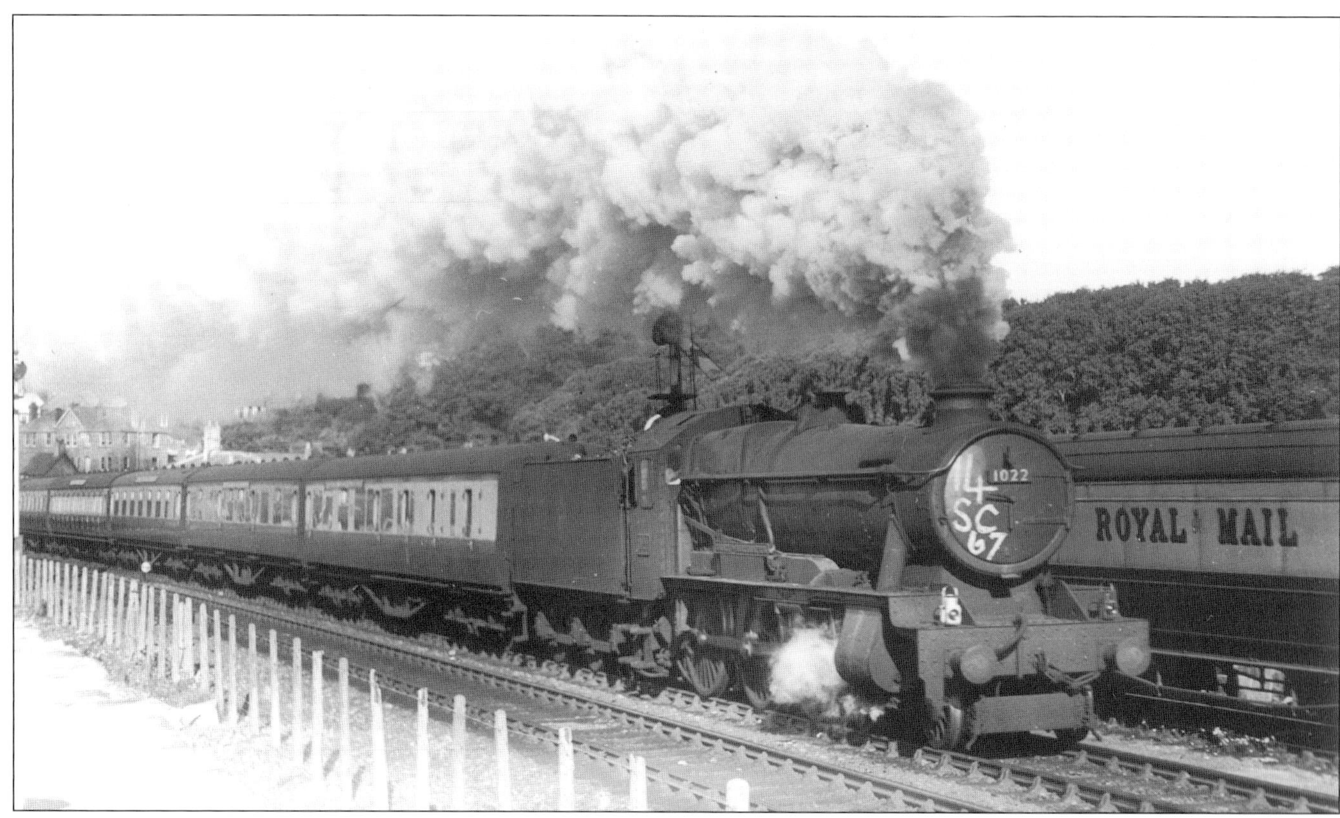

Producing an excellent smoke effect as it accelerates the 8.5am passenger departure out of Penzance, past Ponsondane in July 1951, is Long Rock's 1022 'COUNTY OF NORTHAMPTON'. The first two vehicles are Hawksworth carriages. This engine moved to Chester in November of that year. A GWR mail van is in the siding.

Having run around its stock after arriving at Falmouth in 1947, 1023 'COUNTY OF OXFORD' from Truro shed has shunted the carriages to the departure platform. The engine will uncouple and run out to the yard to turn on the turntable. C.M. & J. M. Bentley.

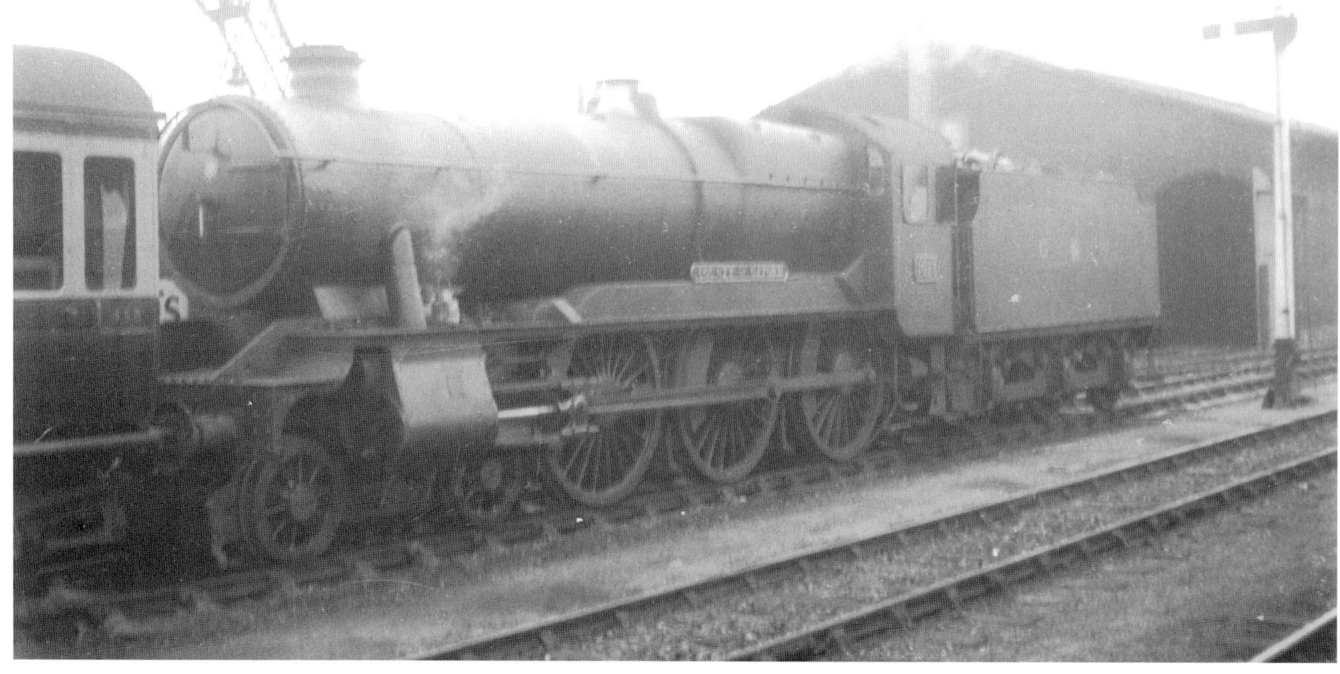

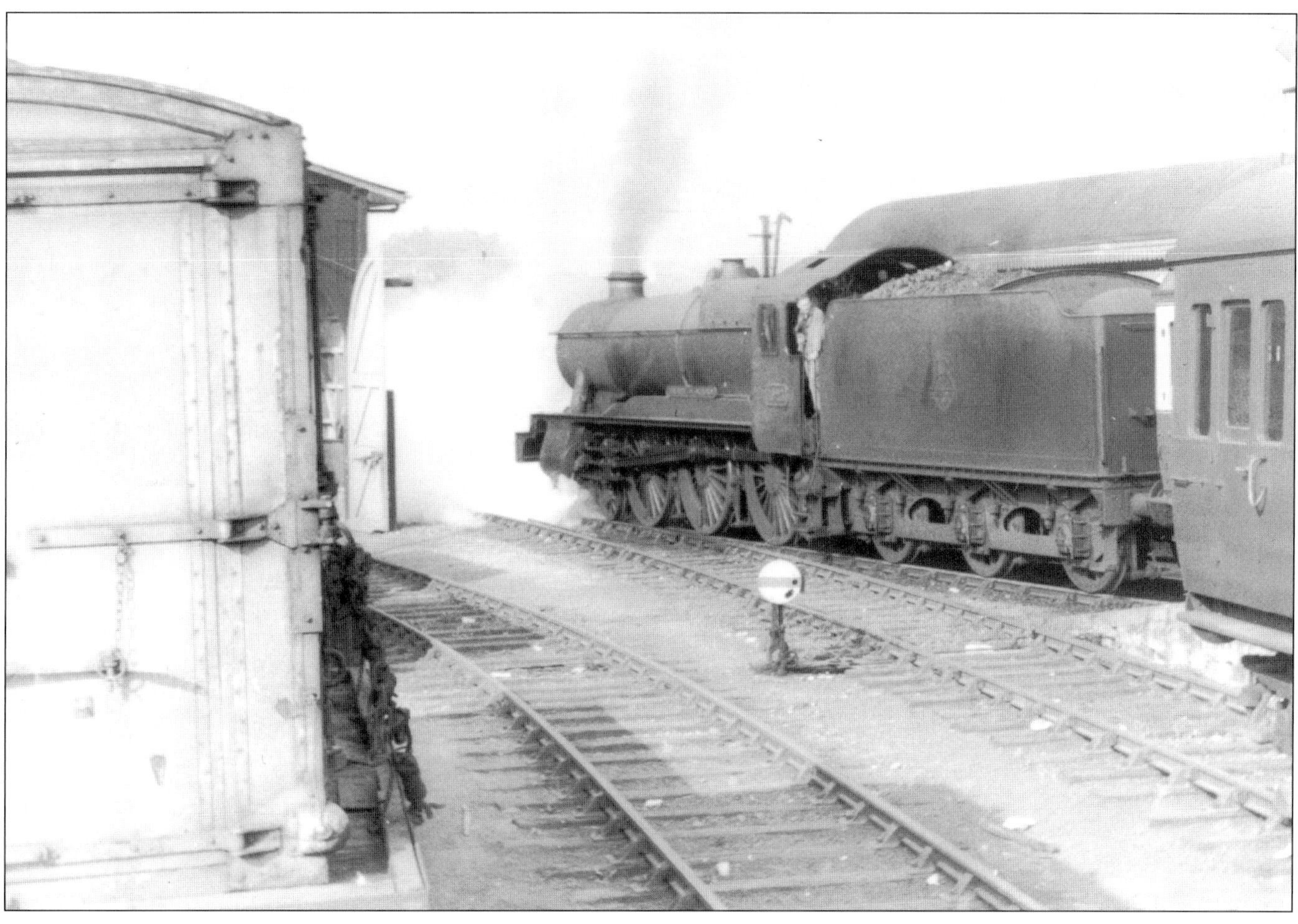

This engine 1023 'COUNTY OF OXFORD' moved around between the Cornish sheds but was back at Truro again when it is seen departing from Falmouth in 1956. On the left is an insulated meat container on a Conflat wagon. D.Buckland.

7

GWR SMALL PRAIRIE TANKS

These were the ideal engines for branch line working and were to be found throughout the county in large numbers. With their 4ft 7½in diameter driving wheels, they were equally at home on passenger or goods work and were well liked by their crews. The most numerous were the 4500 class with small tanks together with their development, the 4575 class. These were fitted with slightly larger tanks with part sloping tops. In the early part of the twentieth century all of the members of the smaller 4ft 1½in diameter driving wheeled 4400 class were also shedded in Cornwall. Together, these two classes of engines revolutionised branch line working, not only in Cornwall but throughout the GWR system.

We start with the first member of the 4500 class and see 4500 itself, running round its train at Falmouth, probably in the 1930s. This engine spent its entire life in Devon and Cornwall and would have been shedded at Truro when this photo was taken.

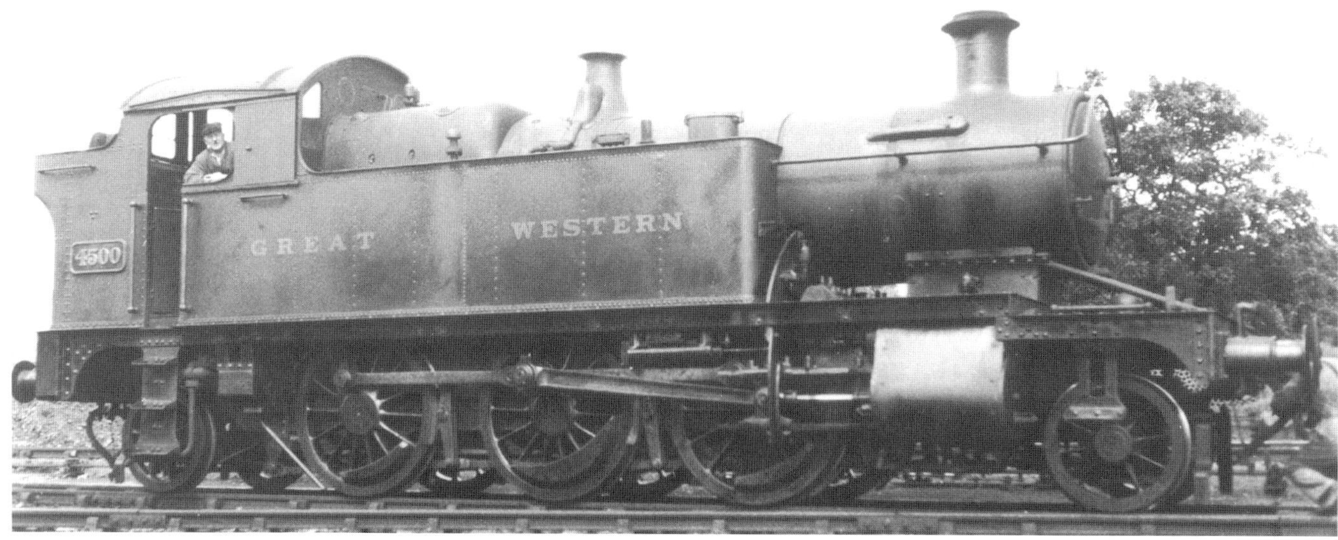

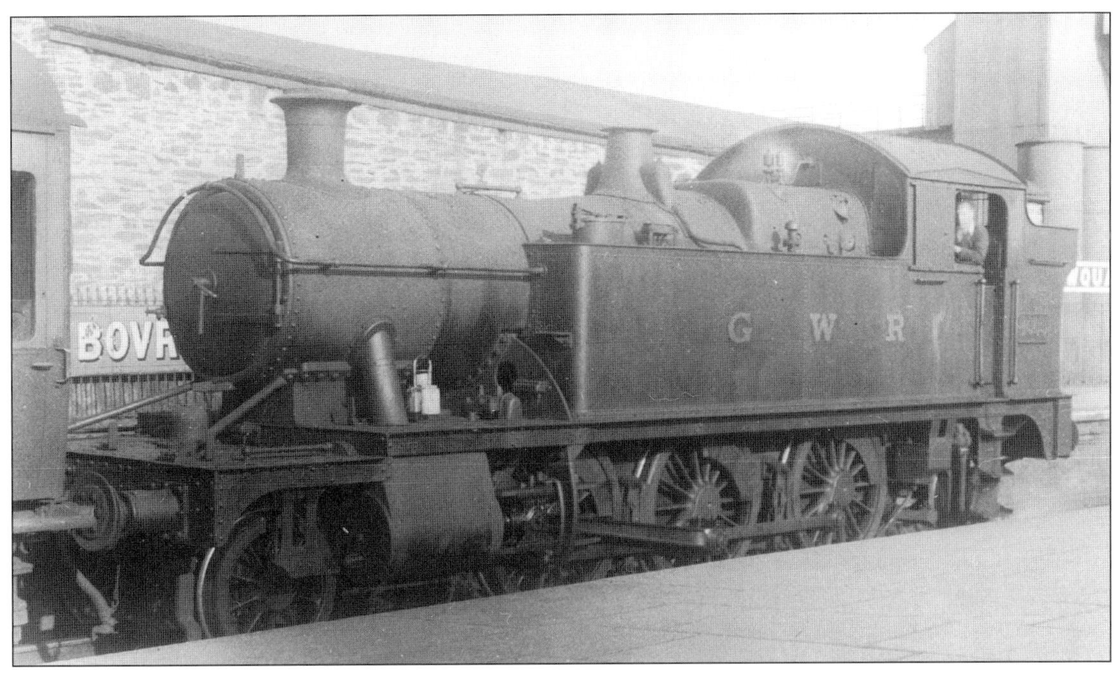

Here is 4503 from St Blazey shed at Newquay awaiting departure on 20 April 1946. The S^{T}B shed stencil is visible on the frame.

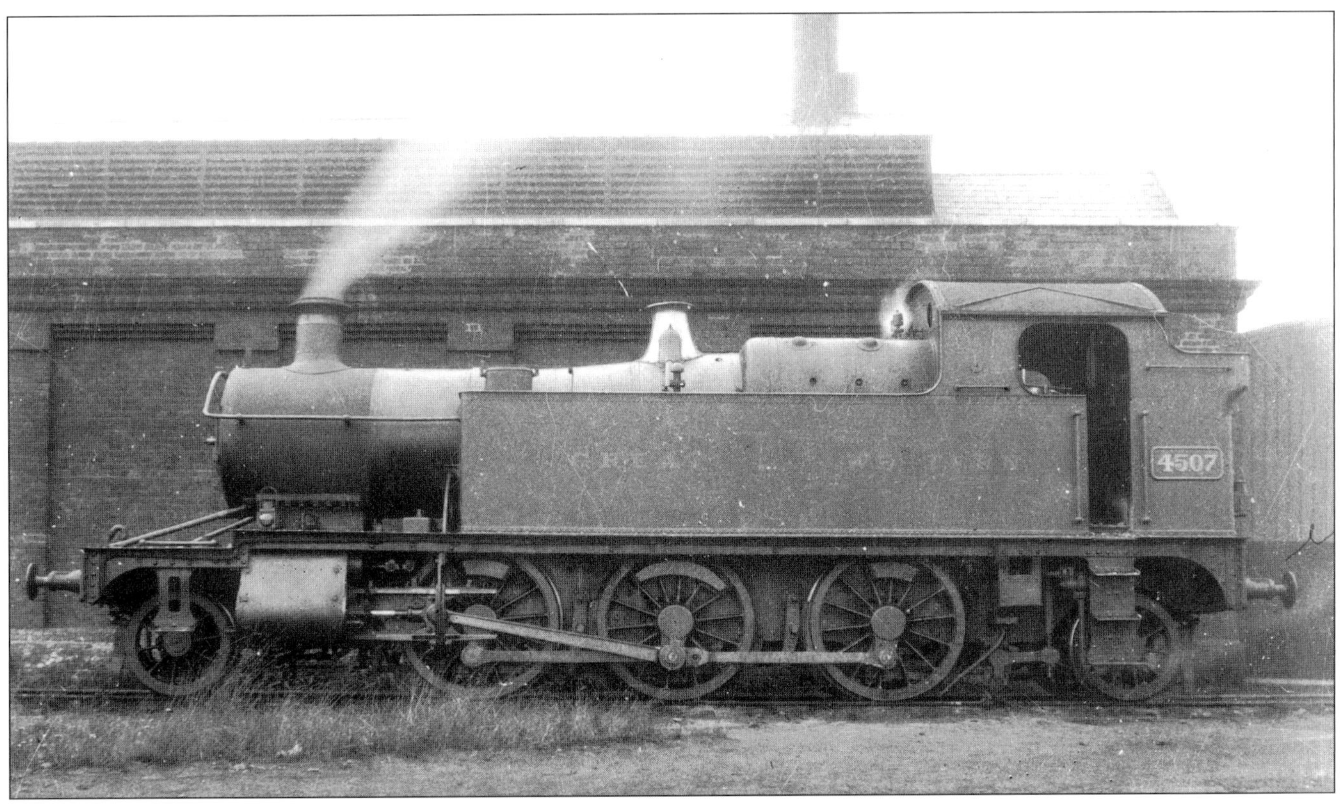

Alongside the shed at St Blazey in 1923 we see 4507 which is still fitted with its original small bunker. P.J.T.Reed.

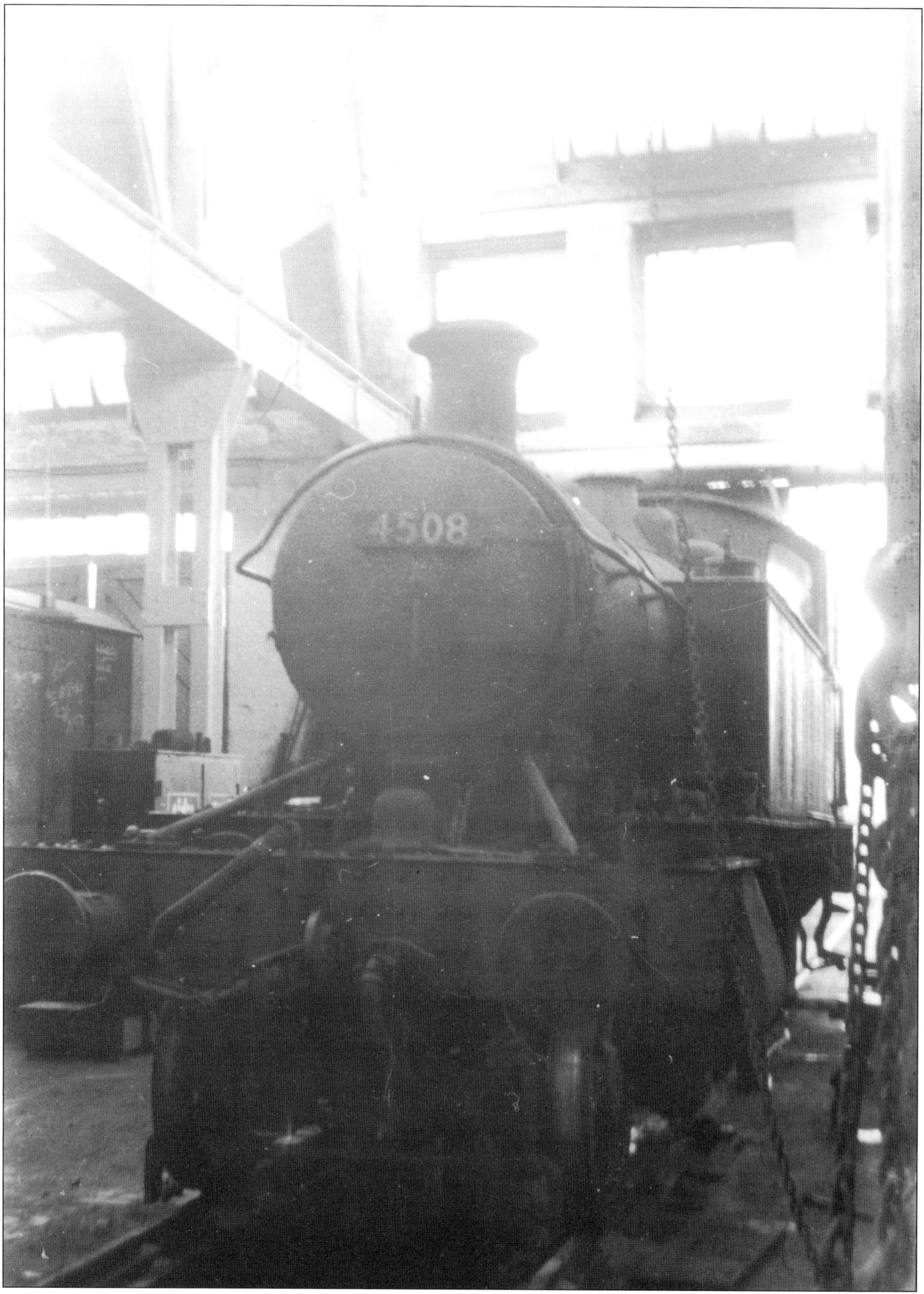

This is an unusual view of 4508 taken inside the one road 'Factory' at Truro shed on 4 May 1957. This engine never gained 'outside steampipes'. Maurice Dart.

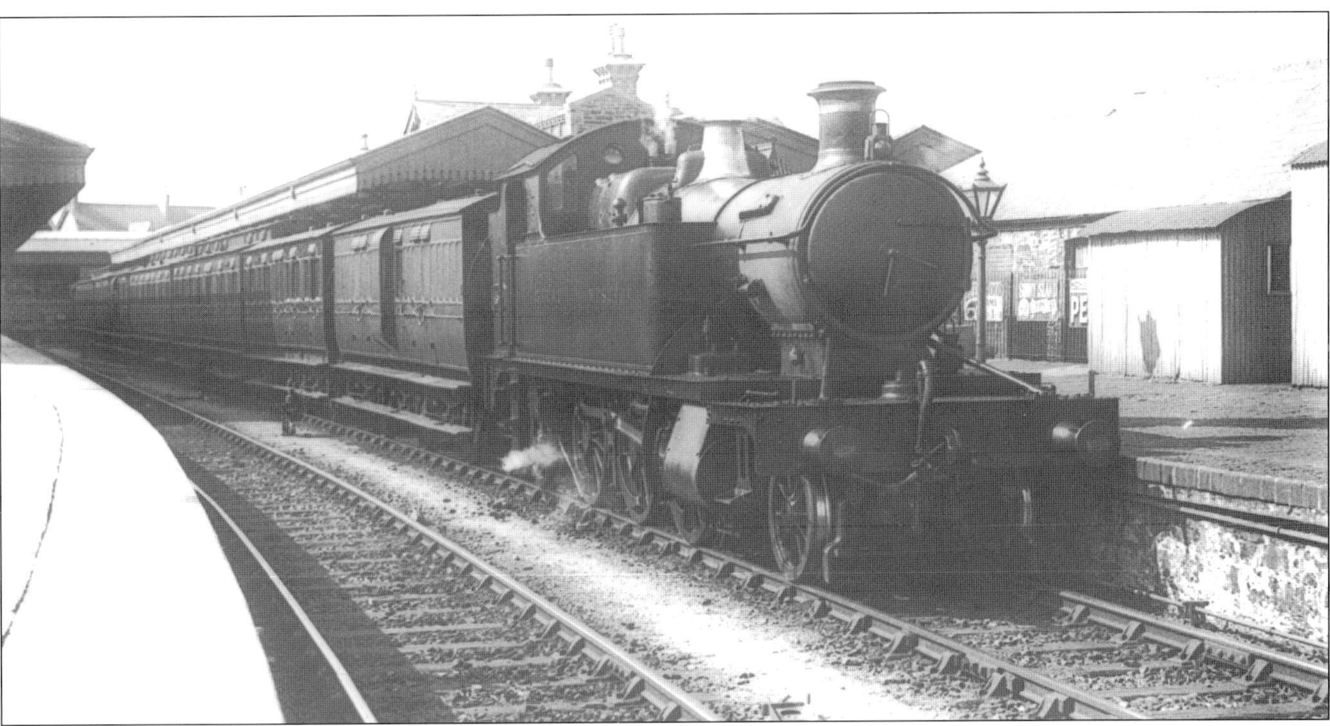

This view from 1 July 1921 shows 4510 waiting to depart from Newquay with a train to Fowey, which would have been routed over the steeply graded route through Pinnock tunnel. The front carriage is a 6 wheeled full brake. The Locomotive Club of Great Britain/Ken Nunn collection.

Here is the same locomotive 4510 outside St Blazey shed in 1935. As there is a crane with its crane match wagon No.606 in front of the loco, it is probably waiting to receive some attention and possibly be 'lifted' under the adjacent hoist which is out of the picture behind the photographer. The ex Cornwall Minerals Railway Wagon Works is prominent behind the engine. Coupling and piston rods have been removed from the engine.

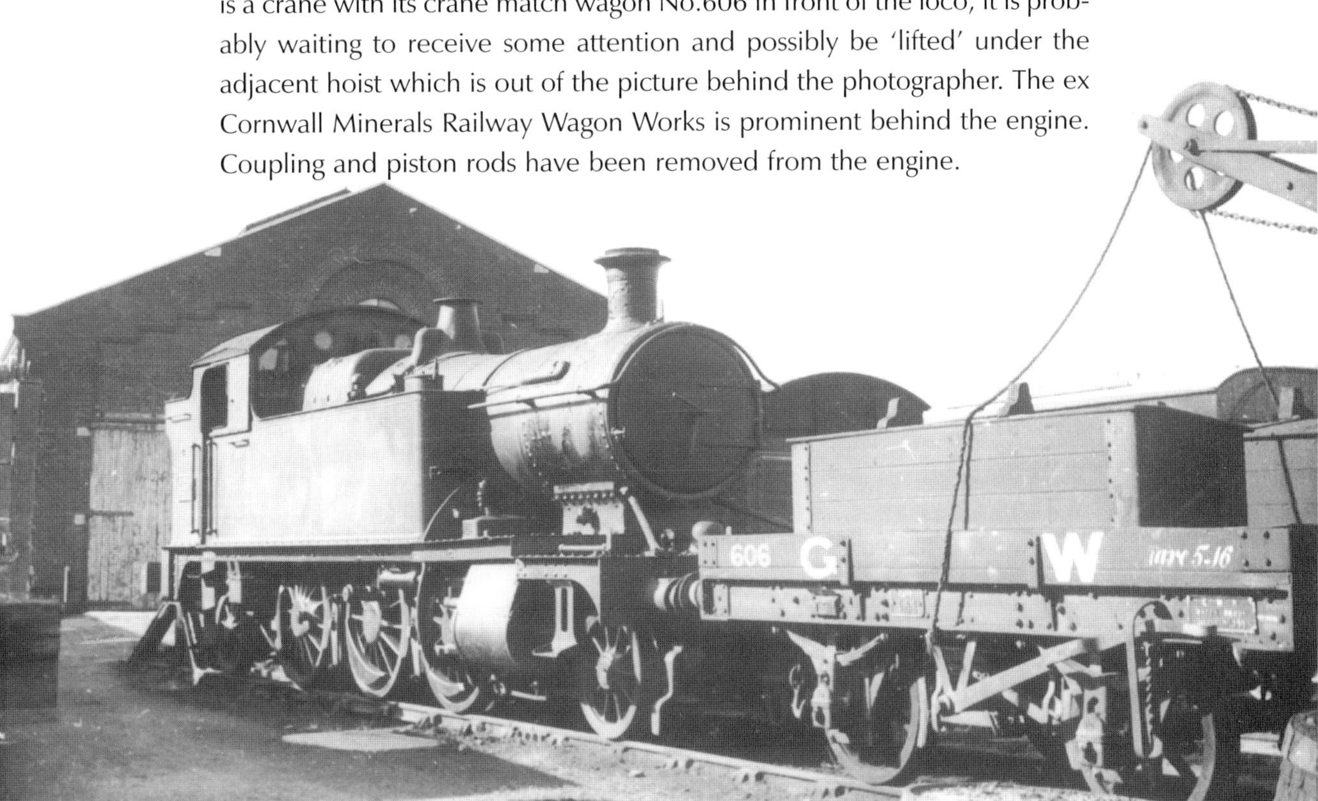

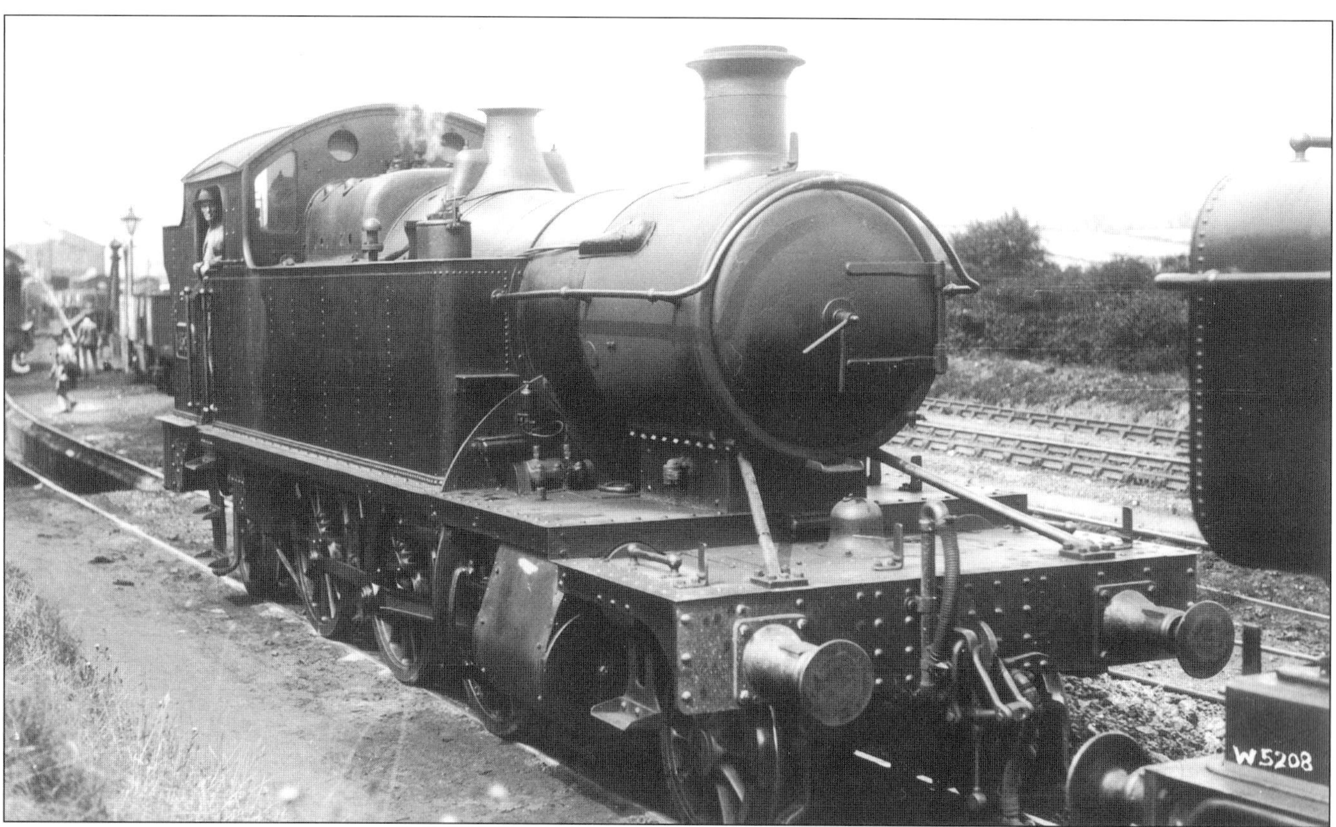

The Wagon Works is again visible in this shot of 4528 on the coaling line at St Blazey shed, probably in the 1930s, complete with its driver wearing a trilby hat. This engine ended its life at Laira shed.

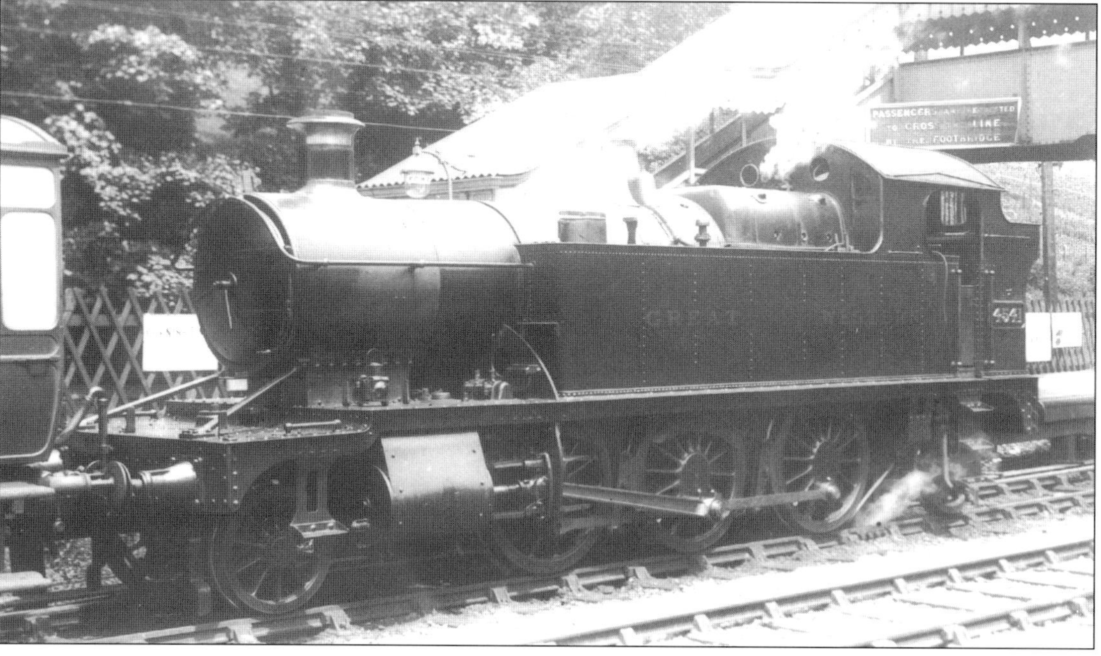

4541 from St Blazey shed has arrived at Fowey with a train from Par routed via St Blazey and Pinnock tunnel on 20 June 1924. The engine has a bright brass safety valve bonnet. The Locomotive Club of Great Britain/Ken Nunn Collection.

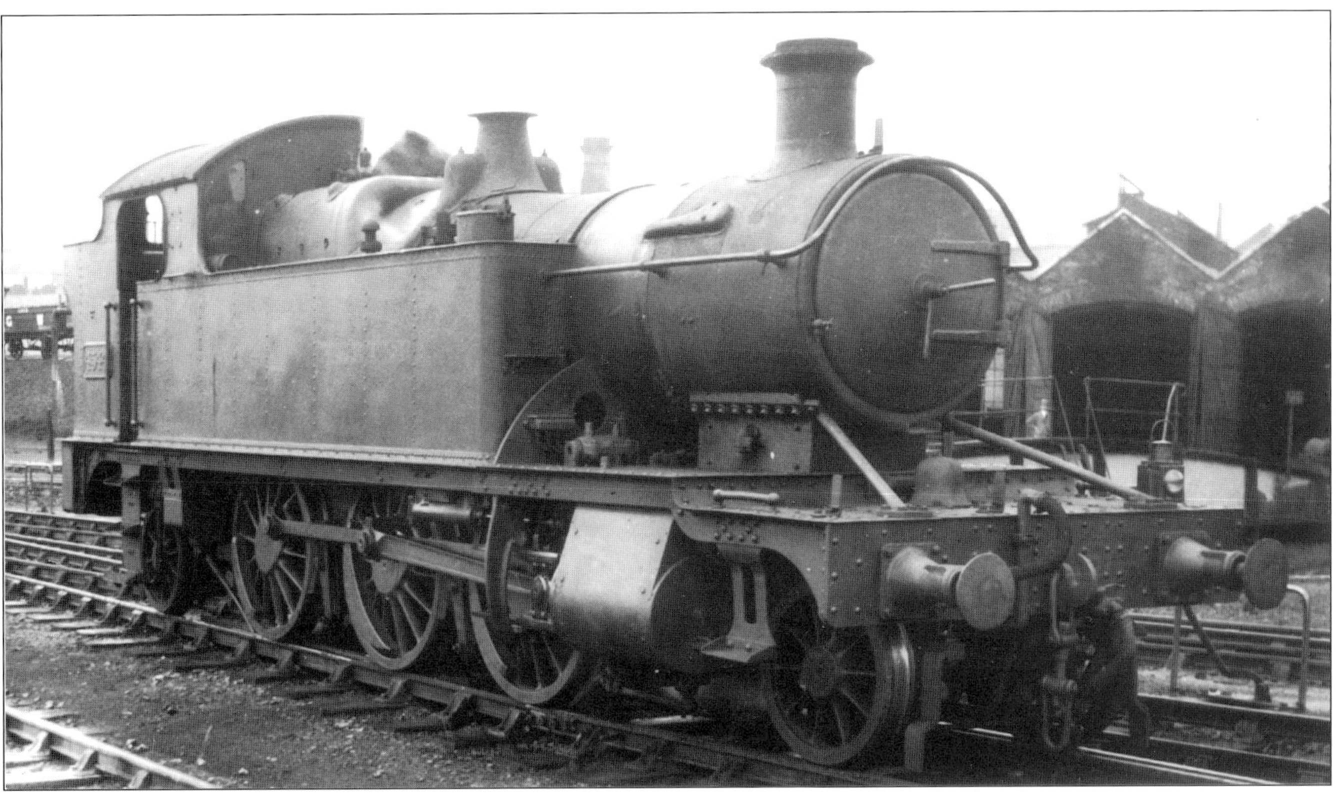

At St Blazey shed in the 1930s, 4544 is opposite the turntable. Rail Archive Stephenson/Photomatic.

4545 from Penzance shed is standing at the short goods and parcels platform at St Erth on a very short mixed goods train on 21 August 1954. The train consists of a GWR Toad brake van, an insulated container on a Conflat wagon and a GWR fish van. L.R.Peters.

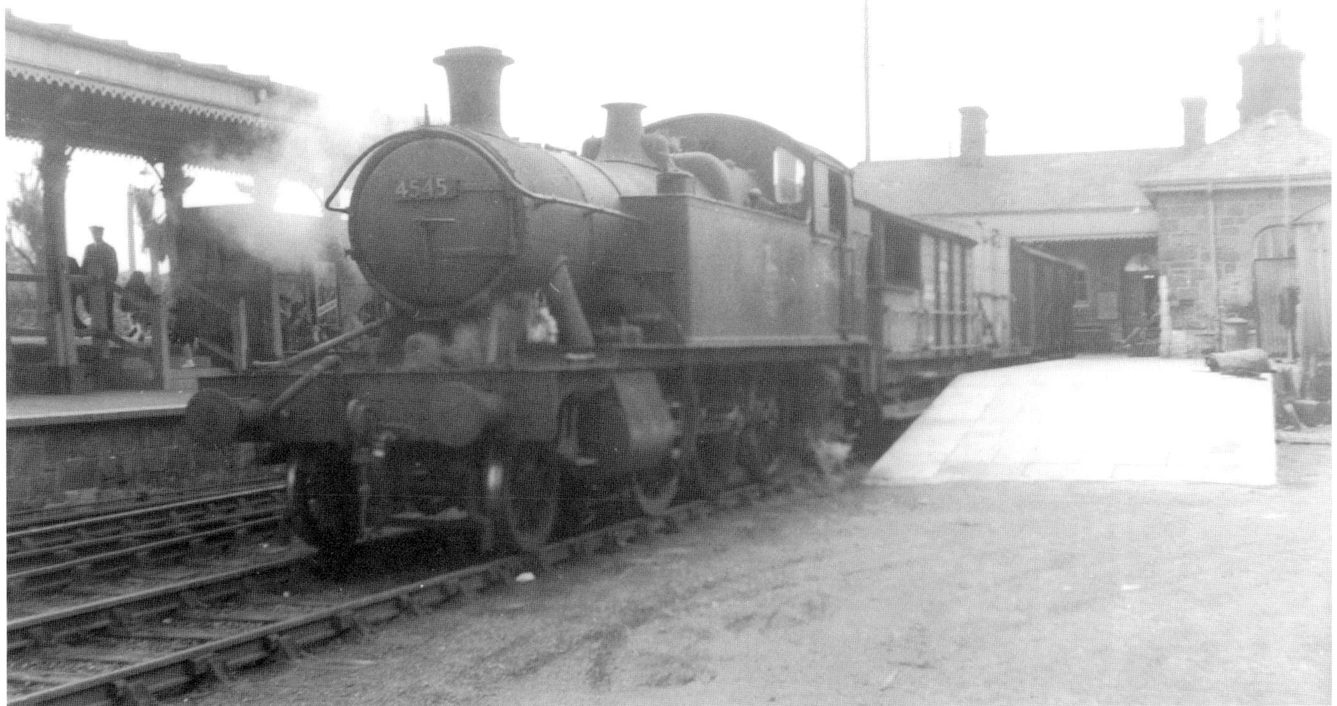

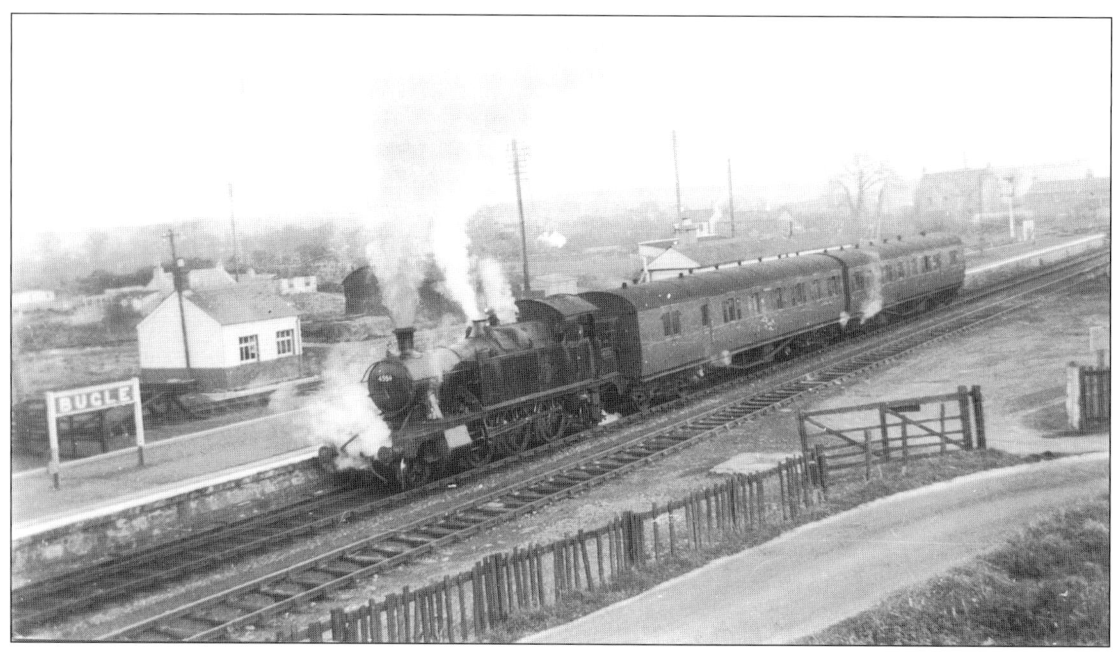

Recently ex works 4559 starts away from Bugle with the 3.50pm Par to Newquay train composed of a standard GWR 'B' set on 24 November 1956.   Maurice Dart/The Transport Treasury.

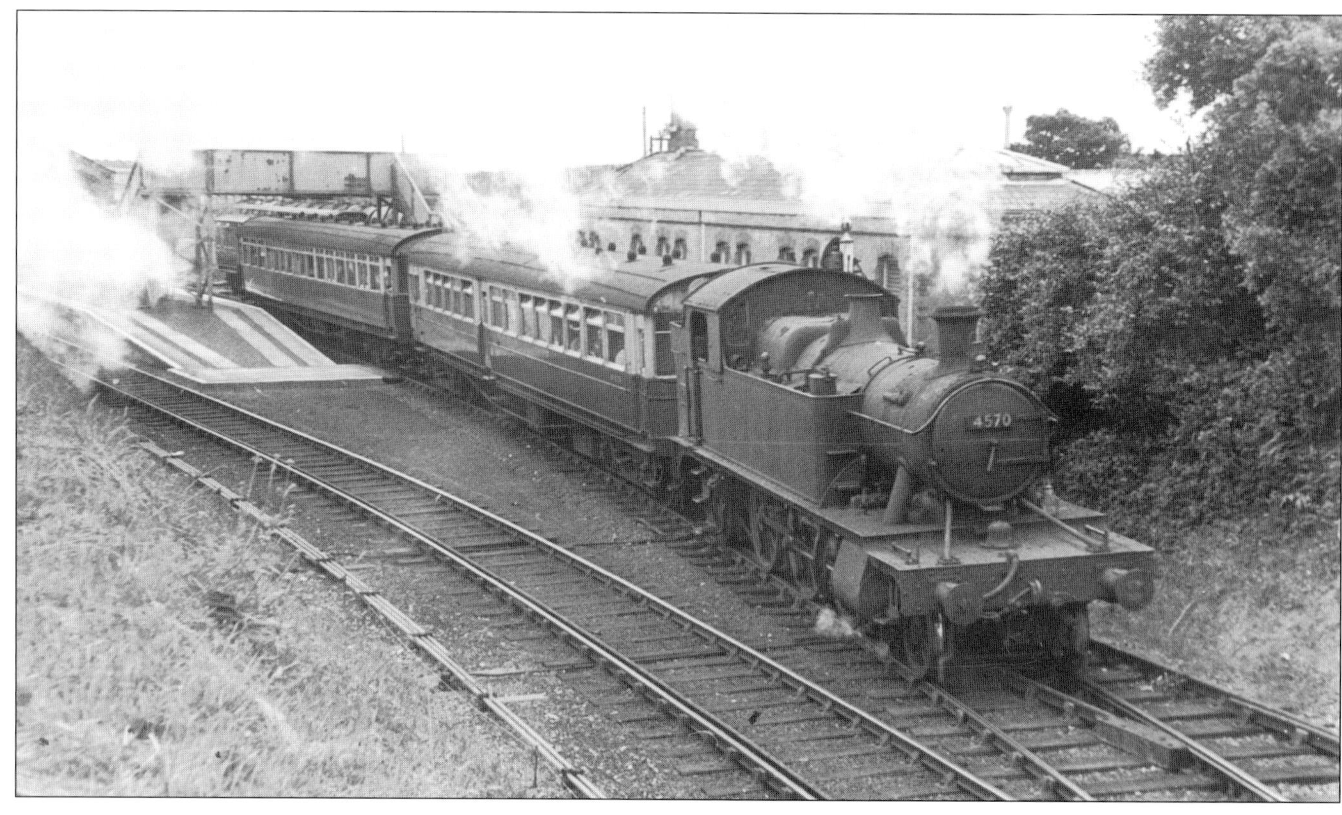

A train from Chacewater to Newquay leaves St Agnes hauled by 4570 from Truro shed on 9 July 1952. It is composed of a pair of Auto coaches in what appears to be GWR livery. Partly hidden by the train is a GWR clerestory carriage, some tank wagons and the goods shed.   G.A.Hookham.

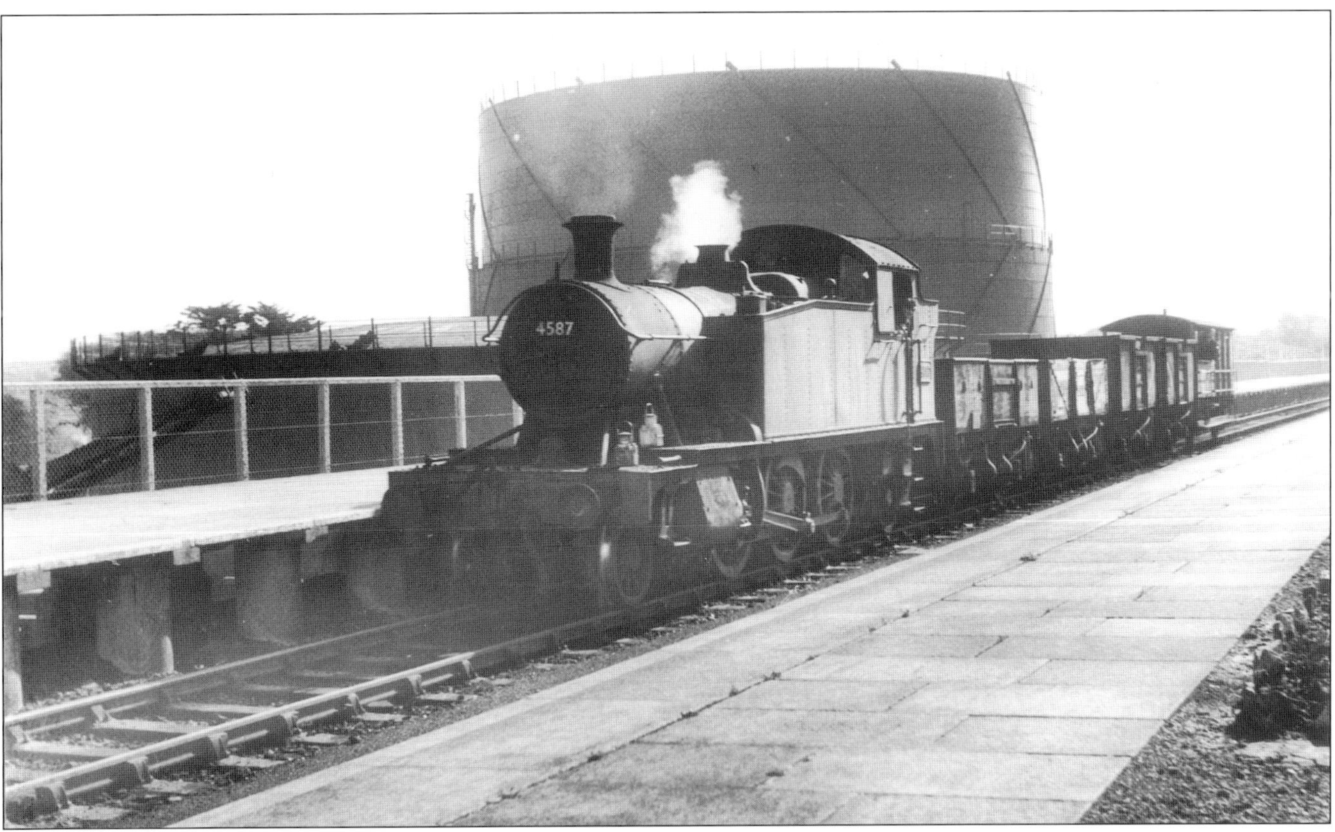

Next we come to the larger tank 4575 class of which 4587 from Truro shed has arrived at Newquay on 19 October 1959 on a short train of open wagons. The gasholders are prominent in the background. R.B.Parr.

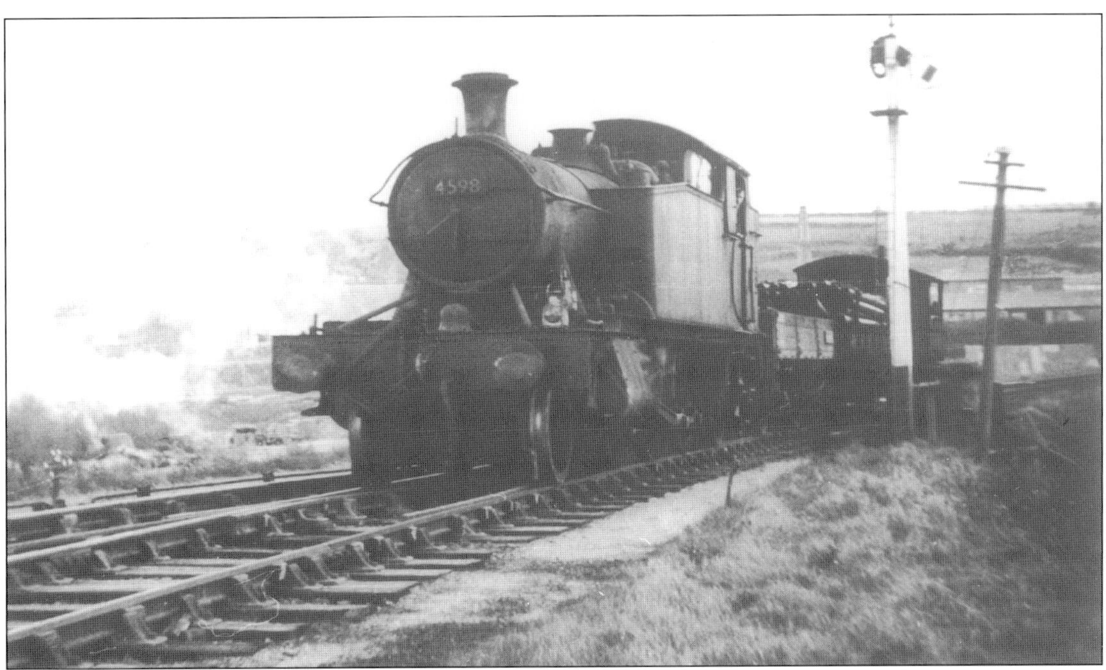

Another very short goods train which appears to be carrying a load of pipes hauled by St Blazey's 4598 is passing Drinnick Mill in 1951. The train is about to start to climb at 1 in 50. West of England Companies siding is diverging on the left and Dubbers No.2 kiln is visible in the right background.

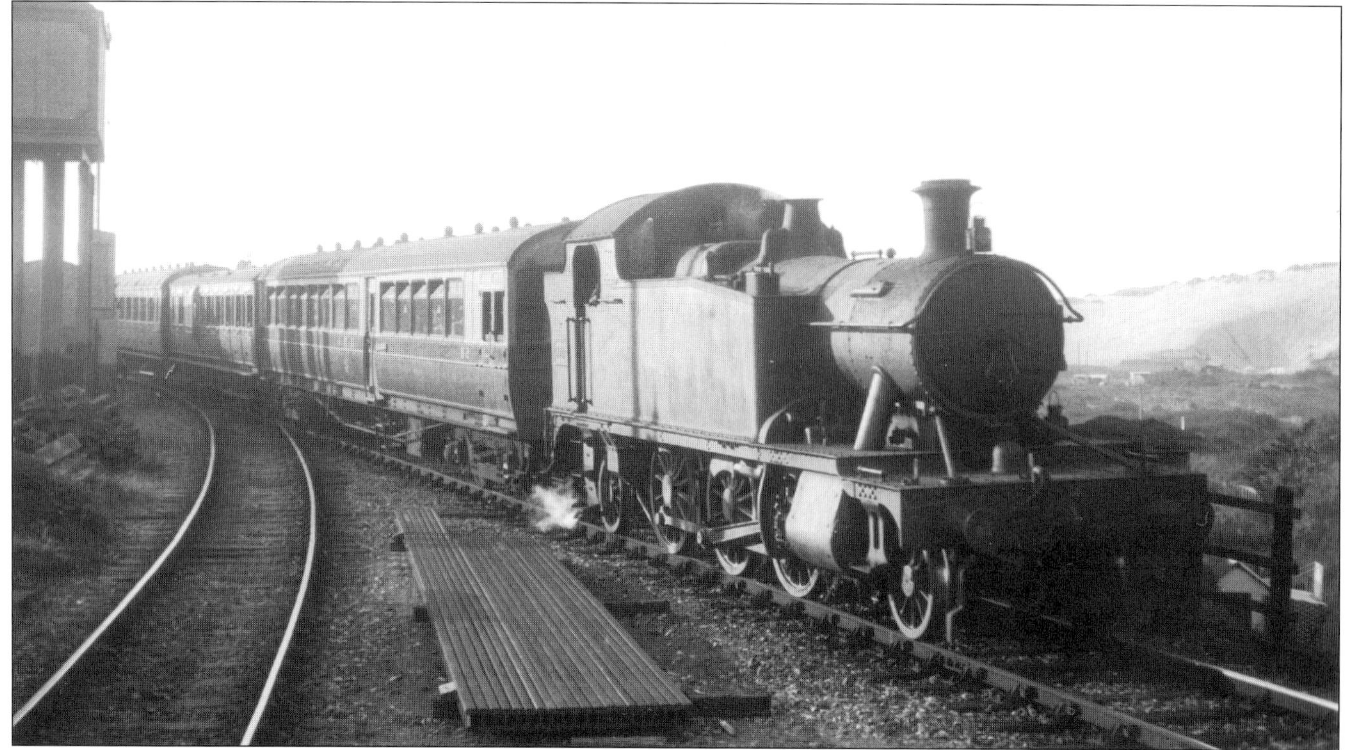

A passenger train composed of three very assorted carriages is passing a water tank as it approaches Perranporth in the early 1930s. Behind the engine is Auto coach No.82. The train is hauled by 5504 from Truro shed. J.C.Allen.

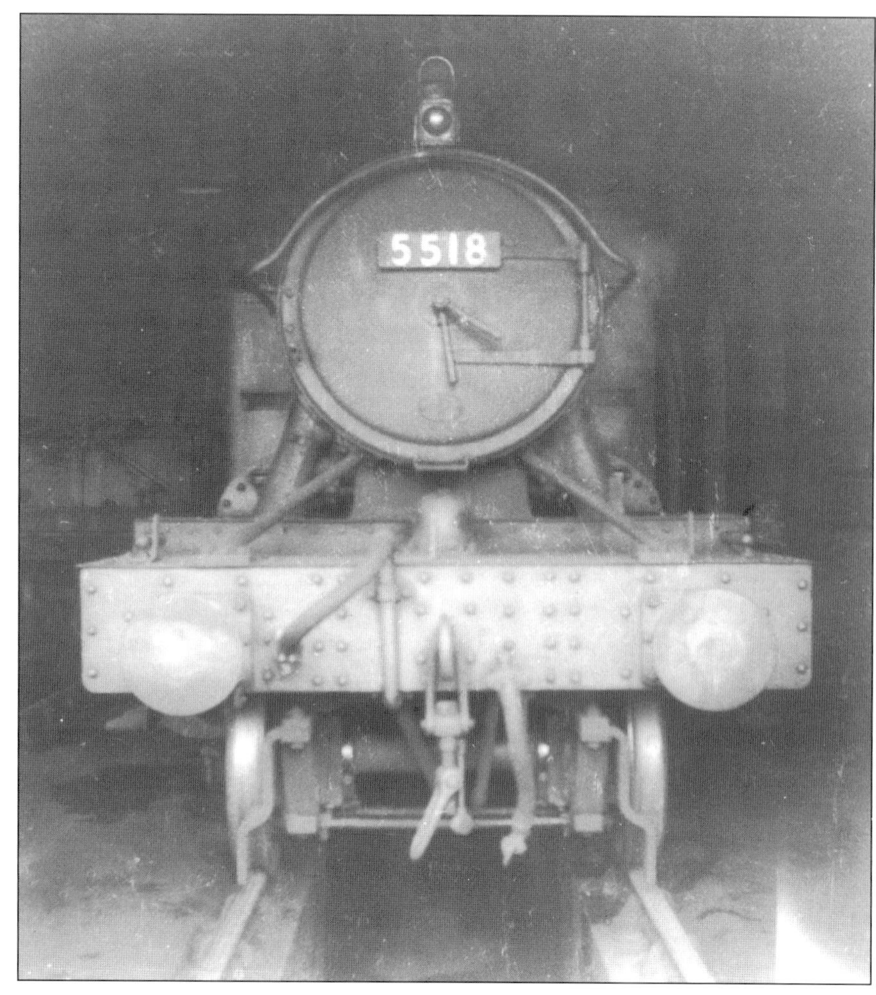

Towards the end of steam operation in the area 5518 from St Blazey shed stands inside the tiny sub-shed at Moorswater during the evening of 7 June 1961. Maurice Dart.

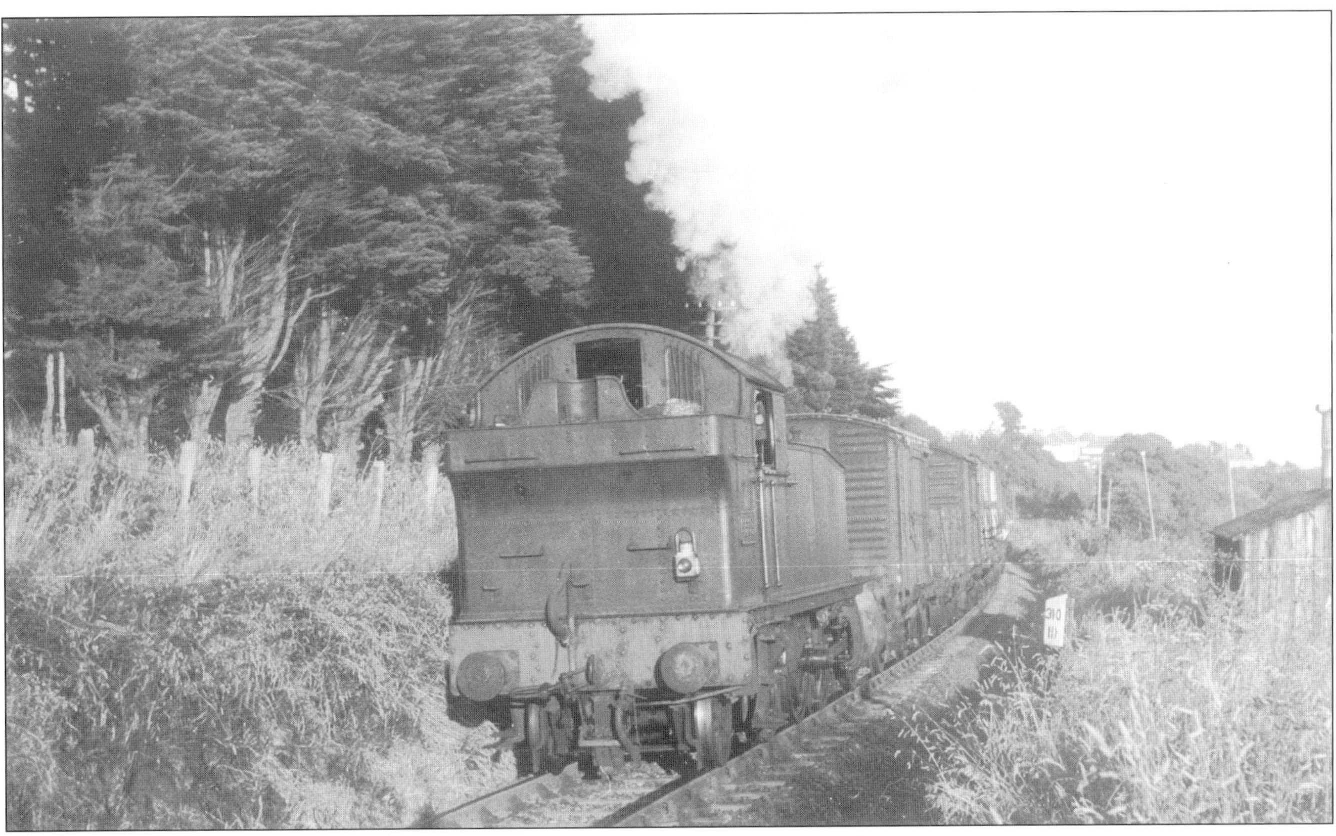

Approaching Tregoniggie crossing, shortly after departing from Falmouth, 5559 from Truro shed is on the 8.12pm goods train for Truro on 7 September 1959.

During September 1962 a train for Plymouth hauled by 5564 from Laira shed awaits departure from the ex SR station at Launceston. Leading the train is a Stanier full brake followed by a pair of BR Mark 1 carriages. Colin Judge.

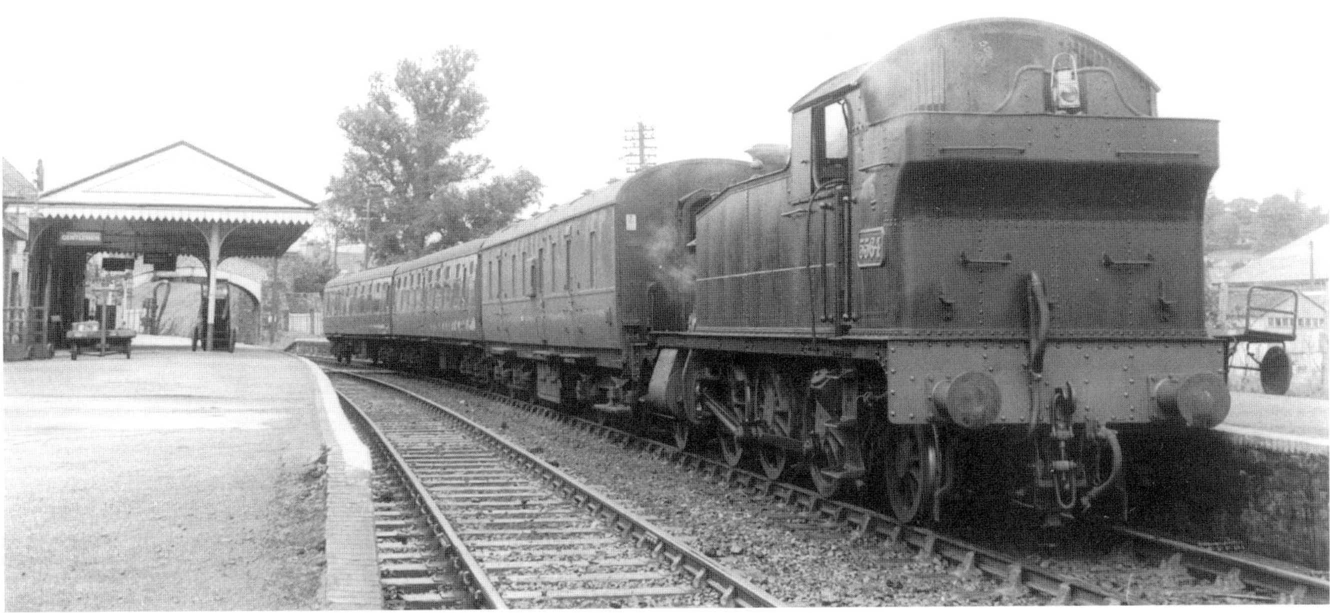

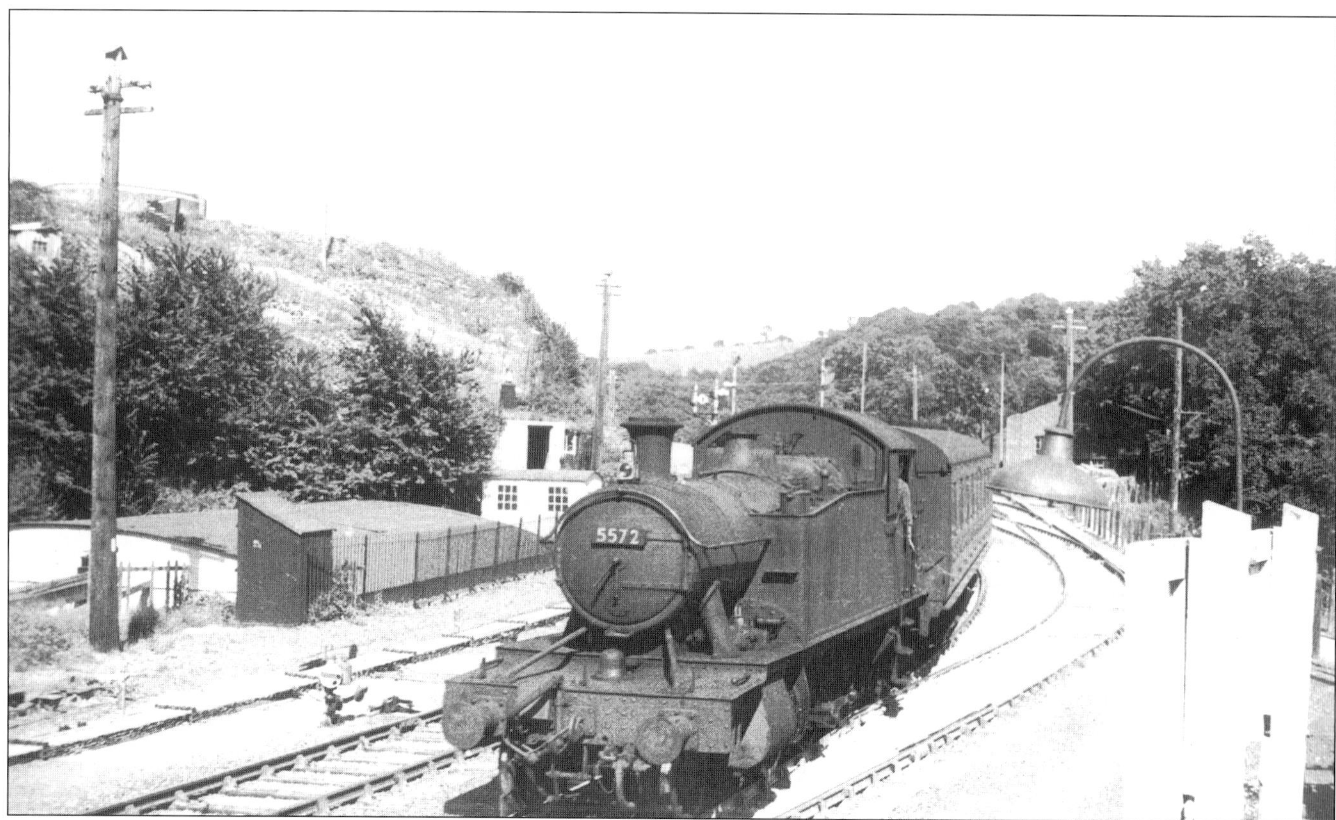

During the mid 1950s several members of the 4575 class were fitted with auto gear for working regular interval trains in the South Wales valleys. Later, when those services were turned over to working by new diesel multiple units, the auto fitted tank locos were dispersed. One of the locos was 5572 which spent periods at Laira and at St Blazey sheds and is seen arriving at Fowey on an auto train from Lostwithiel early in 1961.

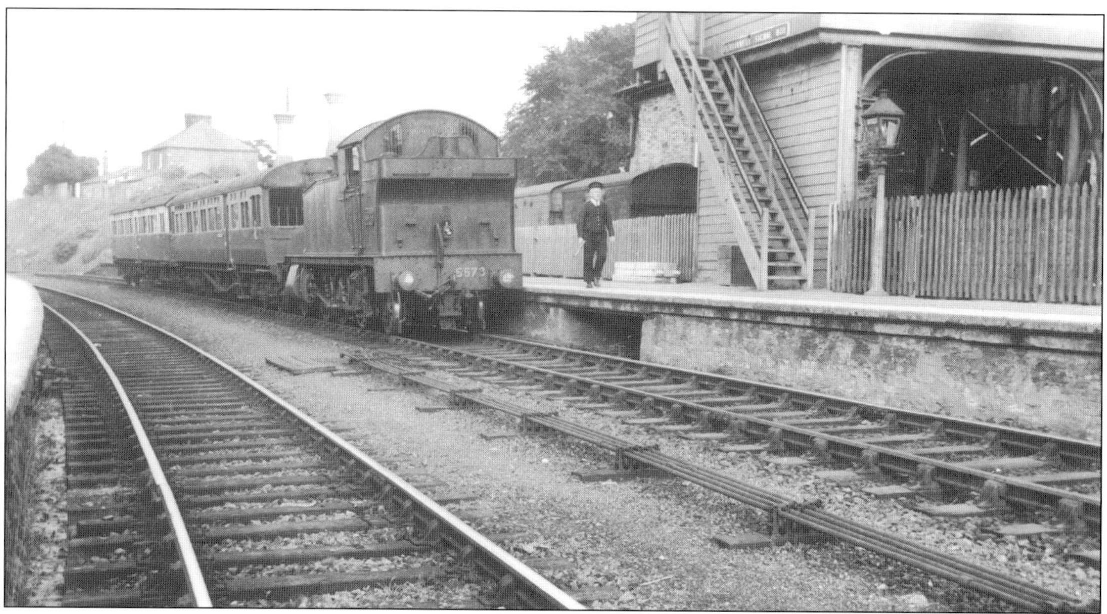

During the early 1930s 5573 has stopped at Perranwell on a train bound for Falmouth composed of two different Auto coaches. The rear carriage looks quite old. It appeared to be normal practice to work non-Auto trains using Auto coaches on the branch lines from Truro to Falmouth and from Chacewater to Newquay. Part of the elevated signal box is visible, to which the signalman is returning with the token for the single line section from Penwithers Junction.

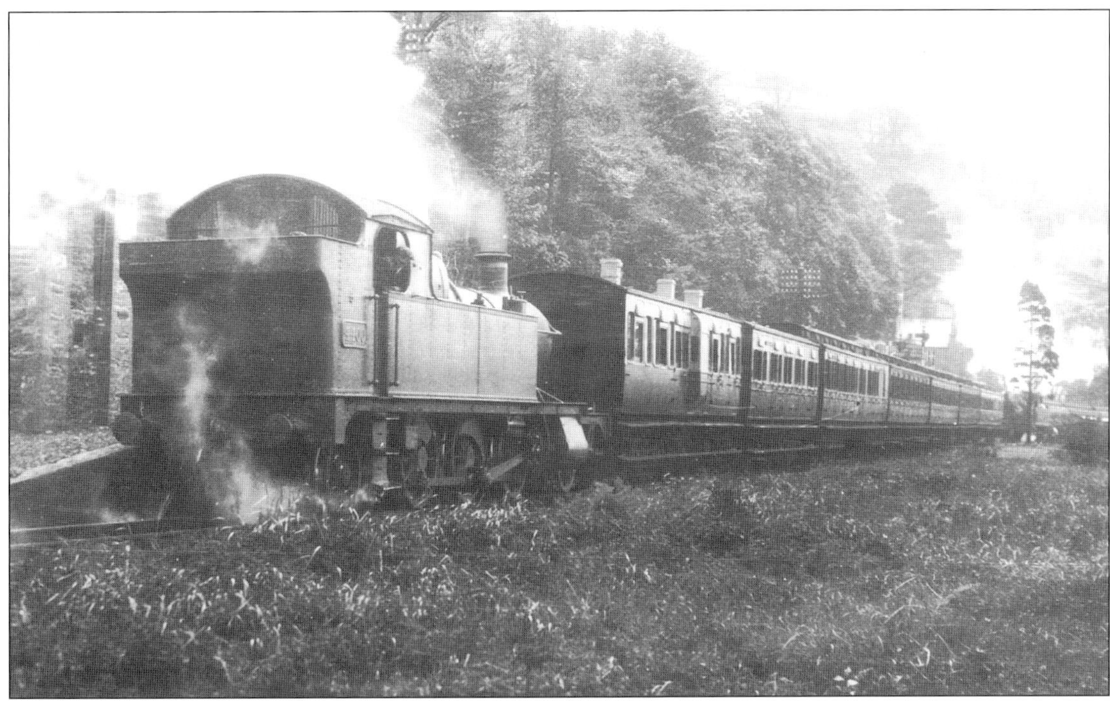

Now we progress to the smaller 4400 class tank locos and start with the first member of the class, 4400. The engine is seen at Looe in 1931 and is at the head of a train composed of very mixed stock which includes several clerestory vehicles. Most unusually, a second train is waiting in the background to follow the first train up the line to Coombe Junction and Liskeard. This engine was sub-shedded at Moorswater from May to June 1931 and again from August to October that year. It left the area in September 1935 for Wellington and Much Wenlock and was the only member of the class of eleven that eluded the author.

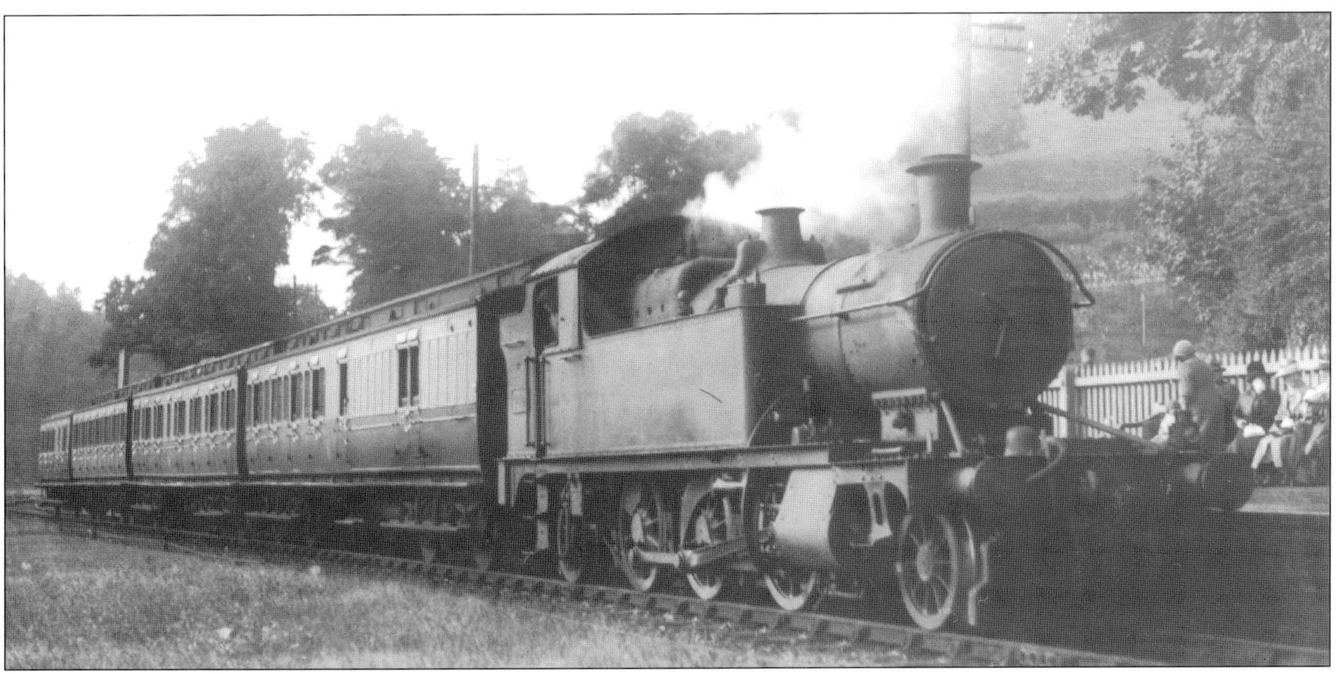

Here, the next member of the class, 4401 has arrived at Looe on a train of four carriages, three of which are clerestory vehicles. As this engine was sub-shedded at Moorswater for various periods between 1928 and 1934 the photo was recorded during that period. These locos with their small driving wheels were excellent power for the Looe branch line with its 1 in 34 gradient between Coombe Junction and Liskeard. R.K.Blencowe collection.

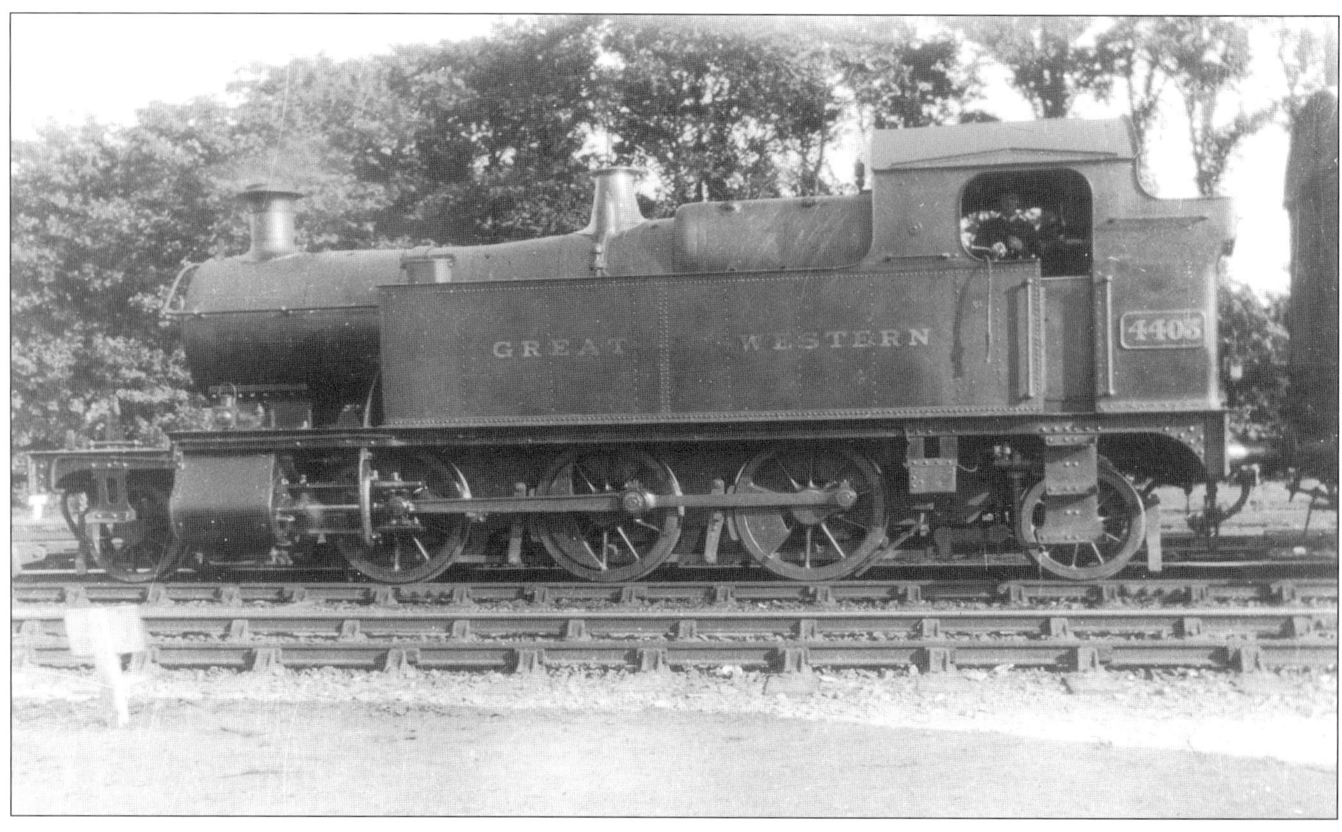

In this view 4403 is standing at St Erth ready to work a train to St Ives on 9 August 1923. The driver is watching the photographer in action. P.J.T.Read.

The driver of 4406 is also watching the photographer at work as the engine pauses in the shed yard at Long Rock, Penzance. This engine worked in the Penzance area from 1928 to 1933.

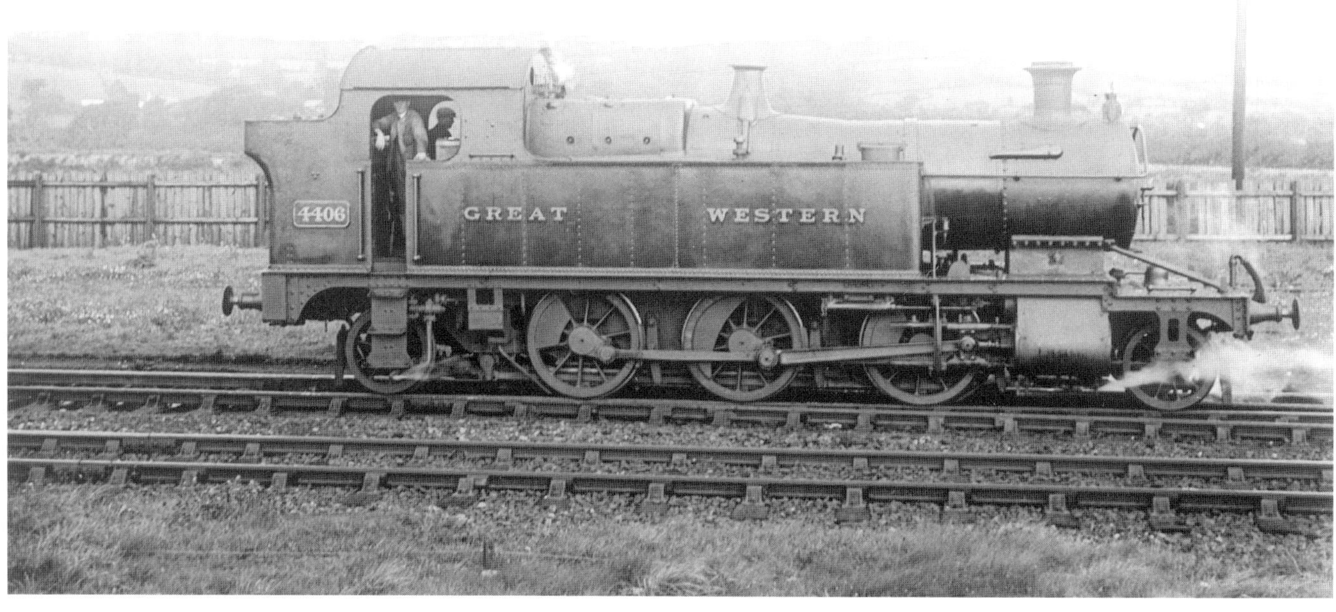

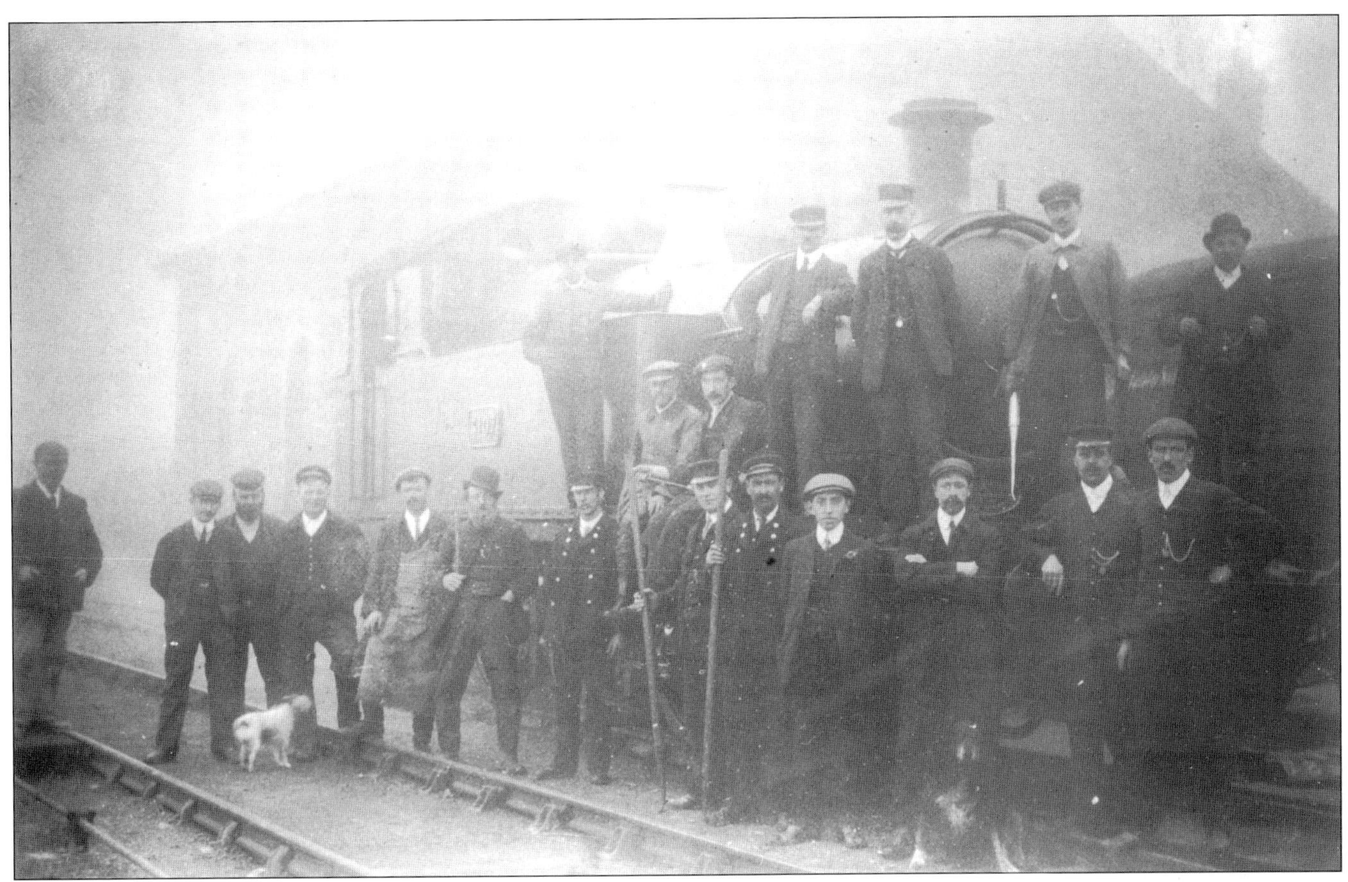

This is an interesting record of 3107 at St Blazey by the small shed which was later demolished. The engine went new to St Blazey shed on 30 April 1906 and judging by the gathering of railwaymen and dogs this photo could well have been taken shortly afterwards as they all wished to be photographed by the 'New Engine'. The numberplates were, up to this period, affixed to the centre of the side of the tanks. On 28 December 1912 at midnight the engine was renumbered to 4407.

Now we see the same engine by now numbered 4407 just entering Long Rock shed yard. This engine spent periods in the Penzance area in 1917/1918 and between 1932 and 1937.

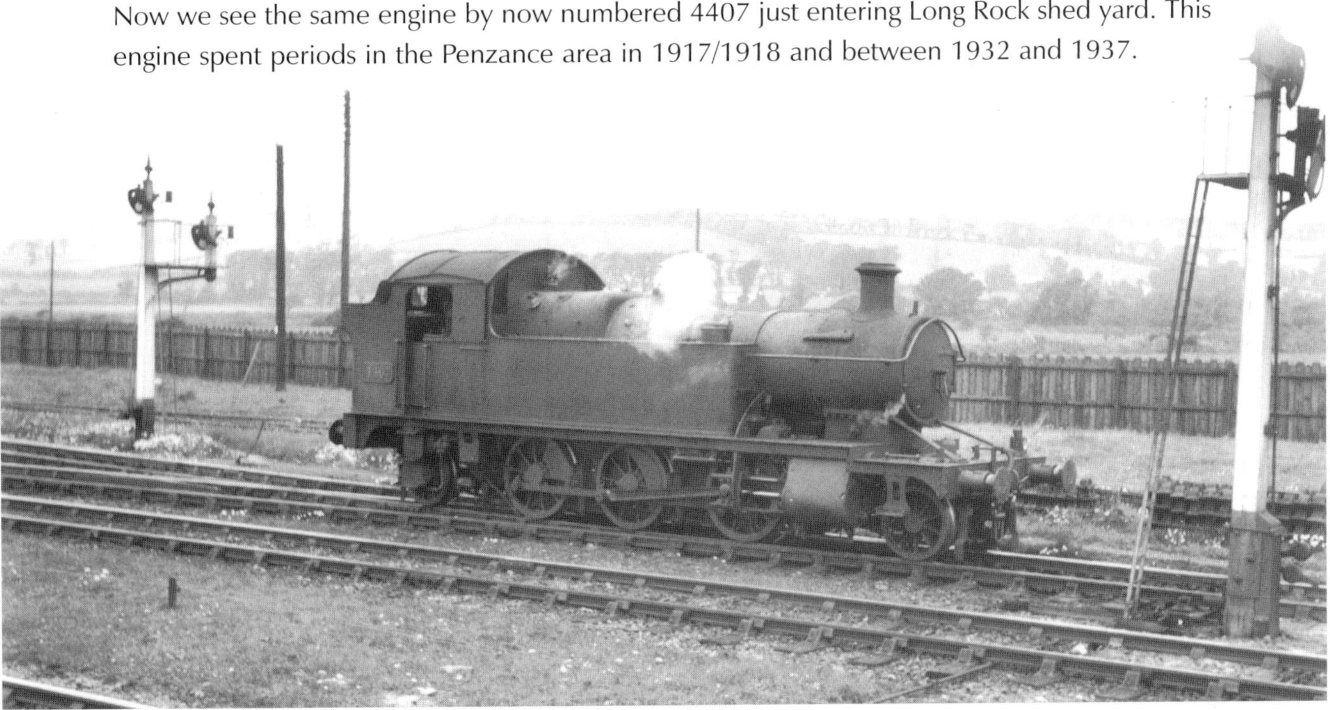

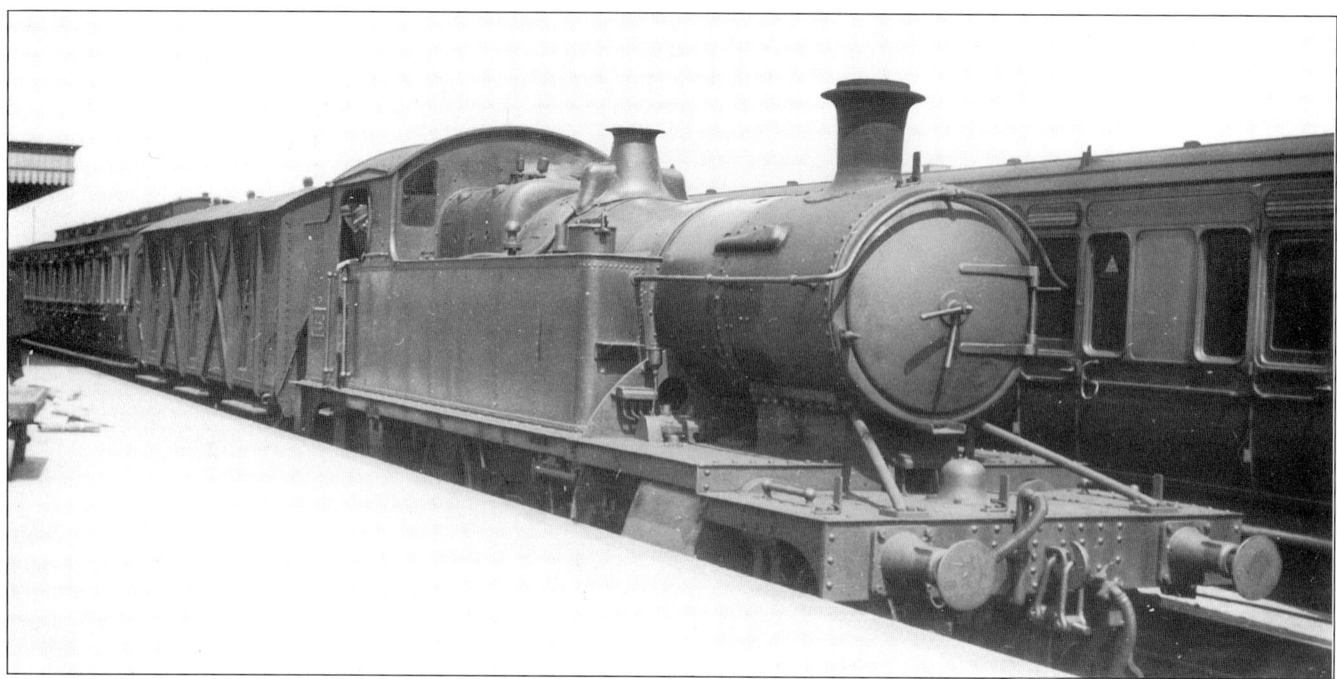

Heading what appears to be a 'mixed' train, 4408 has arrived at Helston from Gwinear Road. A fish van is behind the engine. Both members of the crew watch the photographer from the cab entrance. This engine spent the period from 1921 to 1931 working in the Penzance area and was frequently sub-shedded at Helston.

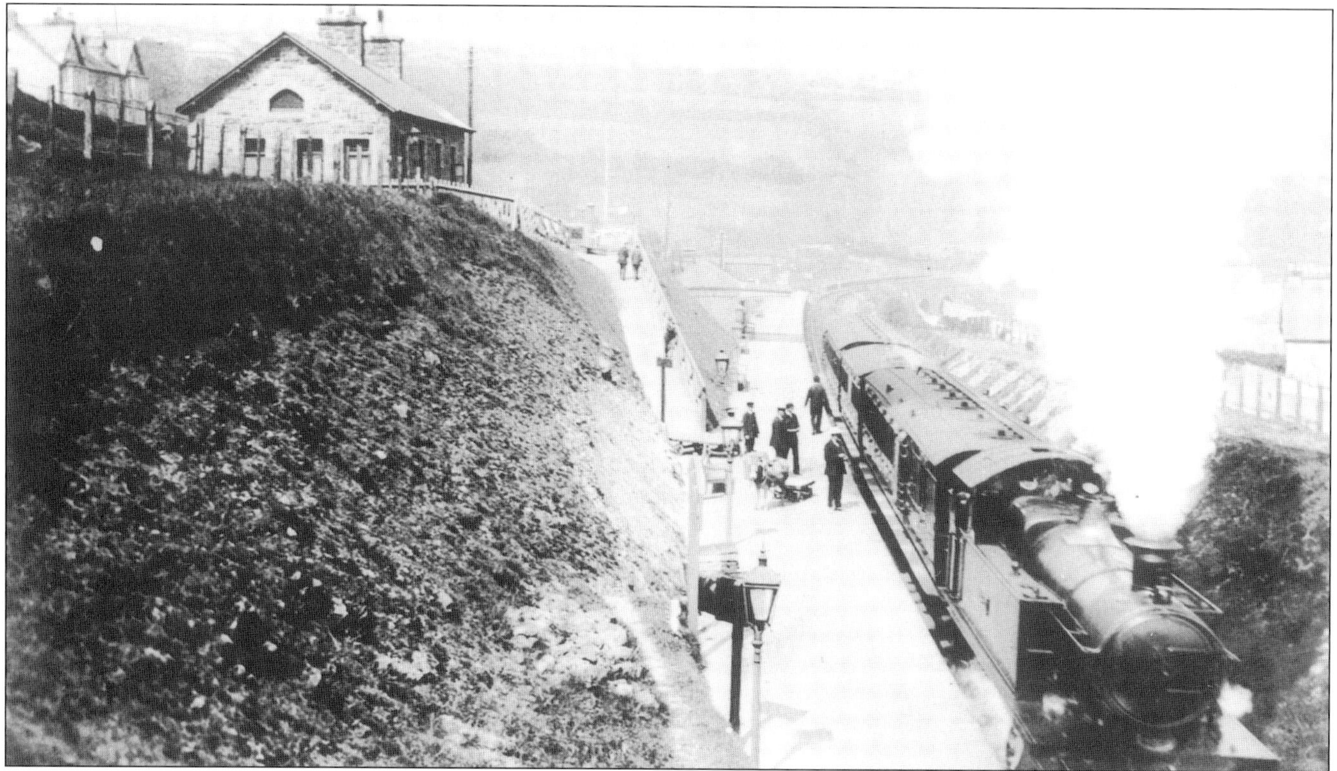

This early scene depicts 3110 stopped at Carbis Bay with a train from St Ives to St Erth. The engine was renumbered to 4410 in 1912. As this engine only worked from Penzance and St Ives sheds from 5 July 1910 until May 1911 this dates the photo fairly well. Note the main station building at the top of the approach ramp.

8

GWR LARGE PRAIRIE TANKS

Only a few representatives of this type of engine were allocated for long periods in Cornwall. There was usually a couple divided between St Blazey and Truro sheds which used them to work trains between Truro, Par and Newquay but not on the line via Perranporth from which they were barred. A batch of five members of the 6100 class was sent brand new to Truro and Penzance sheds in October 1935 but they did not remain long. This may have been in connection with work on the turntable at one of those sheds which would prevent the turning of tender engines. Large Prairies were drafted in to Truro and Penzance from a variety of sheds in 1948 and again in 1956 when work took place on the turntable at Long Rock shed. Another pair, namely 5140 and 5158, were transferred to St Blazey during the early 1940s. They were to work any GWR trains which may have had to be diverted from Bodmin Road via Bodmin to Wadebridge and over the SR North Cornwall line due to enemy action causing damage to the GWR route through Plymouth. They were both transferred to Newton Abbot after hostilities ceased. Photos taken during that period and of the 1935 visit by 6100 class members are virtually non-existant.

One of the last three members of the 5100 class was 5148 which was shedded at Laira and was frequently used to work the 'St Austell goods' from Tavistock Junction yard. It is crossing Bolitho viaduct, a short distance east of Liskeard with this train in 1955. This engine outlasted the other members of the class by four years, being withdrawn from service in December 1959.

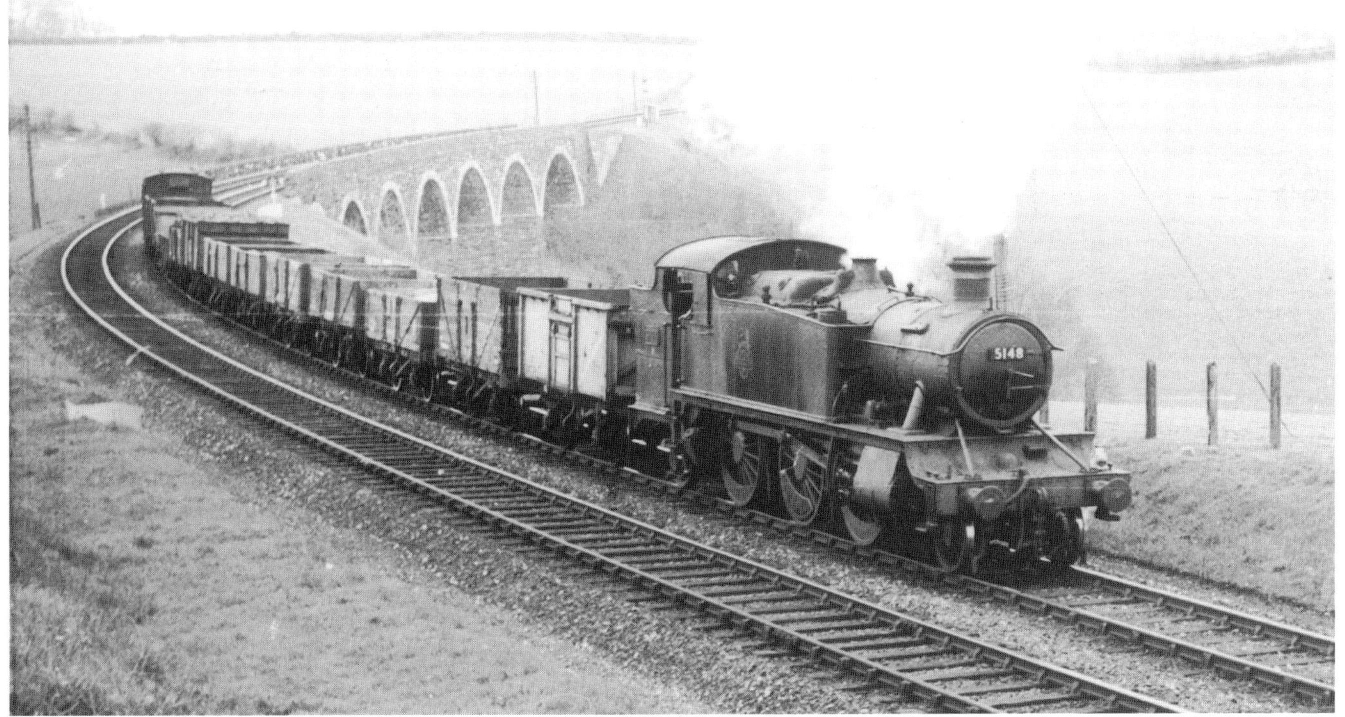

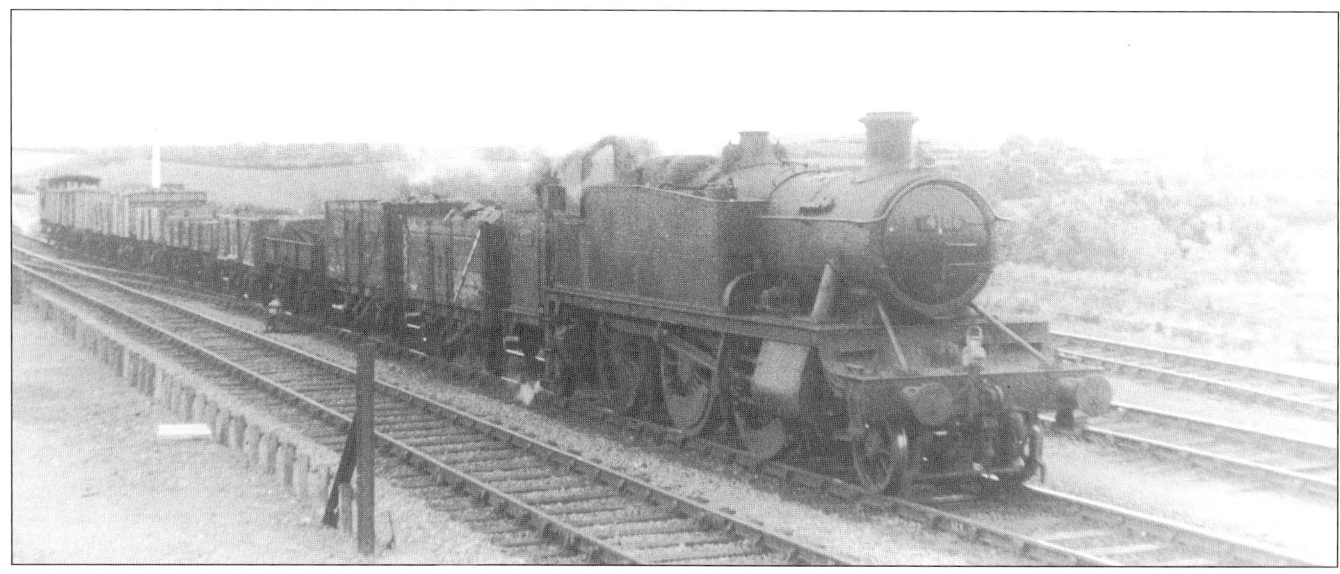

During the period when Penzance turntable was out of action in 1956 several large Prairies were transferred into the area. One of these was 5101 class 4106 from Landore shed, Swansea, which is entering Liskeard with what could well be the 'St Austell Goods' on 14 June of that year. This engine was officially transferred to Truro for just over a month.

Truro shed yard was full of engines on 24 May 1956 when 4107, also from Landore shed but briefly transferred to Truro, was present. To the right are 1007 'COUNTY OF BRECKNOCK' from Truro shed and Penzance allocated 1018 'COUNTY OF LEICESTER'.   Maurice Dart.

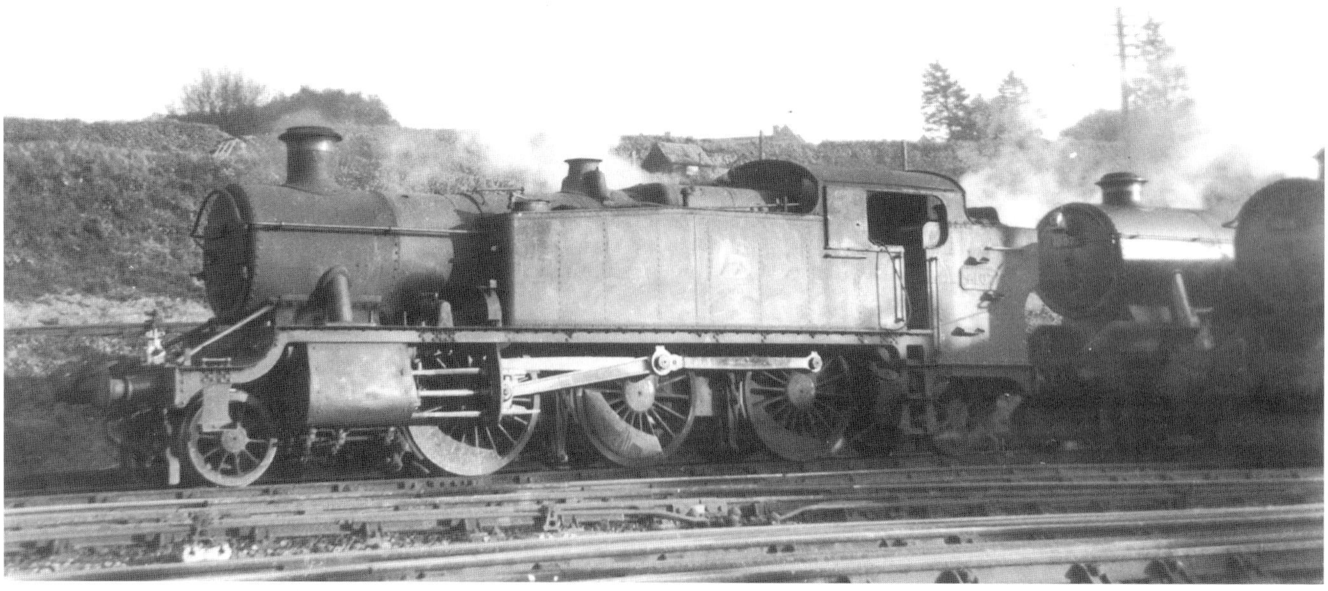

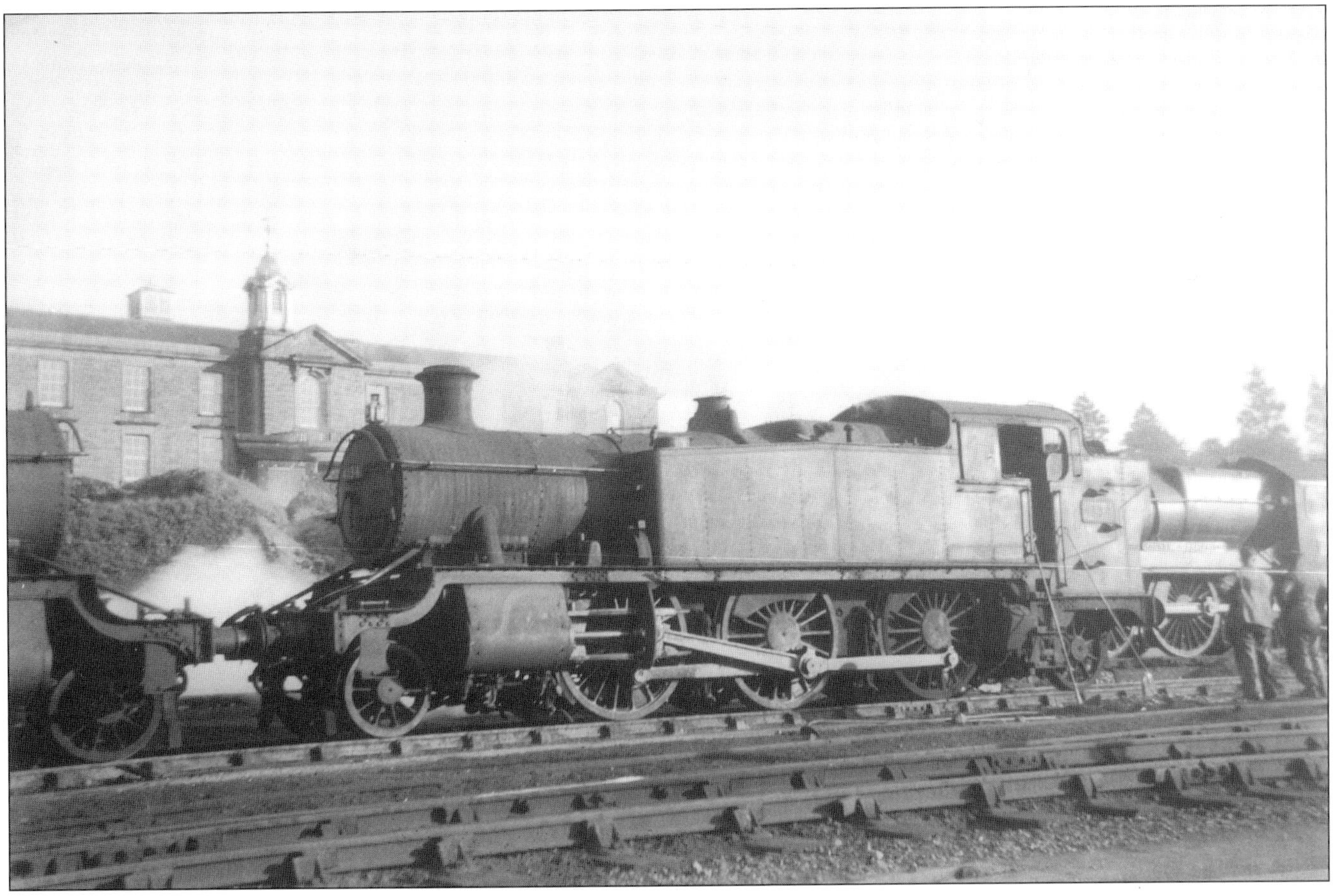

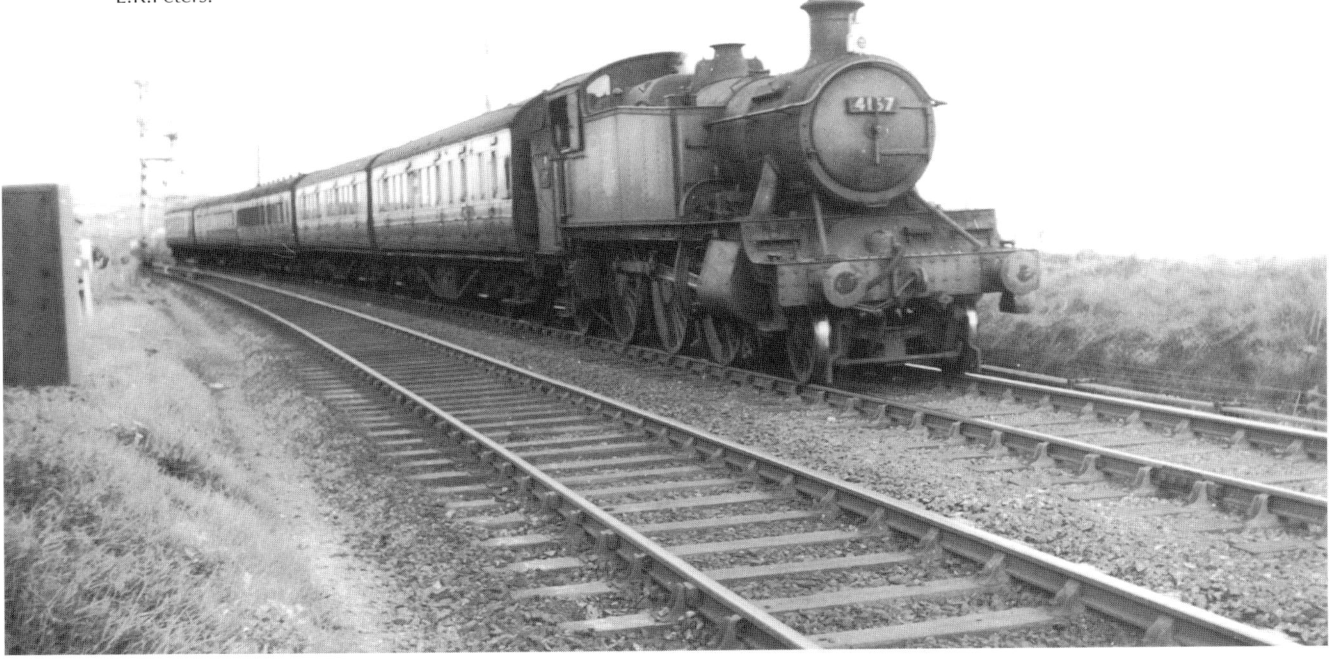

On the same date another rare visitor at Truro shed was 4134 from Carmarthen shed. This engine was also working from Truro shed for the same short period. 'COUNTY OF LEICESTER' is present in the background. Maurice Dart.

Near Ponsondane, east of Penzance, 4167 from Truro shed is heading an up stopping passenger service on 2 September 1952. A pair of LMS carriages are at the front of the train.
L.R.Peters.

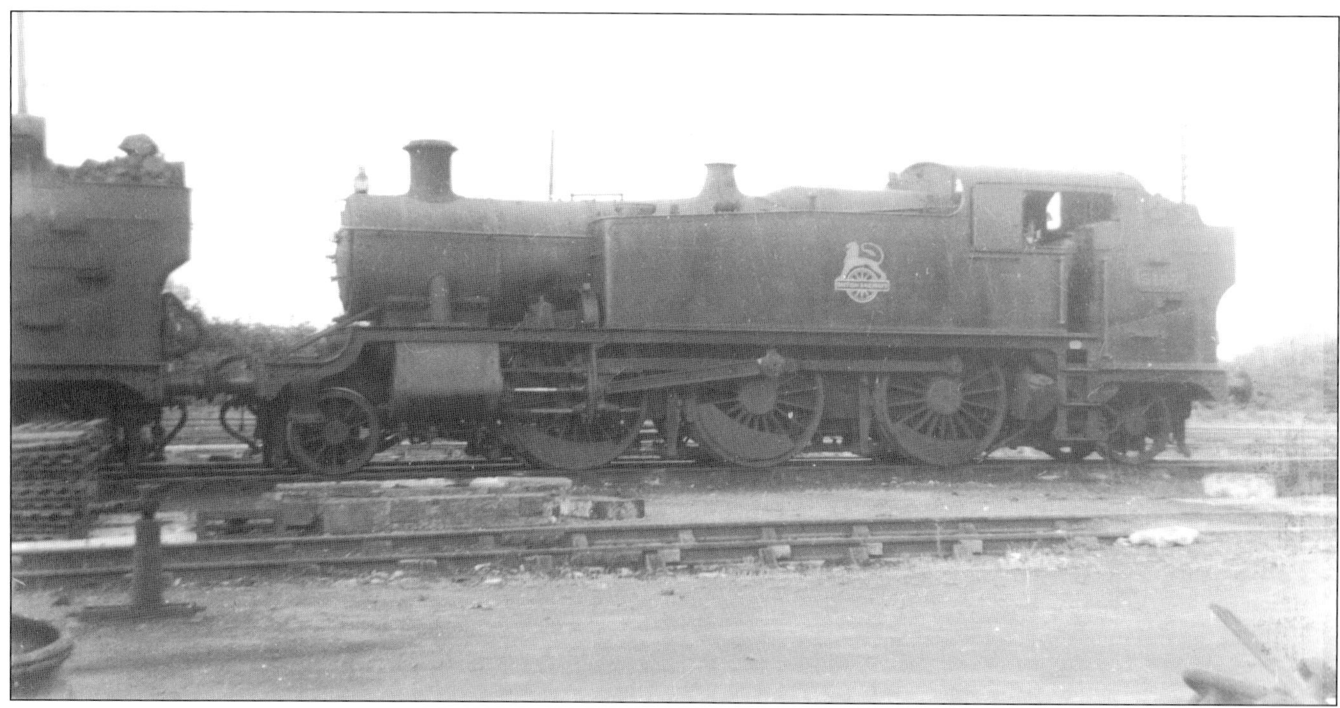

Stabled at St Blazey shed on 13 June 1956, on the way back home after the work on Penzance turntable had been completed, is 5101 class 5107 from Stourbridge shed. It had been temporarily working from Penzance shed. Maurice Dart.

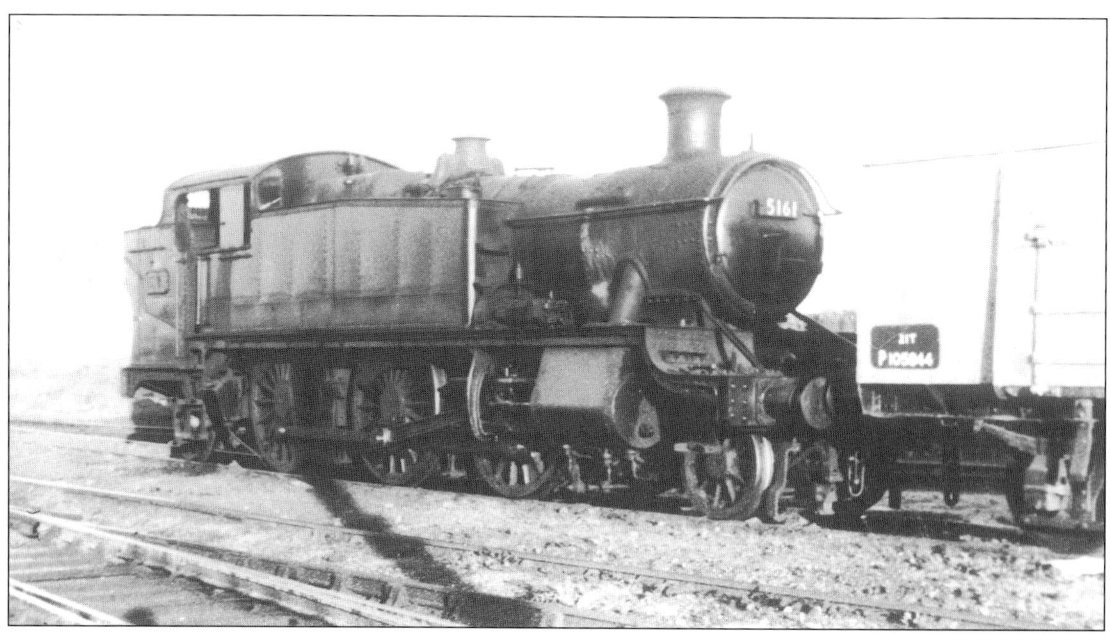

Standing in the yard on 12 June 1956 at Long Rock shed, Penzance where it had been based for a short period is 5161 from Leamington shed. In the background is a 21 ton former Private Owner steel mineral wagon. Denis Richards.

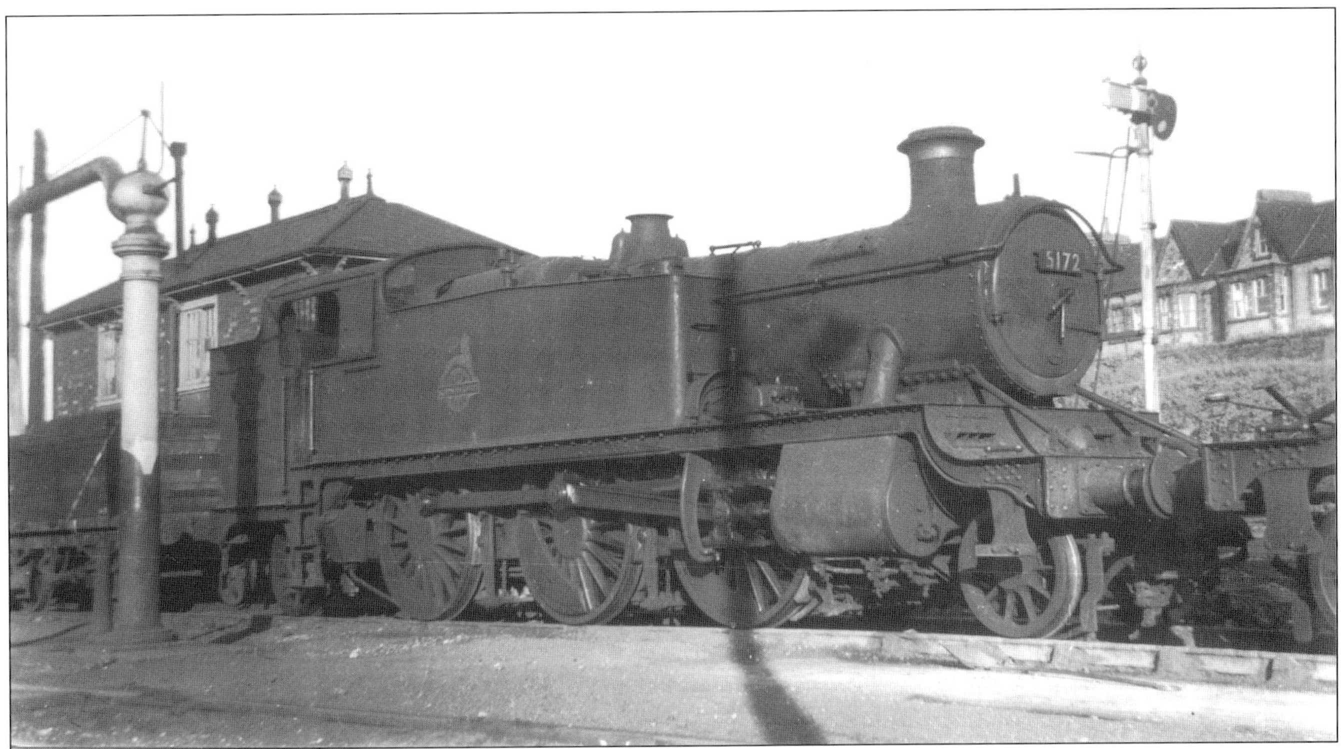

Another of the large tanks that appeared in the same period was Taunton shed's 5172 which is in the shed yard at Truro 24 May 1956. This engine was classed as 'on loan' so was not officially transferred to Cornwall. Maurice Dart.

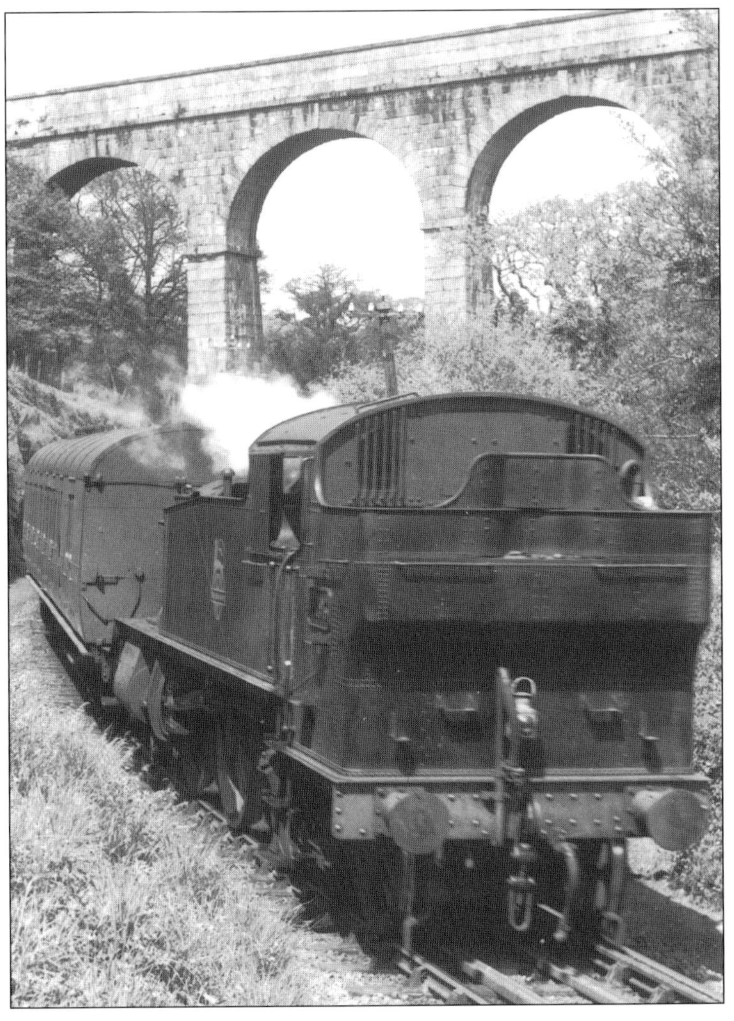

A train from Newquay to Par is descending the bank from Luxulyan hauled by 5195 in May 1956. This engine was officially transferred from Treherbert to Newton Abbot at the end of September 1956 so did the loco arrive in Devon earlier or was it yet another which came down briefly as cover during the work on Penzance turntable? Part of the Treffry viaduct which spans the Luxulyan Valley appears in the background. Rail Archive Stephenson(Photomatic).

A surprise occurred late on in steam days when 5198 was transferred from Gloucester to St Blazey. The transfer was officially recorded as taking place on 18 June 1960. I arrived at St.Austell, from Plymouth, on that date around 8am and was amazed to see that engine standing in one of the up sidings at the station. Despite quite misty conditions, I hastened over the road bridge and took this photo. The typical GWR water tank on the up platform is prominent. The engine moved to Taunton at the end of December of that year. Maurice Dart.

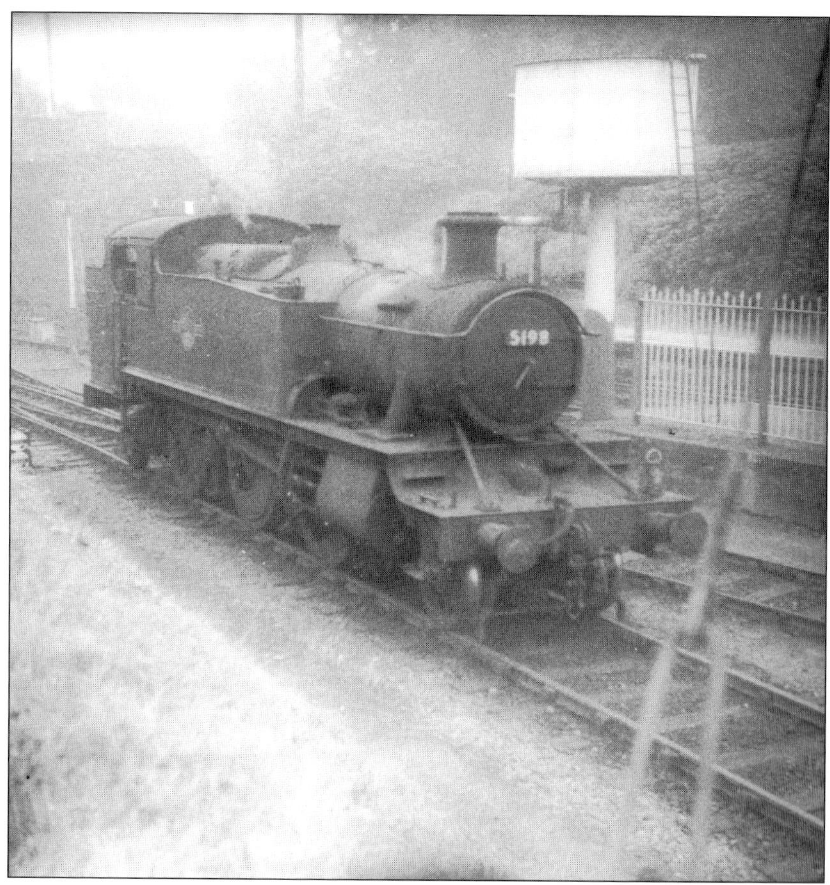

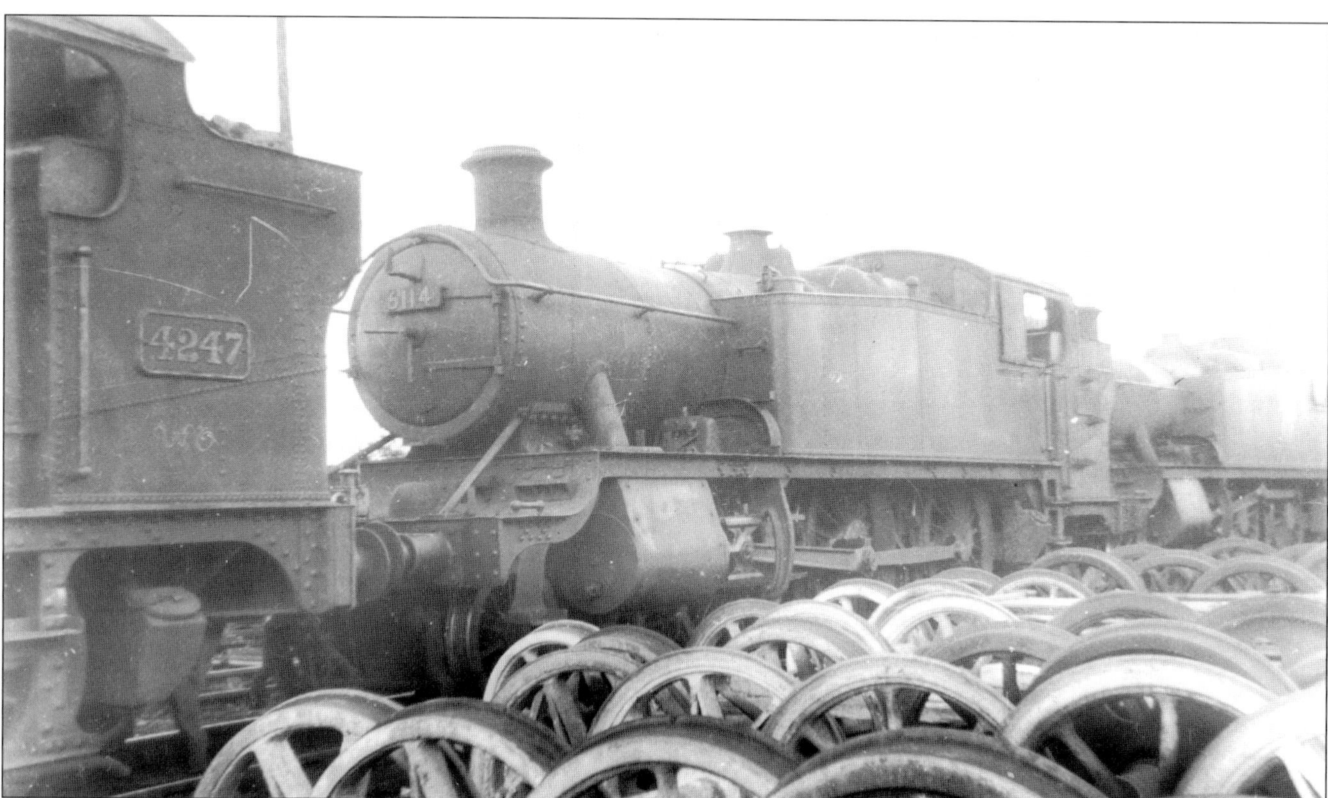

Sandwiched between 2-8-0T 4247 and previously seen 5107 at St Blazey shed on 13 June 1956 is 6100 class 6114. It was returning to Ebbw Junction shed, Newport after being temporarily transferred to Truro for a short period. Maurice Dart.

9

LMS AND STANDARD 2-6-2 TANKS

LMS Ivatt 2MT locos appeared in Cornwall during the early 1950s when a couple of them were transferred to Plymouth Friary shed and were used on the branch line from Bere Alston to Callington. In the early 1960s a couple worked from Wadebridge shed but these will be included in a later section in this book covering lines in that area. In the 1960s BR Standard 2-6-2Ts appeared at Bude being sub-shedded at Okehampton form Exmouth Junction.

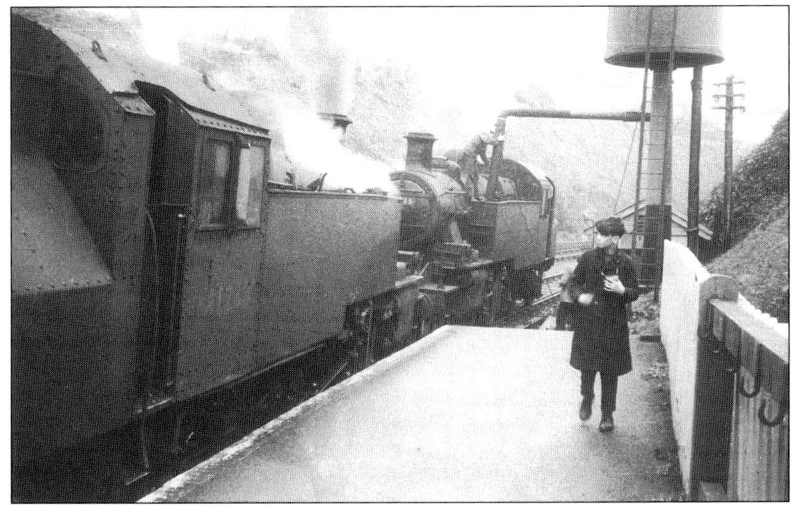

On a wet day at Calstock in the early 1960s a pair of Ivatts, 41238 and 41315, head a passenger train for Callington. Mike Daly.

During the 1950s LMS Ivatt tank 41316, shedded at Friary, waits to depart from Callington with the daily goods train to Bere Alston. The front wagon is a BR standard 12 ton van. The engine does not appear to be carrying a shedplate on the smokebox door.

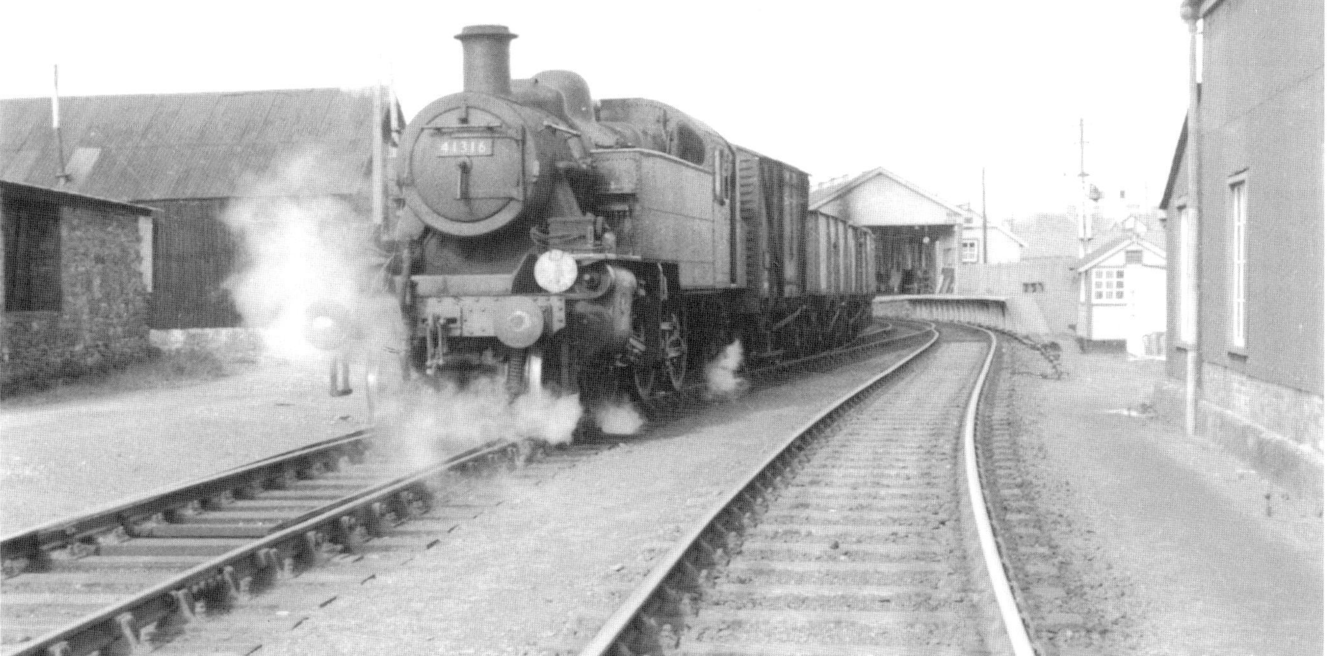

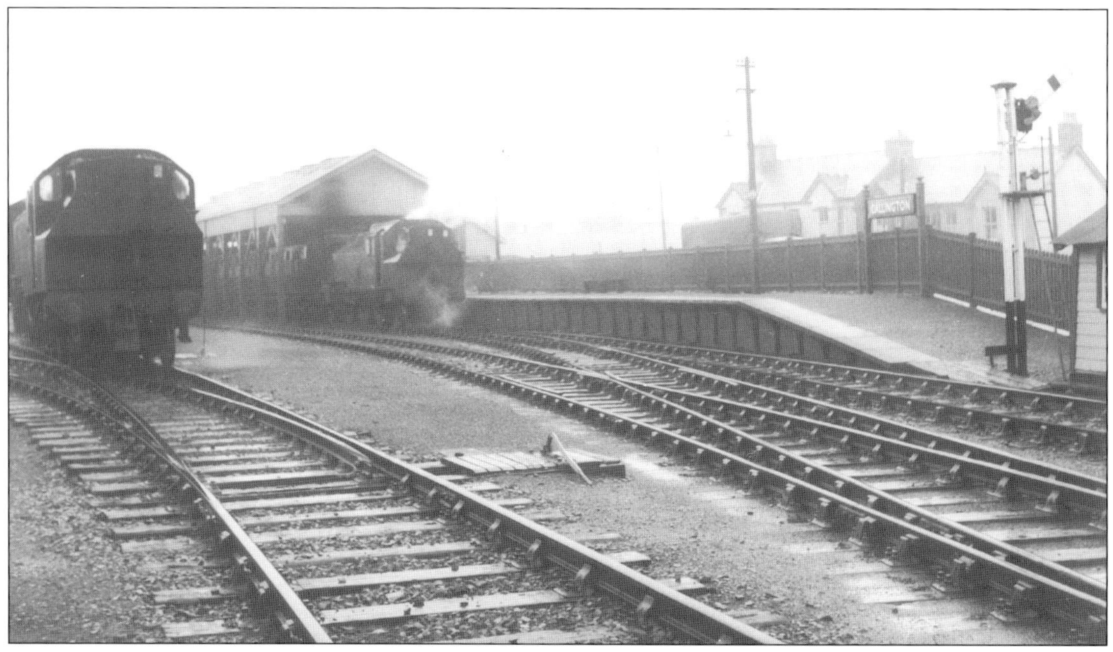

Another pair of Ivatt tanks feature in this photo which was taken on a murky damp 24 September 1963 at Callington. On the left, 41307 is standing on a goods whilst 41238 is ready to depart to Bere Alston on a passenger train. N.D.Mundy.

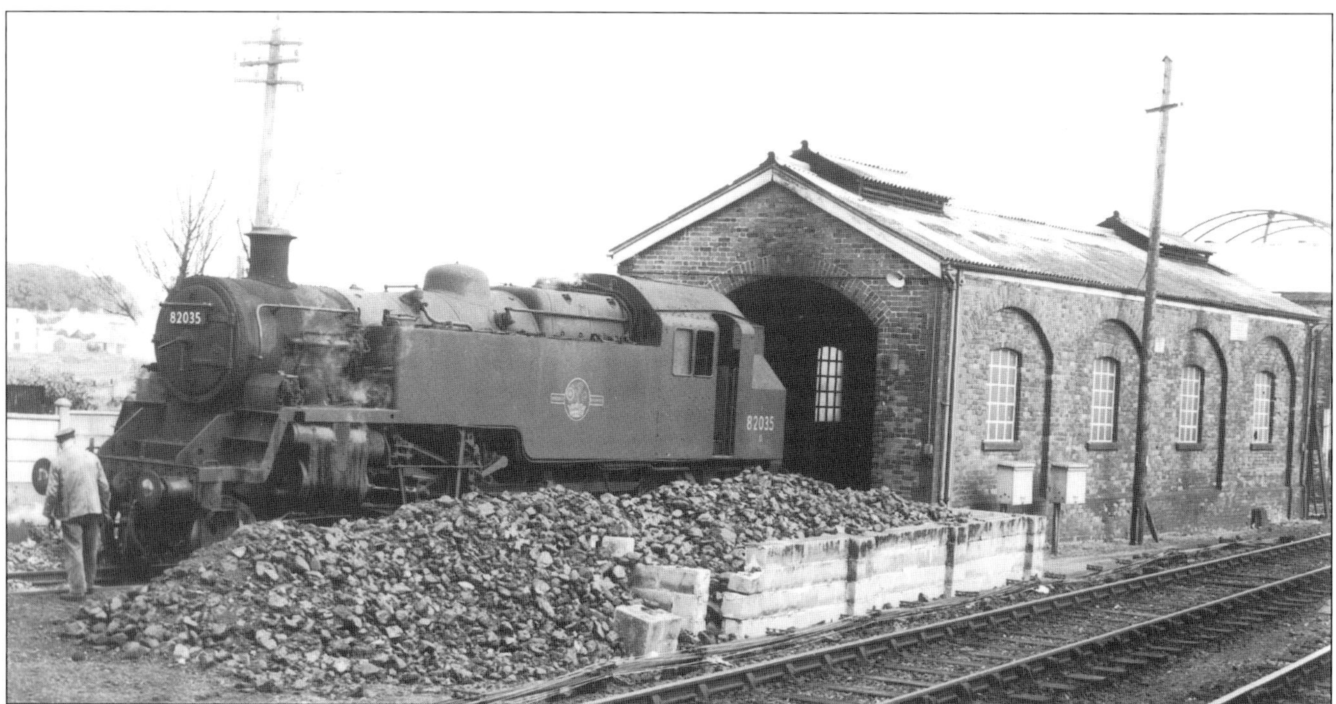

Standard class 3MT 2-6-2T 82035 rests outside the small loco shed at Bude during July 1964. The small bunker that holds the shed's supply of coal has been somewhat overfilled!

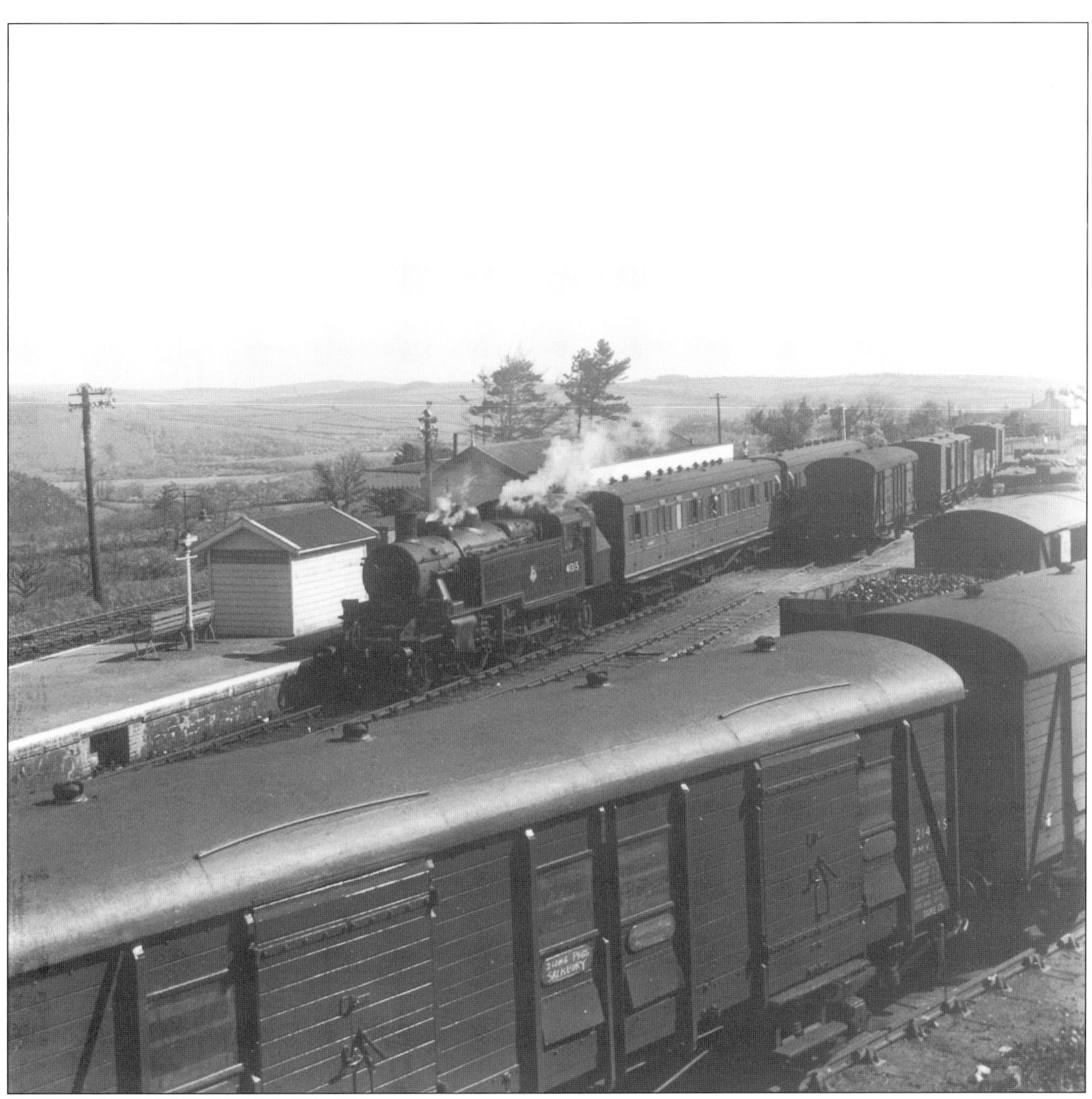

An undated scene in the 1950s has Ivatt 41315 at Gunnislake with a train bound for Callington. The sidings contain an assortment of vans and wagons. Two SR PMVs are visible. The station seen here was closed on 31 January 1994 and the bridge over the main road was removed on 6 February. A new station was constructed on the opposite side of the road and opened on 9 June of that year. Mike Daly.

MOGUL 2-6-0s

10

For many years the standard GWR 4300 class Moguls maintained a presence in Cornwall and during the 1920s regularly worked passenger trains on the main line. Several of the 8300s, which were 4300s and 5300s modified with additional weight behind the front bogie, worked in the county. The additional front end weight eased wear on the leading pair of driving wheels caused by engines negotiating many sharp curves in areas such as Cornwall. Moguls worked goods trains in Cornwall until almost the end of steam in the county. Several of the earlier 'Aberdare' class 2-6-0s worked in Cornwall but photos of these have so far eluded me. On the SR when the 'Woolworth' N class Moguls arrived at Exmouth Junction shed, they soon became regular performers on the North Cornwall line. In later years, examples of the U class Moguls appeared at times and for a couple of brief spells a few of the 3 cylinder U1 class worked from Exmouth Junction. However. photos of this latter type in Cornwall have not, as yet, been located. As far as is known, there were no visits to Cornwall by LMS Ivatt or Standard Moguls.

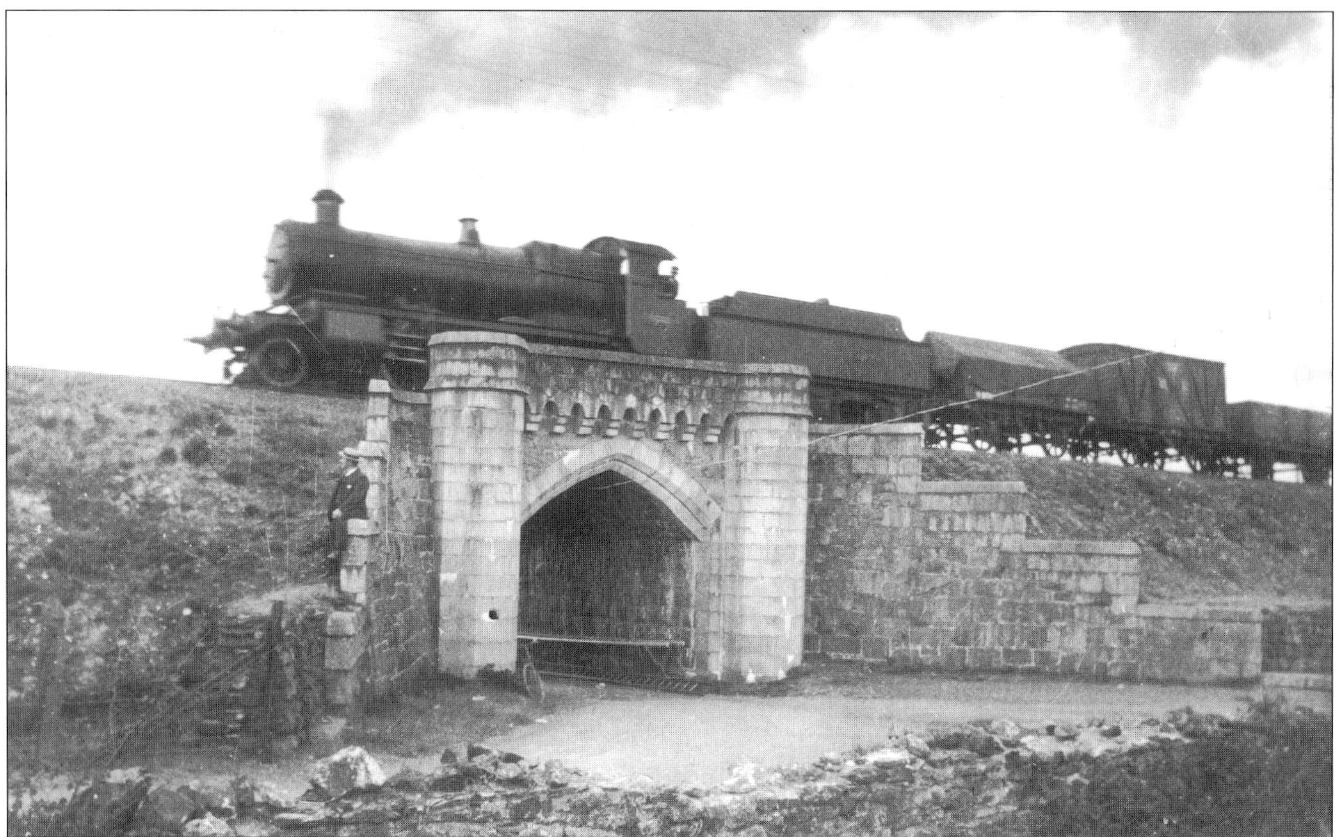

This is an action shot of 4300 class 4352 passing over the ornamental 'Crinnis Arch' whilst climbing the bank from Par to St Austell with a down goods on 10 August 1921. At the front of the train is a GWR open wagon fitted with a tarpaulin bar which is followed by an ex Midland Railway 10 ton box van. The parapets of the bridge were designed as such because the structure spanned a private road. The fireman appears to have spotted the photographer whose companion has found a convenient perch from which to watch as the train passes. This engine was withdrawn in August 1937 and certain parts of it were incorporated in Grange class 6855.

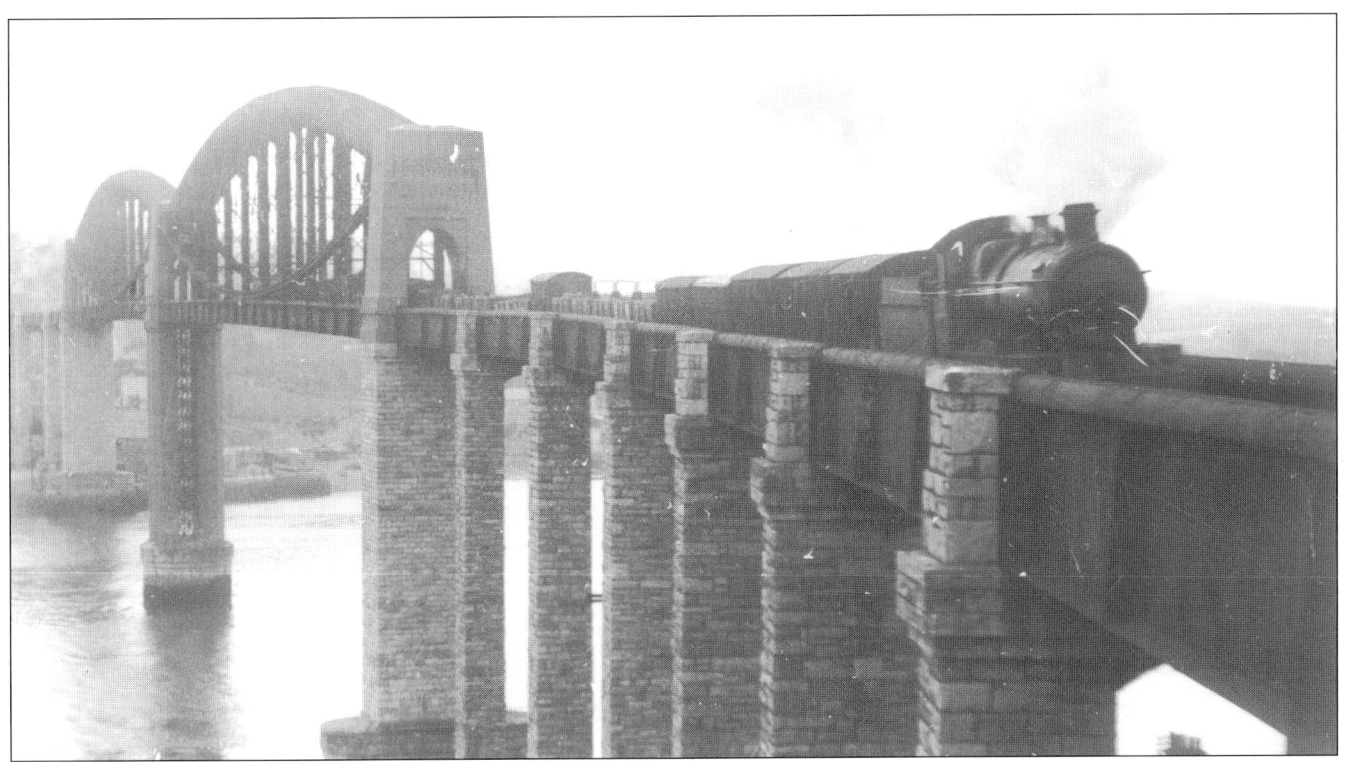

As the official boundary between Devon and Cornwall is the Devon bank of the River Tamar or the Devon end of the Royal Albert Bridge, this train is still in Cornwall as it crosses the structure on a lengthy up goods. The train is the 11.10am Penzance to Plymouth 'Fast Goods' hauled by 4358 on 6 April 1919. *Locomotive Club of Great Britain/Ken Nunn Collection.*

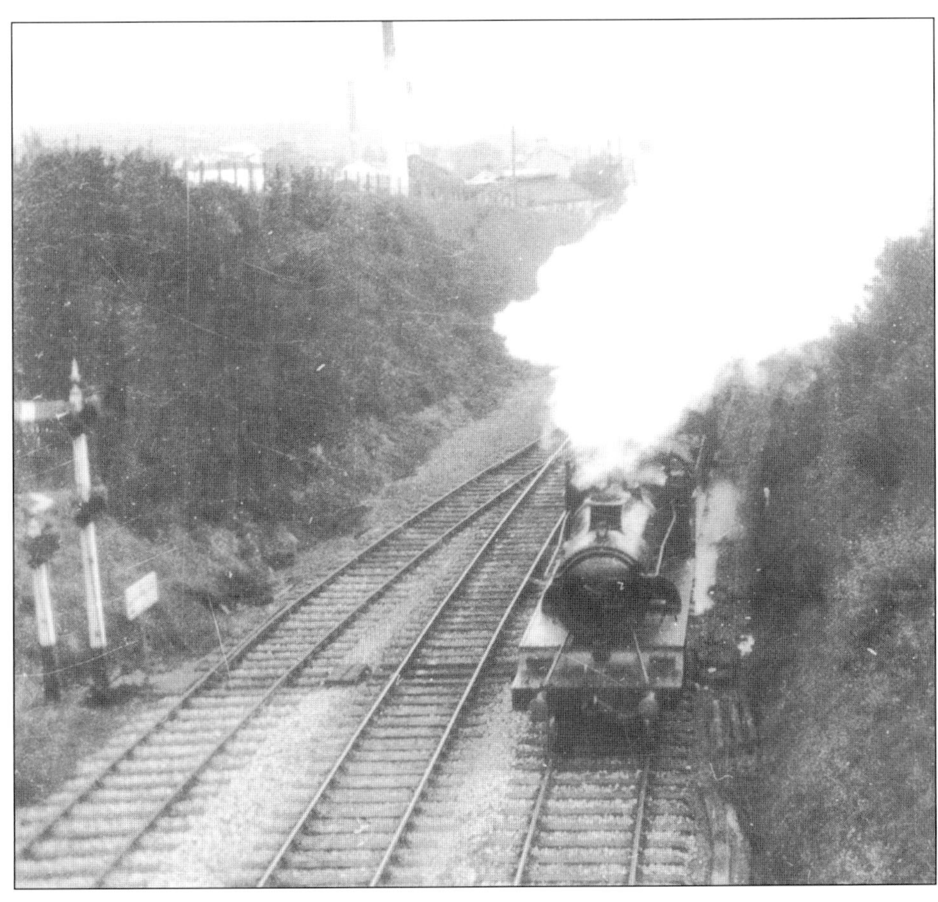

The 11.10am passenger from St.Austell to Penzance has passed through Burngullow hauled by 4378 on 11 October 1921. Burngullow up siding is on the left and in the left background the stacks of West Burngullow and Burngullow china clay kilns can be seen. In the centre of the picture part of the small engine at Burngullow is visible. The signal arms, which have been freshly repainted, are all red which was standard GWR practice until the late 1920s. Parts of this engine were incorporated into Grange 6832. *P.J.T.Reed.*

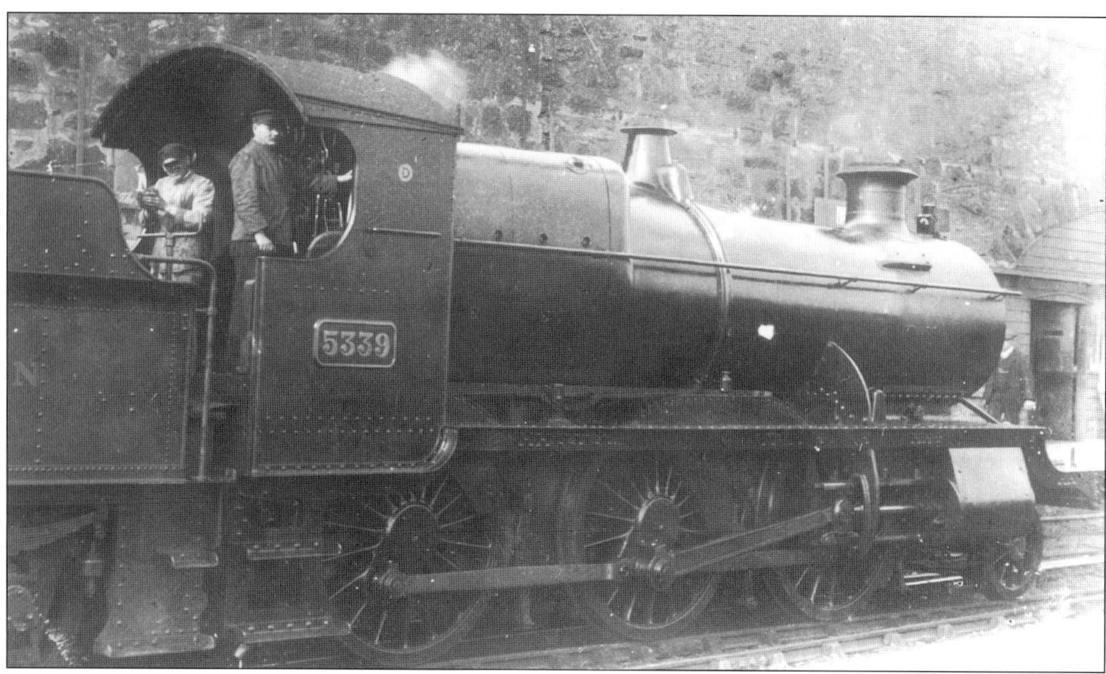

The fireman and driver on 5339 gaze at the photographer as they wait on 5339 ready to depart from Penzance on a passenger train in 1928. A.C.Roberts.

During May 1956 6300 from St Blazey shed climbs Luxulyan bank on a local stopping passenger to Newquay. Rail Archive Stephenson(Photomatic).

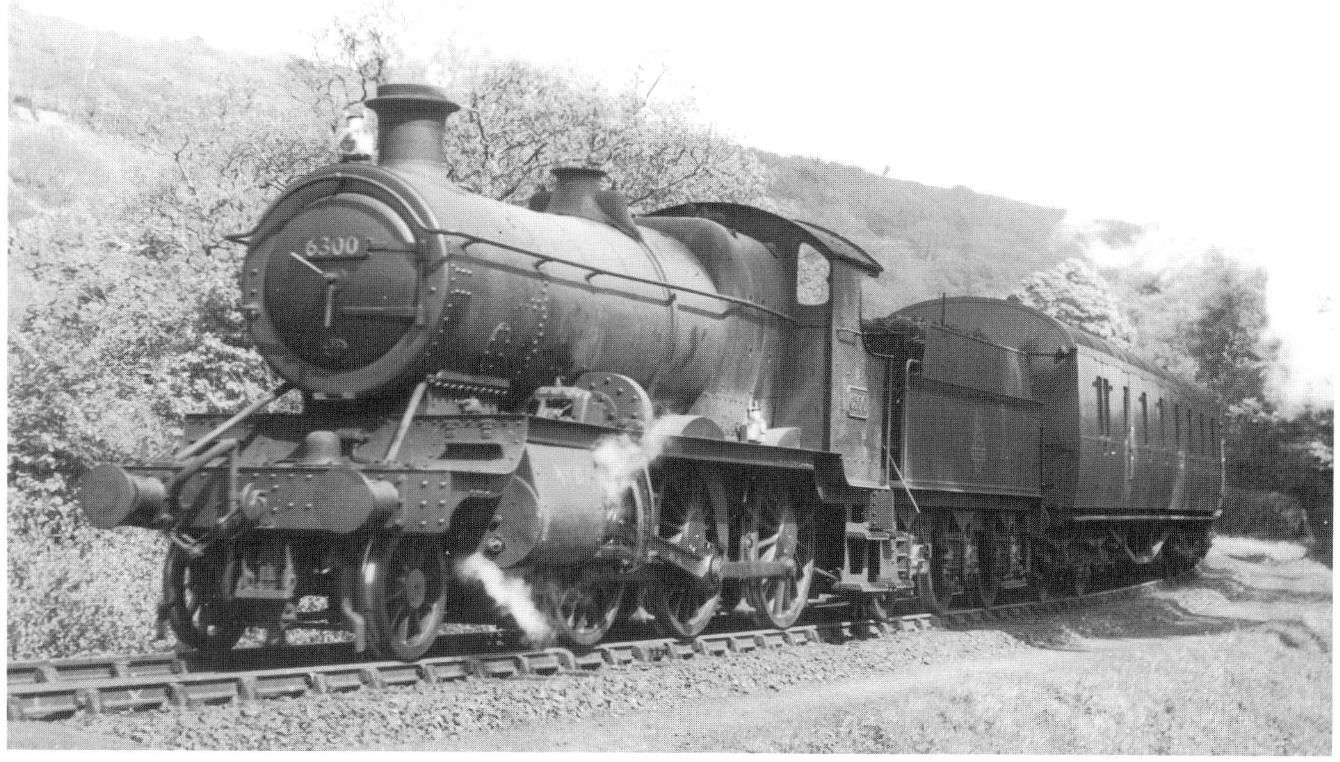

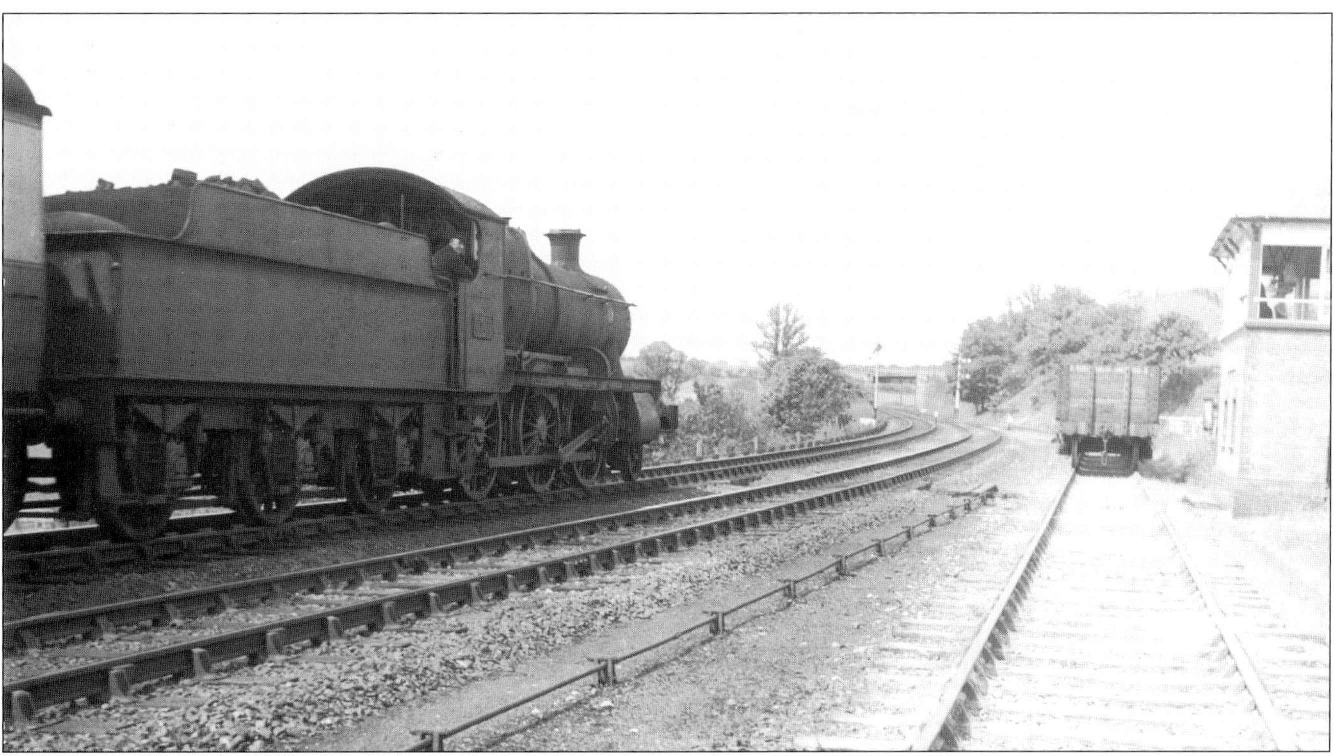

As 6305, also from St Blazey shed, passes Trenance sidings signal box on a down local passenger on 20 June 1956, the driver glances backwards at the photographer. The line on the right is the up Refuge loop and sidings behind the signal box served a clay kiln and a clay store. This engine was fitted with outside steampipes during July 1948.

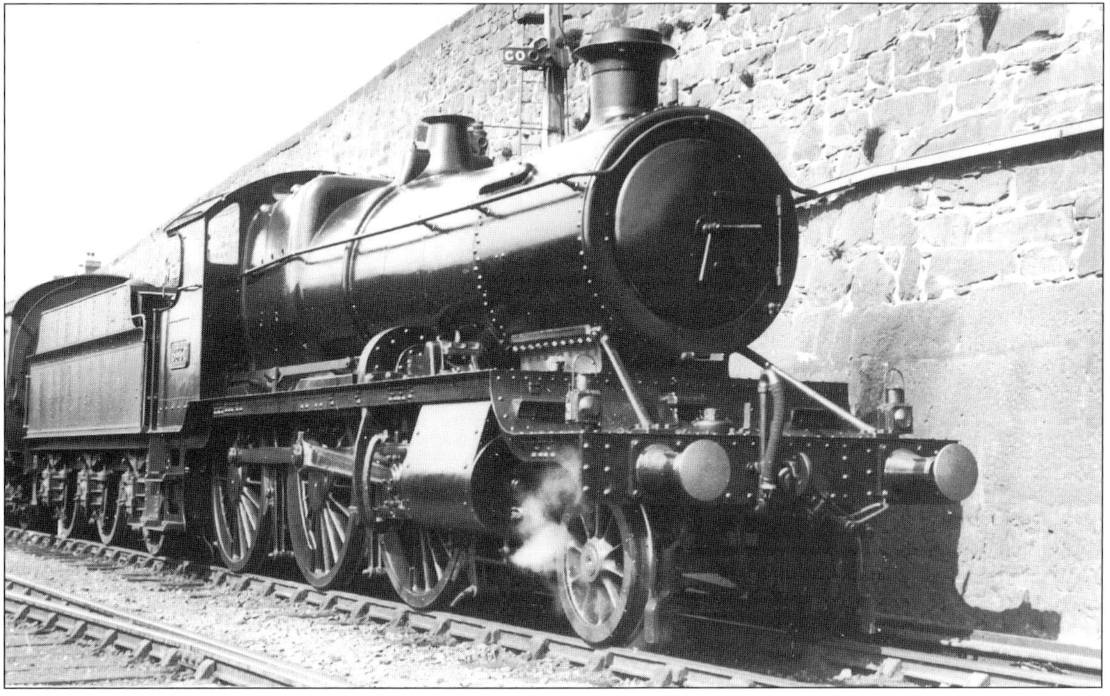

At Penzance waiting to depart for Plymouth with an up express in the early 1920s is a very clean 6331which went new to Penzance shed in April 1921. A.G.Ellis.

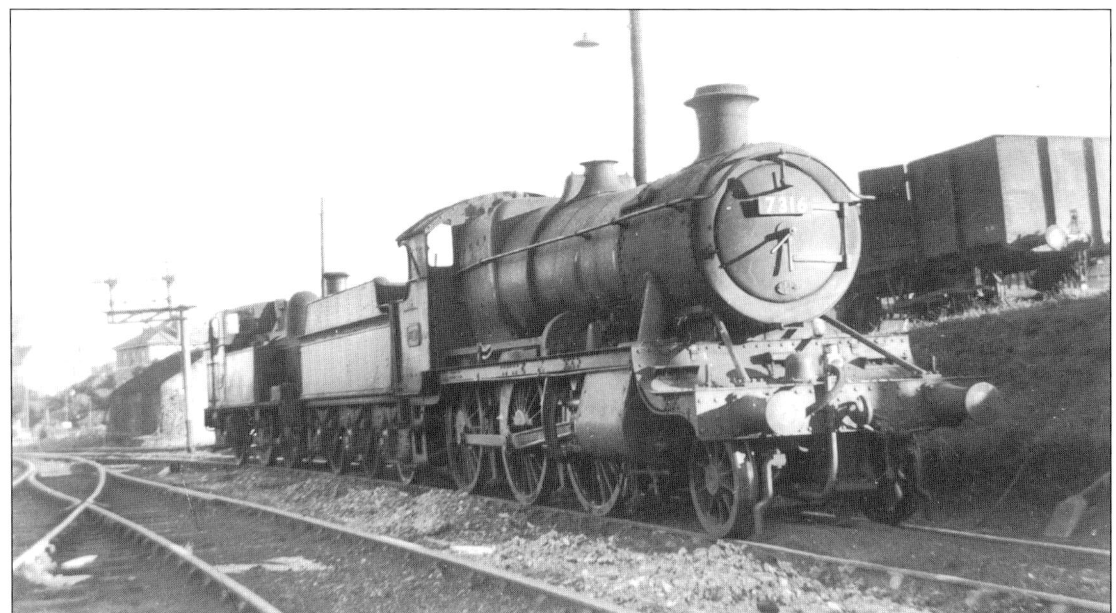

It is mid-evening at St Blazey shed on 7 August 1956 with 4800 class 0-4-2T 1419 and Exeter Mogul 7316 awaiting their turn to be coaled. 1419 had returned after completing the day's duties working the Lostwithiel to Fowey Auto train. The Mogul was fitted with outside steampipes during November 1947. On the coal stage is one of the 16 ton mineral wagons fitted with cupboard doors which were built for the SNCF to replace war damaged stock. However they were found to be unsuitable to operate in France and were repatriated by 1952. They were reconditioned and used by BR. Maurice Dart.

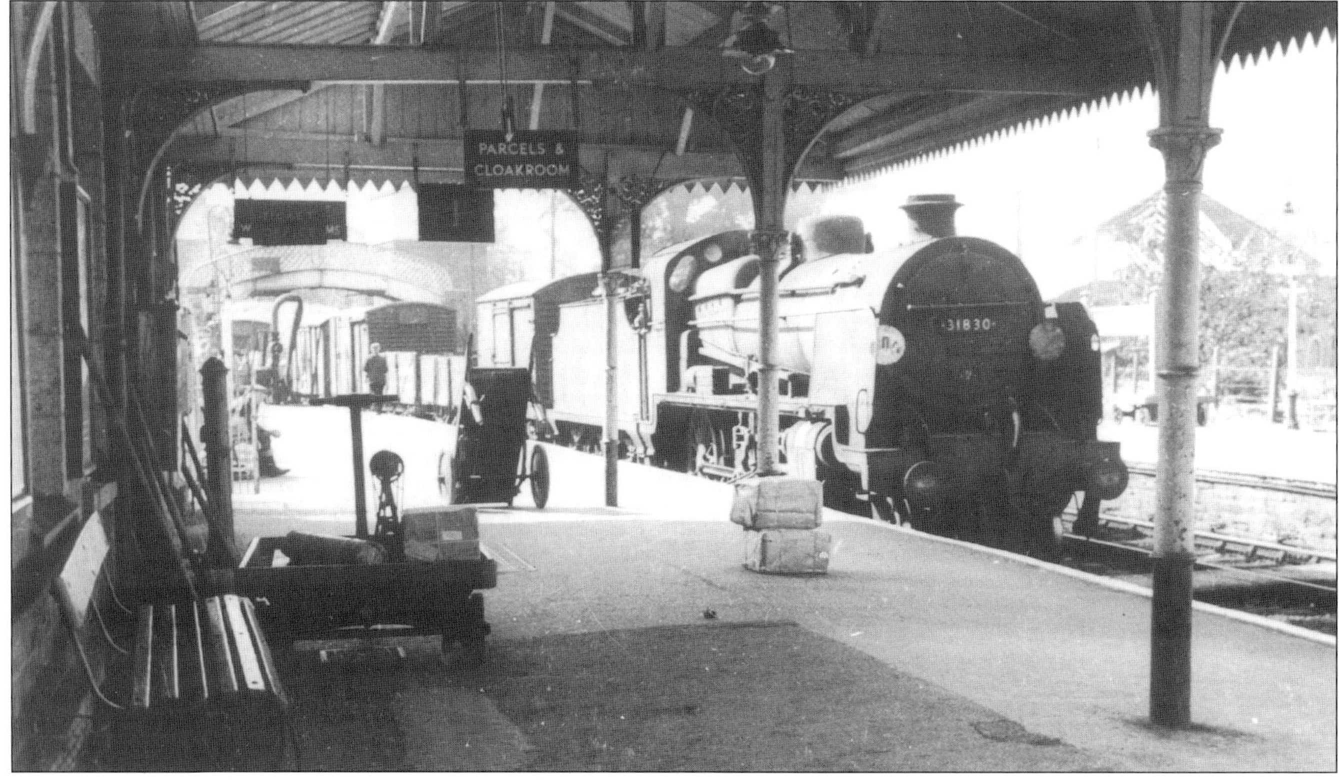

Ex SR N class 2-6-0 31830 from Exmouth Junction shed brings an up mixed goods through Launceston on the down line in the 1950s. At the front of the train is a 12 ton LNER van. A typical SR water column is prominent on the platform together with various platform trolleys.

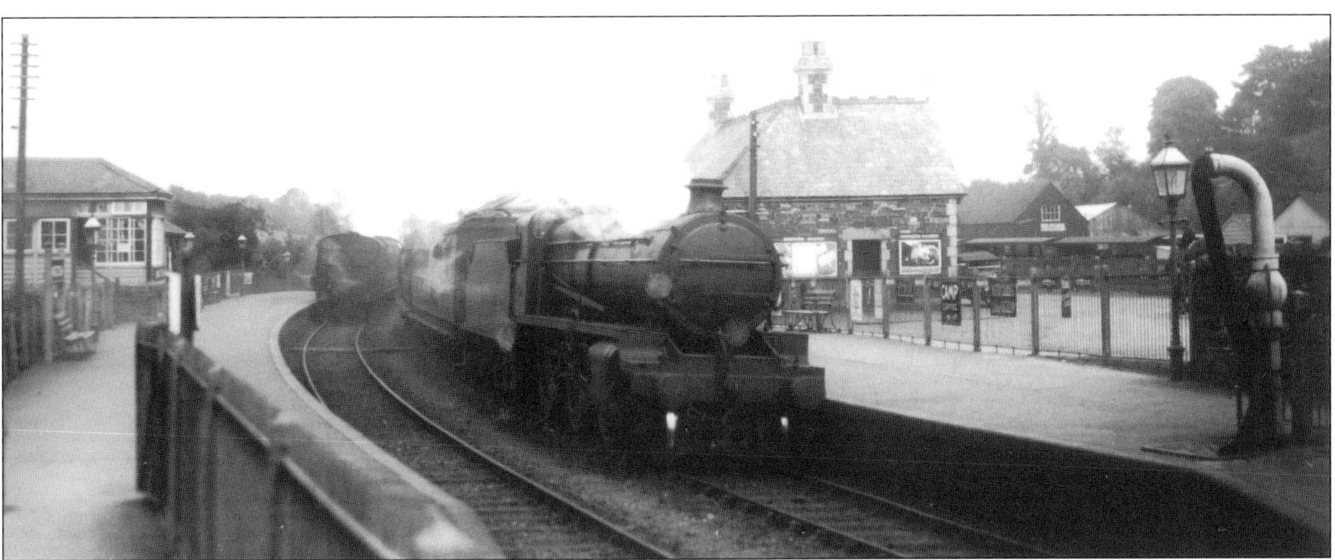

Two passenger trains are passing at Launceston in the early 1920s. The down train is hauled by fairly new N class 833 from Exmouth Junction shed. The loco was renumbered to 1833 in SR days and gained smoke deflector plates.

Heading an up goods through St Kew Highway in the late 1950s is N class 31844 from Exmouth junction shed. The signal box is of typical LSWR design.

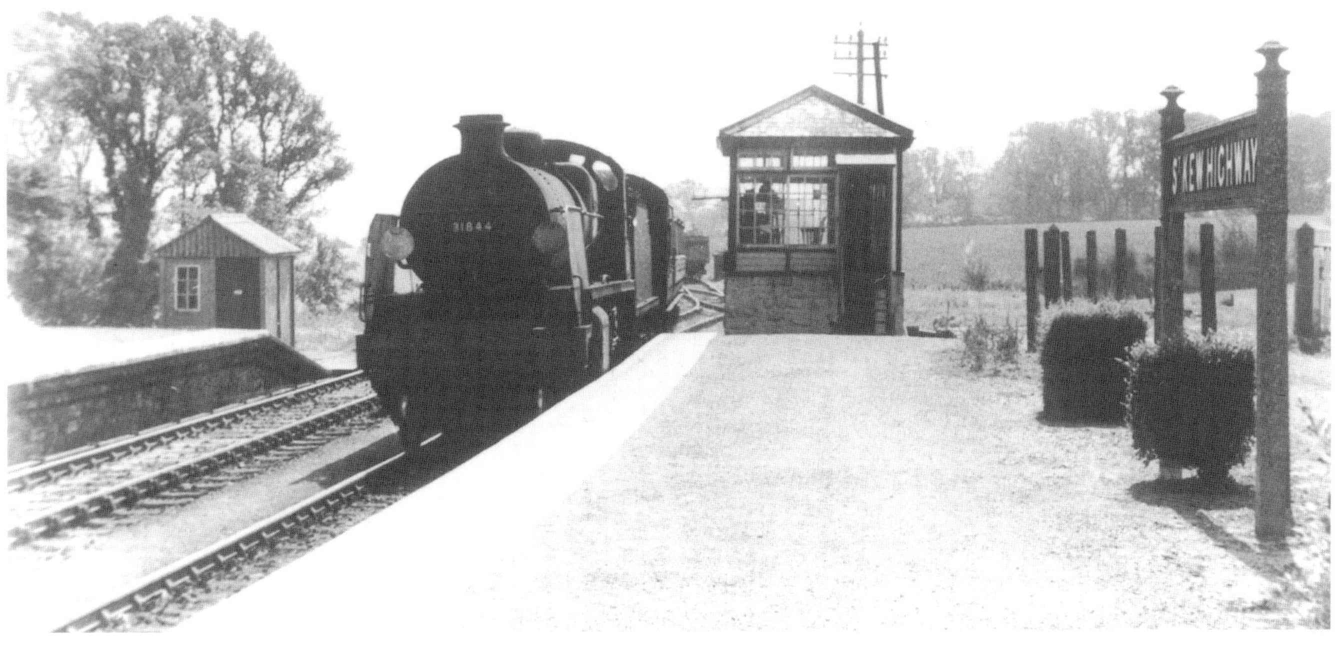

11

0-6-2 TANKS AND
0-6-0 TENDER ENGINES

To the author's knowledge there were only two 0-6-2T locos of this type that regularly worked in the county. They were the two ex Plymouth, Devonport & South Western Junction Railway engines that worked the Callington branch from Bere Alston for many years.

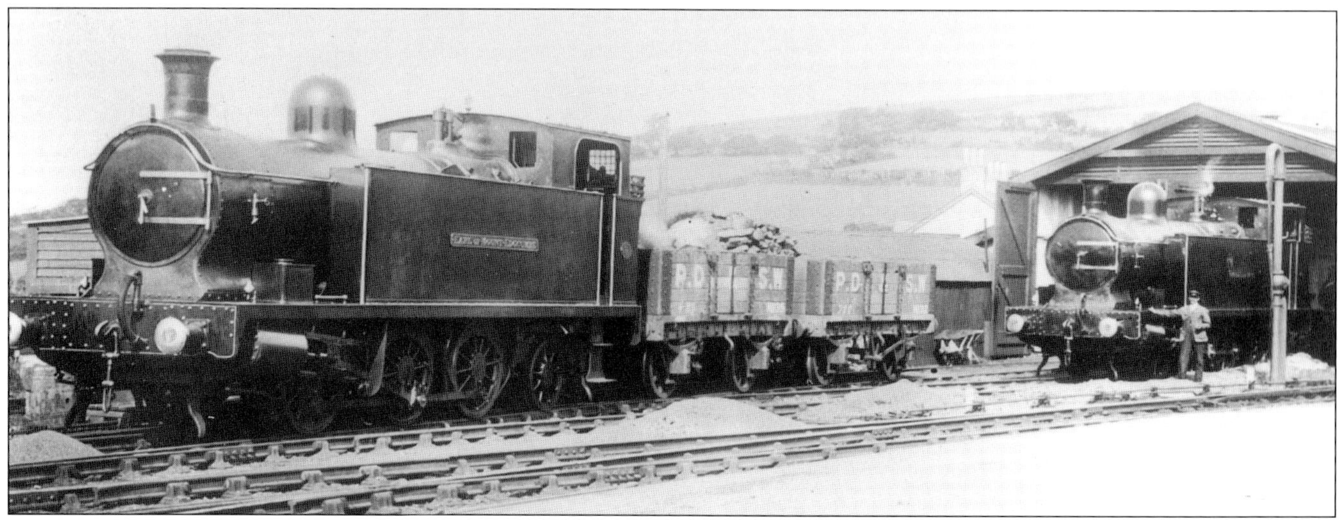

Here we see both of the engines standing outside the shed at Callington in PDSWJ days soon after the line opened in 1908. Also present are PDSW 5 plank wagons Nos.35 and 32 bearing the company's initials. No.3 'EARL OF MOUNT EDGCUMBE' is nearest to the camera with No.4 'LORD ST LEVAN' to its right. In later years the engine shed was rebuilt facing in the opposite direction.

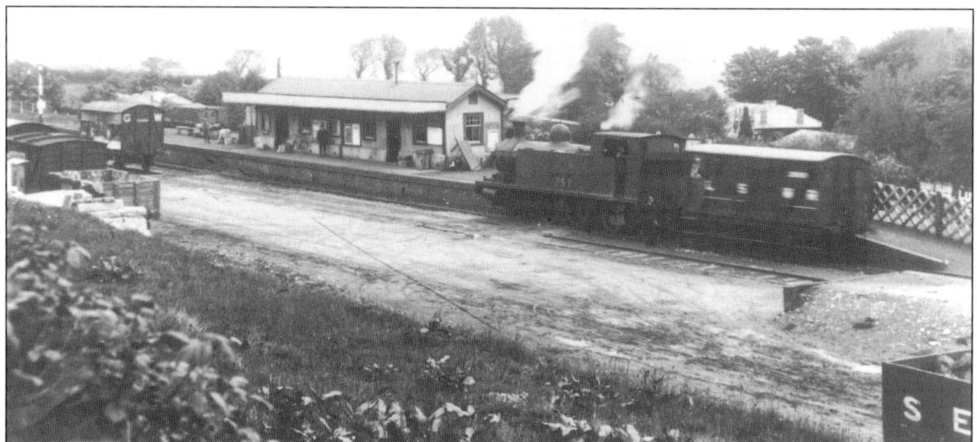

Rolling stock which includes a GWR cattle wagon, an SE&CR open wagon, a LSWR Road van designed for carrying small packages between stations and a vehicle from the Cramlington Colliery Co. is present at Gunnislake in this photo. The brake van at the platform is hauled by a rather grubby 'EARL OF MOUNT EDGCUMBE' which is lettered LSWR and carries the number E757. The letter 'E' indicates that the SR has taken over at the Grouping and that Eastleigh Works is responsible for overhauling the engine which is a SR Western section loco. It also points to the photo being taken soon after 1923.

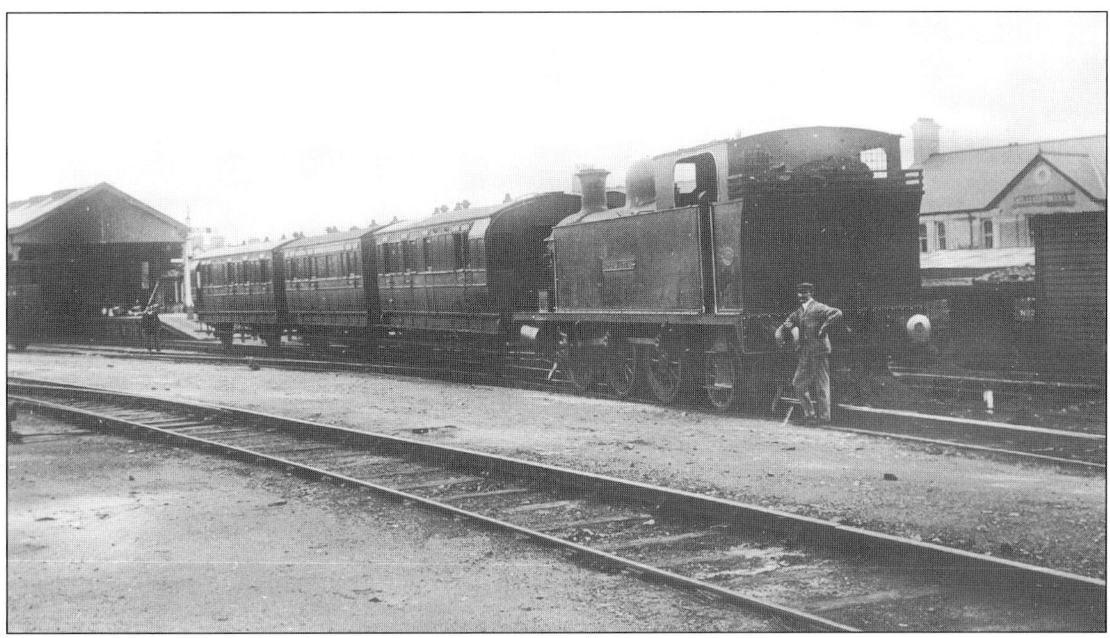

This is a photo taken in 1908 at Callington which has driver 'Natt' Neil standing behind No.4 'LORD ST LEVAN' ready to back a three coach passenger train into the platform to form a service to Beer (Old spelling) Alston. When the author made his first trip from Bere Alston to Callington in 1946, the train was hauled by this engine.

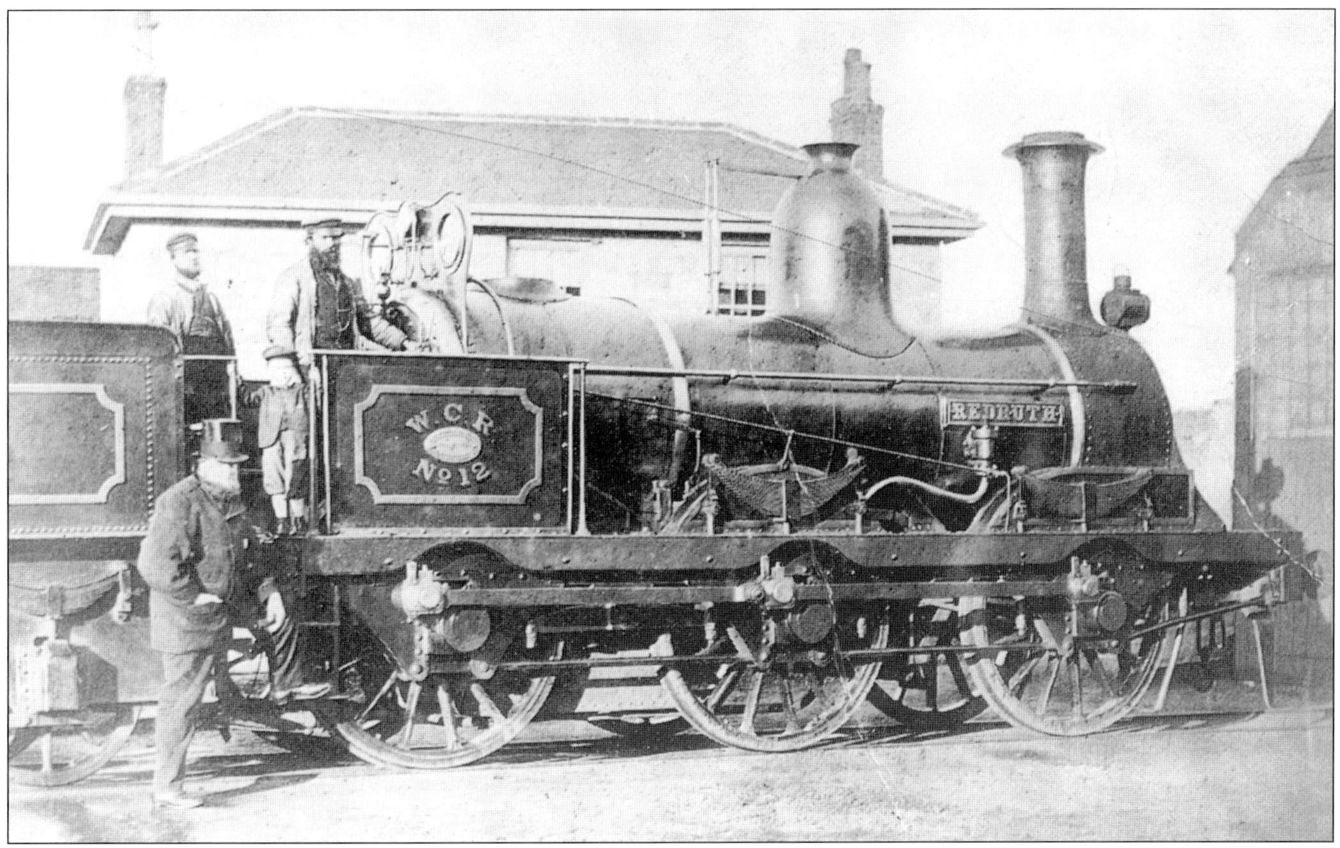

We end this short section with West Cornwall Railway 0-6-0 No.12 'REDRUTH' outside Carn Brea engine shed. This engine was built by R.Stephenson & Co. and was purchased by the WCR in 1852. When delivered it was described as "being probably the most useful engine on the line". It was replaced by a four coupled engine in 1865 so this photo must pre-date that. Royal Institution of Cornwall. Courtney Library.

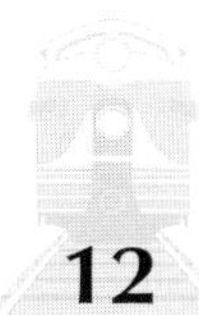

12

0-6-0 TANK ENGINES

The first engines of this type to work in the county were saddle tanks which were gradually replaced by the more well known pannier tanks. Almost all of the GWR classes appeared through the years and a representative selection of the various types are included, on shed and at work. The 'pannier' was synonymous with the very thought of the GWR and worked in every nook and cranny of the system. Some examples from companies which were absorbed by the GWR are included. A lone representative of the SR is included as, to the authors knowledge, no others regularly worked in Cornwall and photos of any others have not been located.

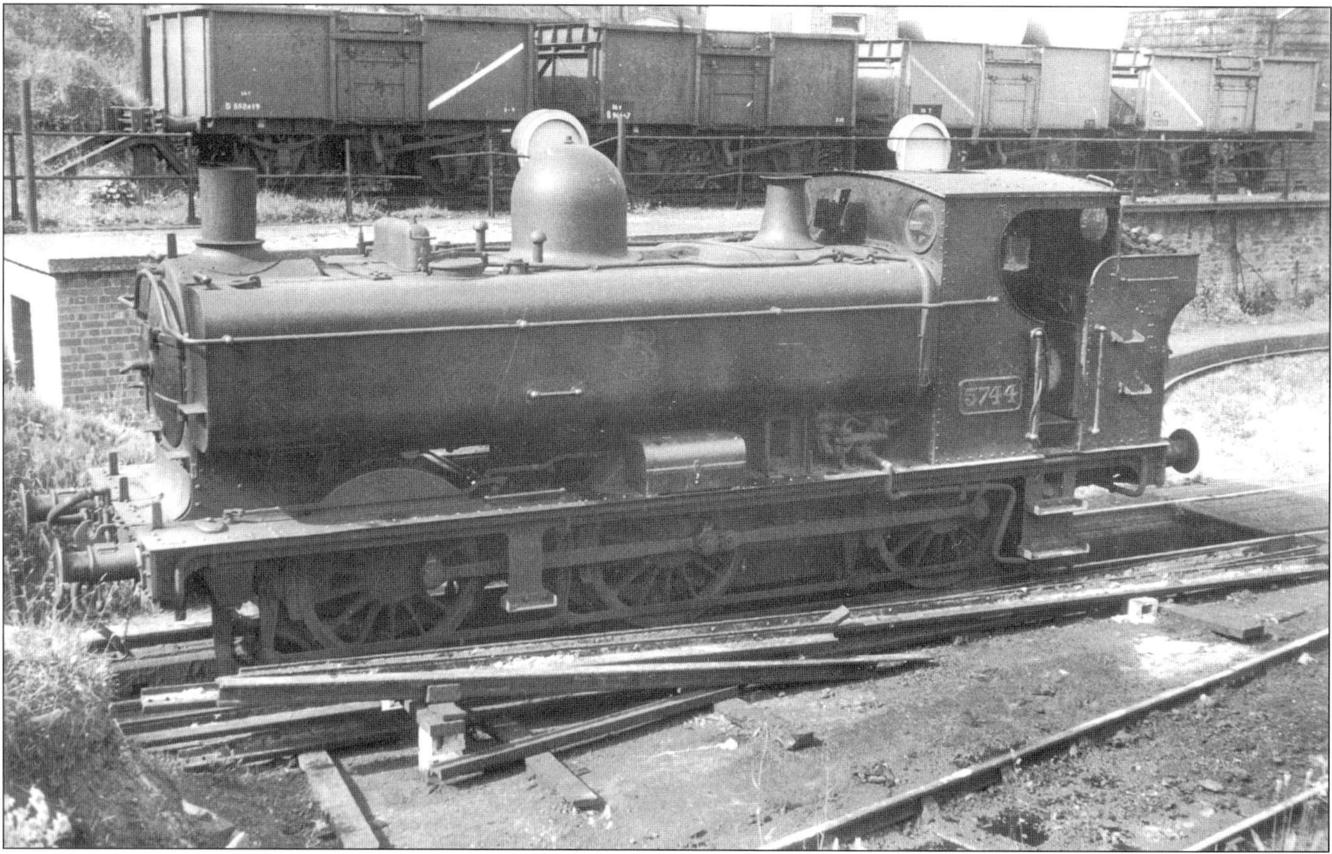

This section starts with a selection of the GWRs 5700 class standard pannier tanks. Standing in the shed yard at Truro during late 1961 is 5744. The engine is stabled on one of the two short stub sidings which were just beyond the turntable. It will be noted that the engine has a 'stovepipe' chimney. Before it came to Truro in 1960, this engine spent several years working from Didcot shed where some of the work involved shunting at a munitions depot. As a precaution some of the engines at Didcot were fitted with a 'Spark Arrester' on their chimney and 5744 was one of these. This was a large cowl fitted over the top and the engine still carried it when it arrived at Truro. Soon after arrival the cowl was removed leaving the funnel as seen. The coal wagons in the background are at the end of the coaling stage ramp. The white, arc shaped fittings visible on the railings were fuelling points for diesel multiple units. Fuel tanks can be seen above the BR 16 ton mineral wagons.   Mike Daly.

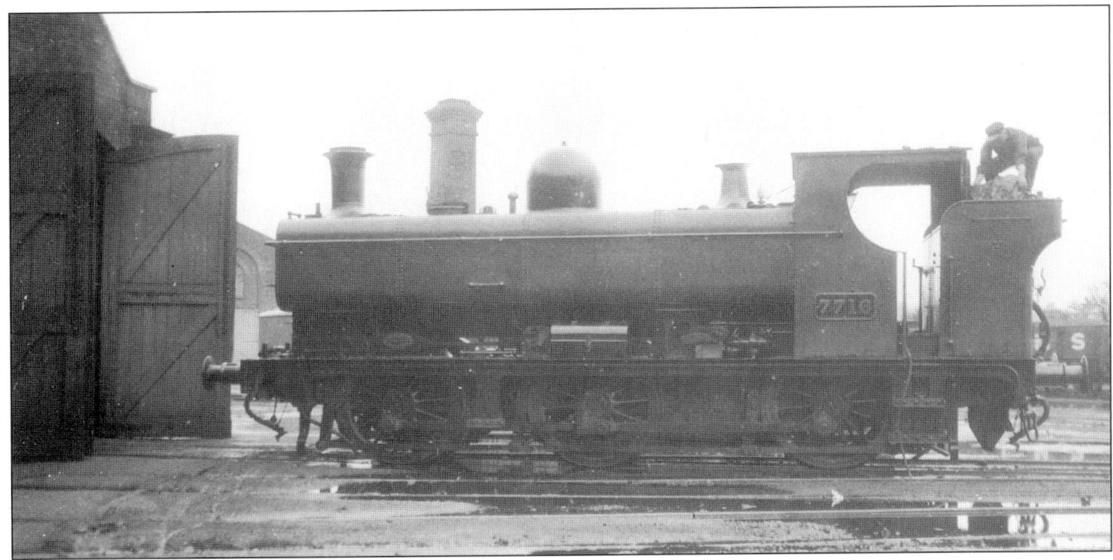

The fireman of 7716 appears to be wrestling with an extra large lump of coal which had been deposited in the engine's bunker. The engine is outside the semi-roundhouse shed at St Blazey during the early 1930s among numerous pools of rain water. The chimney of the sand drying house is behind the engine. This engine moved to Exeter within a few years and remained there until it was withdrawn in December 1959.

Here are pannier tanks outside the shed at St Blazey on 5 September 1959. Nearest to the camera is 8713 which was on loan from Tyseley shed, Birmingham. To its left is 1600 class 1627 which was on loan from Gloucester shed or Lydney sub-shed whilst far left is local resident 1624. The engines were on loan, as were several others, to cover for some of the shed's own engines which were away receiving attention at Works and were here for around seven weeks. Maurice Dart.

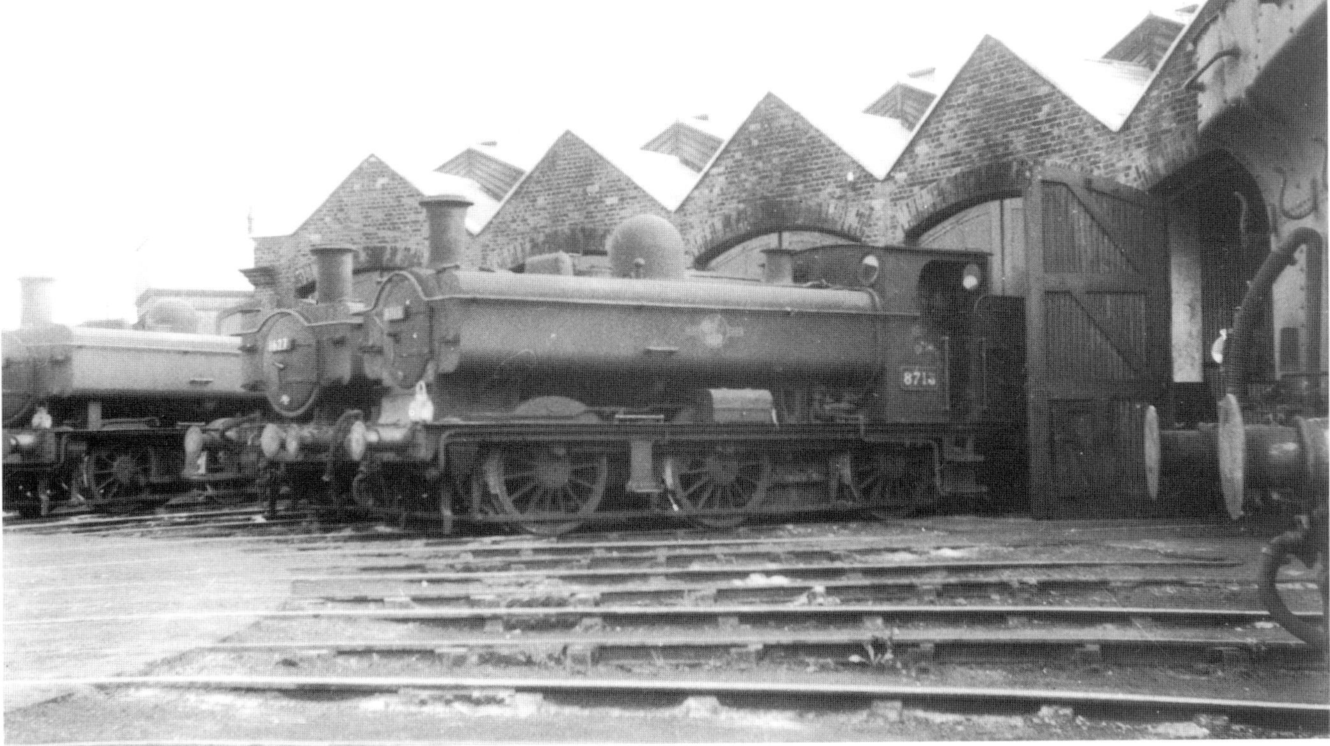

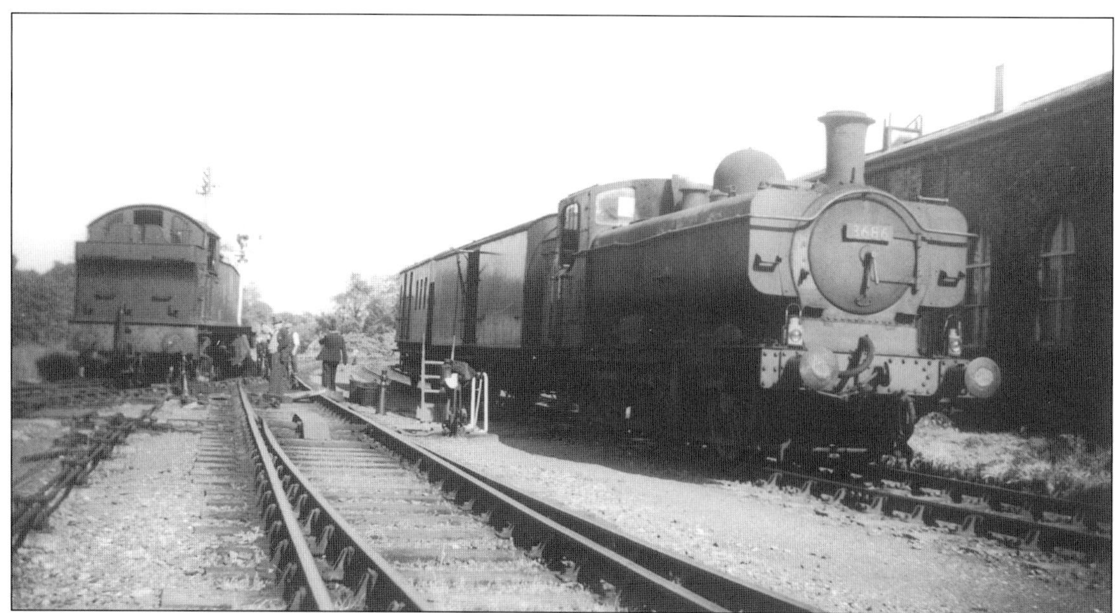

We move on to the 8750 class which were a development of the 5700 class, identifiable as they were fitted with a cab which had a rounded, instead of a flat roof. This interesting photo, taken on 28 May 1960, shows Laira's 3686 in the GWR yard at Launceston with the shed's 'Breakdown train'. On the left is 4575 class 2-6-2T 4591 which had become derailed. The loco is being re-railed using jacks and blocks. One of the jacks can be seen almost under the right hand rear buffer of the loco. Another jack is on the ground near the trolley. The gentleman wearing a trilby hat and a black suit is Harold Luscombe who was Shedmaster at Laira. He was supervising the operation. The small GWR sub-shed is on the right. The author once saw this engine bring a train of 93 empty wagons, vans and a brake van into Laira yard from Tavistock junction yard. This was quite a feat for a lone pannier tank. The engine was opposite Mount Gould Junction signal box and the brake van was just past Laira Junction box.

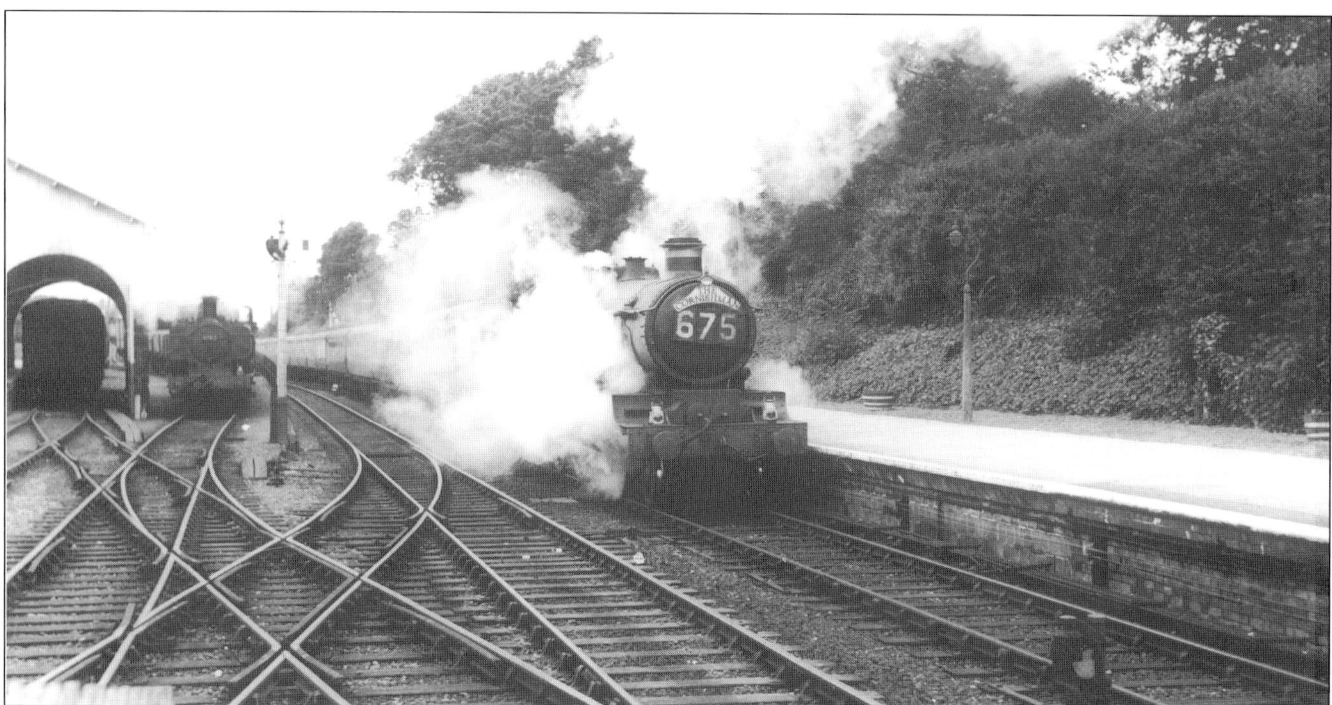

There was plenty of steam blowing around at Camborne on an unspecified date in 1957. Viewed from the end of the down platform, Truro shed's 3702 shunts beside the goods shed as an unidentified 'Castle' class 4-6-0 storms up the rising gradient with the up 'Cornishman'.

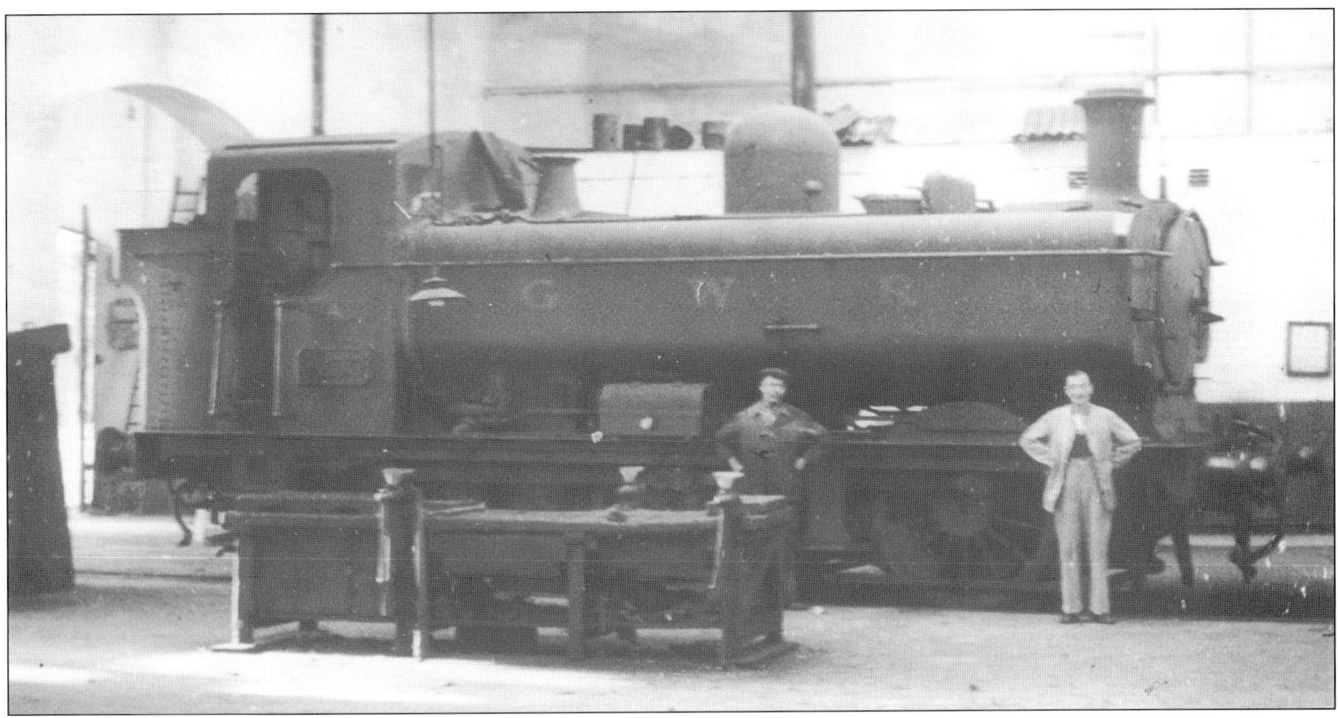

This scene inside the 'factory' at St Blazey shed was taken on 13 September 1947 when 9655 was present for some attention. Two of the fitters obviously wished to be part of the photo. The shed contained nine lines which radiated off an outside turntable. The three centre lines continued through archways to reach this spacious workshop. A.C.Roberts.

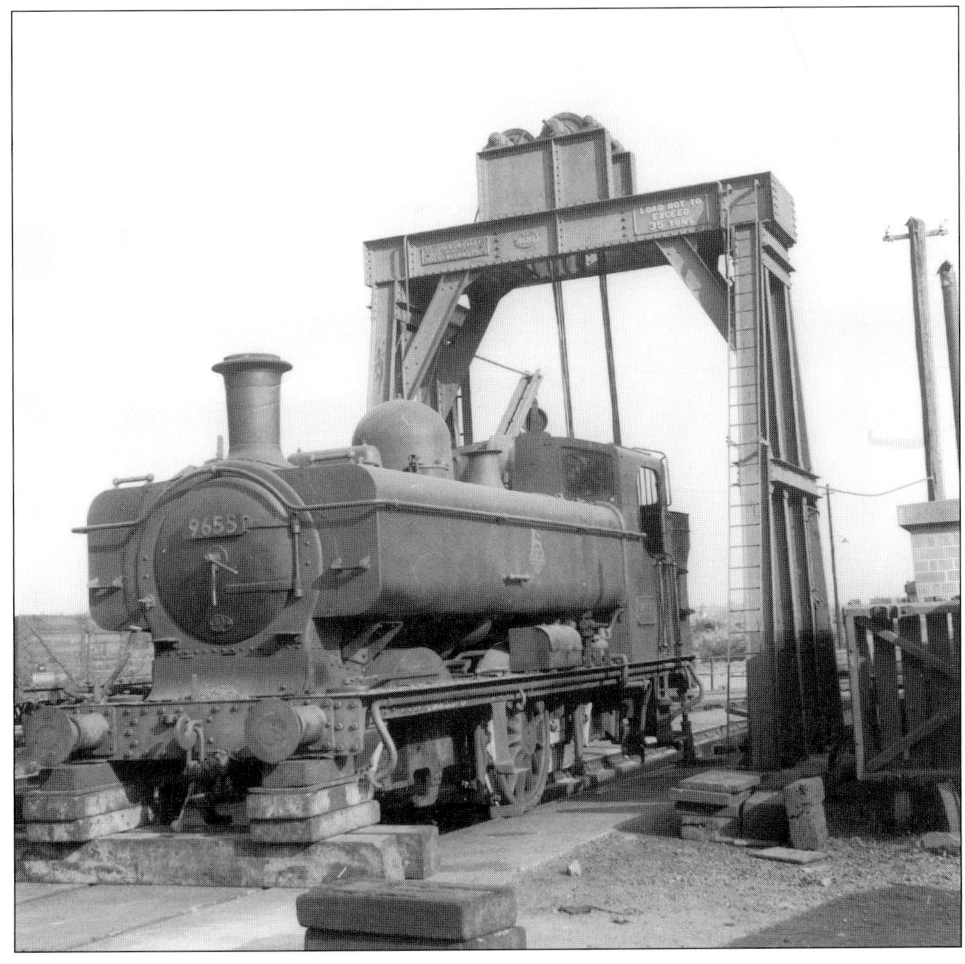

This is a photo of the same engine, taken on 4 May 1957 at St Blazey, when it was 'under the hoist' with its front and rear driving wheels removed for attention. It is supported on blocks at the front and on jacks at the rear with the hoist's chain holding it up. The plates on the hoist proclaim that it was built by Stothert & Pitt Ltd of Bath in 1909 and that the load must not exceed 35 tons. The oval plate carries FE 4688. To the left of the engine is a 13 ton Private Owner 7 plank wagon.

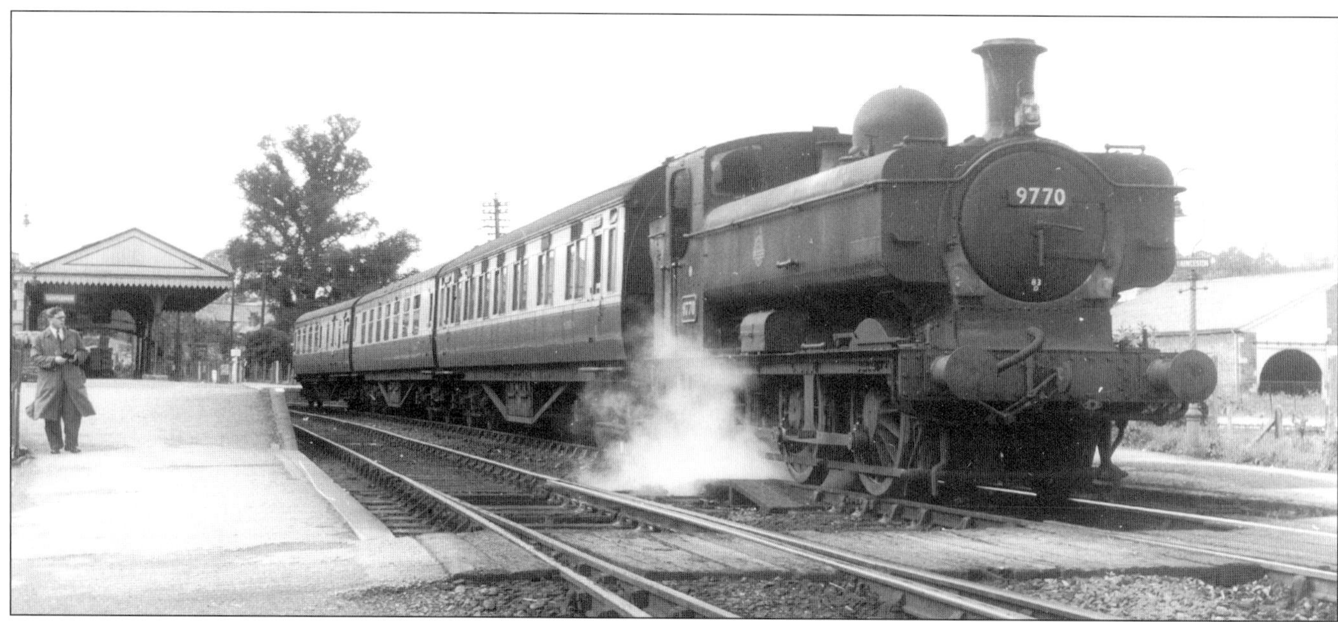

We end the batch of 8750 class locos with a shot of Laira's 9770 ready to depart from Launceston SR station with a train for Plymouth North Road in the mid 1950s. The train is composed of LMS stock. As an economy, passenger trains ceased to use the GWR terminal station at Launceston and utilised the SR platforms. The GWR goods shed is in the right background. In December 1959, this engine was one of a batch of the 8750 class that were transferred to the Southern Region and for several years it worked from Nine Elms shed on empty stock workings between Clapham Junction and Waterloo.

Next we look at a few of the lighter pannier tanks which were used for working Auto trains, branch passenger trains and local goods work. During a visit by Plymouth Railway Circle to the Royal Albert Bridge on 26 May 1956, an Auto train from Saltash to Plymouth, North Road is propelled over the bridge by 6400 class 6414. This was a Laira engine for all of its existence.   This was well before stringent health and safety regulations were introduced!
Mike Daly

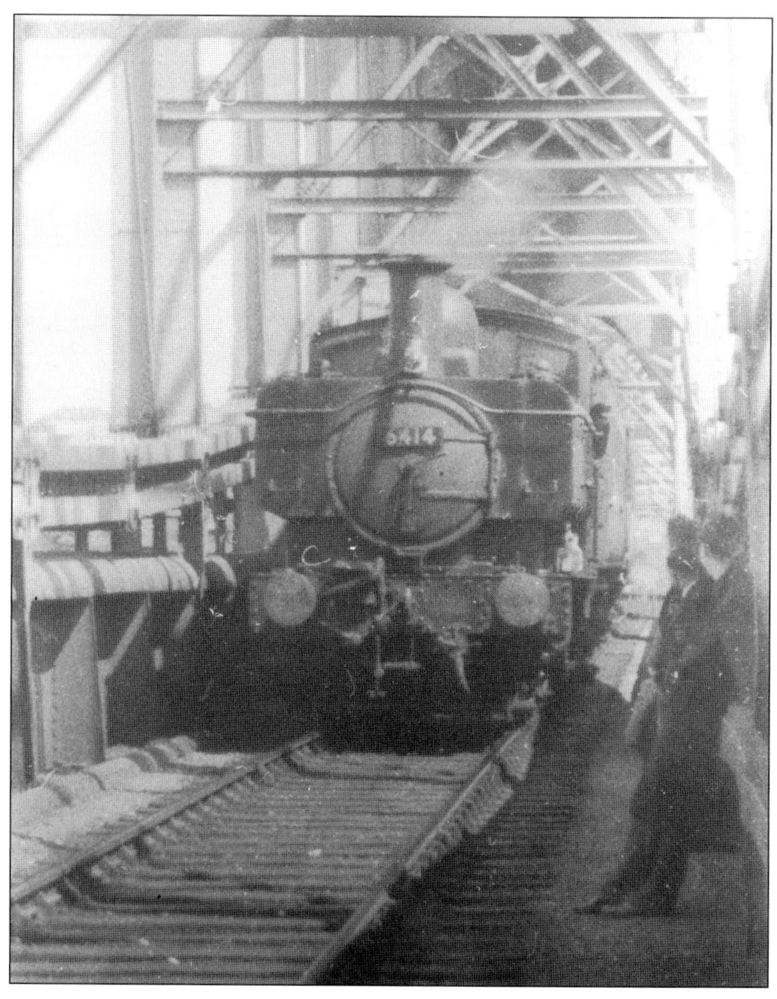

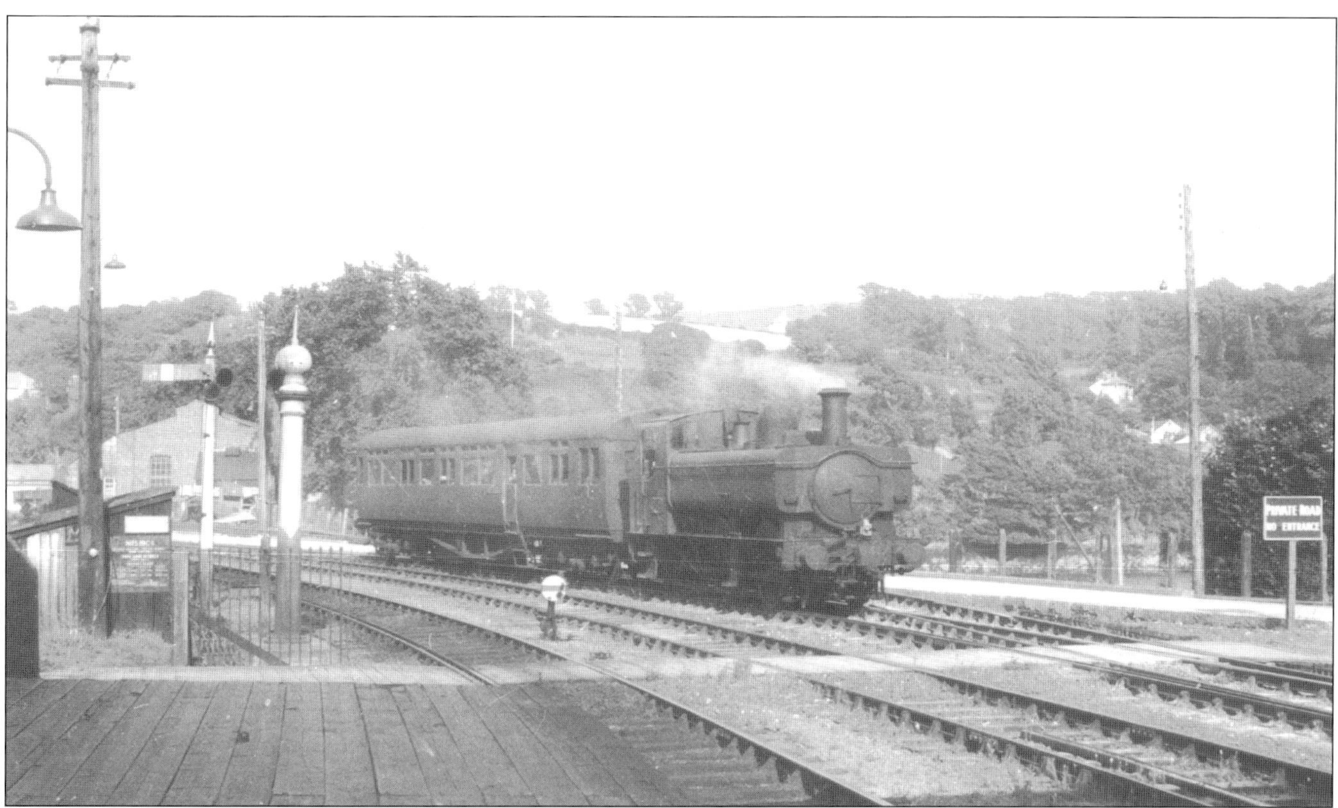

During 1946, 5400 class 5412 replaced withdrawn 2-4-0T 3581 on the Fowey Auto train for a period and in 1947 6400 class 6420 was transferred from Taunton to St Blazey for a brief period to cover this work but no photos of these locos working the branch have been found. 2-4-0T 3582 was transferred from Taunton and worked the line until it was withdrawn in November 1949. When the regular engine for the branch was under repair it was the usual practice for Laira to send a replacement down 'on loan'. This occurred early in 1948 when 6400 class 6417 officiated. That engine is approaching Fowey with the single Auto coach. This photo was taken from the Up platform which had been taken out of use for passenger trains. Joe Moss Collection.

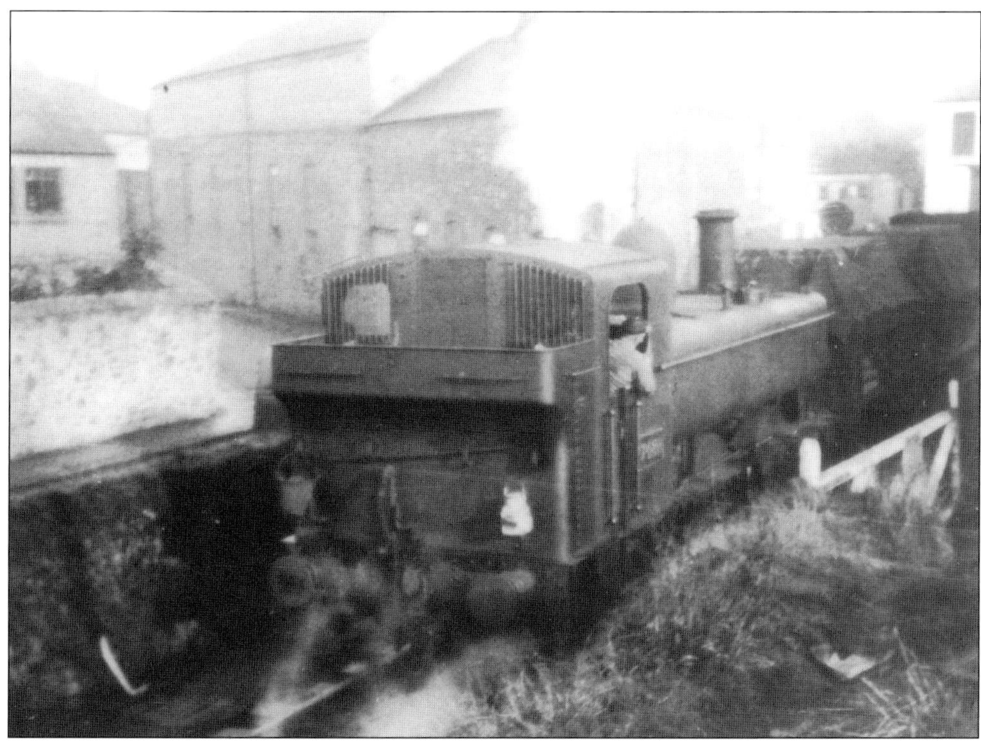

Not many representatives of the 7400 class were seen in Cornwall but 7422 was transferred from Laira to Truro where it spent many years. Although not photographically perfect, this is a very rare photo taken on 8 October 1947 of 7422 propelling a short train over Foundry Road level crossing on the Roskear branch. This is the only photo that I have seen of a train on this line. Kenneth Brown.

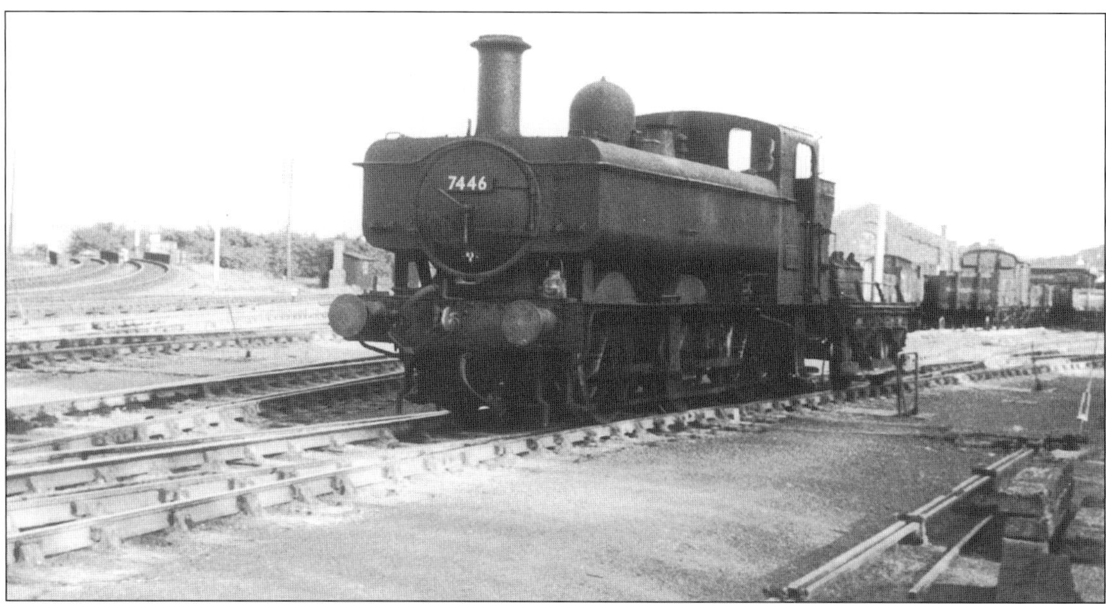

Built in British Railways days in 1950, 7446 came new to St Blazey. It is shunting in the goods yard there on 14 June 1957. The line to Par is curving off to the left and the ex Cornwall Minerals Railway Wagon works is visible in the background to the right of the engine.

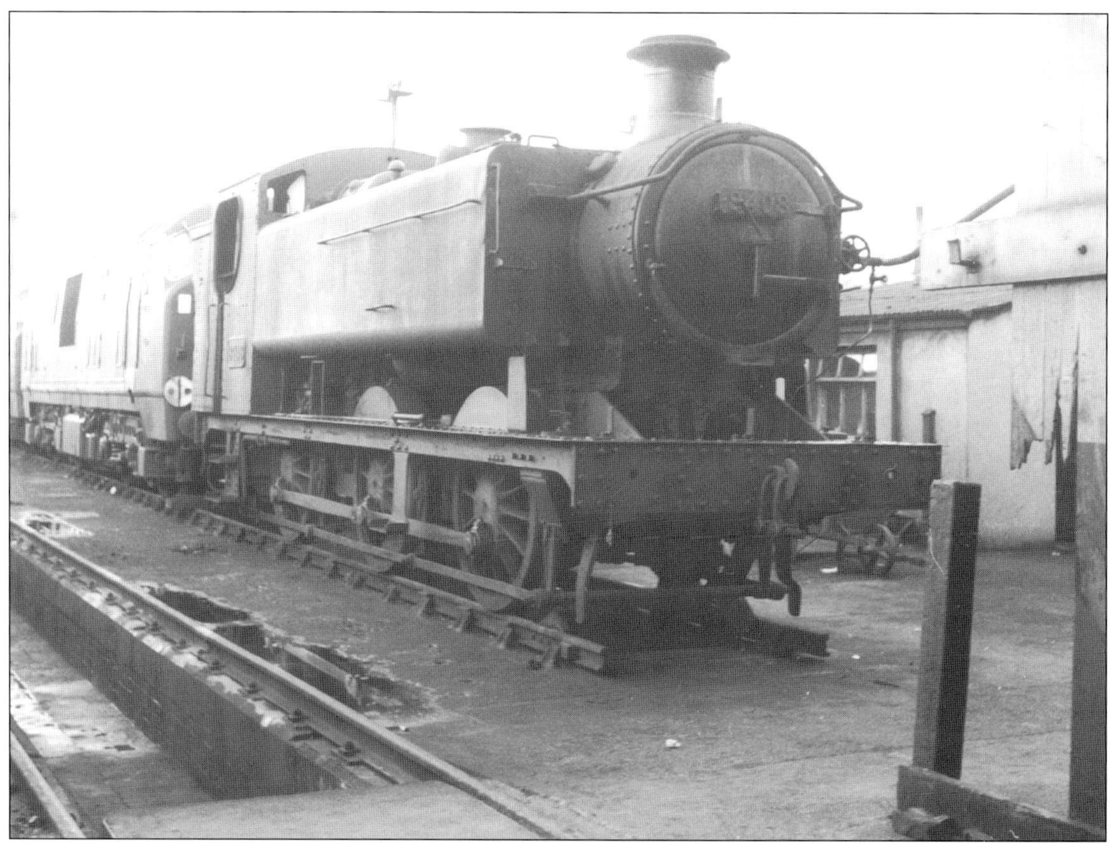

In 1947 the 9400 class, a new type of heavier pannier tank was built followed by many more of the type from 1950 and several were based in Cornwall. However, after Truro shed had closed to steam locos and was servicing diesel multiple units 8408, which had been withdrawn from Swansea East Dock shed in September 1959, arrived to act as a stationary boiler to supply steam. The arrival of this rare engine caused great excitement among local enthusiasts. It is seen outside Truro shed devoid of buffers in 1962. The valve and steam pipe connection are visible to the right of the smokebox. Two North British type 22 diesel hydraulics, one of which is D6330, are behind the steam loco.

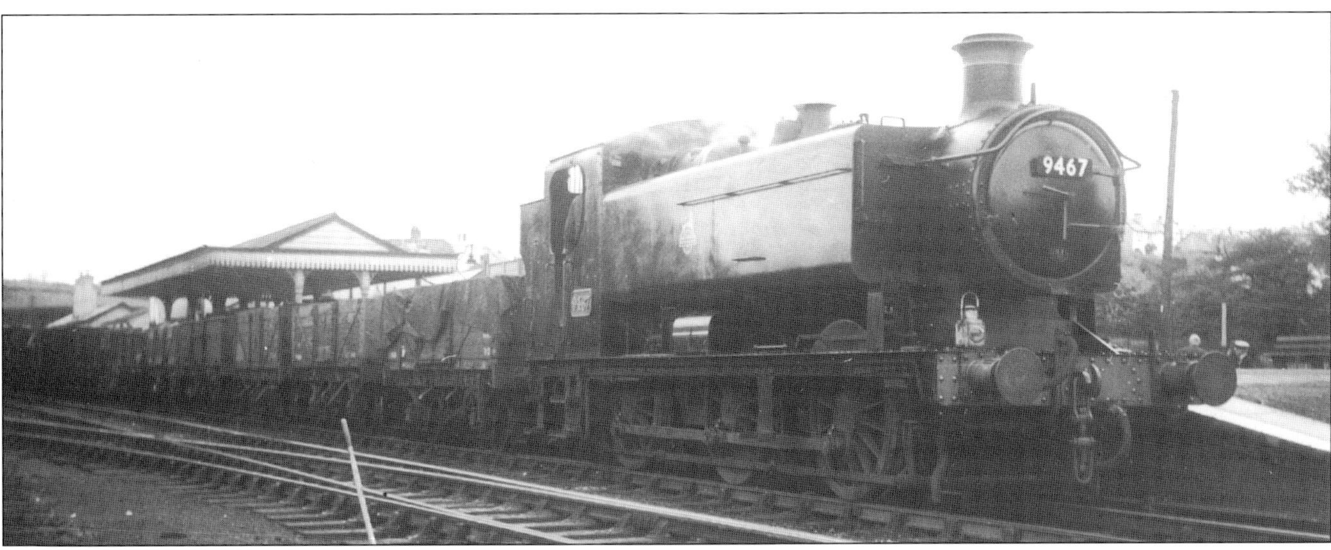

Laira received 9467 new in February 1952 and it remained there until it was withdrawn in May 1962. It is seen at Par on a down goods on 6 May 1952 'awaiting the road to St Blazey'. The first vehicle behind the engine is a LNER vacuum fitted 5 plank wagon. A.G.Ellis.

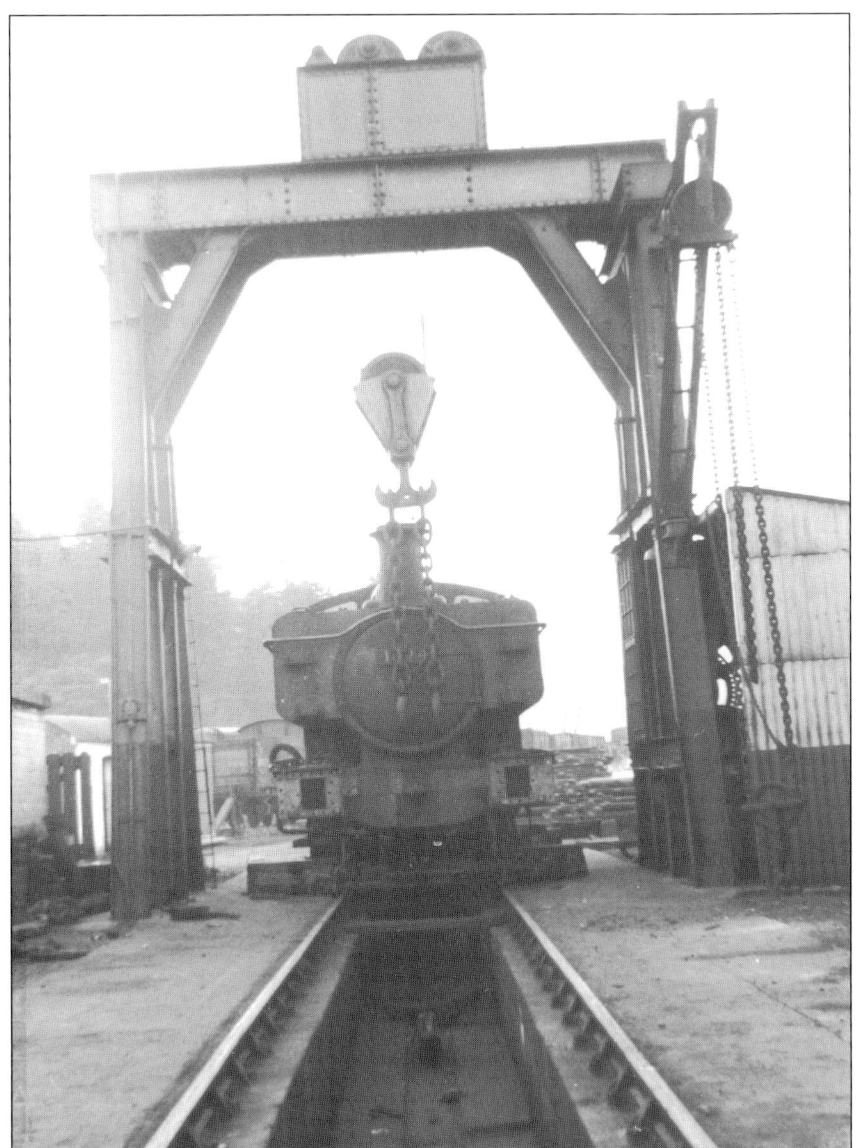

A new type of lightweight pannier tank, the 1600 class, emerged from Swindon late in 1949 to replace the older types on certain lines. One of these, 1624, was sent new to Croes Newydd shed, Wrexham in June 1950. After moves to Stourbridge, followed by Machynlleth, it arrived at Laira in May 1953 and in October of that year it moved to St Blazey to join 1626. 1624 is raised up on blocks at St Blazey, suspended 'under the hoist' with its front buffer beam removed during the evening of 23 April 1956. Maurice Dart/Transport Treasury.

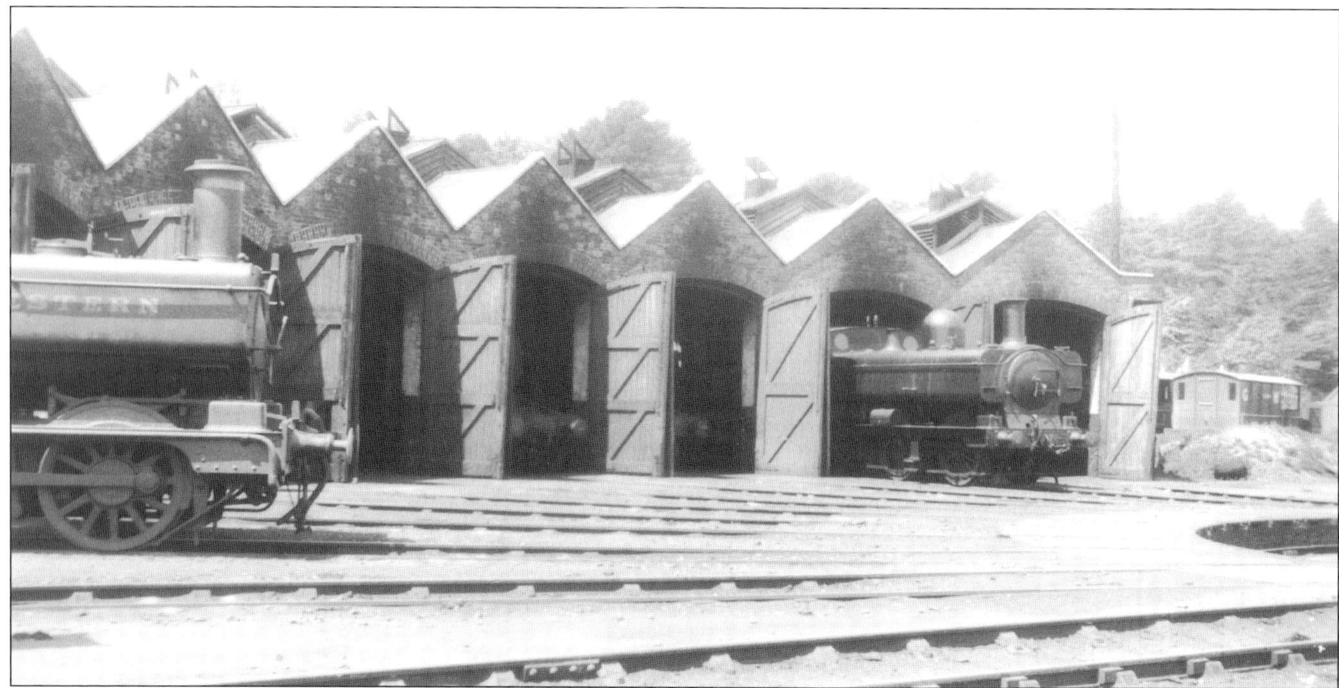

Now we start to look at the multitude of older types of pannier tank which used to inhabit the Cornish sheds, being particularly prevalent at St Blazey for working the china clay branch lines. This view of St Blazey shed in 1936 has an 850 class pannier on the left. Inside the shed are 4500 class 2-6-2Ts 4559 and 4565, whilst partly outside is 2721 class 2725. The author saw this engine working around St Austell during 1943/44. It was withdrawn from Truro shed in January 1946. A GW 'Toad' brake van emblazoned 'St Blazey' can be seen to the right of the loco shed. Rail Archive Stephenson(Photomatic).

This undated photo of 2721 class pannier 2750 in the yard at St Blazey shed was probably taken before the early 1920s as the loco has an early type of bunker. It is standing at the back end of a siding containing GWR 10 ton loco coal wagons and a thin pipe can be seen trailing out from within the cab. There is a 'Not to be moved' notice above the buffer beam so the loco is probably receiving some attention to some fitting within the confines of the cab or the firebox. The piece of equipment that is standing on the ground alongside the engine is probably a Point Indicator. This engine was withdrawn from Treherbert shed in the Rhondda valley in November 1945.

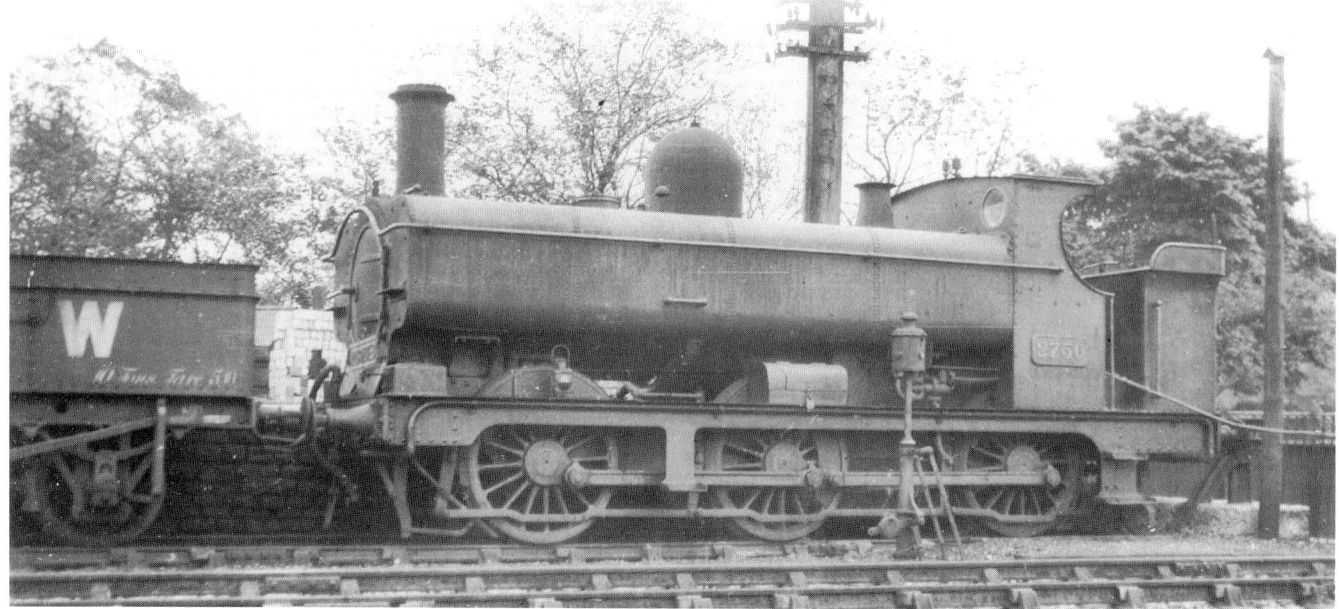

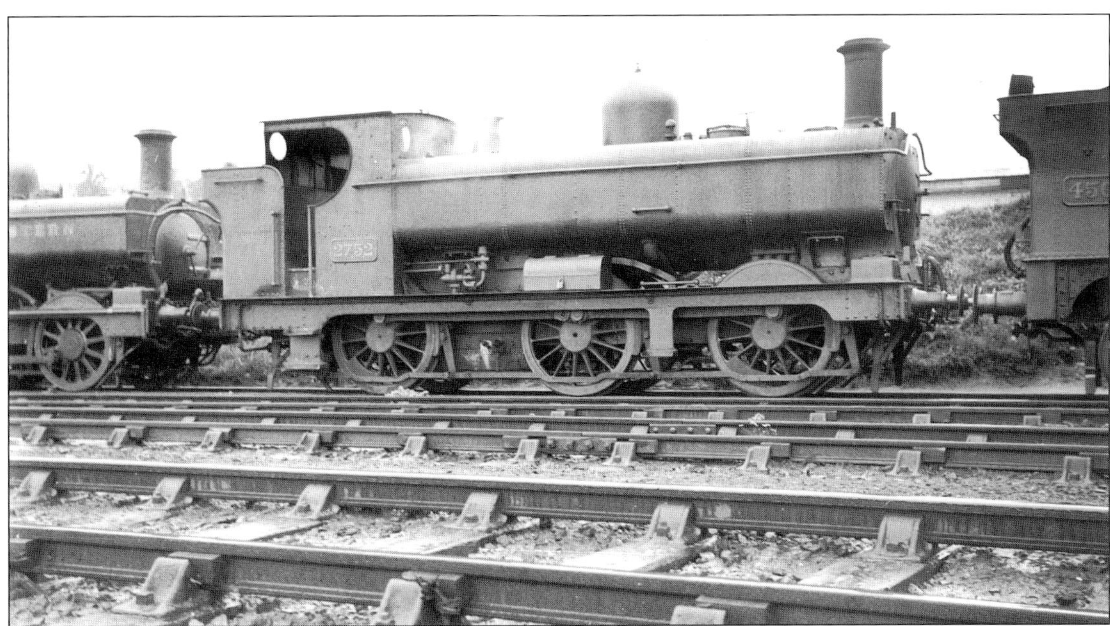

Sandwiched between a pannier tank of either the 850 or 2021 class and one of the early 4500 class 2-6-2Ts on the coaling line at St Blazey shed is 2721 class pannier 2752 on 18 July 1936. This engine was at Laira during 1946 and 1947 and ended its days at Penzance shed in March 1948. Ken Davies.

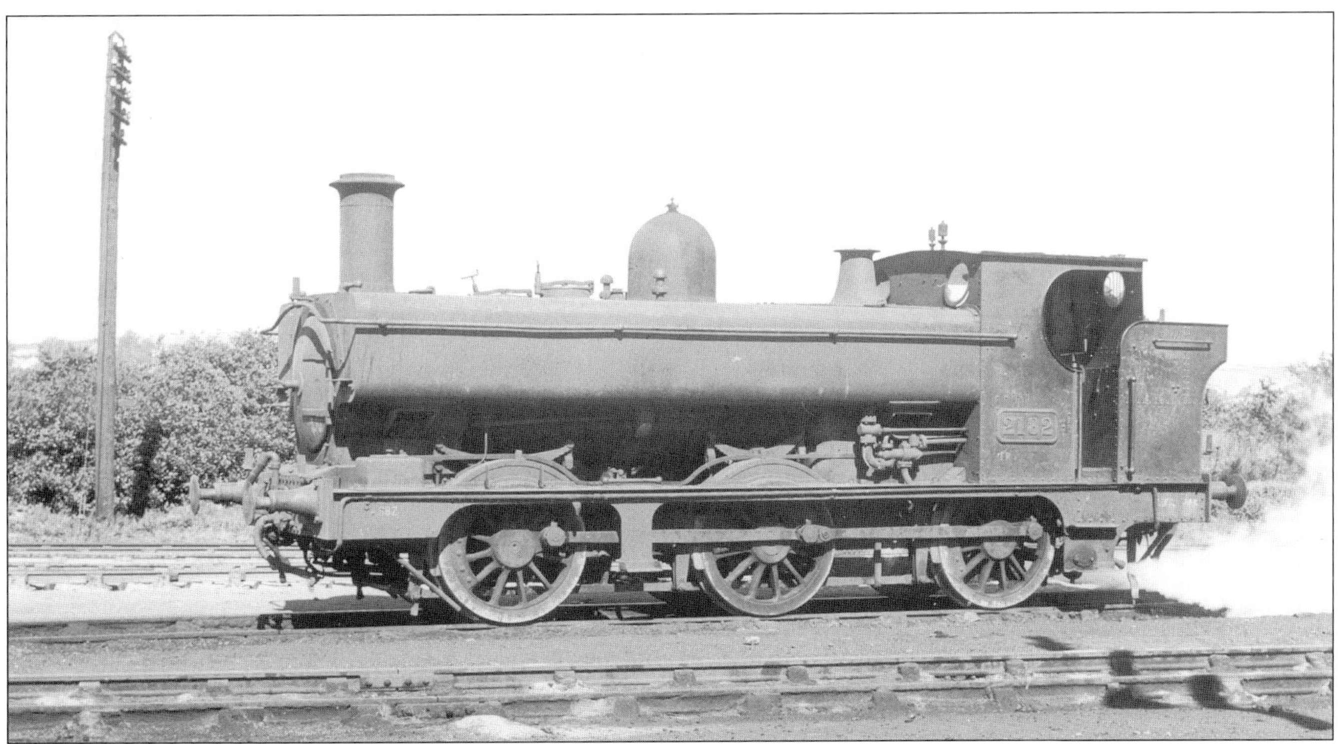

Now we see 2182 shunting at Goonbarrow Junction on the Par to Newquay branch line. This is one of ten members of the 2021 class which were fitted with increased brake power in 1939 to work on steeply graded lines. They were known as the 2181 class and St Blazey received 2181 and 2182 for working on the Goonbarrow branch. This engine had originally been numbered 2125. The photo was taken between 1945 and 1948 as the engine has a SBZ shed stencil on the side of the frame. This stencil superceded the S^{T}B stencil that had been used from the early 1940s, which had replaced the earlier SBLZ code. Notice the white clay on the rims of the wheel tyres which typified many St Blazey engines. J.H.Aston.

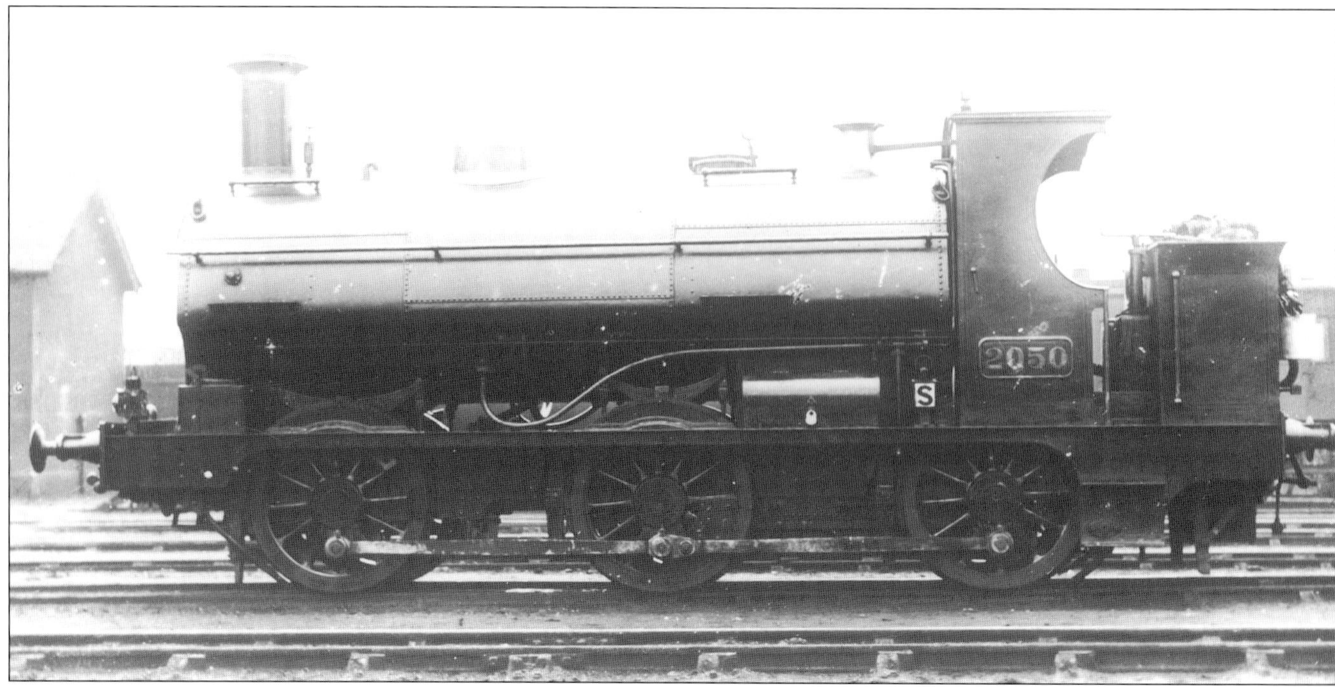

Next we look at some members of the 2021 class. Here is 2050 running as a saddle tank in the yard at St Blazey before 1914. The purpose of the prominent letter 'S' is unknown. The engine is in a remarkably clean condition so is probably recently 'ex-works'. The shunters cabin, the end of which can be seen on the left, is still in use in 2007. A.G.Ellis.

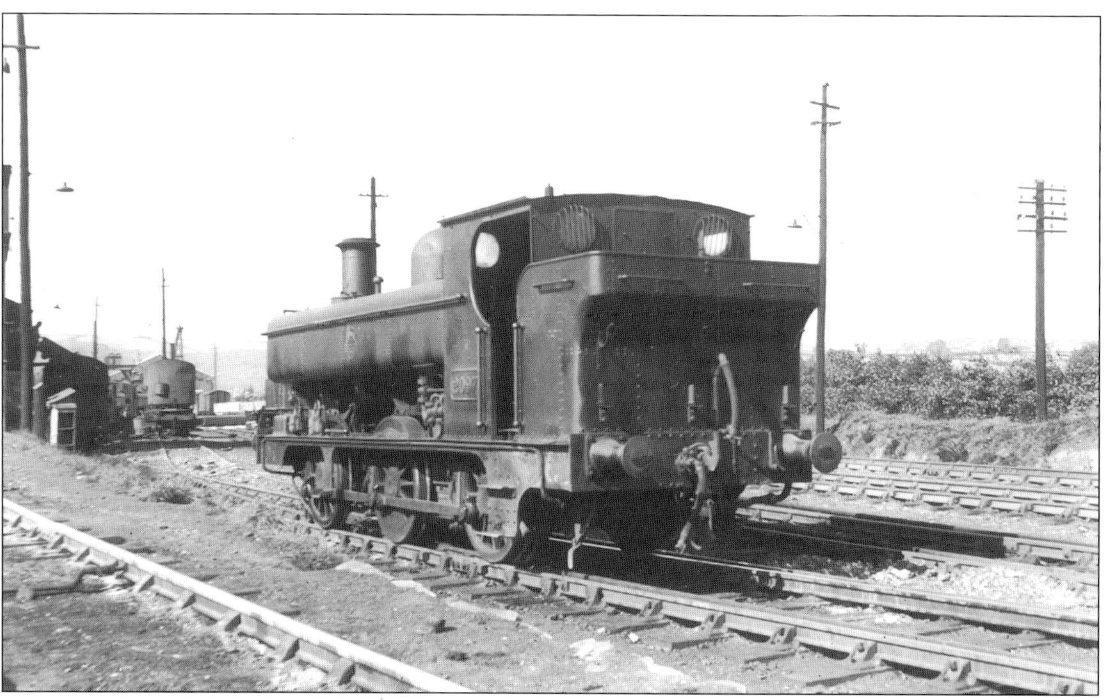

On 14 September 1952, 2021 class 2097 is waiting to be 'coaled' at St Blazey shed. The steam powered 'grab' for used for scooping up ash is in the distance, along with a couple of pannier tanks on the line under the hoist. The Wagon works is in the far distance. Ian Duncan.

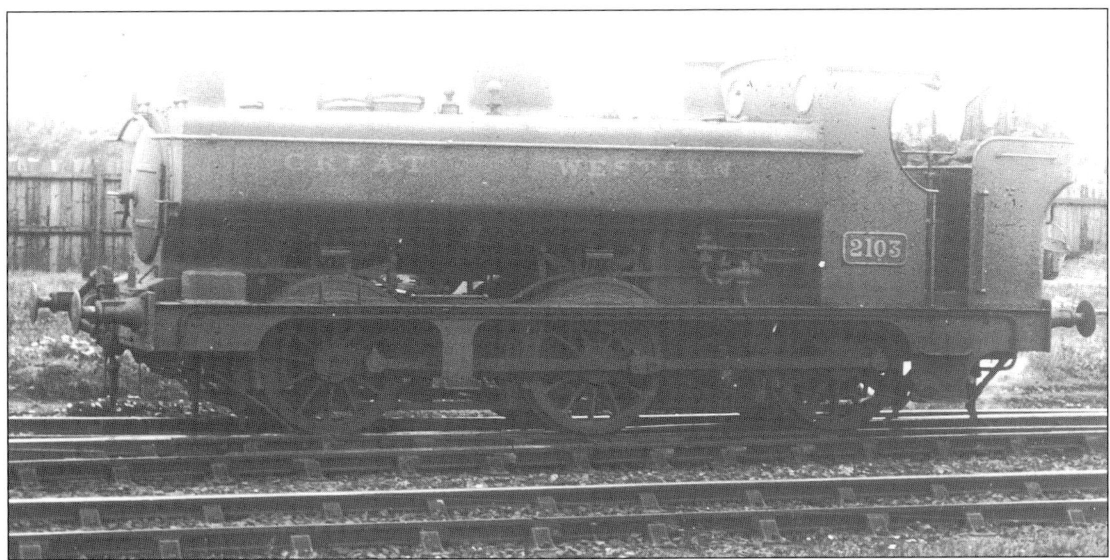

2021 class 2103 is in the yard at Long Rock shed, Penzance probably in the early 1920s. It received pannier tanks in November 1917 but retained a 'half cab' and is fitted with a 'cab back plate' on the bunker. I saw this engine in September 1945 in an immaculate condition, painted green, working a train on the Sutton Harbour branch line at Plymouth. I was returning to Friary on a train from Turnchapel and passed above it. It was withdrawn from Laira in March 1946.

Here is 2021 class 2118 standing outside St Blazey shed on 4 August 1926. It is also in a very clean state and was fitted with pannier tanks in February 1930. During 1939 it received increased brake power and was renumbered 2186. The centre one of three wagons in the right background is a GWR wooden loco coal wagon.

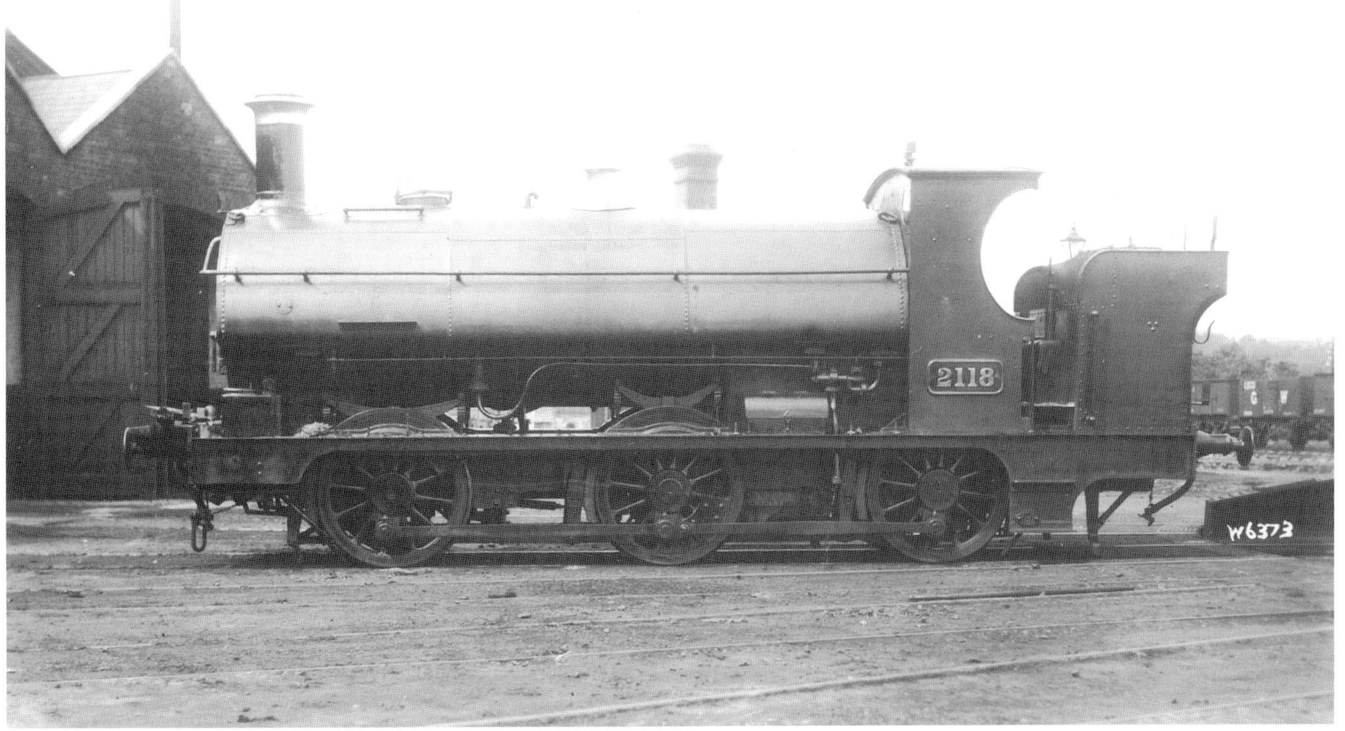

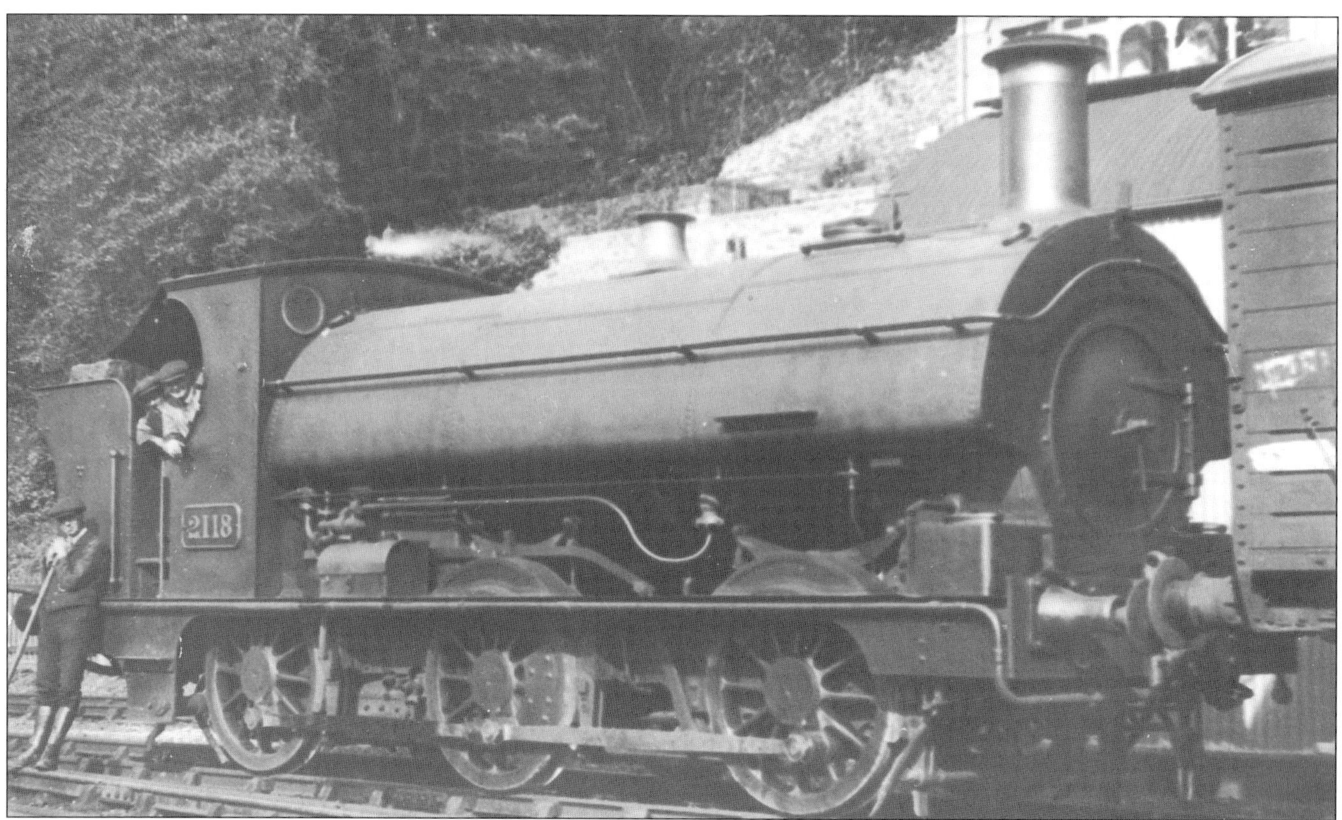

Here is an undated shot of the same engine, 2118, shunting goods wagons in the yard immediately south of the station at Looe. The crew have tied the 'weather sheet' over the half cab to provide some degree of shelter when running bunker first.

Now we see 2021 class 2148 shunting at Ponsondane sidings between Penzance and Long Rock in the mid 1930s. In July 1934 this engine was fitted with a Belpaire firebox, the top of which can be seen forward of the cab. This loco ended its days at Laira.

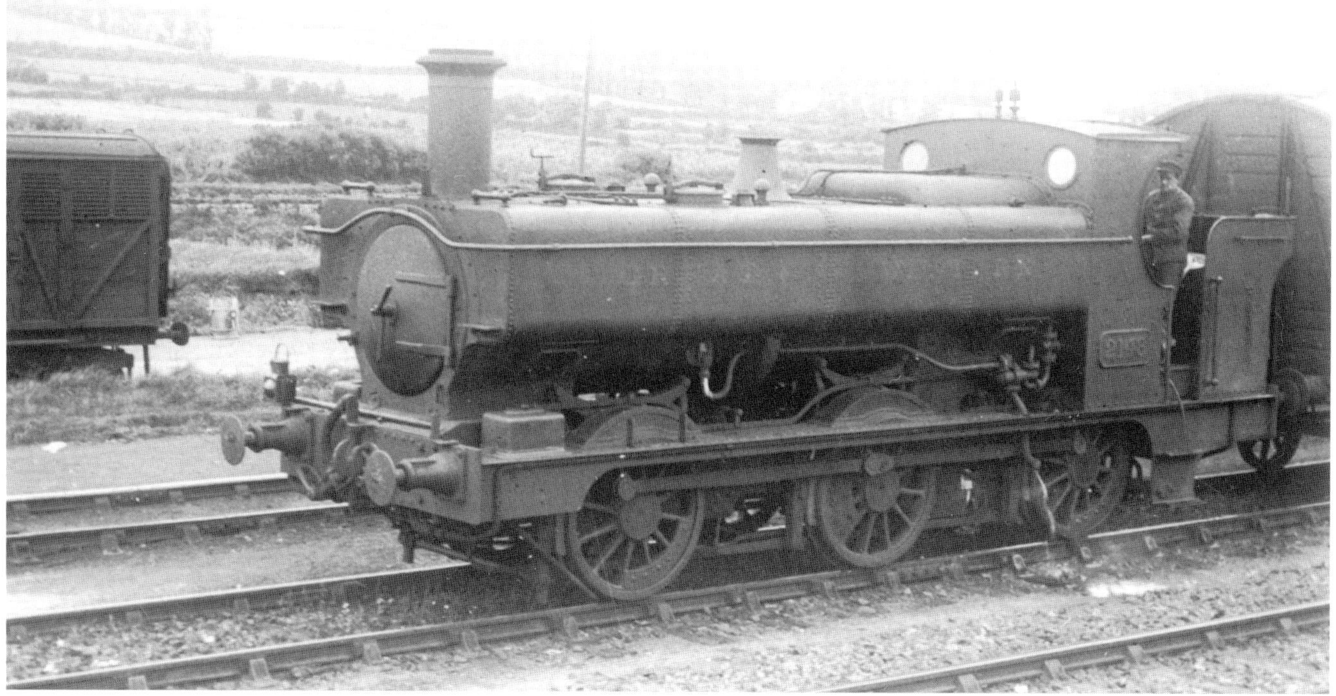

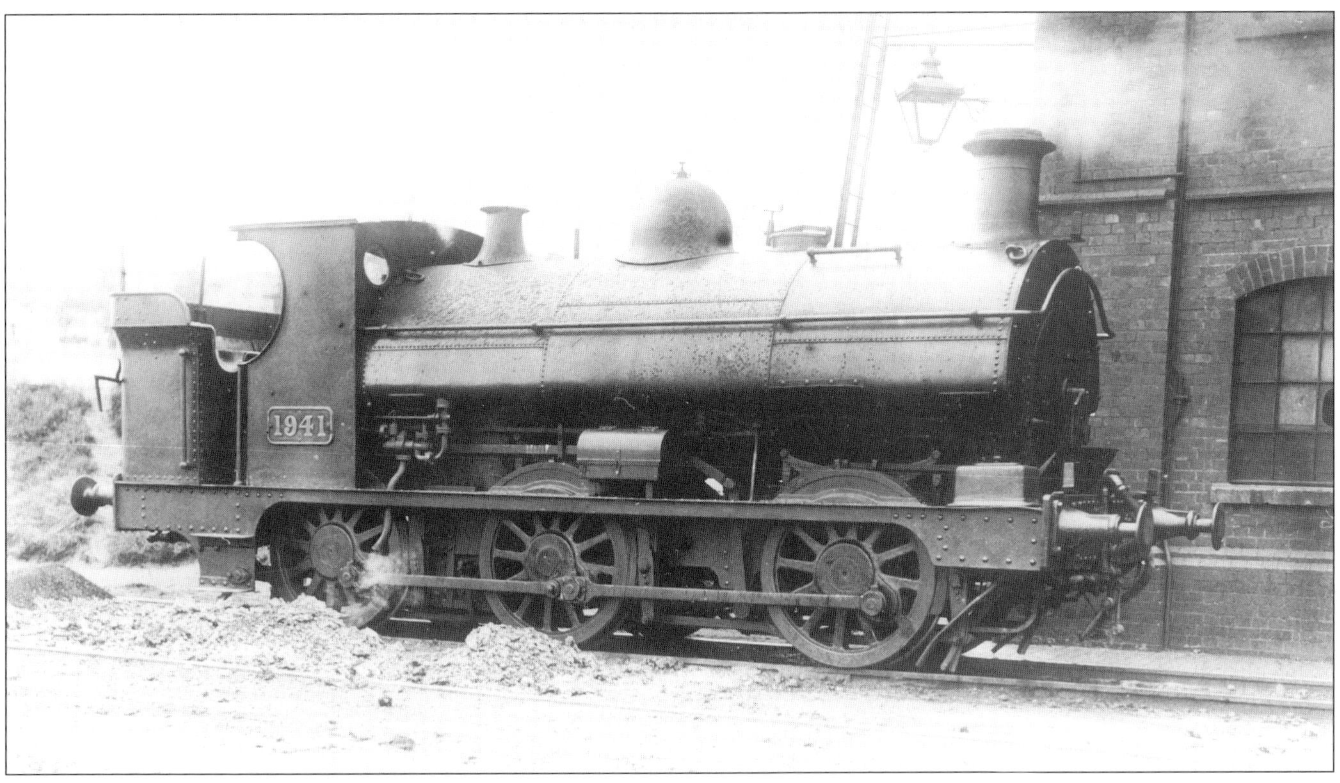

The saddle tanks at St Blazey certainly appear to have been kept in a remarkably clean state as shown by this photo of 850 class 1941 awaiting coaling at the shed. As the loco received pannier tanks in September 1929 the photo dates from before then.

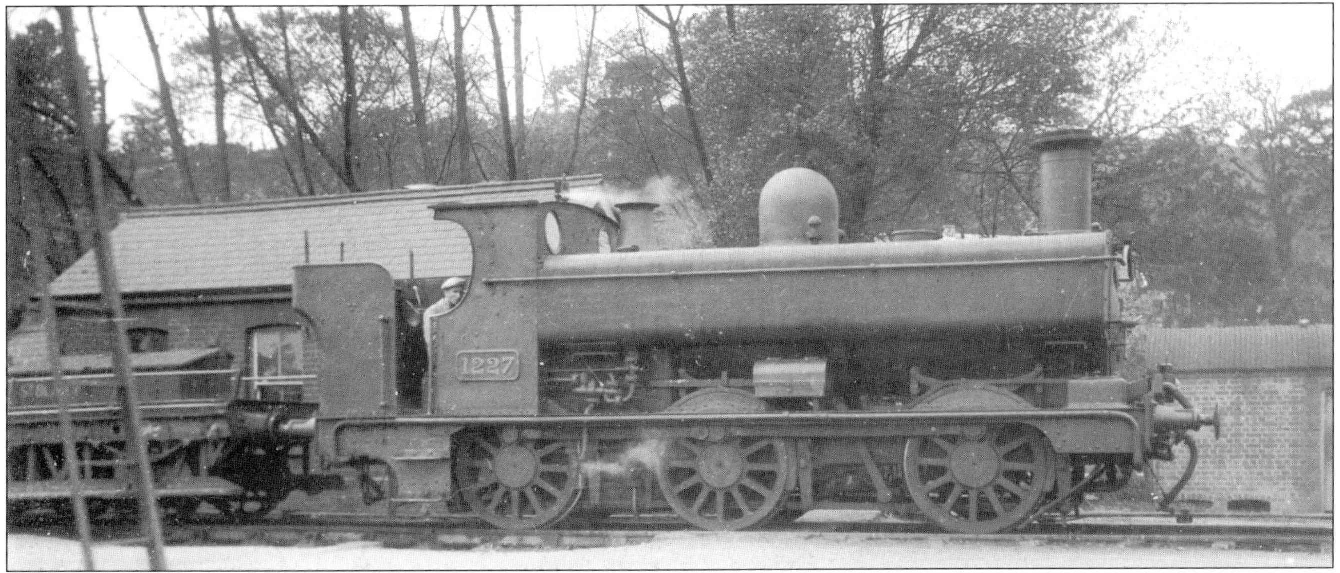

850 class pannier 1227 is standing in the yard at St Blazey coupled to a shunters runner truck. The fireman is crouching down but is glancing at the photographer. The photo post dates March 1914 when the engine received pannier tanks. It was at St Blazey when withdrawn in April 1938.

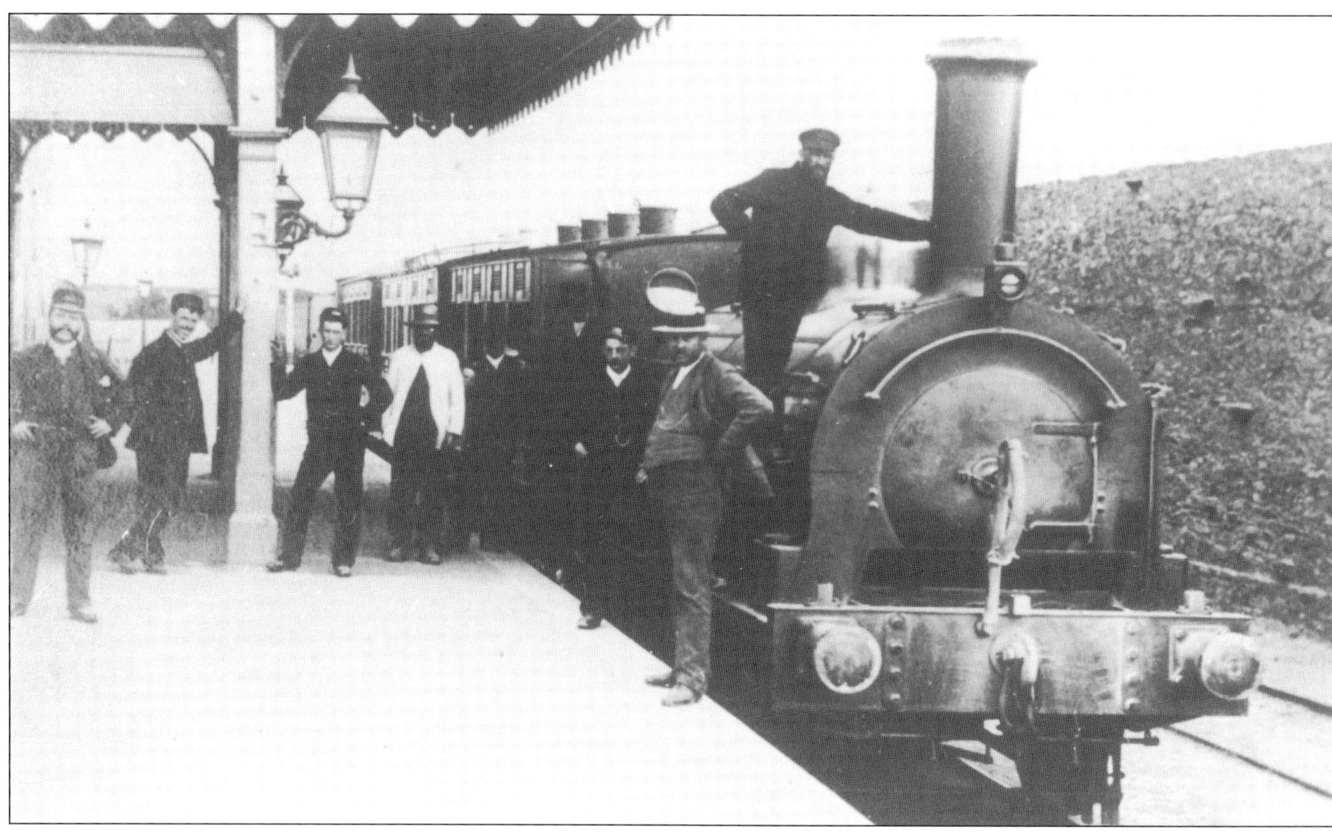

This photo shows an unidentified 850 class saddle tank on a passenger train which has arrived at Newquay in the early 1900s. Passengers, engine and train crew and station staff all pose, wishing to be included in the photo. Notice the cylindrical ventilators protruding from the roofs of the carriages.

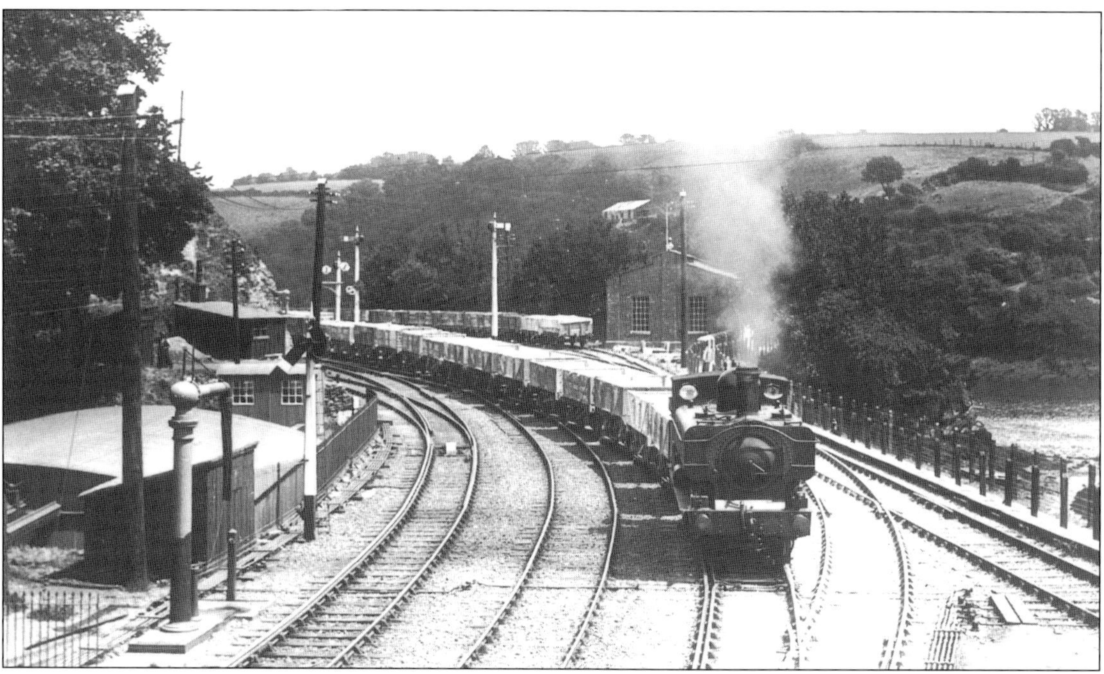

This photo was taken on 7 July 1921 from the footbridge which linked the platforms at Fowey station. It shows 655 class pannier tank 1746 hauling a train of empty china clay wagons from the jetties towards the station. It will tackle the steep climb to Pinnock tunnel on the line to St Blazey. The Locomotive Club of Great Britain/Ken Nunn Collection.

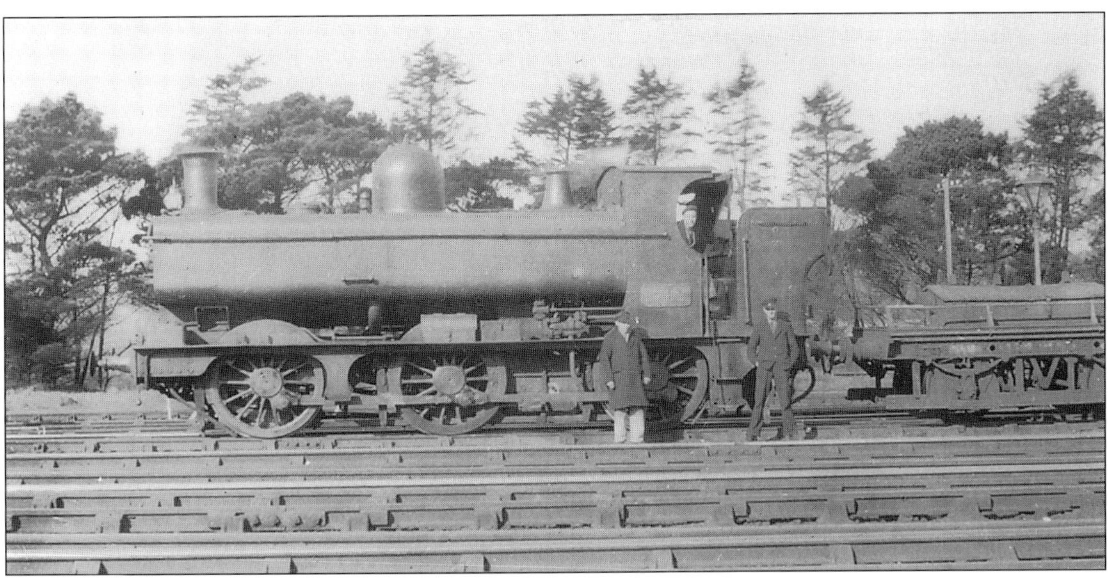

Another 655 class pannier tank, 1782, is shunting in the goods yard at Truro early in 1948. The engine carries a TR shed stencil on the side of the frame. Staff, including the shunter, who is wearing an overcoat, pose for the photographer. John Humphrey/Kenneth Brown Collection.

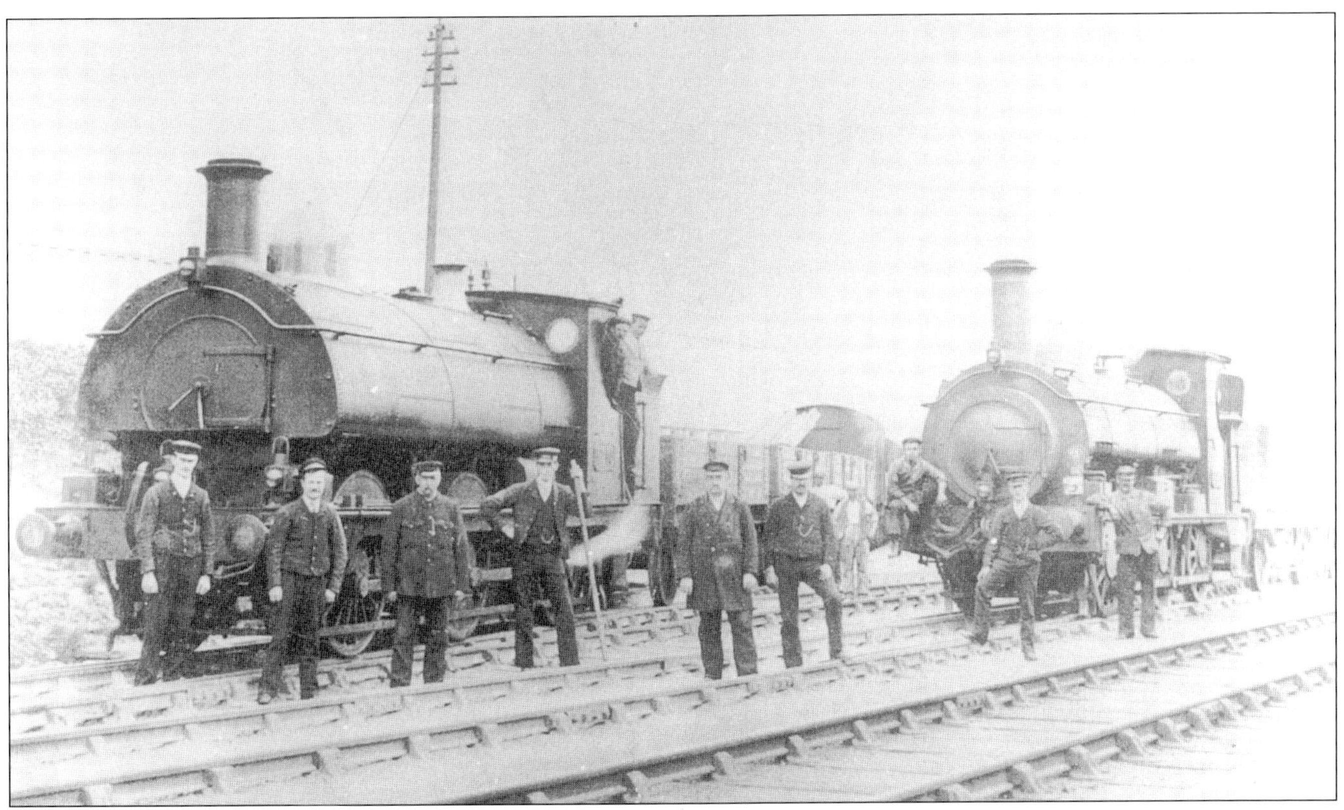

This is an interesting undated photo taken at Burngullow, two miles west of St Austell. On the left, 1854 class saddle tank 1718 is shunting a train into sidings which served china clay kilns. It received pannier tanks in October 1920 and was withdrawn from service in October 1936. On the right is one of the two members of the 2021 class saddle tanks which were fitted with a 'drum head' extension to the smokebox. It also has a cab 'back plate' fitted. One of the two locos was 2044 which was noted in 1911. The identity of the other has never been ascertained but it appears to possibly be either 2052 or 2092. The shunting staff and train crew pose for the camera.

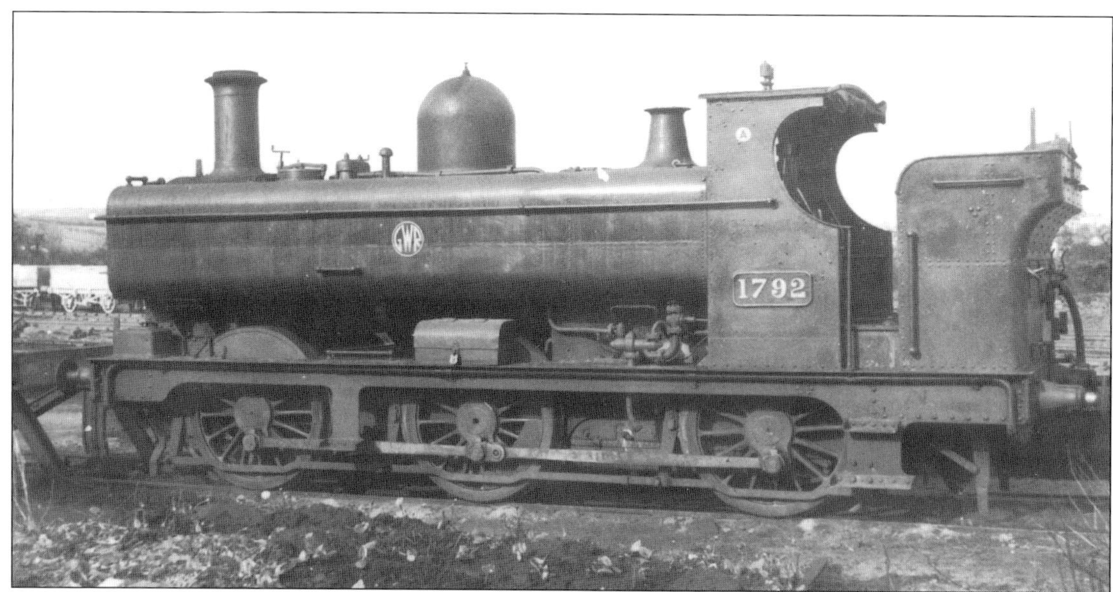

Now we see a portrait of 1854 class pannier 1792 at the buffers adjacent to the turntable in the yard at St Blazey shed. As the engine does not carry a shed stencil on the frame, the photo was taken before 1939. This engine was very familiar to me between 1943 and 1945 when it regularly worked trains up the Trenance Valley branch. It was withdrawn in November 1945. W.A.Camwell.

This view of St Blazey shed probably dates from the late 1930s as none of the engines carry shed stencils on their frames. From left to right are an 8750 class pannier, 2021 class pannier 2050, both inside, a 4500 class 2-6-2T and another 8750 class pannier partly outside and on the right the real gem which is 1854 class pannier 1794 which ended its days at Truro in December 1946. B.Roberts.

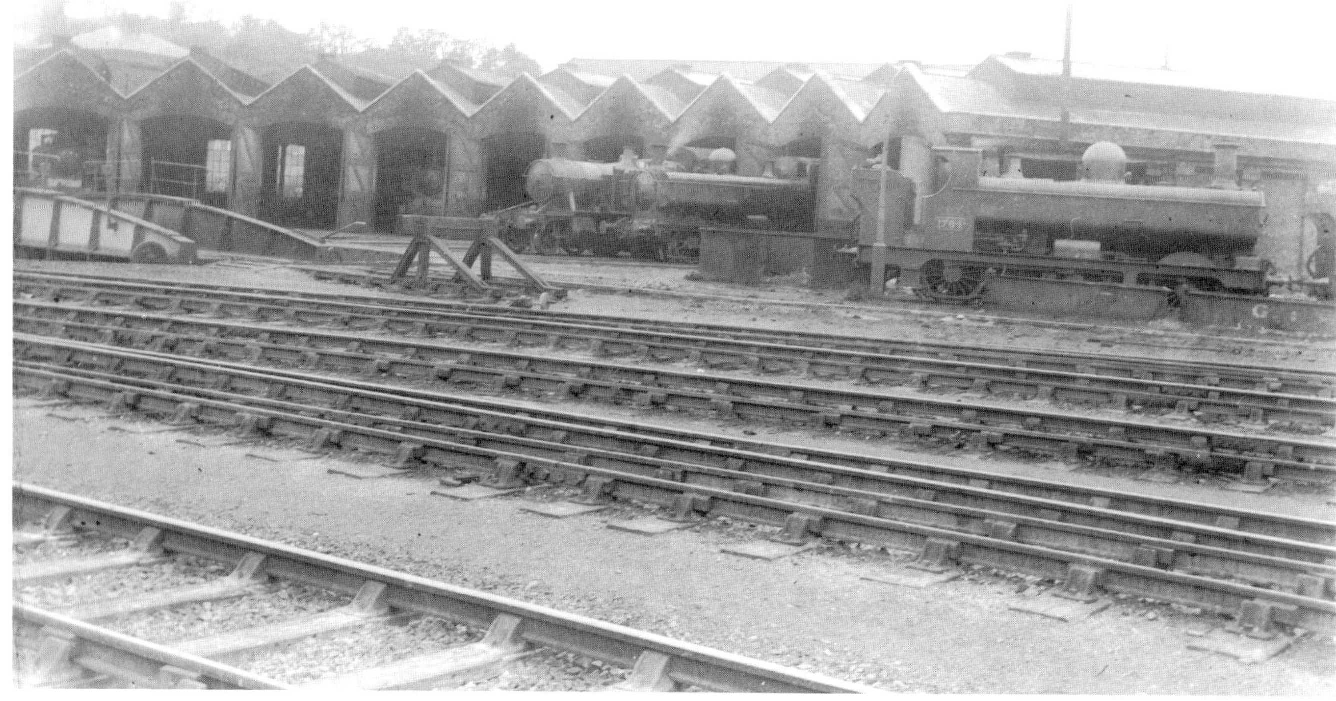

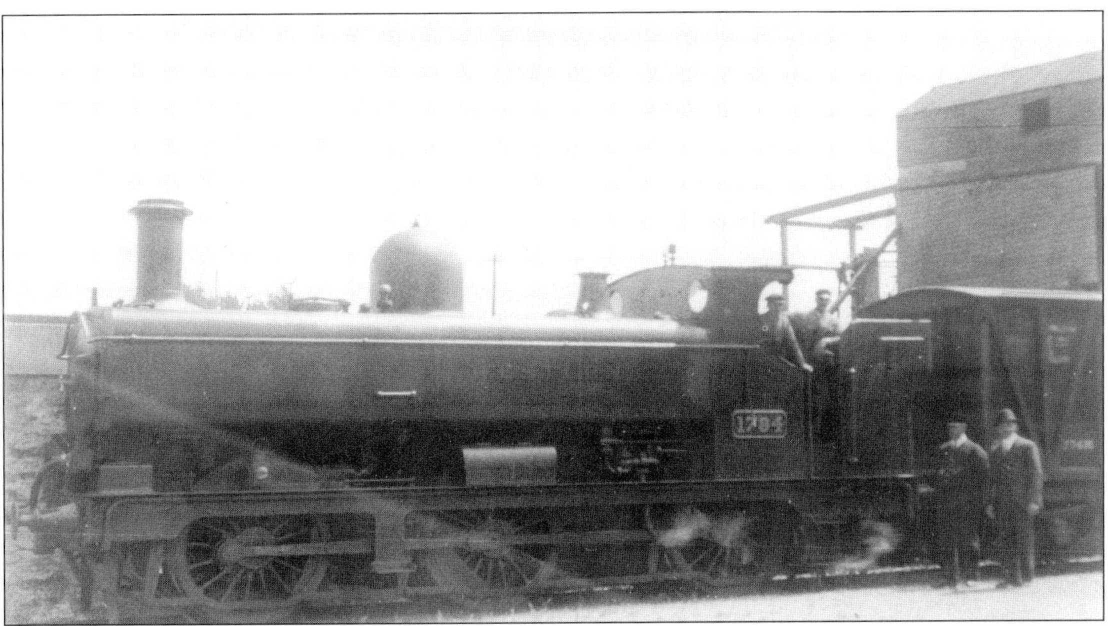

This is a shot, probably taken about 1938, of 1794 on a train at the rarely photographed non-passenger branch line terminus at Treamble. A Midland Railway van leads the train. Clive Benny Collection.

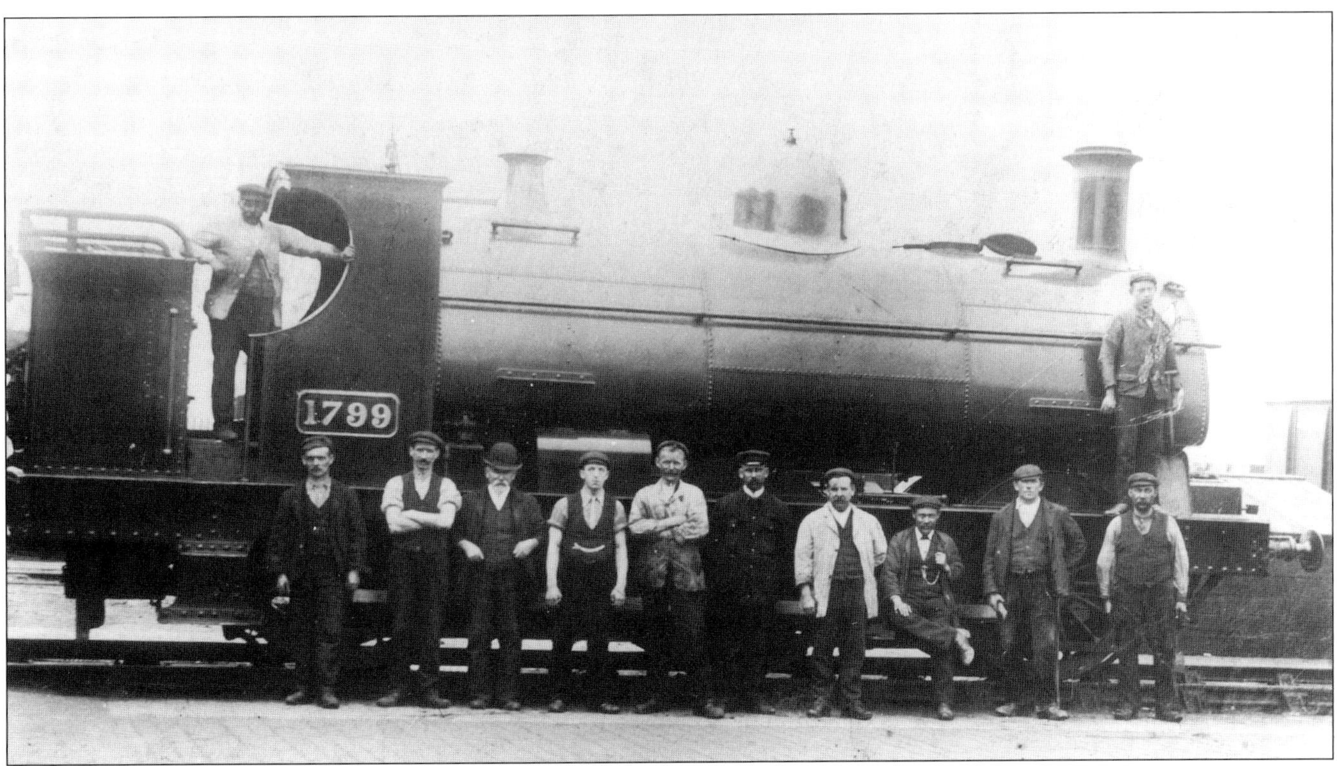

As usual, in earlier days, if the opportunity to be photographed with an engine presented itself, all of the railwaymen who were present wished to be included. Such was the case when 1854 class saddle tank 1799 was recorded outside the loco shed at Carn Brea in 1905. Once again the engine, which was used on the branch line to Portreath, is in a commendably clean condition. It was converted to a pannier tank during October 1919.

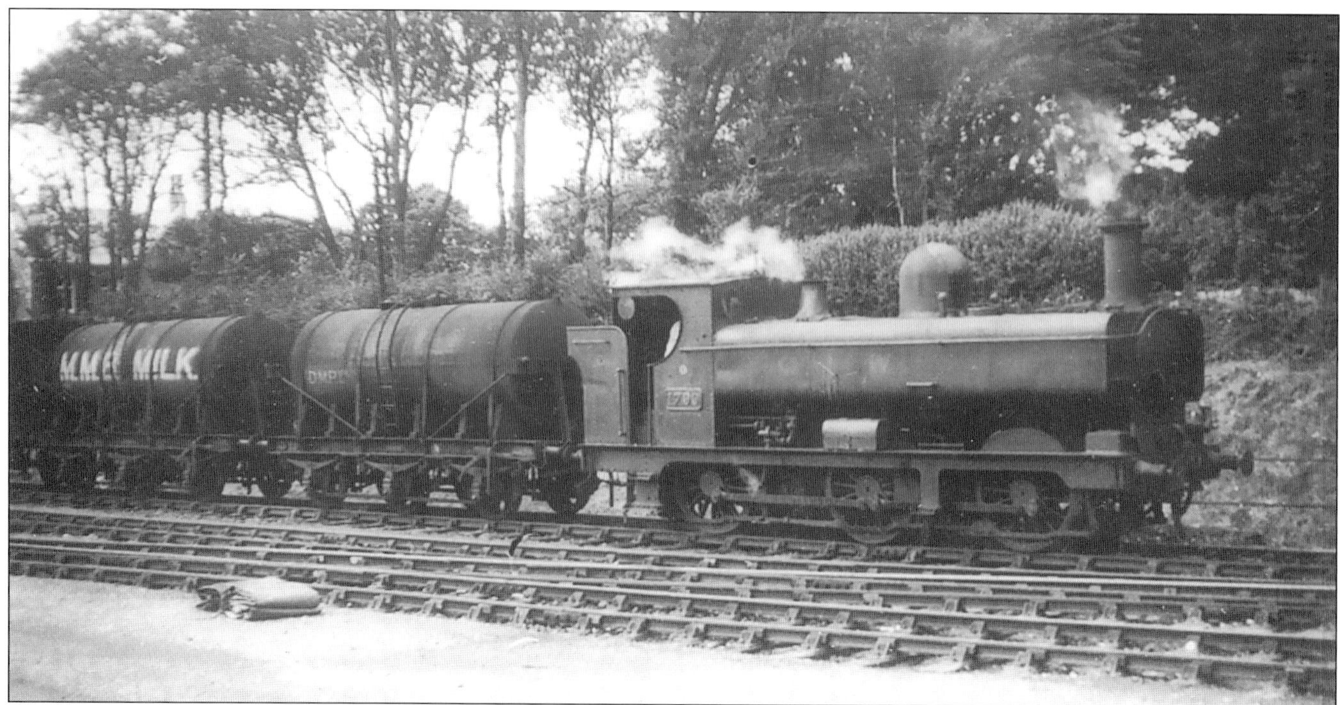

Here is 1799 again, now a pannier tank, shunting at Camborne around 1947. Kenneth Brown Collection.

The deeper frame is obvious on 1813 class pannier 1819 which is near the turntable in the yard at St Blazey shed on an unknown date. This engine was built as a side tank in November 1882. In September 1898 it was fitted with saddle tanks and became a pannier tank in May 1924, being withdrawn from Laira in January 1938.

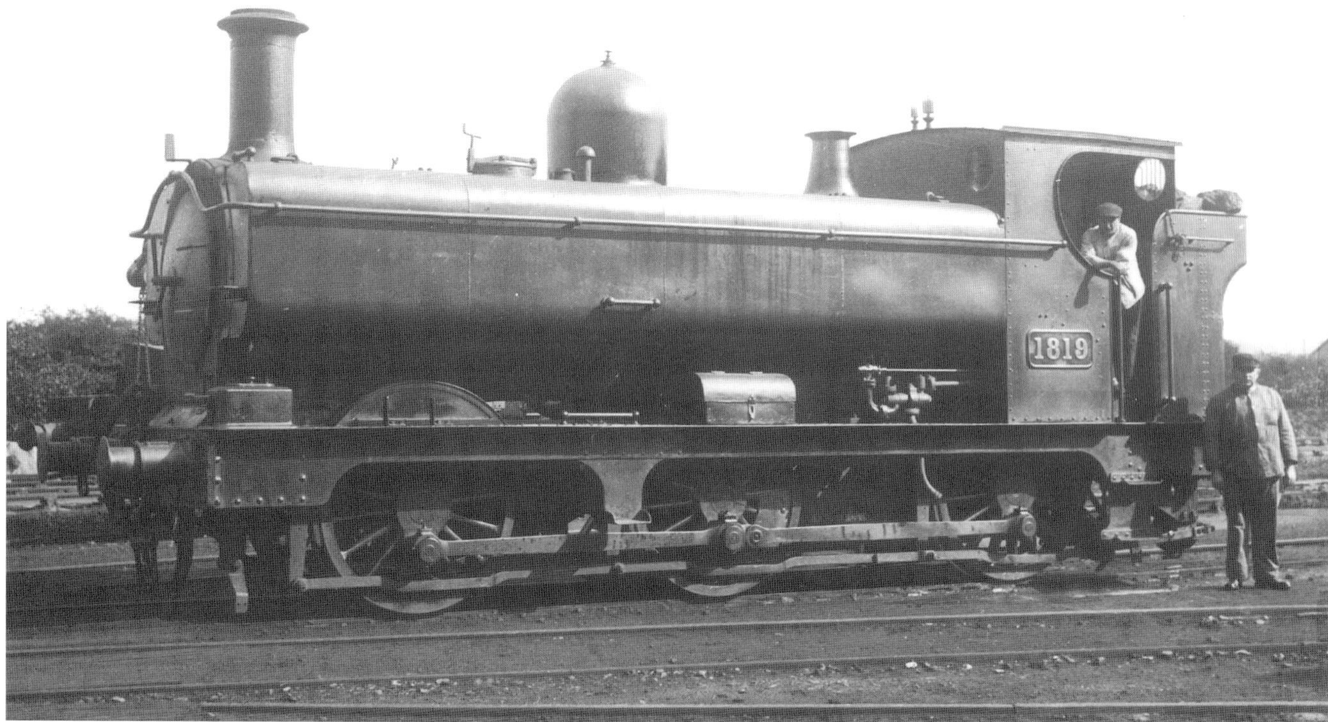

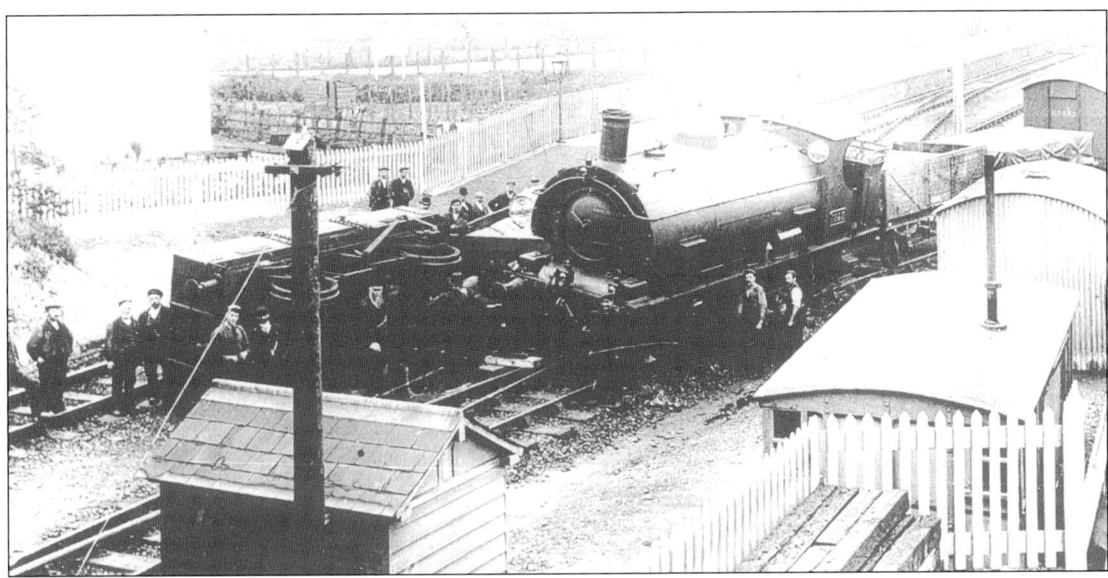

Another of the 1813 class was 1825 which has been involved in a 'mishap' with some open wagons at Par on an unknown date but before October 1923, when it gained pannier tanks. The wagons on their side, including a GWR 4 plank open wagon and the loco, have become derailed. This engine started life as a side tank in December 1882 and lasted until September 1928 after spending around thirteen years in the Rhondda & Swansea Bay Railway's stock.

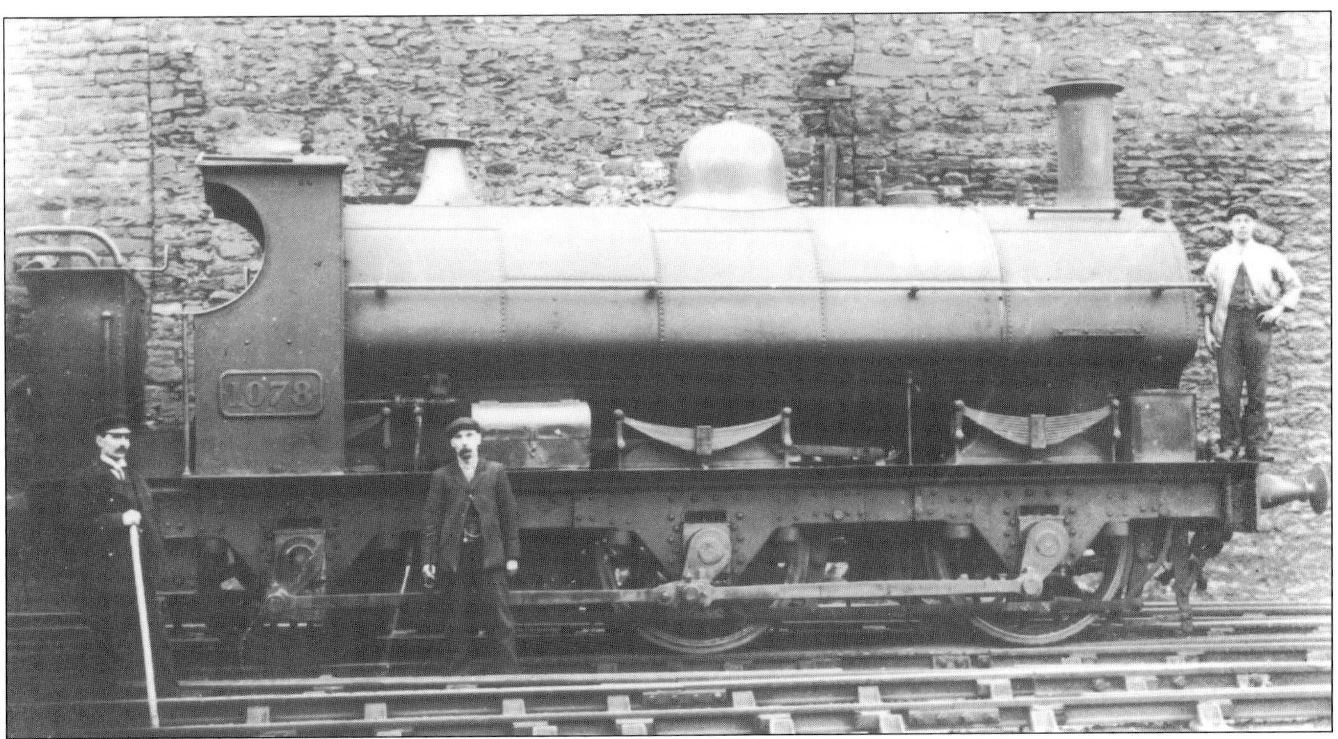

We now look at a few of the outside framed 1076 or 'Buffalo' class engines and to start we see 1078 as a saddle tank at the up end of Penzance station before September 1923 when it was fitted with pannier tanks. It was withdrawn in October 1928.

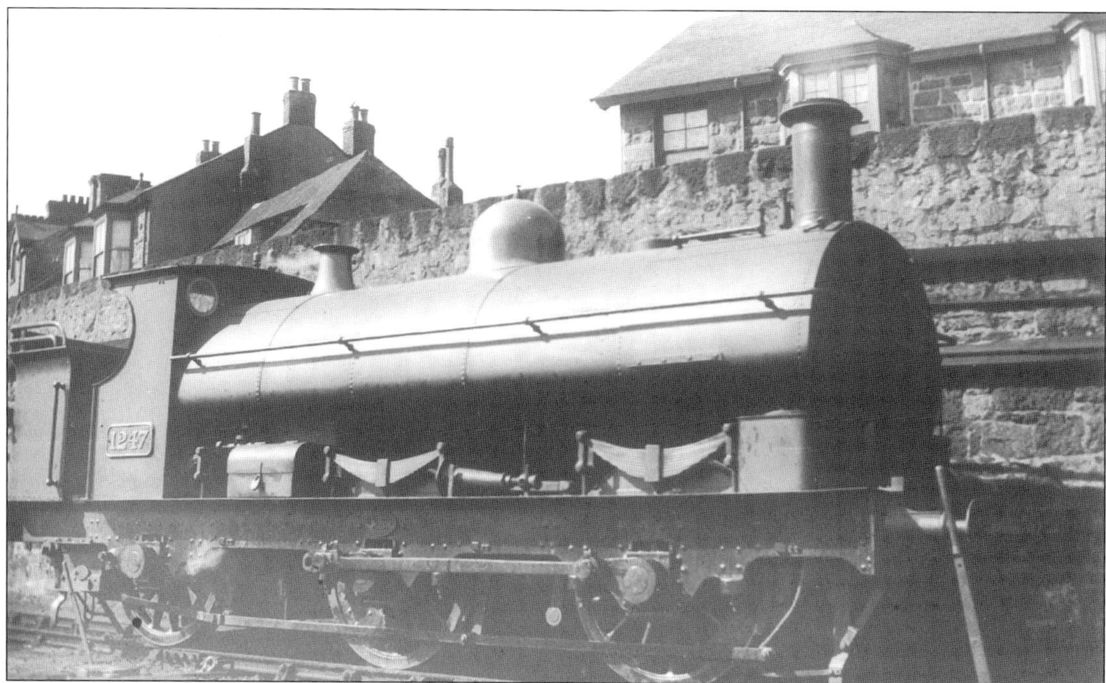

We are at Penzance station again where 'Buffalo' class saddle tank 1247 has had the rear portion of its coupling rods removed and is running as a 0-4-2ST. This was to facilitate traversing some of the tight curves in the area. As the engine was fitted with pannier tanks in March 1914, this photo pre-dates that.

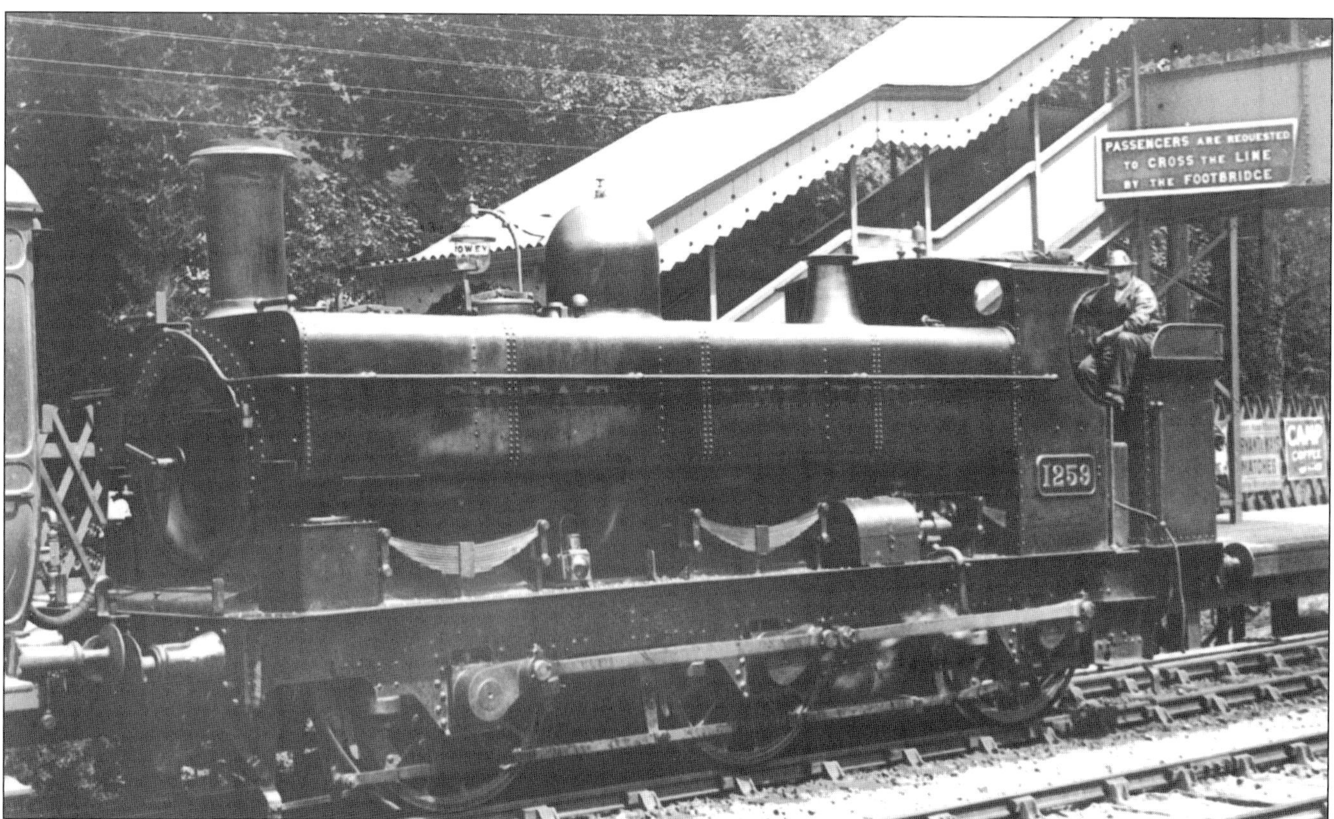

Standing at Fowey station on 7 July 1921 with a train for St Blazey is 'Buffalo' class pannier 1259. The fireman is wearing an unorthodox hat. This engine was withdrawn in July 1932. The engine is noticeably clean. The Locomotive Club of Great Britain/Ken Nunn Collection.

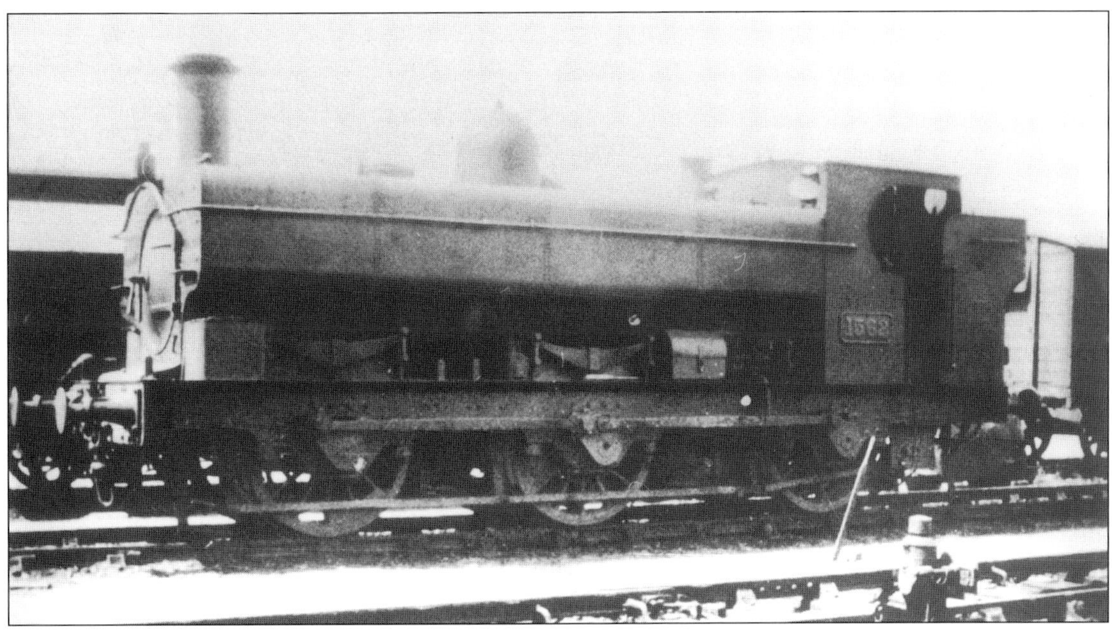

Passing along the east side of the wagon works at St Blazey on 14 July 1934, with a goods train, is 'Buffalo' class pannier 1562. It was withdrawn in July 1938. The external condition of this loco bears a marked contrast to some of those seen earlier in this volume. Brunel University Transport Collection. Locomotive Views.

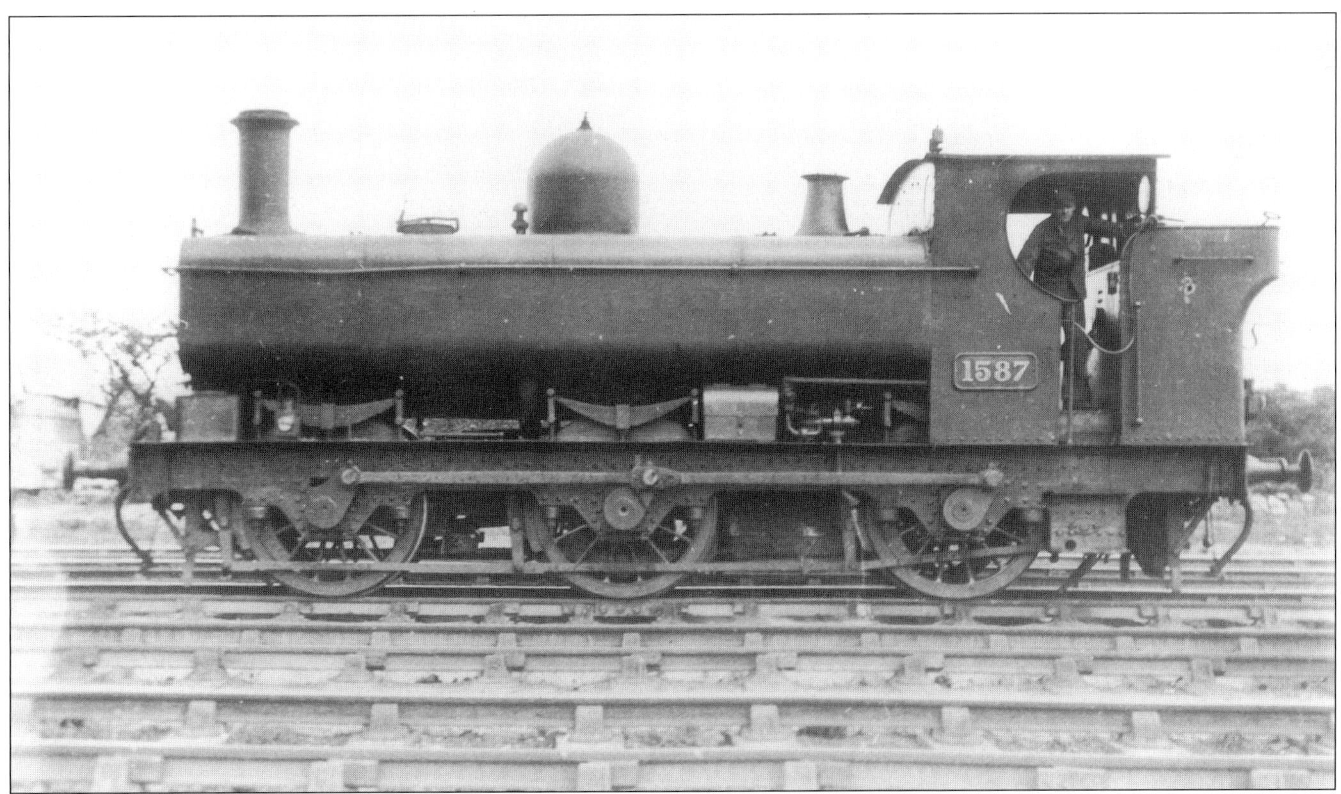

Another 'Buffalo' class pannier, 1587, is shunting in the yard at St Blazey between 1931 and 1933. It was withdrawn from here in January 1934. This engine is in a more respectable external condition.

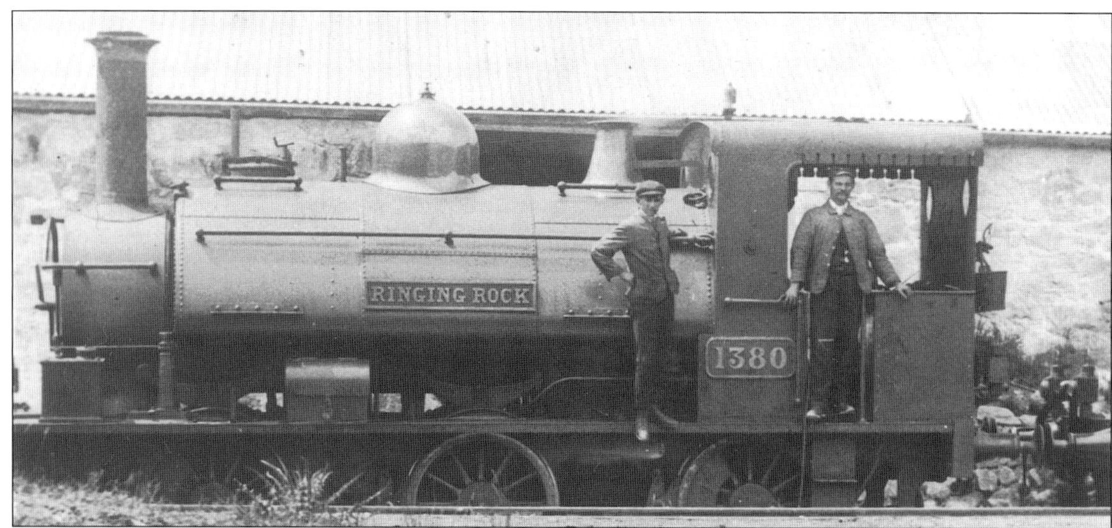

We leave the pure GWR engines and look at examples from minor railways which were absorbed by the GWR. The first is 'RINGING ROCK' which became GWR 1380. This engine was Manning Wardle no.630, built in 1876 for the North Pembroke & Fishguard Railway. When the GWR absorbed that line in July 1898 this engine went to Swindon works for repair, following which it came to Cornwall. It was shedded at St Blazey from where it worked on the Goonbarrow branch. It is seen on that line double heading a train for St Blazey which has stopped at Rock Hill siding. It was rebuilt at Swindon during 1902 and this photo post dates that. The GWR withdrew the loco and sold it to the Bute Works Supply Co. in 1912. From there it was sold to the Kent & East Sussex Railway where it became no.8 and was renamed 'HESPERUS' and survived until 1941.   P.J.T.Reed.

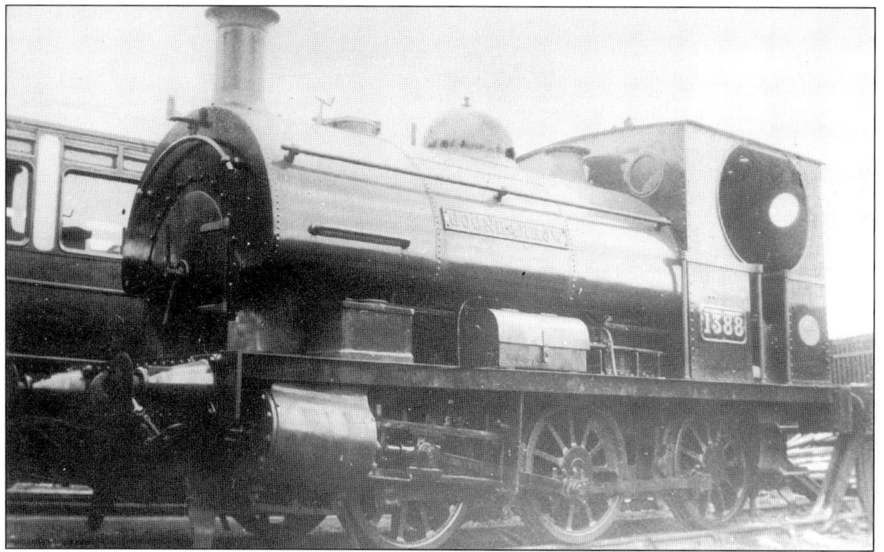

The Cornwall Minerals Railway had been worked by the GWR from 1 October 1877 and was purchased by the company on 1 July 1896. The CMR opened its branch from Goonbarrow Junction, south east of Bugle on 2 October 1893 and purchased a new engine to work the line. It was a standard Peckett design and fittingly was named 'GOONBARROW', and was stationed in a small loco shed at Stenalees. The shed was re-sited a short distance away on the opposite side of the line but when the GWR bought the CMR the shed was closed. The engine was transferred to St Blazey where it is seen carrying its GWR number of 1388. It was sold by the GWR in September 1911 to the Bute Works Supply Co. who sold it on to Cwm Ciwc Colliery at Llanharran where it was reported as being 'cut up' soon after 1918.

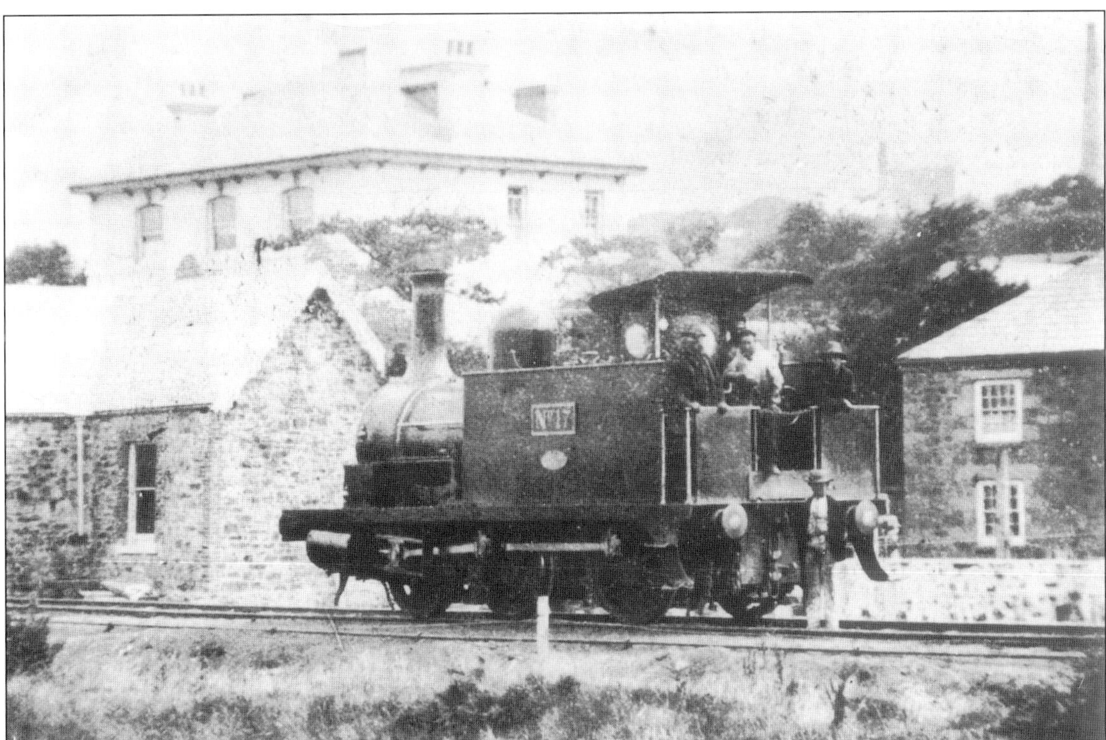

Another photo taken before 1883 shows CMR 17 between St Blazey and Par Bridge level crossing with the engine house and chimney of Par Consols mine in the upper background. The CMR returned this engine to Sharp, Stewart who sold it to the Lynn & Fakenham Railway in 1880 where it became no.1 and was named 'MELTON CONSTABLE'. This company became part of the Eastern & Midlands Railway on 1883 and this engine retained the same name and number.

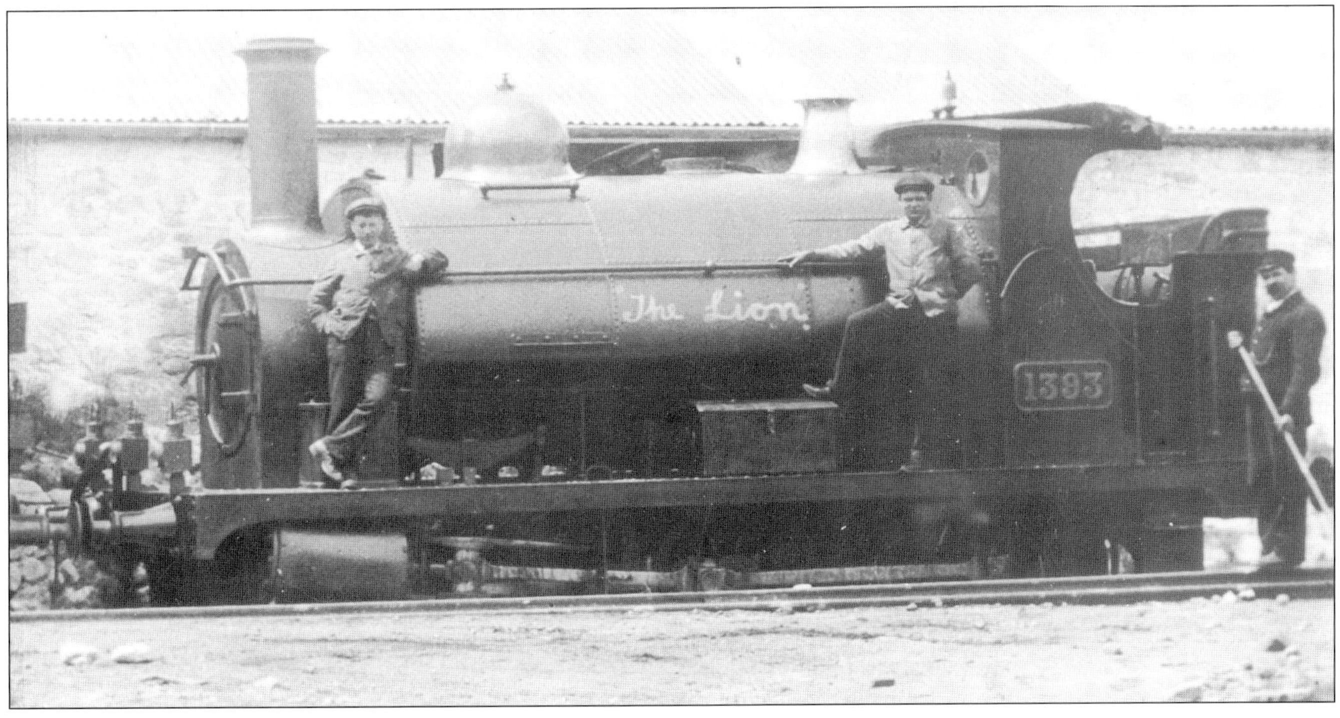

The other engine on the train hauled by 'RINGING ROCK' was CMR 1393. This is similarly taken whilst the train was stopped in Rock Hill siding at Stenalees on the Goonbarrow branch. The engine has been unofficially named 'THE LION'! It survived until May 1933. P.J.T.Reed.

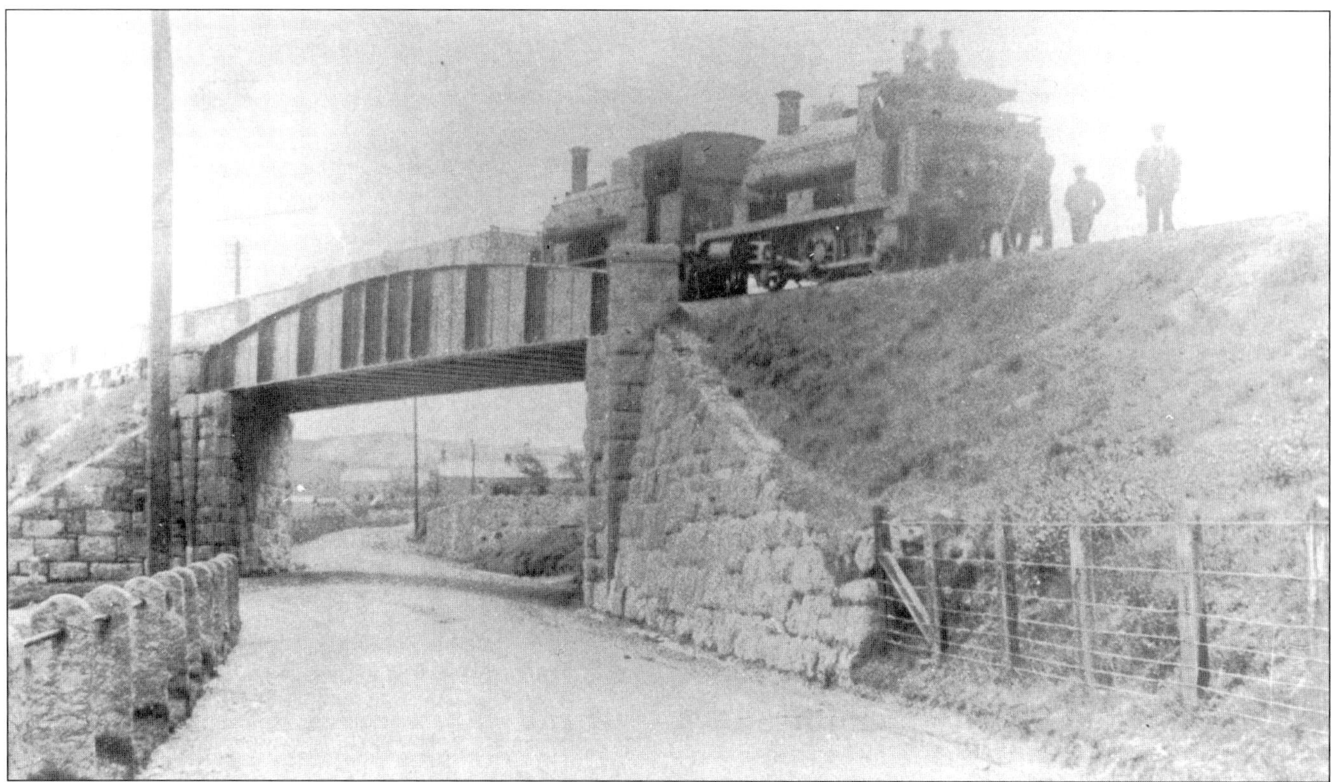

The crew on the train that was shunting at Rock Hill appear to have posed for the photographer at other points on the line. Here the train has stopped on the underline bridge at Lower Stenalees, a few hundred yards south of Rock Hill. The engines are 1380 'RINGING ROCK' and 1393 'THE LION'.

Lower Stenalees seemed to be favoured for photography, probably because the Goonbarrow branch ran on an embankment parallel to the main road. Posed on 24 June 1921 are CMR 1396 and 1361 class 1364. The CMR engine was withdrawn in March 1934 but 1364 lasted until February 1961. P.J.T.Reed.

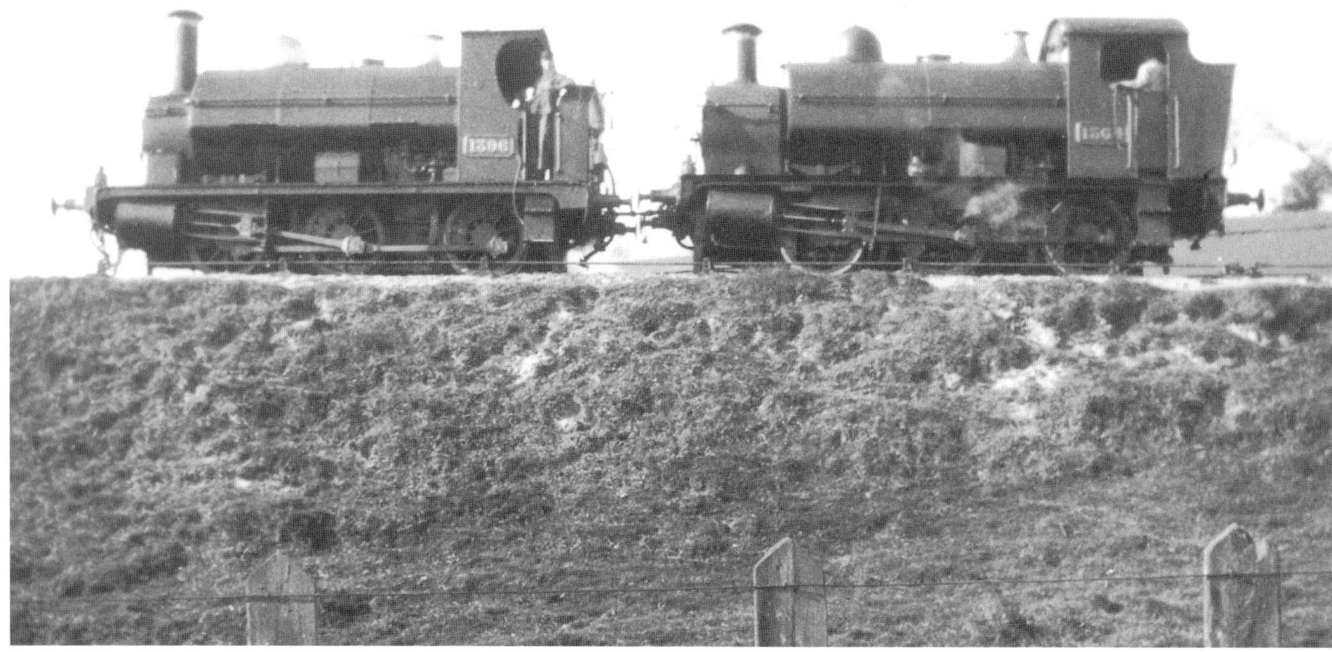

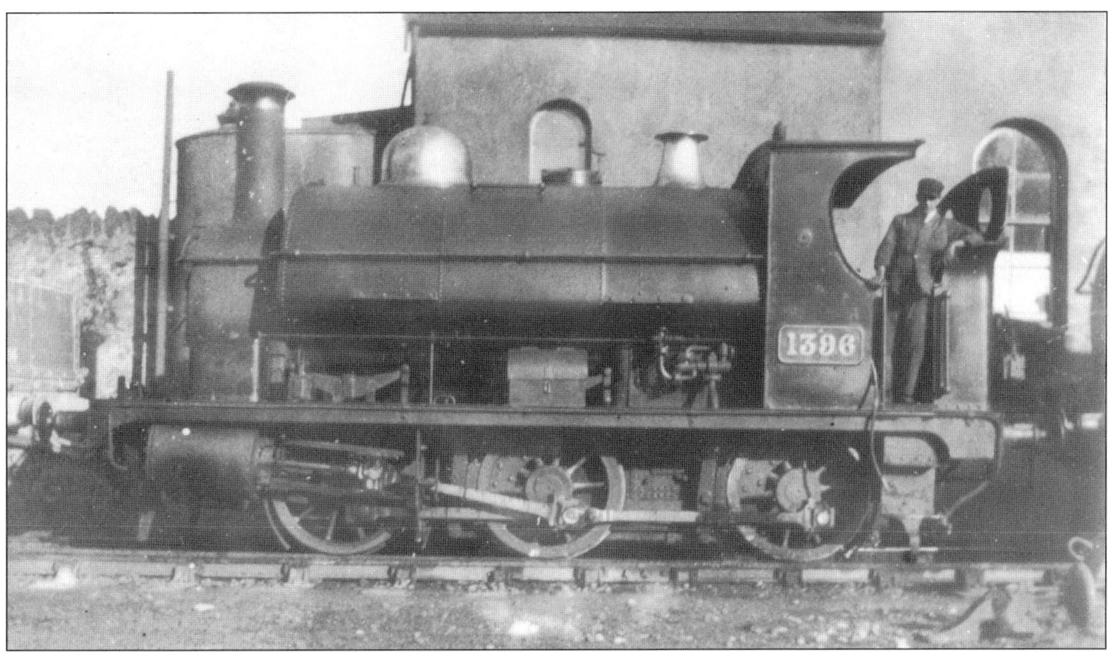

Here we see a close up of the driver posing on 1396 which has arrived in the sidings at St Blazey on 24 October 1921. St Blazey station is behind the engine. As another loco is coupled to rear of 1396, the train may have come from the Goonbarrow branch.

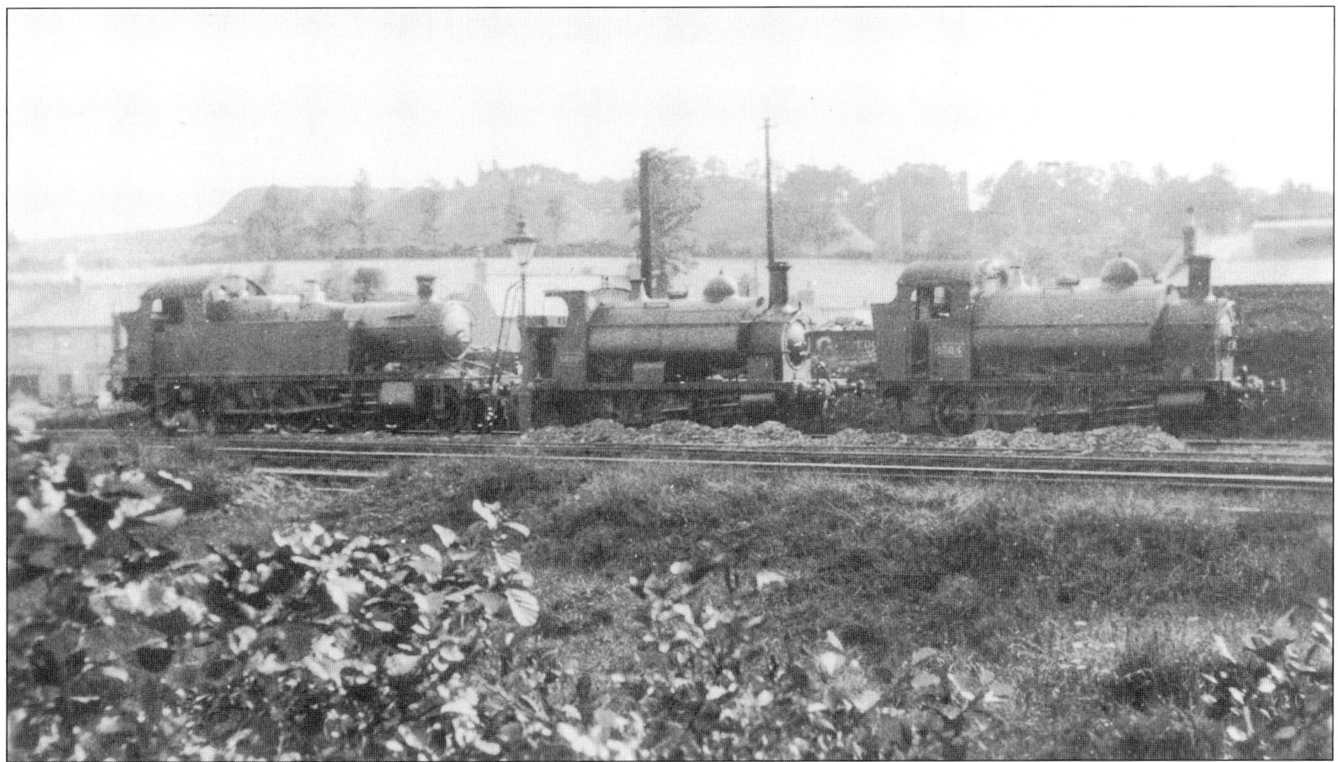

This is a view of locos lined up awaiting coaling at St Blazey shed on 5 August 1922. From left to right they are a 4500 class 2-6-2T, CMR 1398 and 1361 class 1364. 1398 had been numbered 1400 until December 1912 and was withdrawn in October 1936. The original CMR 1398 was sold to the Sharpness Dock Co. in April 1883. The waste tip from Par Consols mine is visible on the top of the hill in the background. P.J.T.Reed/R.S.Carpenter Photos.

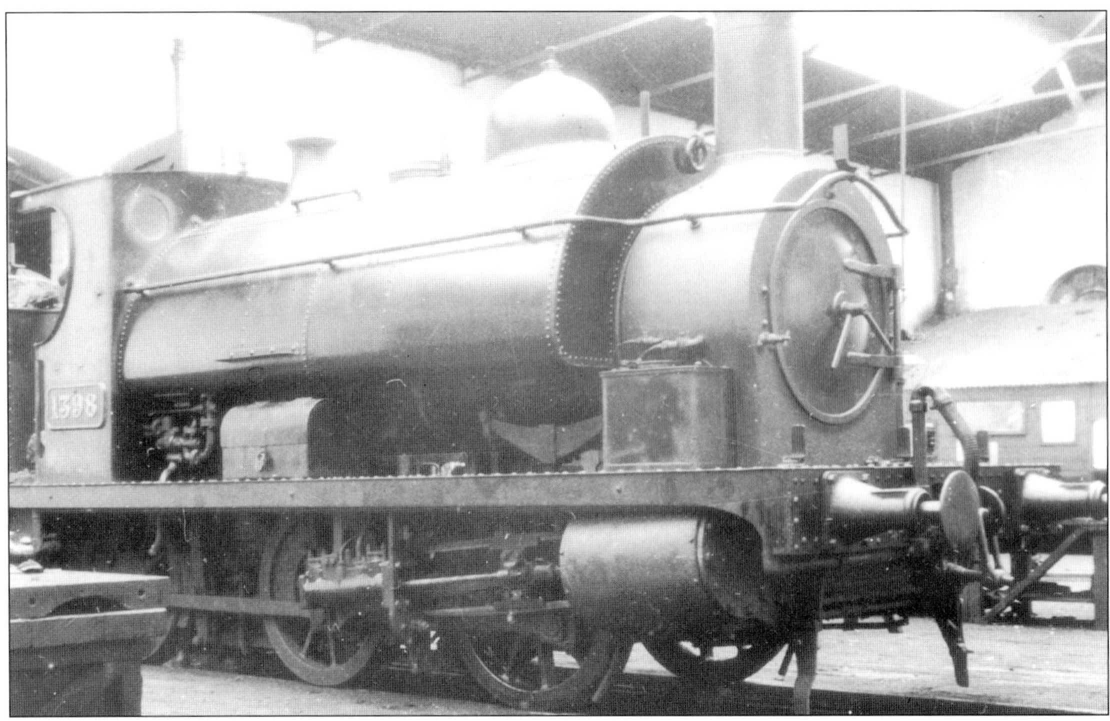

This is a very rare photo of CMR 1398 inside the three road 'Factory' at St Blazey shed on 8 August 1923. The shed had nine stabling lines, which would each accommodate two engines, so all of the eighteen CMR engines could be under cover. The centre three lines passed through arches in a dividing wall and entered the repair shop or, in GWR terms, the 'Factory'.

I make no apologies for doing an 'overkill' as photos of the CMR tank locos in Cornwall are very hard to locate. So here is yet another shot of CMR 1398 standing in the shed yard near the turntable at St Blazey shed on 20 June 1924. Locomotive Club of Great Britain/Ken Nunn Collection.

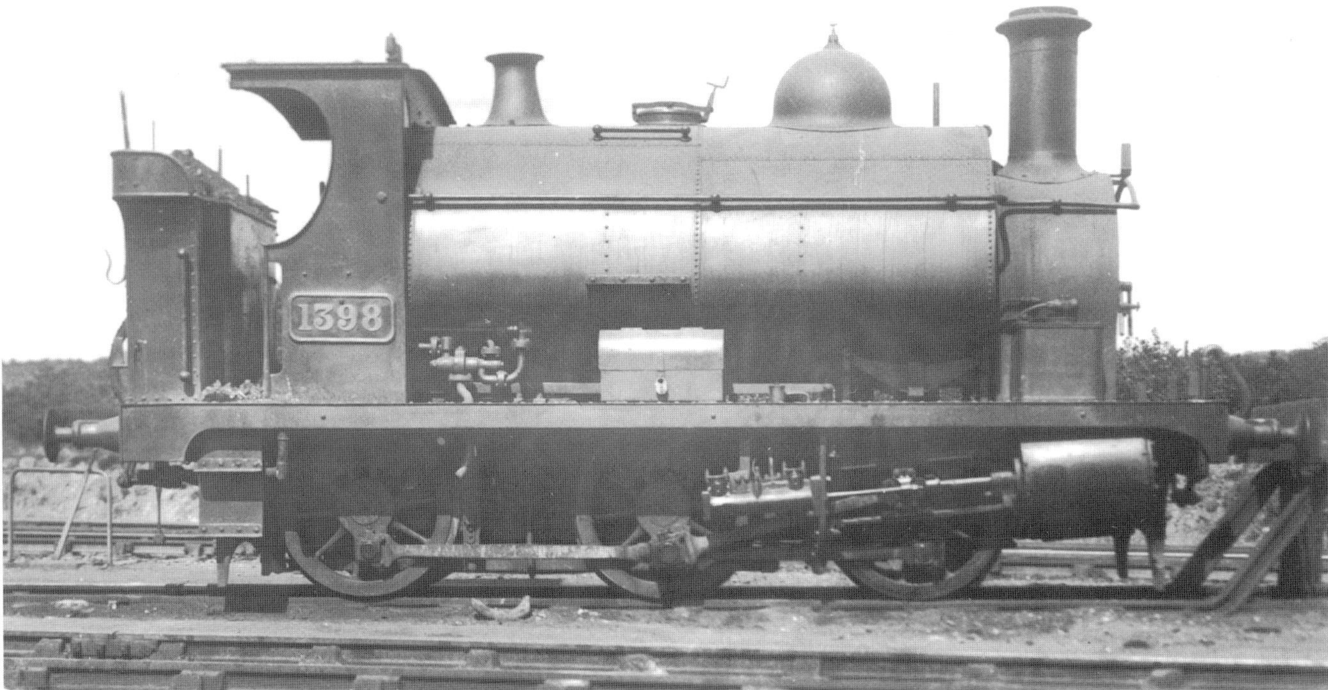

The next few photos are of six coupled tank locos from the Liskeard & Caradon Railway. This line was worked by the GWR from 1 January 1909. The first photo *(right)* shows 'CARADON' at Liskeard opposite the Looe branch platform. It was built by Gilkes, Wilson & Co in 1862 and was withdrawn in 1907 and scrapped at Moorswater, near Liskeard. However, the firebox wrapper plate from this engine was strategically placed over a stream, across one line from the shed, where it functioned as a toilet for the establishment. Fortunately it is still extant and occupies a position near the end of the platform at Bodmin General as a static display item.

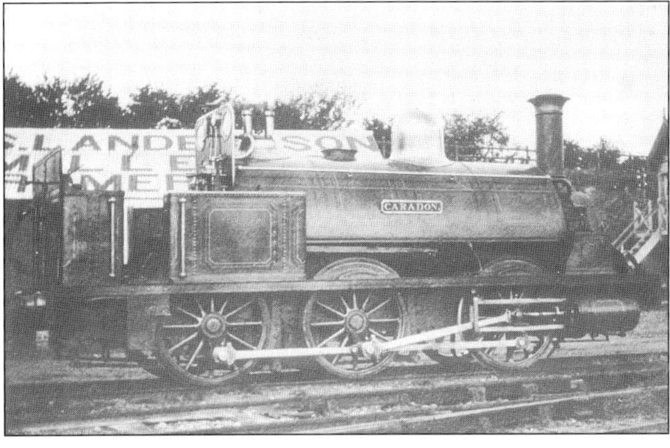

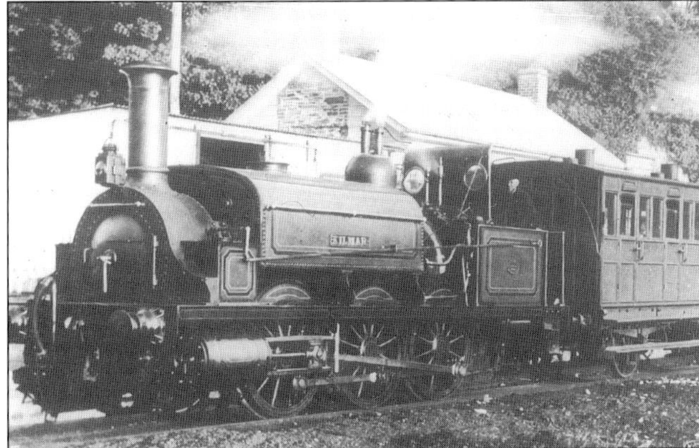

This is a shot of 'KILMAR' at Looe, ready to depart on a passenger train to Liskeard sometime between 1896 and 1901. Built by Hopkins & Gilkes in 1869, it became GWR 1312 and was withdrawn in May 1914.

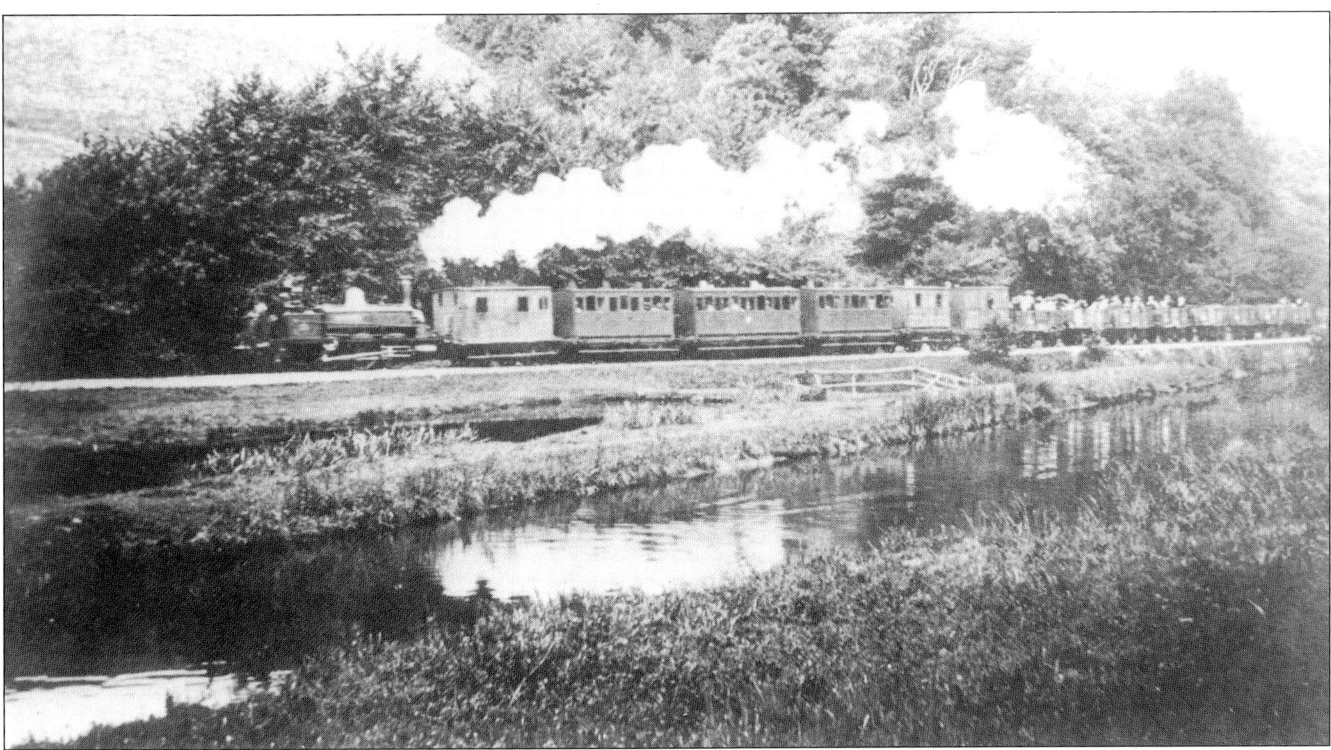

Here is 'CHEESEWRING' which became GWR 1311. It is near Sandplace, hauling a 'mixed' train from Looe to Liskeard in 1901. This loco, built by Gilkes, Wilson in 1864, ended up working in the London area and lasted until August 1919. The train appears to contain the entire passenger stock of the Liskeard & Looe Railway.

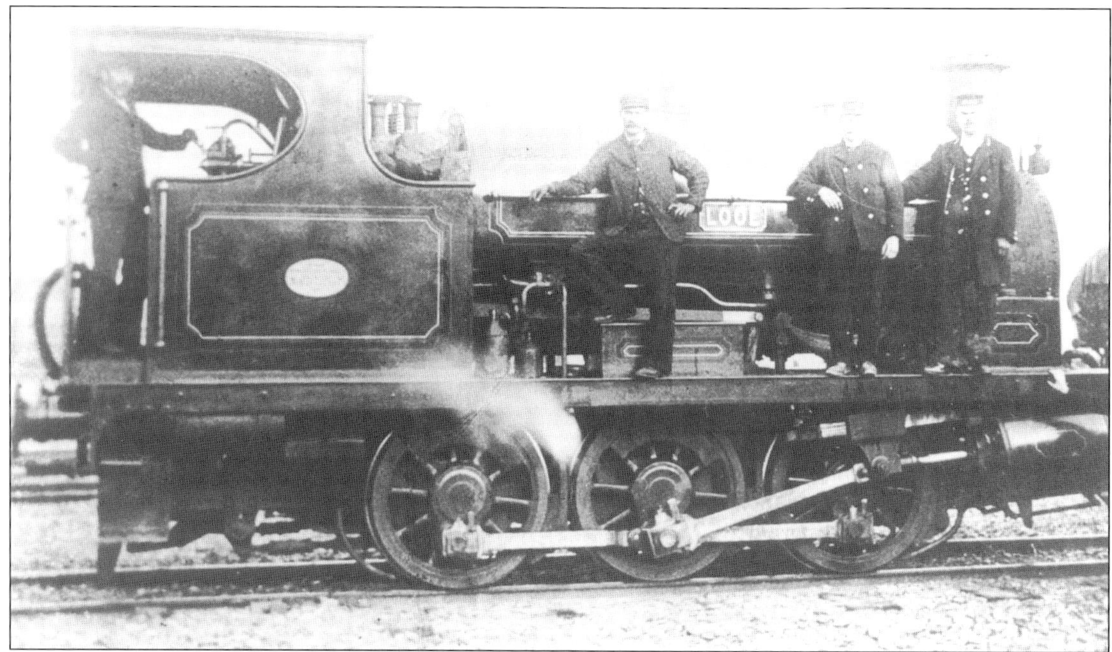

Here we see 'LOOE' at Looe in 1901 with the locomotive crew and station staff posing for the camera. This engine was built by Robert Stephenson & Hawthorn in April 1901 and was purchased to work the steeply graded 'extension line' from Coombe Junction to Liskeard. However, it proved to be unsuitable and was sold to the London & India Docks in April 1902. It went on to work for the Port of London Authority as their no.11 and lasted until September 1950.

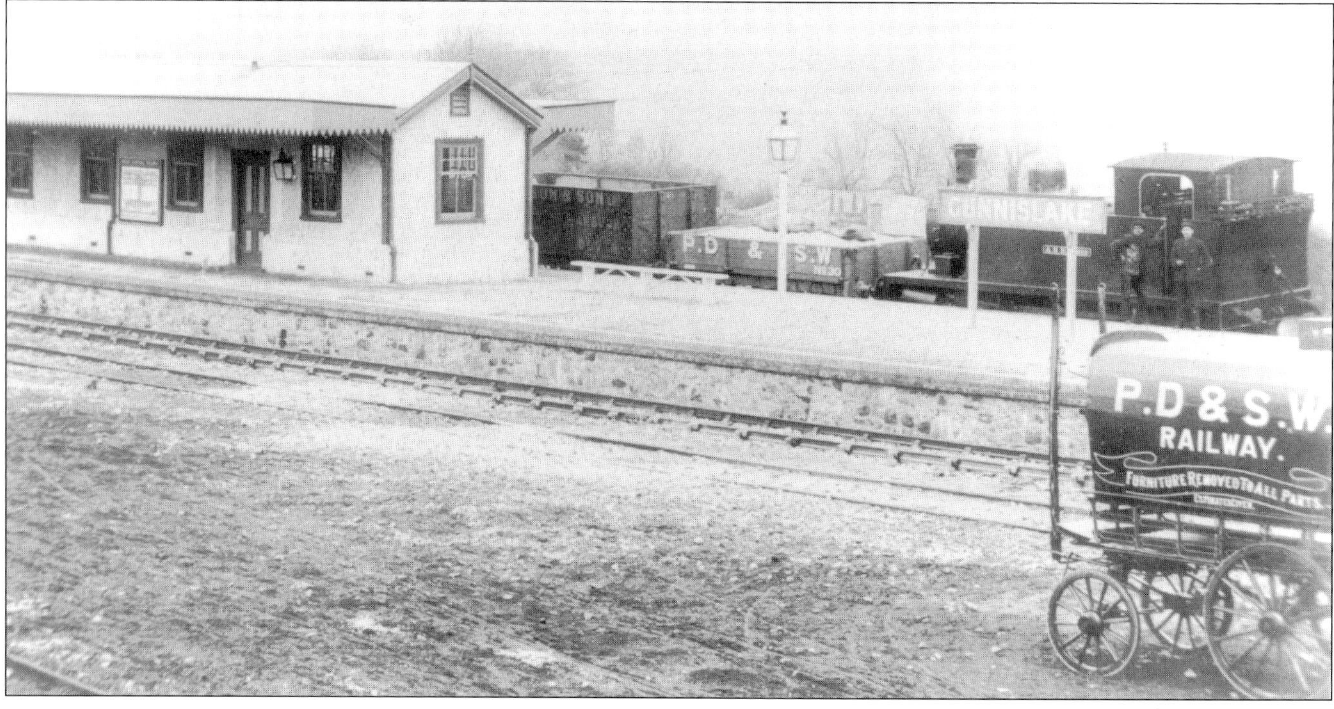

We end this large section of photos of 0-6-0 tanks with an undated shot of the only SR representative to work regularly in Cornwall. This is Plymouth, Devonport & South Western Junction Railway 'A.S.HARRIS' on a goods train at Gunnislake. The loco was built by Hawthorn Leslie in 1907 and became SR 756 and then BR 30756. It was transferred to the London area and ended its days as pilot at Stewarts Lane shed, Battersea where the author saw it in 1950. It was withdrawn on 6 December 1951. Next to the engine is PDSW 3 plank wagon No.30.

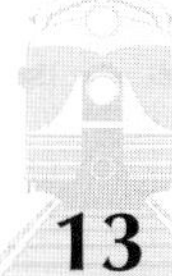

13

BULLDOG CLASS 4-4-0s

These sprightly engines superceded the 'Duke' class 4-4-0s on most of the goods and passenger trains in Cornwall before themselves being displaced by 4-6-0 types. Even then they maintained a presence, being used as pilots through to the 1940s.

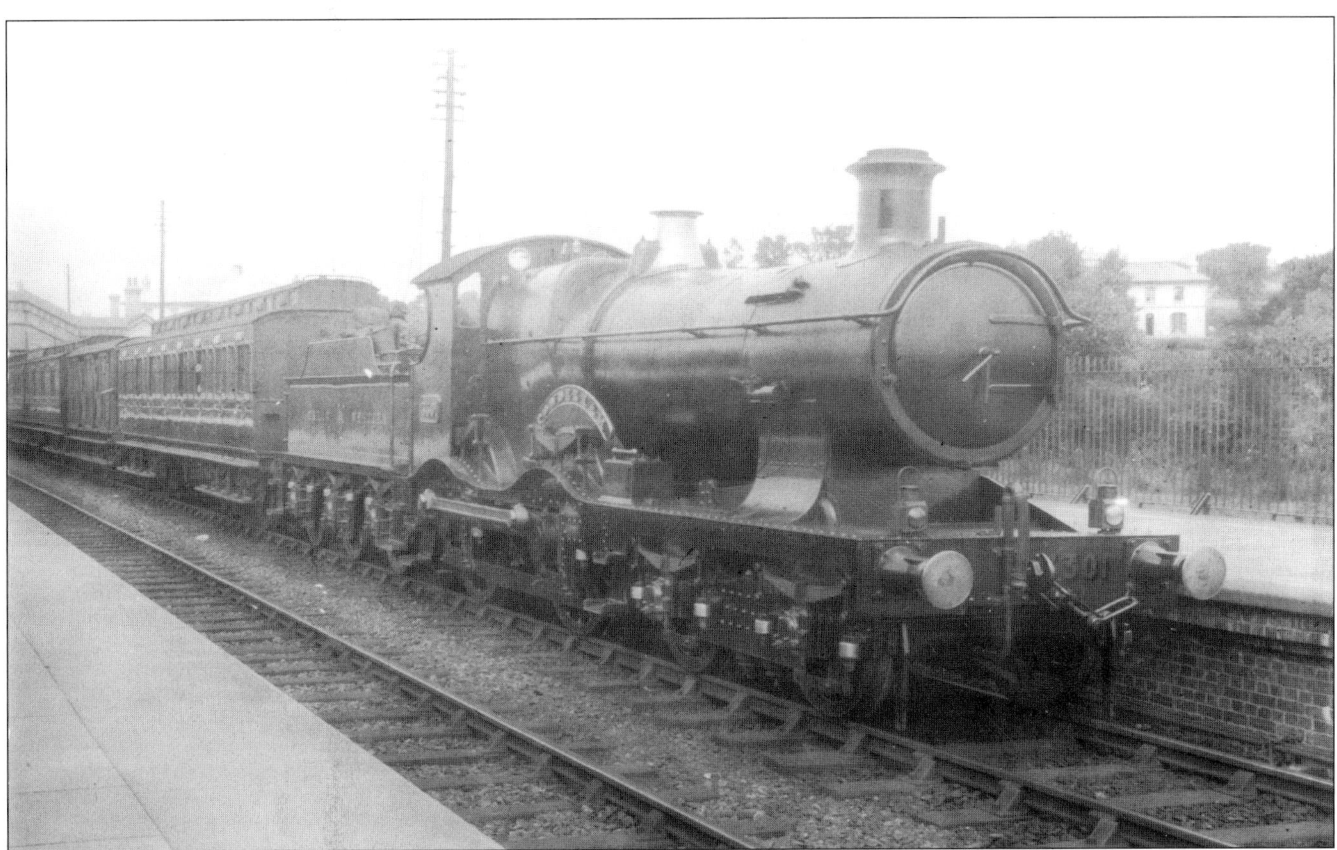

We start this section with a fine shot of 3301 'POWDERHAM' stopped at Par in 1914 on a down passenger train. The front carriage is painted crimson lake, behind which is a 6-wheeled Syphon. This engine started life as a 'Duke' class numbered 3262 and survived until April 1931. These rebuilds were distinguishable by their curved frames over the driving wheels. It would seem to be a little unusual to have a parcels' van coupled between two carriages, so possibly an extra carriage had been attached to the front of the train at North Road. The Royal Hotel is visible above the front carriage. It was, and still is, very conveniently situated to provide refreshment for passengers. P.Brookman/P.J.T.Reed.

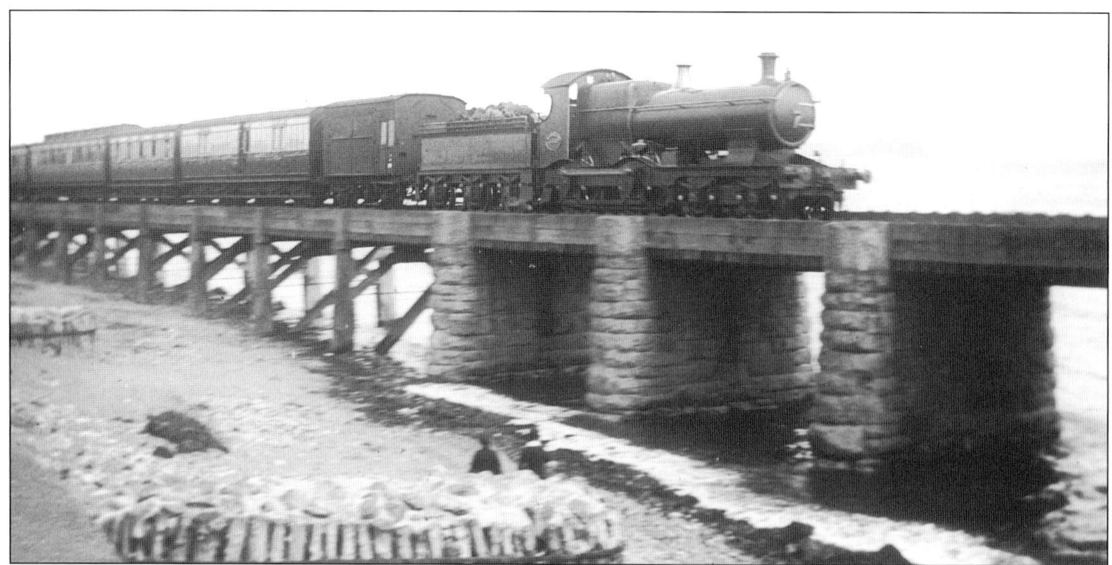

Another 'Bulldog' that was rebuilt from a 'Duke' was 3340 'MARAZION' which is approaching Penzance on the low viaduct across the beach in 1912. The viaduct was replaced by an embankment during 1921. The engine, which retains its original circular combined name and numberplate, was later renumbered to 3328 and worked until April 1934. The train is composed of a mixture of rolling stock which includes a GWR Horse Box and a GWR low roofed bogie full brake. Locomotive & General Railway Photographs.

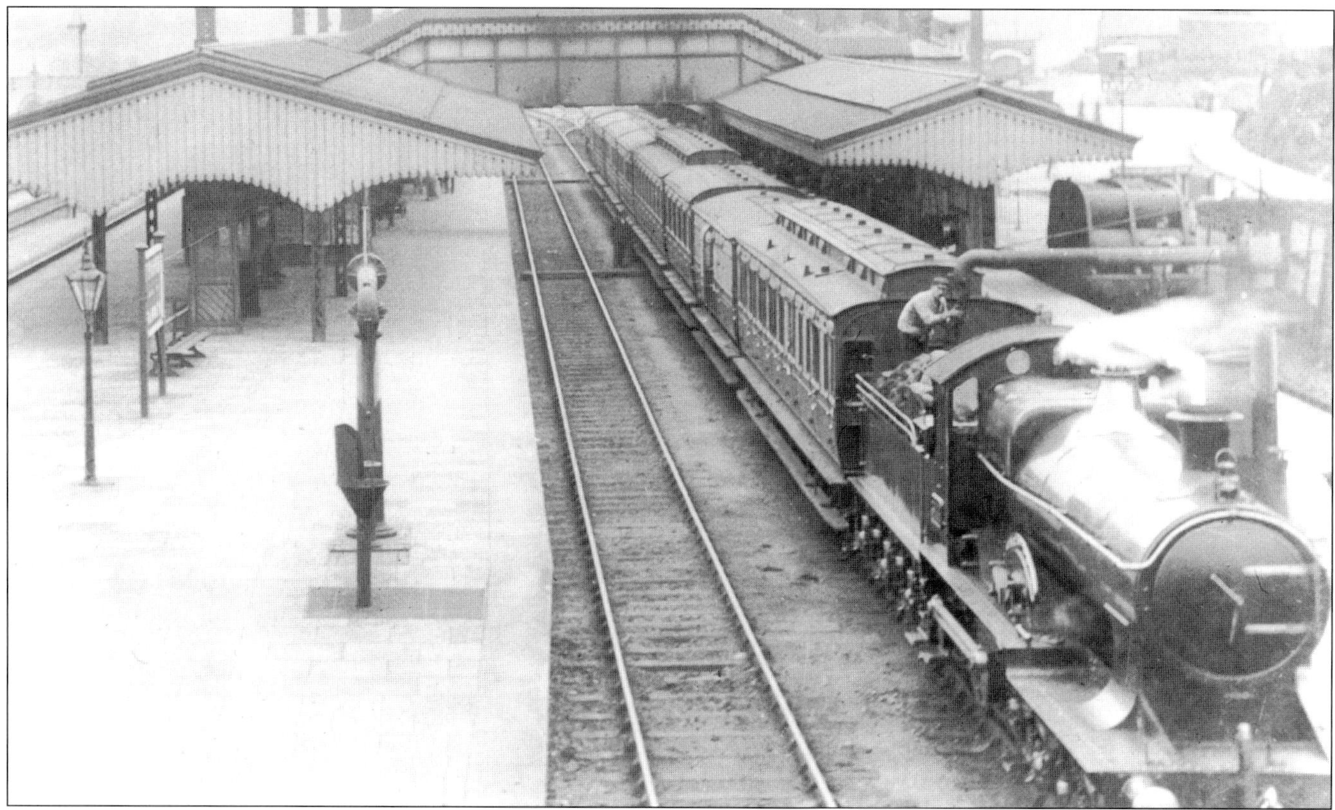

The fireman is filling the tender with water as 3418 'EARL OF CORK' is stopped at Truro with a down stopping train which contains a variety of stock. This engine became 3366 and was not withdrawn until April 1948. Note the Gas Cylinder wagon on the right at the rear of the Falmouth bay platform.

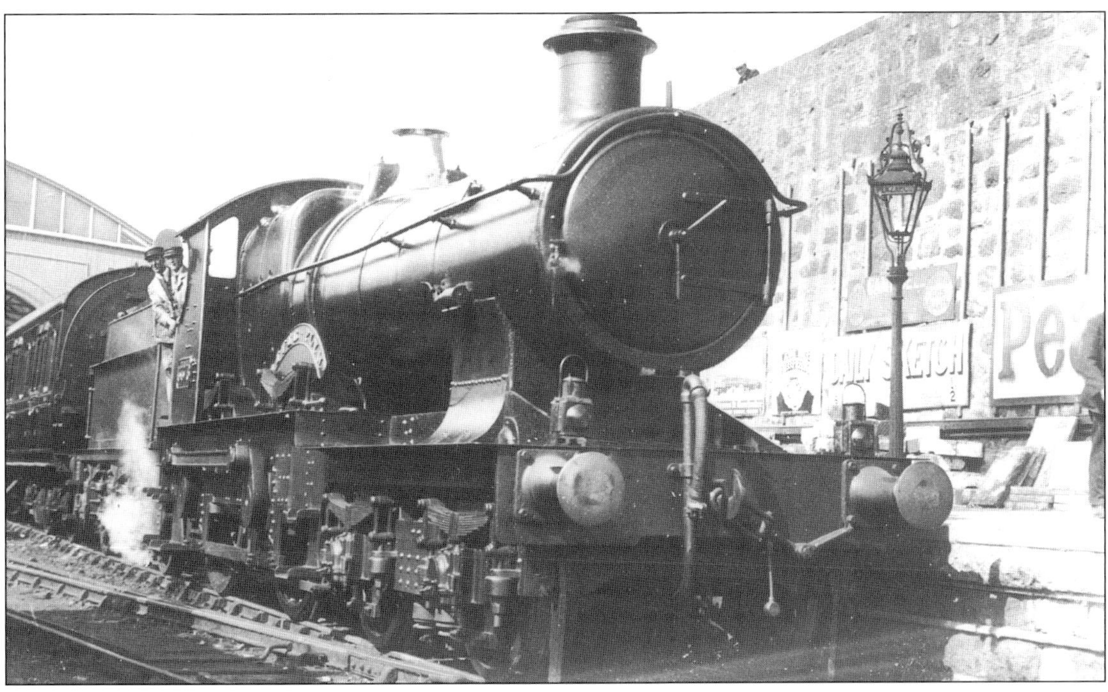

The crew pose in their cab for the photographer as 3376 'RIVER PLYM' awaits departure from Penzance with an up express. As this engine went new to Long Rock shed in 1903 and was shedded there in 1921, this photo probably dates from the latter period. It lasted until September 1948. A.G.Ellis.

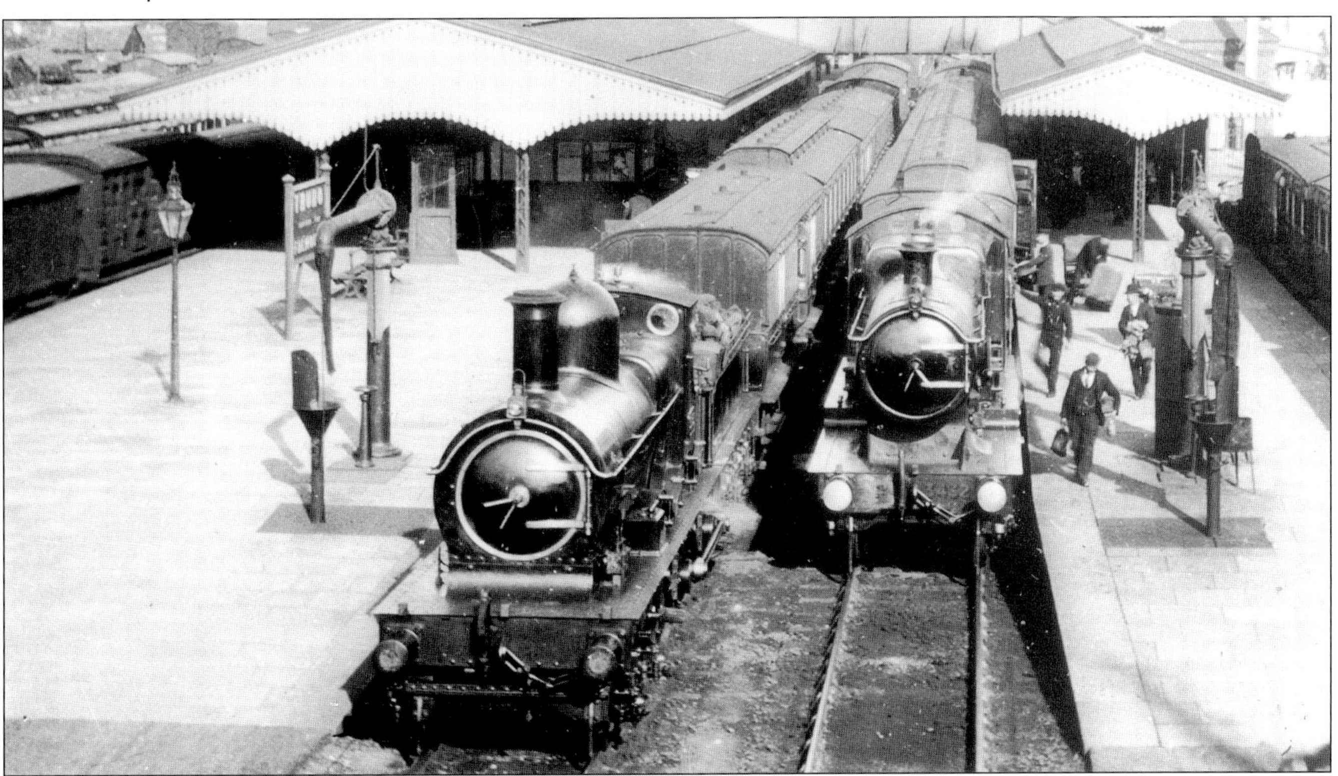

All of the platforms at Truro are occupied by trains in this busy scene which dates from before 1912. On the right, on a down stopping train, is 'Bulldog' 3432 'RIVER YEALM' which became 3380. The train on the left, which is probably for Falmouth, is headed by an unidentified 3521 class 4-4-0. The 'Bulldog' was shedded at either Plymouth, Truro or Long Rock from 1903 until 1923 and ended being withdrawn from Bath Road shed, Bristol in March 1938. I saw this engine several times at Plymouth during 1937. P.J.T.Reed.

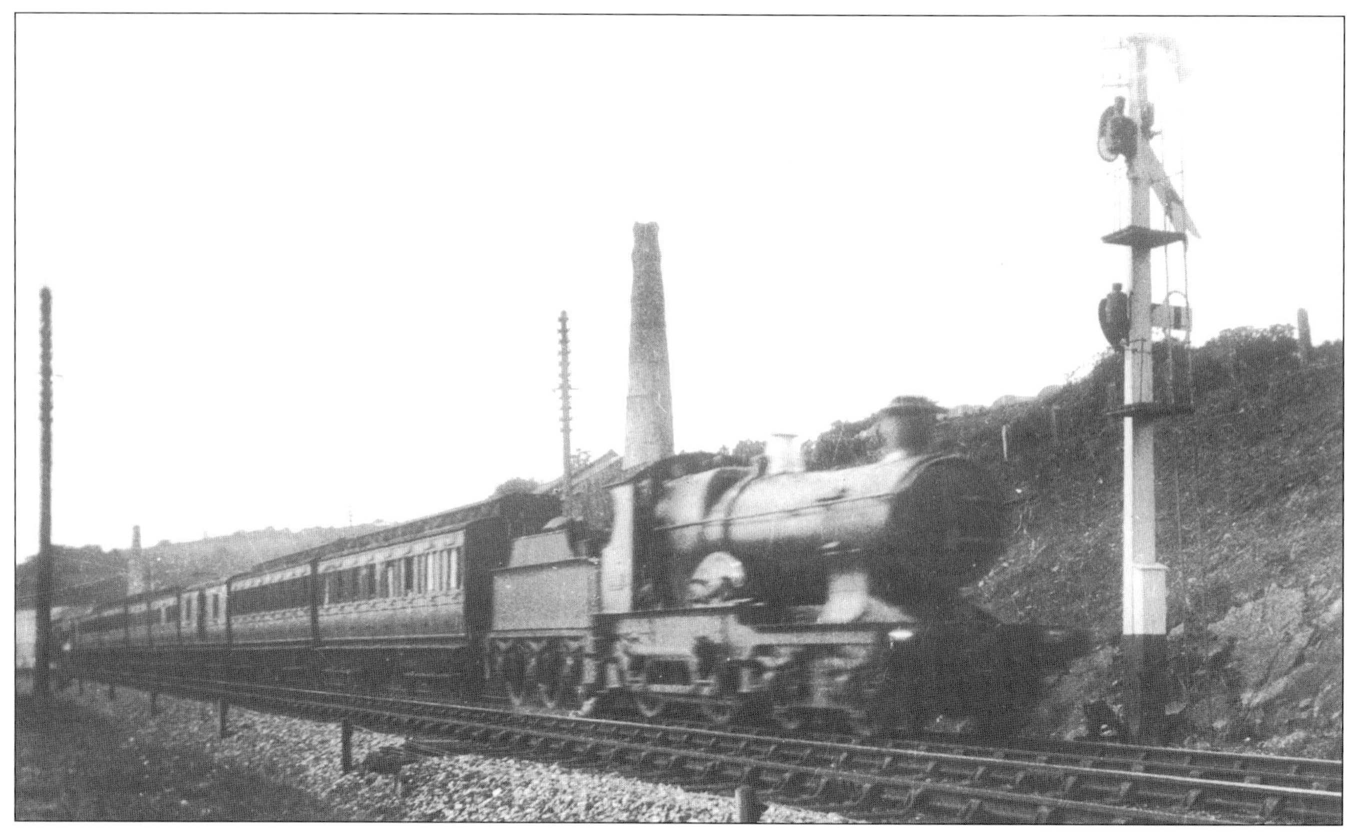

An up stopping train is passing Trenance sidings, west of St Austell, at 3.51pm on 29 July 1921 headed by Long Rock's 3406 'CALCUTTA'. This engine lasted until March 1951 but eluded the author. The 'stacks' of Trenance and Carrancarrow china clay kilns are visible. P.J.T.Reed.

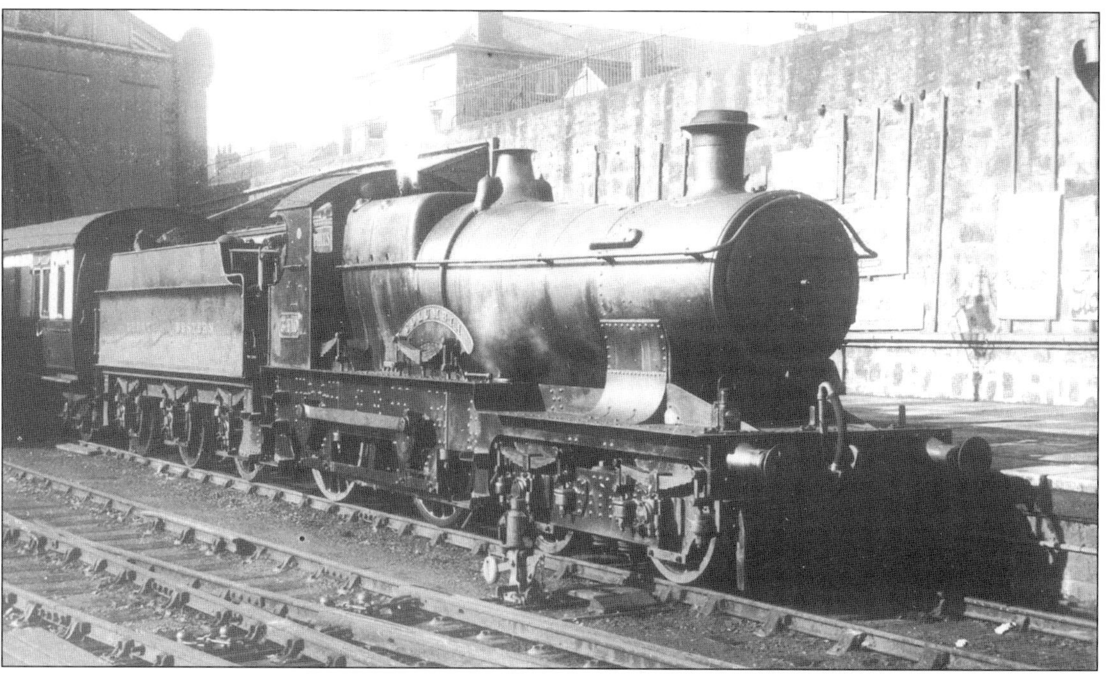

At Penzance on empty coaching stock is 3410 'COLUMBIA' which was not a local engine when new, nor in 1921. It was withdrawn from Stratford-upon-Avon shed in November 1936. A.G.Ellis.

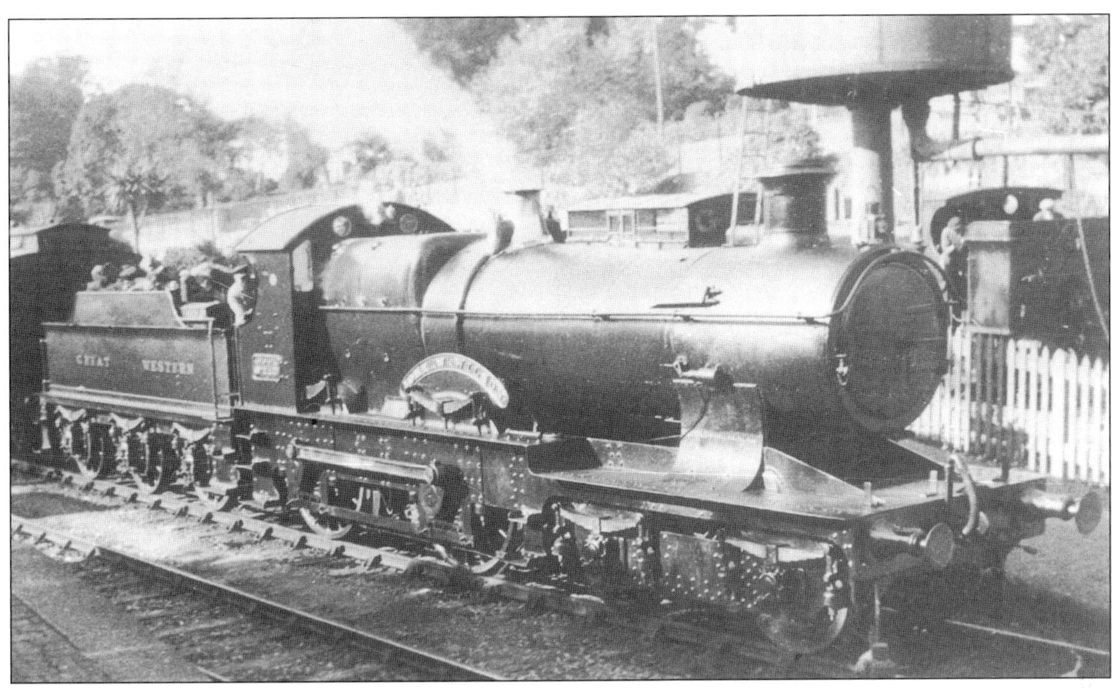

'Buffalo' class pannier tank 1613 shunts at St Austell as 3416 'JOHN W. WILSON' waits to depart with an up stopping train on 28 September 1921. This engine, which was shedded at Long Rock, worked until May 1936. P.J.T.Reed.

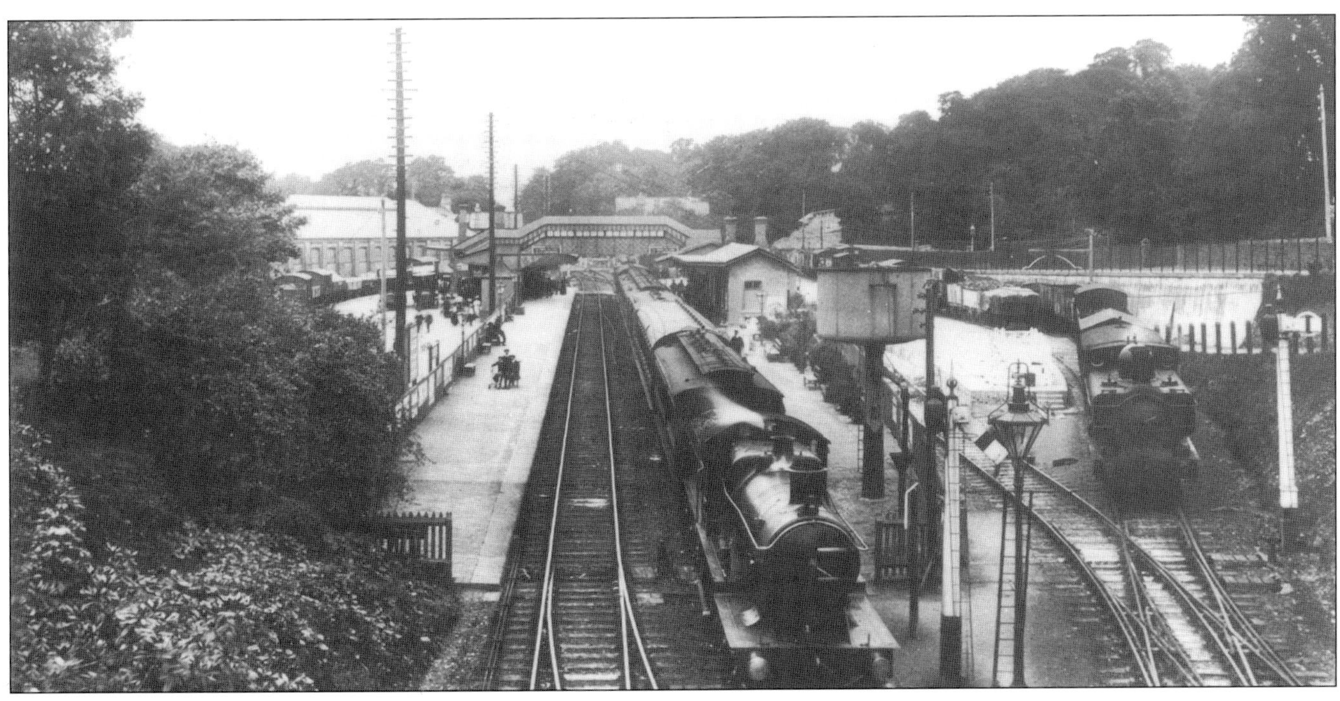

Another scene at St Austell, before 1912, has 3720 'INCHCAPE' on an up stopping train. This engine became 3430 and was withdrawn from Newton Abbot shed in December 1948. It was very familiar to me from the late 1930s. An unidentified pannier tank is in the sidings. Plenty of wagons are in the sidings on the left alongside the goods shed. As the level crossing, visible at the far end of the station, presented a hazard when shunting was taking place, during 1921 it was replaced by a footbridge which had originally spanned rails at St Blazey to link the platforms with the booking office. Pamlin Prints.

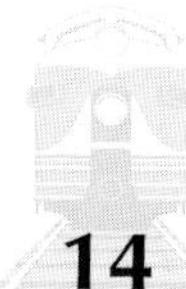

14

DUKE CLASS 4-4-0S

These elegant locomotives revolutionised working passenger trains over the hilly routes westwards from Newton Abbot to Penzance. They were introduced from 1895 and were originally known as the 'Pendennis Castle' or 'Duke of Cornwall' class. They handled most of the main line passenger trains in Cornwall until the arrival of the more powerful 'Bulldog' class engines. They continued in use on some of the branch line trains into the 1920s.

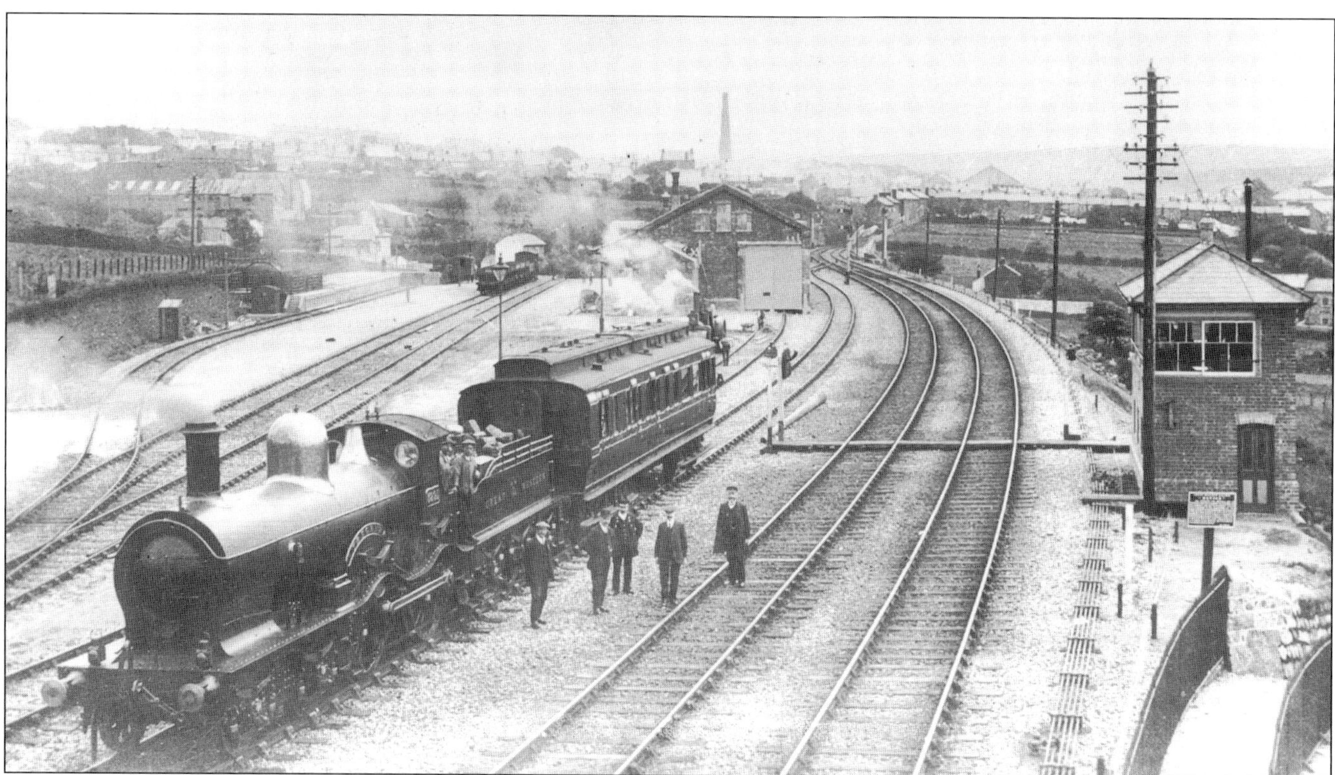

A small group of officials gaze up at the camera as 3291 'TREGENNA' waits with a one coach Director's Inspection special. It is near to the entrance to the new goods yard at Drump Lane, east of Redruth tunnel, shortly before the yard opened to traffic in 1913. Construction work is still in progress as a steam roller is working in front of the goods shed. The engine was renumbered to 3280 shortly after this photo was taken and was de-named in July 1930. It was withdrawn in May 1939.

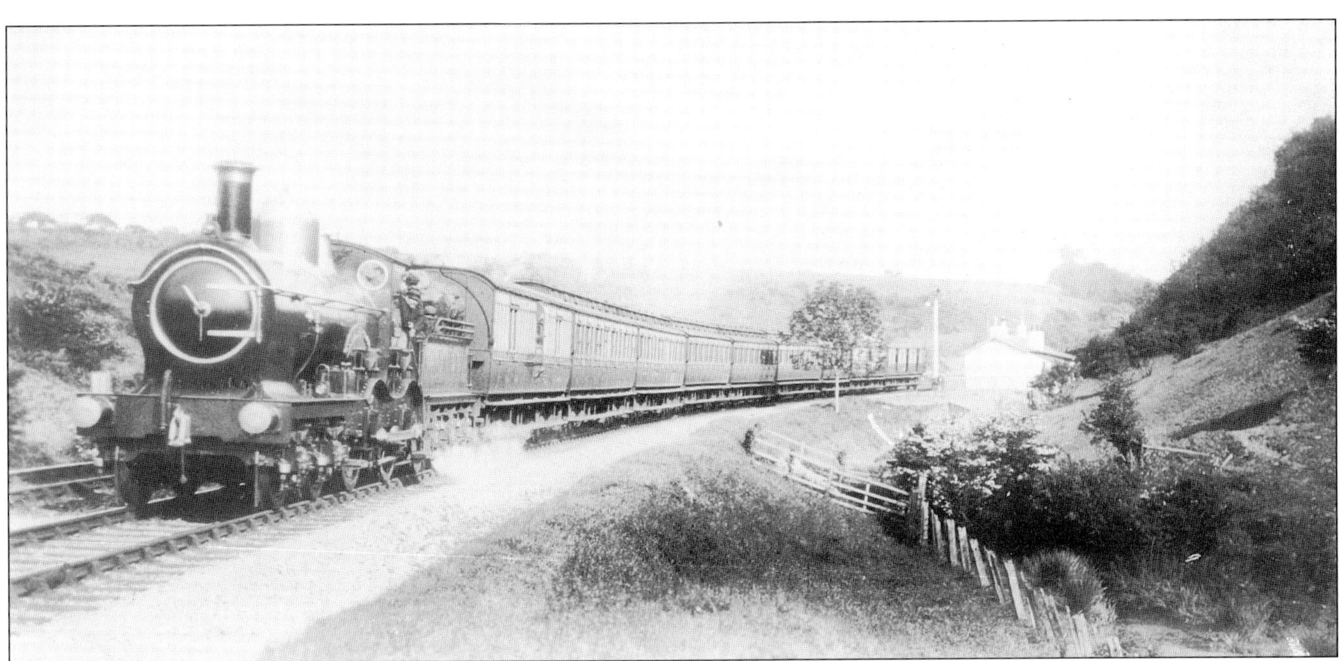

A train from Falmouth to Truro has departed from Penryn on an unknown date but prior to about 1912. It is hauled by a 'Duke' class loco which appears to be 3314 'CHEPSTOW CASTLE' which became 3282. The engine was de-named in May 1923 and was in service until October 1937. The leading vehicle is a GWR full brake. The lines were re-aligned slightly to the east of this formation and new platforms were built during 1922/23.   Locomotive Publishing Co.

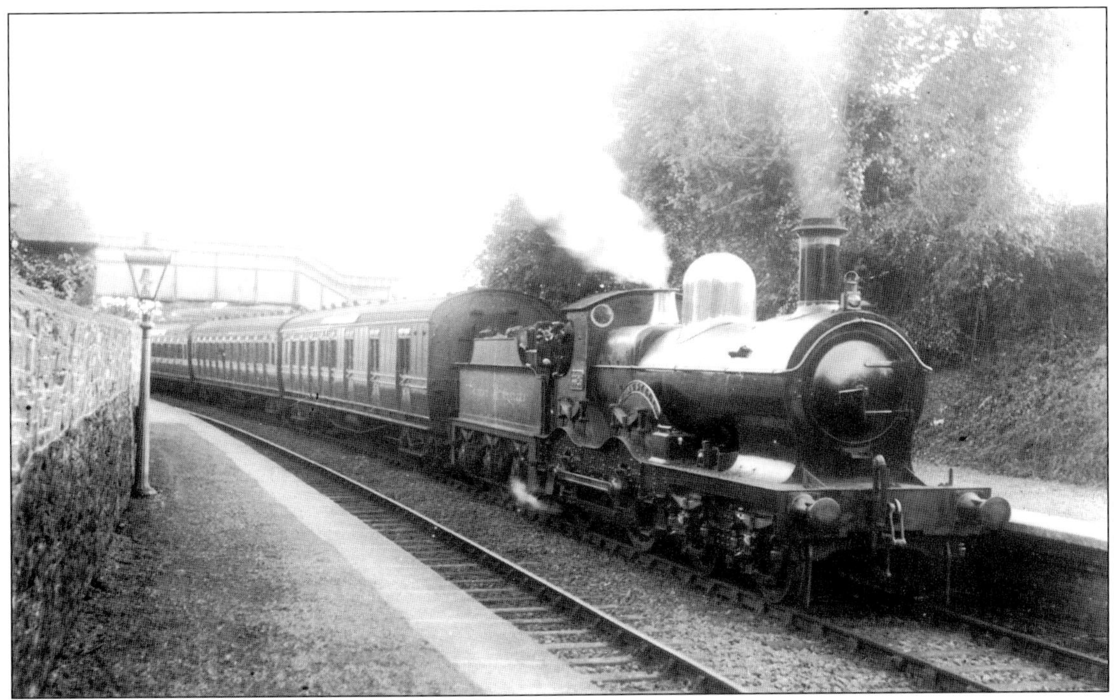

The large brass dome cover was a distinctive feature of the 'Dukes'. It is seen to advantage in this shot of 3326 'ST AUSTELL' passing through St Germans with a down stopping train prior to around 1912/13 when it became 3289. Along with other members of its class it was de-named in July 1930 as the Traffic Department considered that the engine's name may lead some passengers to believe that the town was the destination of the train. I saw this engine inside Gloucester Horton Road shed during 1947.

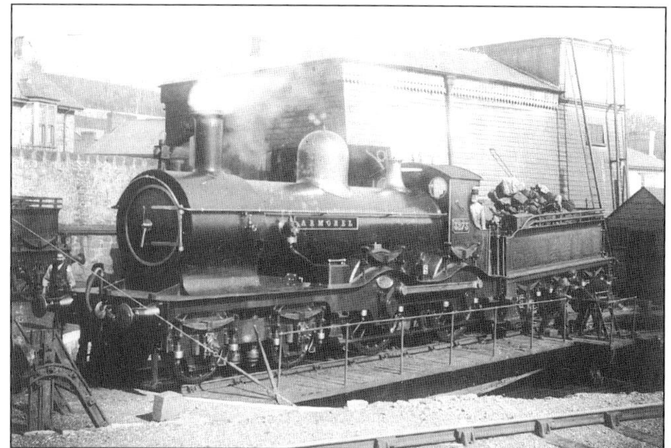

This very interesting scene has 'Duke' 3273 'ARMOREL' on the turntable at the small loco shed near the east end of Penzance station. It is being turned with the use of 'extension bars' underneath the tender. This small shed closed in June 1914 following the opening of new, much larger shed at Long Rock. This engine has an interesting history as it was built as shown in November 1896. In February 1902 it was rebuilt as a 'Bulldog' class loco and during 1912/13 it was renumbered to 3306. During these changes it lost its early straight nameplate for one of the standard GWR crescent shaped pattern. I saw this engine in 1937 regularly at Plymouth when it was shedded at Swindon but it was withdrawn from service in January 1939. Extension bars had to be used at sheds where short turntables were provided.   Locomotive & General Railway Photographs.

This is a broadside view of 3331 'WEYMOUTH' at Truro in 1900. This loco has a straight nameplate which is affixed in a different position to the similar one carried by 'ARMOREL'. This engine was built in August 1899 and was rebuilt to a 'Bulldog' class in July 1907. During the renumbering it became 3319, had its replacement crescent shaped nameplate removed during May 1930 and was withdrawn in May 1932.

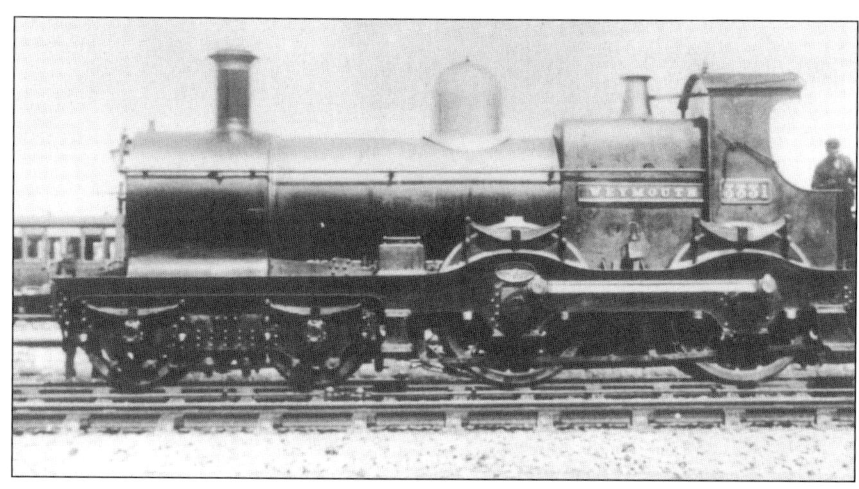

Now we have an unidentified 'Duke' class engine departing from Penzance across the viaduct with a stopping train, formed from clerestory stock, in the early 1900s. The small loco shed can be seen to the left of the cloud of steam.

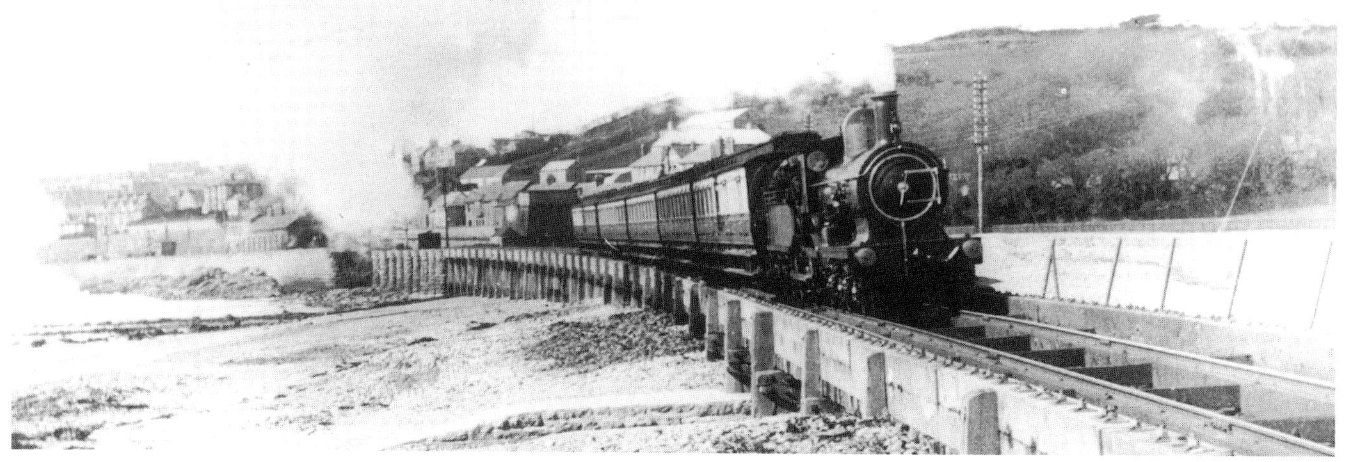

OTHER GWR 4-4-0s

Members of the larger wheeled 4-4-0s were not regular visitors to the Duchy as the smaller wheeled locos were better suited to the sharp gradients and curves. Nonetheless a few photos of some have been found and are shown in this short section.

A railwayman, who is probably a loco inspector presents himself in full glory to the photographer as he records the cabside detail of 'Atbara' class 3380 'LADYSMITH' at the east end of Penzance station. The oval cabside combined name and numberplate shows up well. It became 4127 in the renumbering scheme and survived until September 1929.

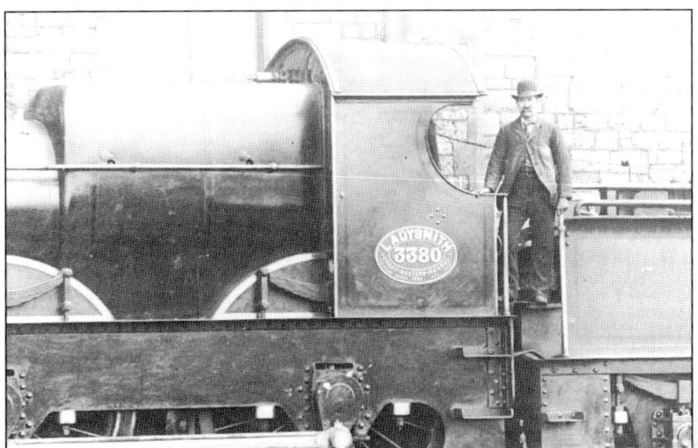

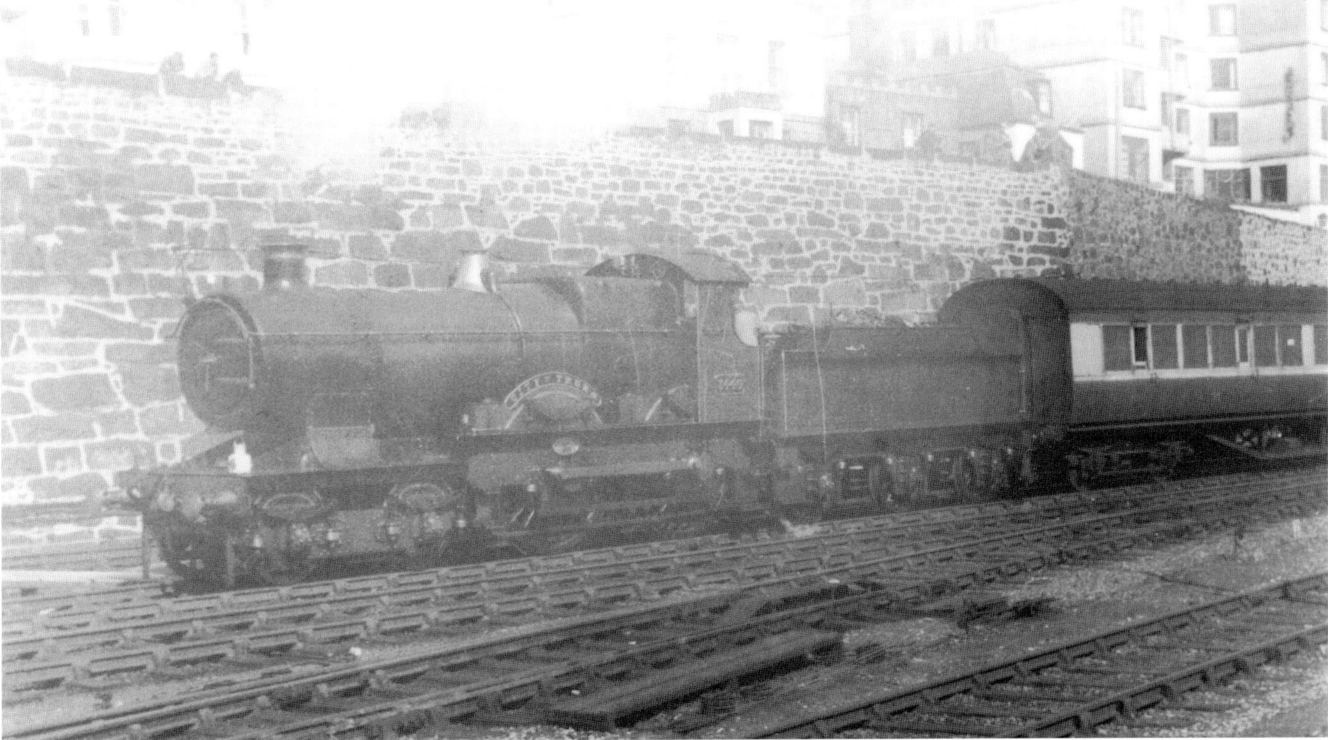

Compared with many of the previous photos dates, this one is relatively modern! It depicts the world famous 3440 'CITY OF TRURO' backing out of Penzance station after working a special excursion from Plymouth on 15 September 1957. An ex LMS carriage is behind the engine. I rode on this train but was unable to take any photos. This was because I had arrived home the previous night (a Saturday), from a two week holiday travelling around railways in Wales during which I had used all of the films which I had taken with me as well as extra ones which I had purchased in the Principality. As I had been on trains all of Saturday, on a Sunday it was impossible in those days to purchase a film anywhere! Mike Daly.

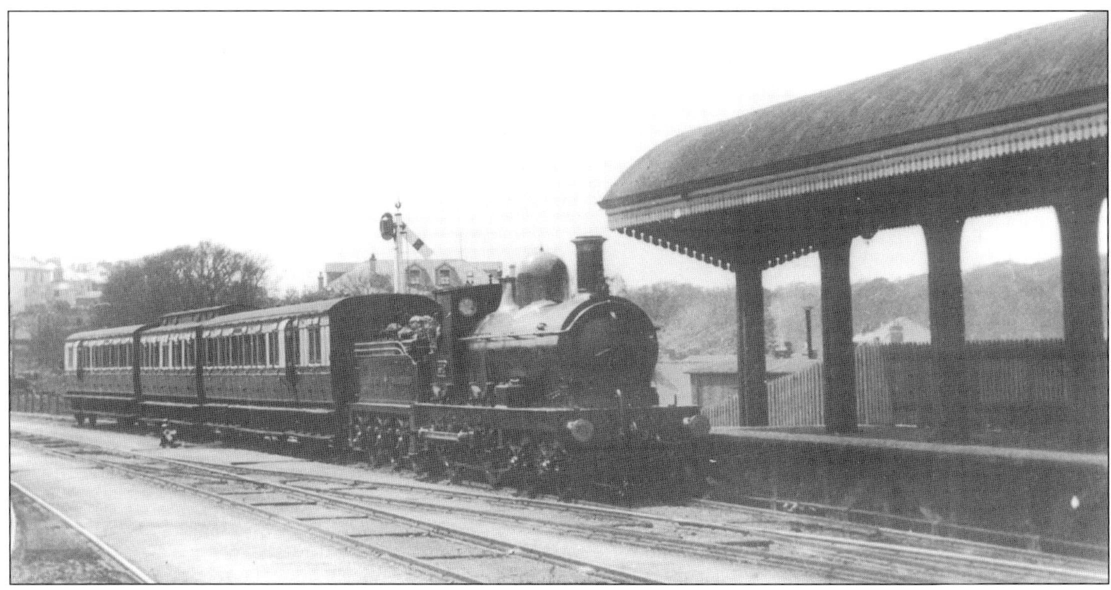

Here is 3521 class 3542 entering Falmouth on a train from Truro probably around 1910. This engine was built as a Broad Gauge 'Convertible' 0-4-2ST in 1888 and was converted to a 0-4-4 side tank in 1890/91. It became Standard Gauge in 1892 and in March 1899 it was rebuilt as seen. It lasted until March 1926.

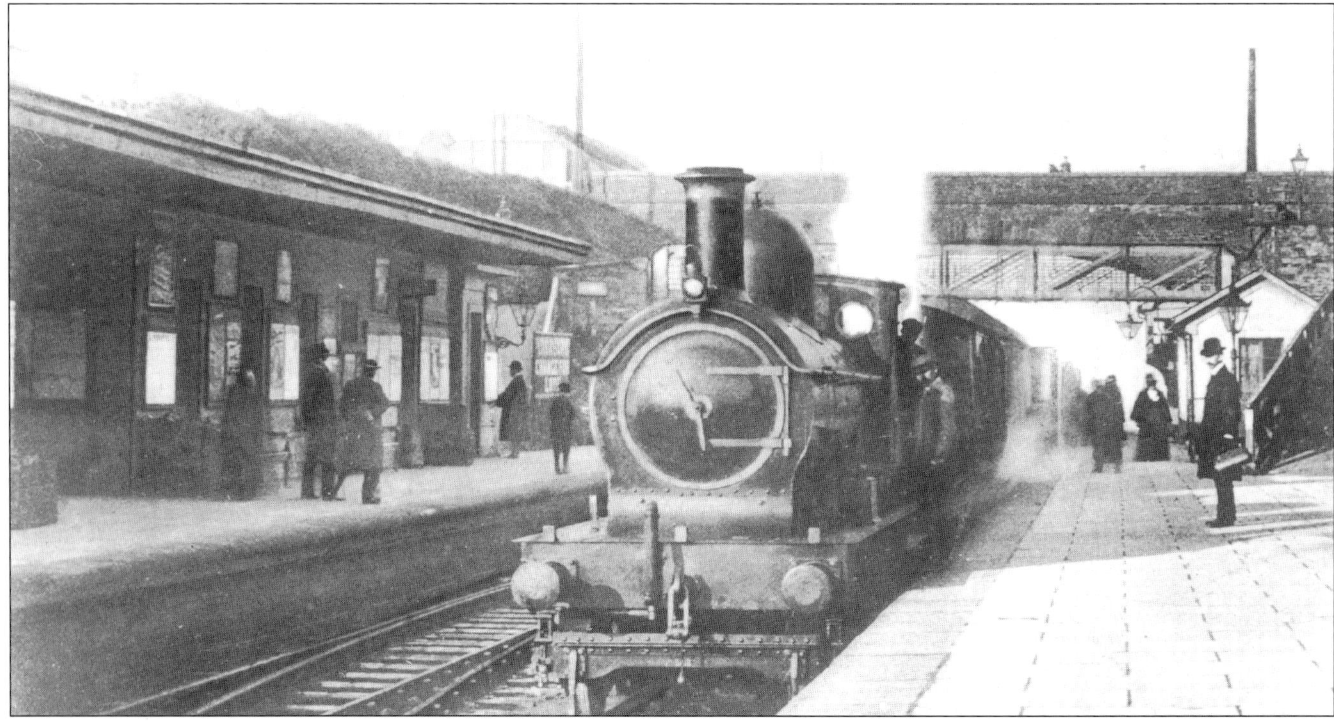

Now we see an unidentified 3521 class 4-4-0 at Liskeard at the head of an up stopping train for Plymouth probably in the early 1900s judging by the attire of some of the passengers.

16

SOUTHERN 4-4-0s

Early examples of LSWR engines worked most of the passenger trains over the North Cornwall line until they were displaced by the well liked sprightly 'Greyhound' T9 class 4-4-0s. A selection is contained in this short section.

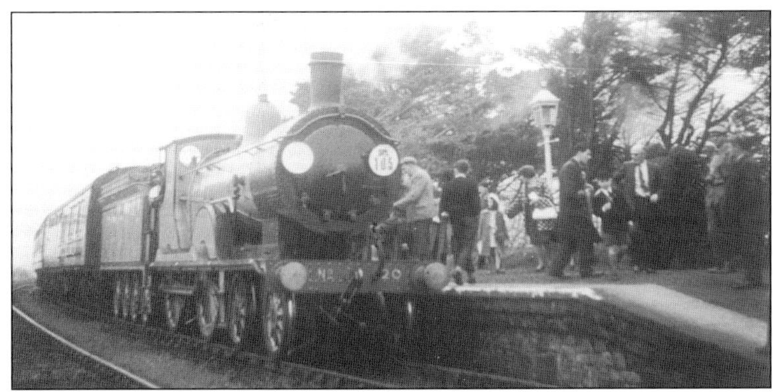

The preserved T9 class 120 worked a special train, composed of BR standard stock, from Exeter Central to Padstow on 27 April 1963. It was organised by Plymouth Railway Circle and the West of England branch of the Railway Correspondence & Travel Society. Here 'The North Cornishman' has stopped at St Kew Highway to permit an up passenger train to pass. Many passengers detrained to inspect the engine, take photos, have a leg stretch and discuss how the engine has been performing. Maurice Dart.

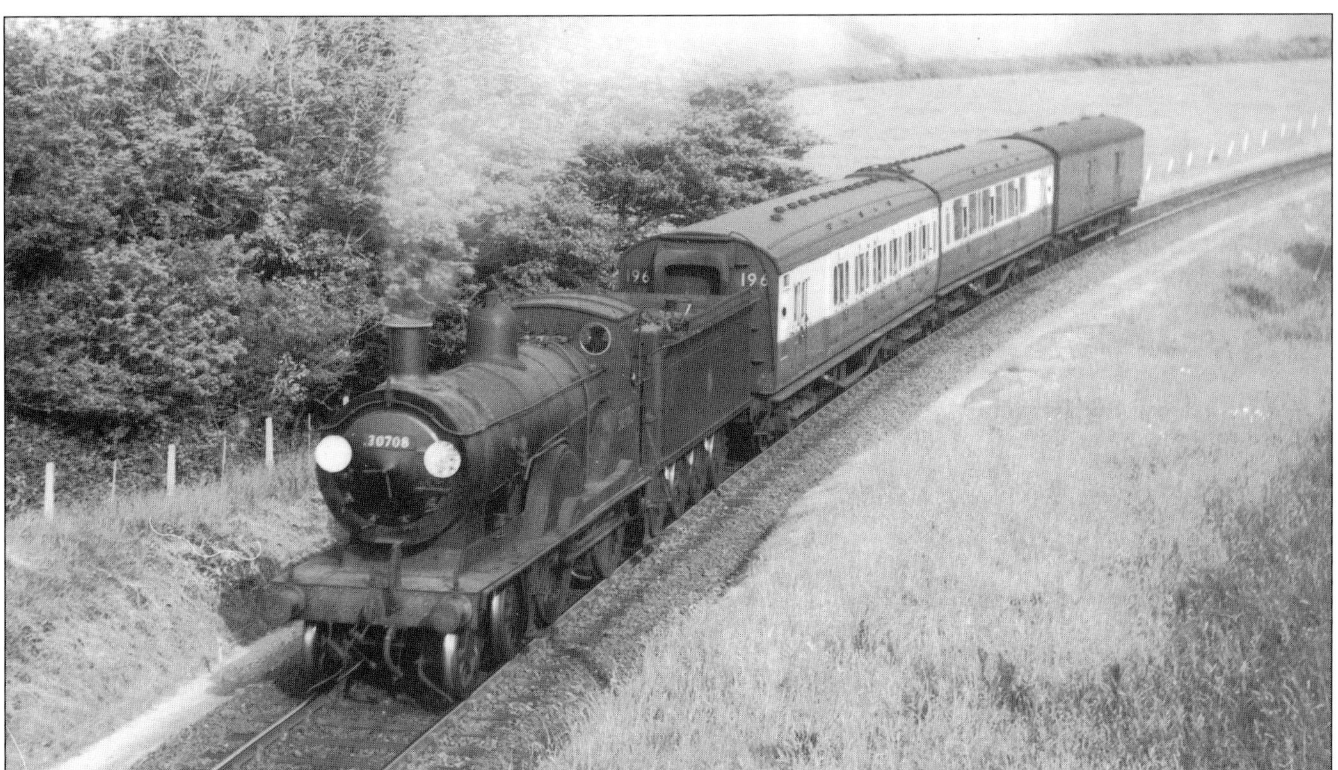

A typical North Cornwall line train, hauled by T9 class 30708 from Exmouth Junction shed but sub-shedded at Okehampton, is near Port Isaac Road in May 1957. The carriages are a pair of Maunsell brakes which formed SR set 196. Rail Archive Stephenson(Photomatic).

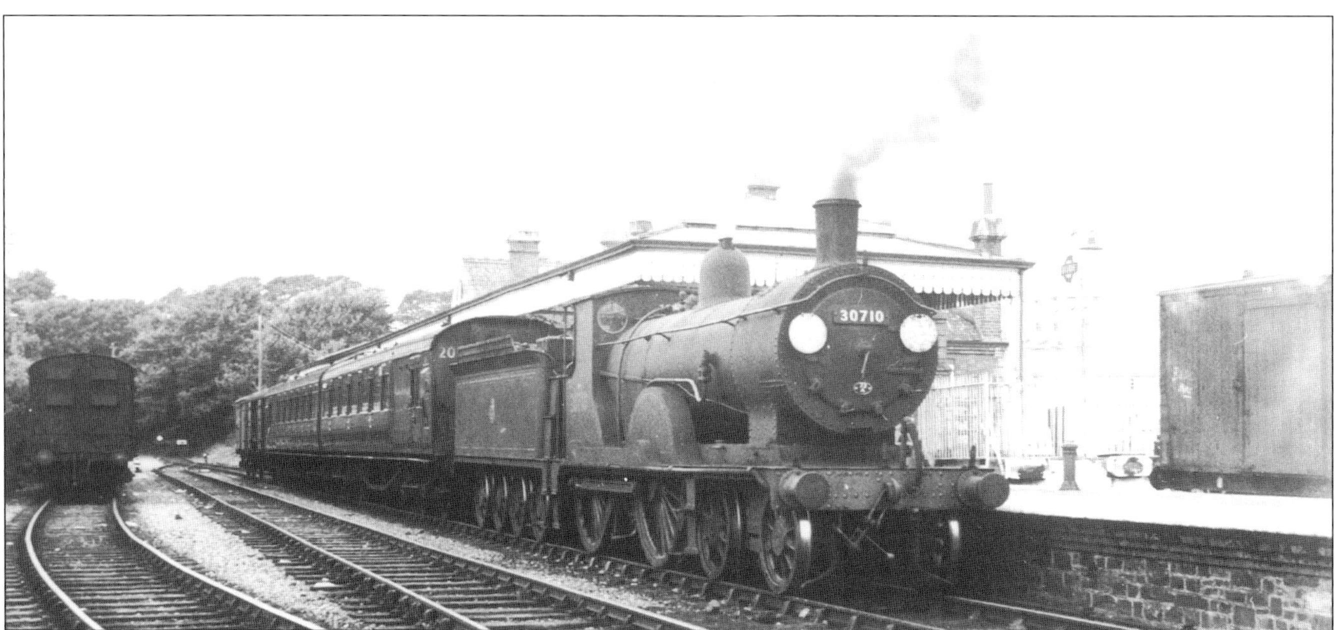

Another Okehampton based T9 was 30710 which waits to depart form Bude with the 3.18pm to Okehampton on 19 July 1957. The train is formed from an SR Maunsell set. On the right a LMS 12 ton van can be seen and an SR CCT is on the left. The author was evacuated to Bude for almost two years following the Plymouth blitzes and the journey out was by train from Friary station. Pamlin Prints.

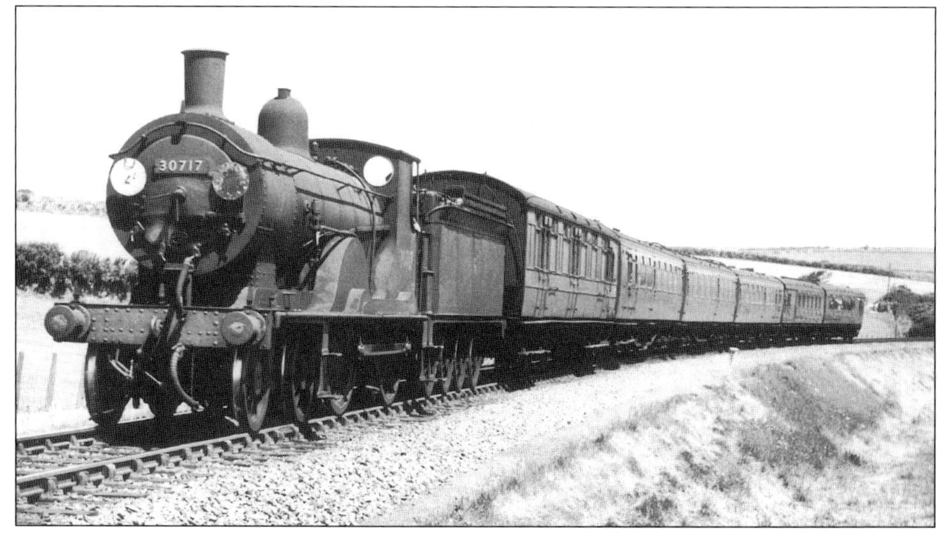

Another long standing T9 based at Exmouth Junction was 30717 which is between Camelford and Delabole with the 9.56am Okehampton to Padstow train on 19 June 1959. The train appears to be formed from a Great Eastern Railway coach followed by a Bulleid three coach set. A.C.Roberts/Pamlin Prints.

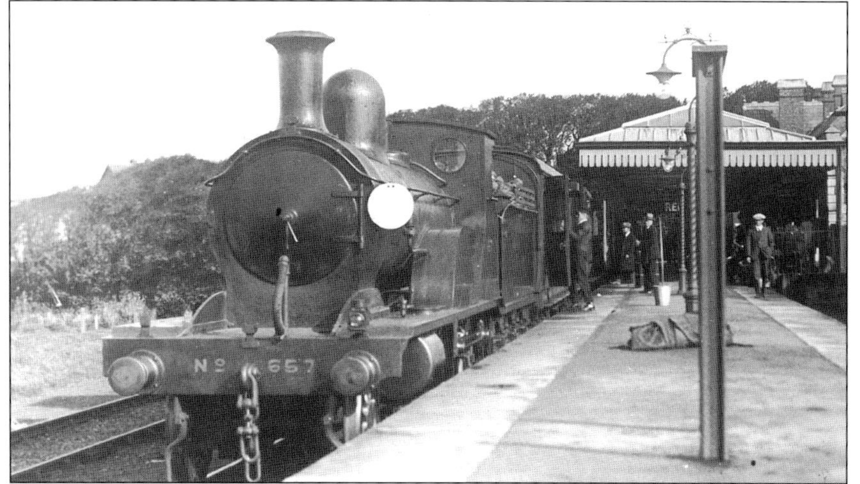

Now we see earlier X6 class 4-4-0 657 at Bude waiting to depart with the 10.50am train to Okehampton on 15 September 1923. This engine remained in service until February 1940. The Locomotive Club of Great Britain/Ken Nunn Collection.

FOUR COUPLED TANK ENGINES

This is a larger section which includes the many diverse smaller locomotives that mainly worked on branch line duties or performed shunting work. Most of the types are ex GWR but a few ex SR also appear.

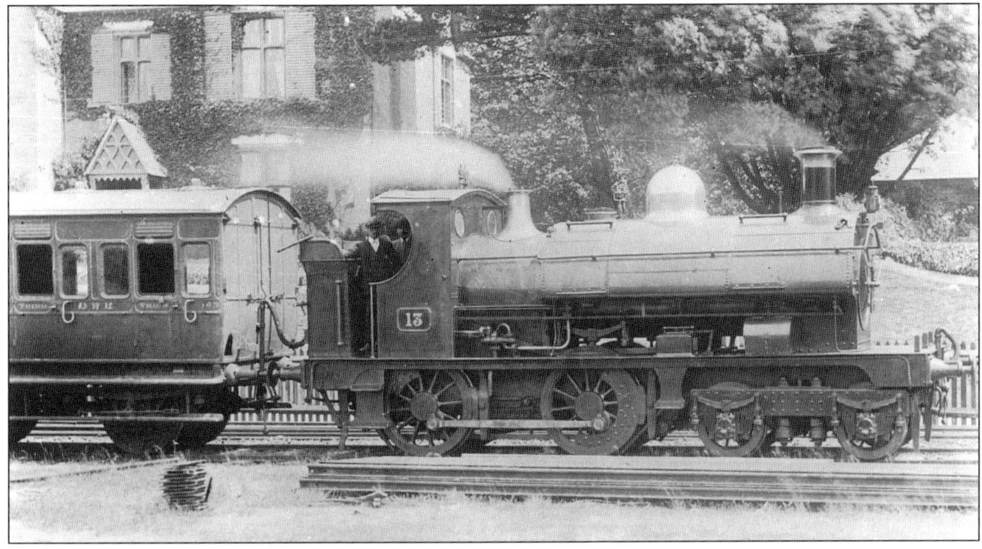

We start this section with a really unusual engine. GWR 4-4-0ST 13 has arrived at Looe with a train from Liskeard during 1922. This engine was unusual for the GWR as it was a 'one off' design which was built in 1886 as a 2-4-2 tank. The tanks were at the back and underneath and it was fitted with a plain square bunker. It was rebuilt to this design in 1897 and from 1901 to 1908 it went on loan to the Liskeard & Looe Railway. When the GWR took over this railway in 1909 it continued to work the line until 1922. From Cornwall it went to Swindon as a Works shunter and was withdrawn in May 1926.

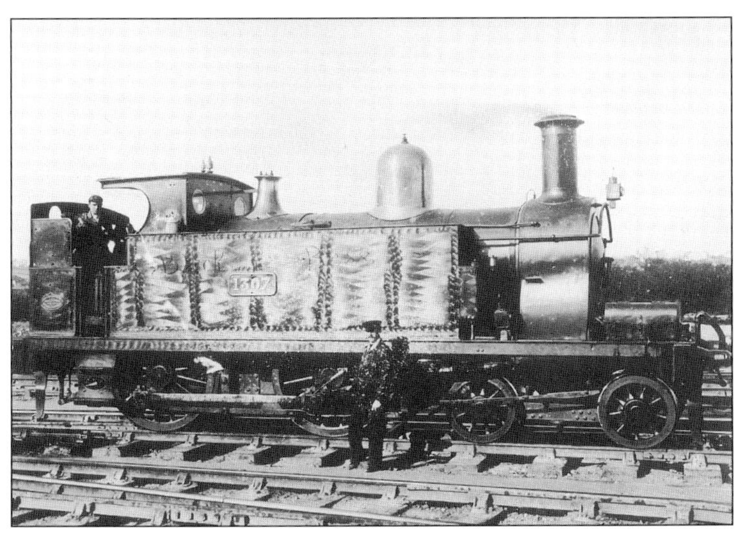

We continue this section with another unusual engine. This is GWR 4-4-0T 1307 at St Blazey shed around 1904/05. This engine was originally no.10A of the Monmouthshire Railway & Canal Co. and was reported as working from Truro shed in 1904/05. It succumbed in November 1905.

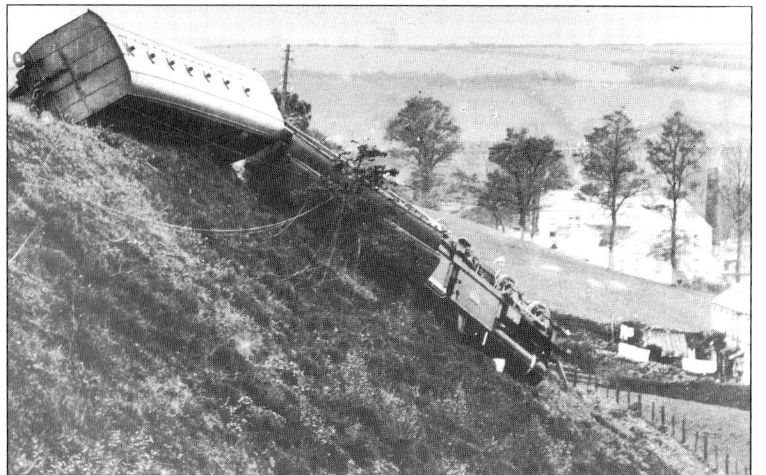

Next we look at a 'mishap' as the GWR never had 'accidents'! Here is 3521 class 3542 running as a 0-4-4T. This engine appears in photo after conversion to a 4-4-0. Whilst running as 0-4-4Ts they were found to be somewhat unsteady at speed and developed a distinct 'rolling' motion. There were two derailments involving them which led to the decision to rebuild them into 4-4-0 tender locos. Whilst working a train on the Falmouth branch on 31 October 1898, 3542 derailed near Penryn and fell partly down an embankment where it is seen on 1 November. P.J.T.Reed.

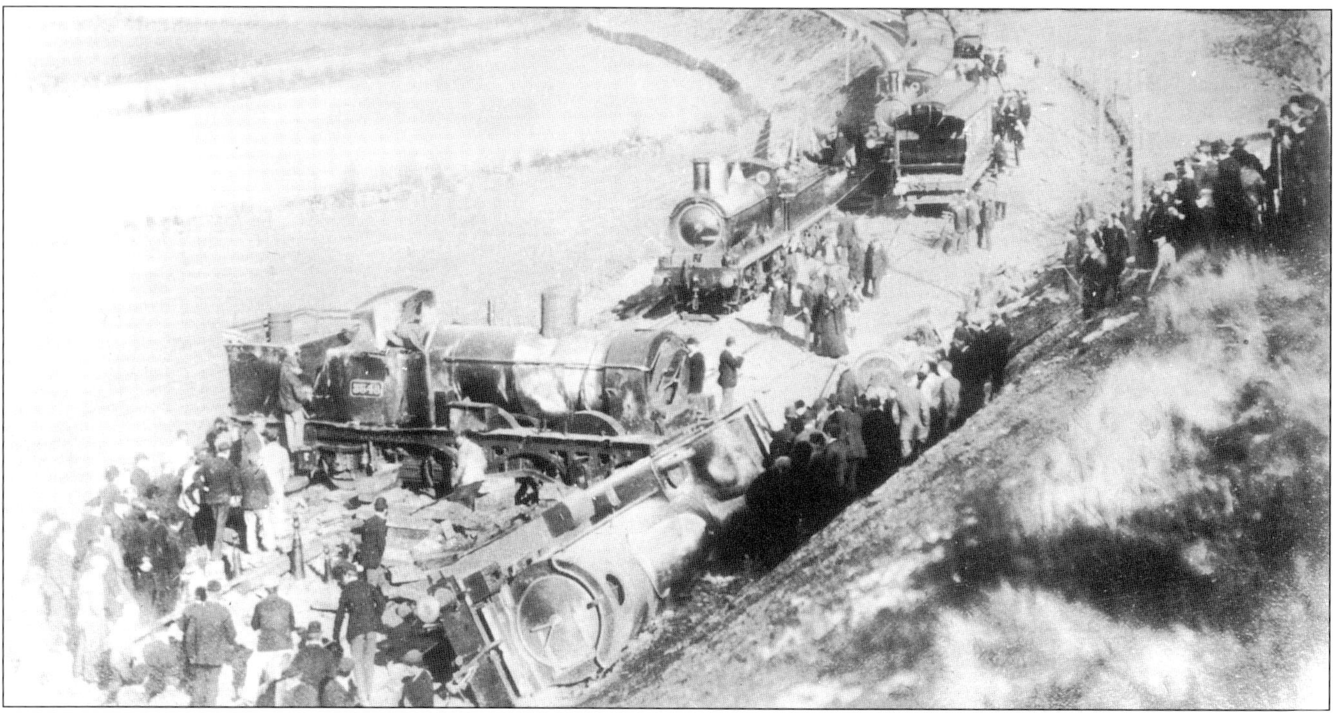

This was the scene recorded on 16 April 1895 following a far more serious derailment. It occurred when 3548 and 3521 were double-heading the 5pm Plymouth to Penzance passenger train on the Charlestown curve near Doublebois on 13 April 1895. 3521 was leading 3548 when they became derailed between Derricombe and Clinnick viaducts. 3521 left the rails followed by 3548 and the first four coaches. 3521 ran for one hundred yards, hit the side of a cutting and turned over on to its side with its crew still on the footplate. 3548 went into a field on the right side of the line and turned over. The driver on 3521 said that he felt the engine start to 'oscillate'. A ganger stated that this class of engine tended to' knock the track about'. Also the previous train on the Down line had been 'The Cornishman' which was hauled by two other members of the same class, 3536 and 3537. That train had departed four minutes late from Liskeard but was only one minute late arriving at Bodmin Road. The guard estimated the train's speed through Doublebois to have been 42mph but the signalman there made it 58½mph. The Inspector concluded that the train had exceeded its booked speed of 34mph and passed at between 50 and 60mph. Also because the driver on the second engine had done the braking instead of the driver on the leading engine, this had caused oscillations which damaged the track for the following train. The only fault found in the track was a 'slight crook in a rail joint'. Following this incident locos of this class were not permitted to work coupled together and were restricted to working over branch lines.

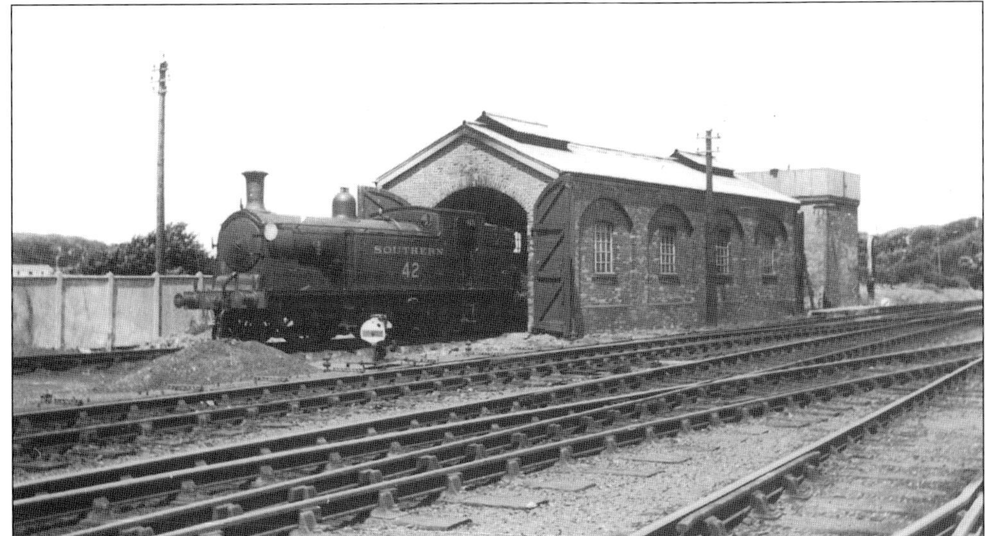

Now we change to the SR and see M7 class 0-4-4T 42 standing outside the small engine shed at Bude probably during the 1920s.
R.K.Blencowe collection.

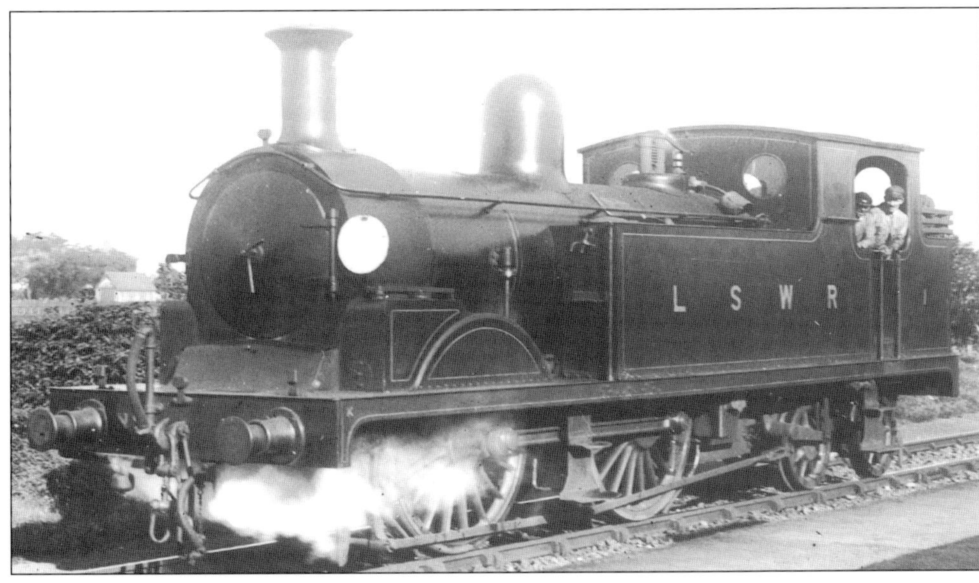

Despite the date being 11 September 1923, T1 class 0-4-4T 1 is still lettered LSWR when standing at Bude between duties. Apparently SR loco crews also posed for photographers! Locomotive Club of Great Britain/Ken Nunn Collection.

Still on the SR we see 231 which was one of the smaller O2 class 0-4-4Ts standing outside the small engine shed at Callington, probably during the 1930s. Visible inside the shed is 0-6-2T 757 'EARL OF MOUNT EDGECUMBE'. The O2 remained in service until February 1953. In the yard are two SR and one LMS 5 plank wagons.

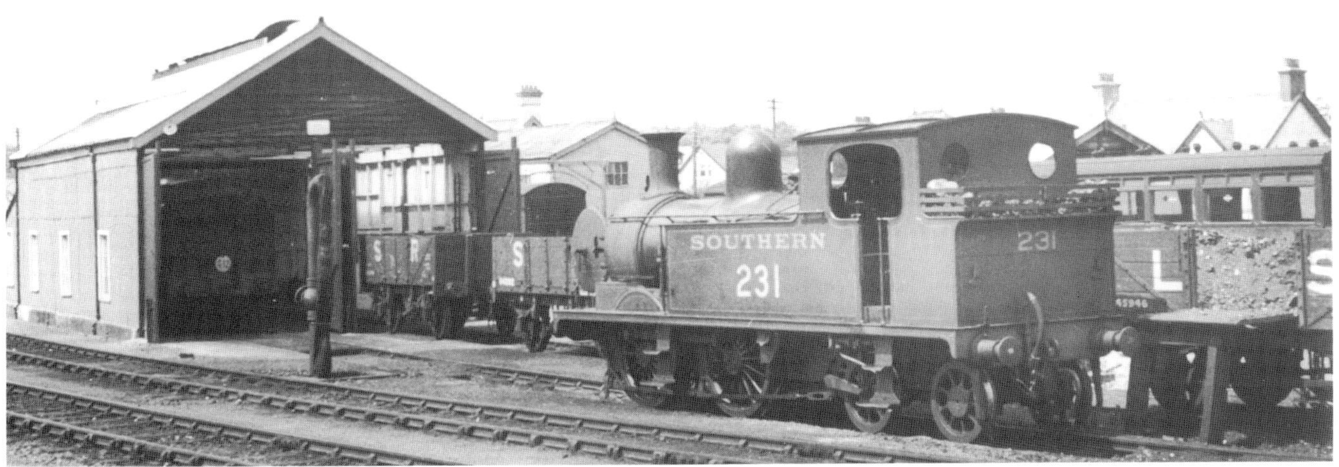

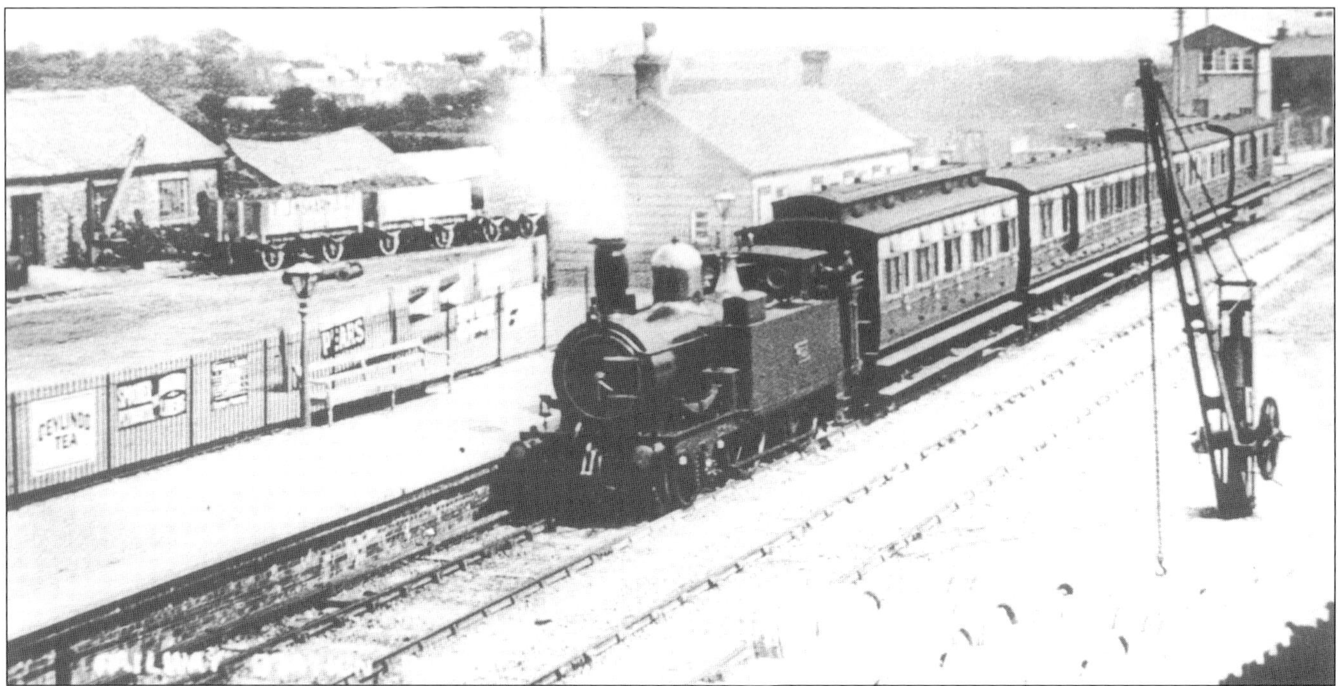

We return to the GWR and see a shot taken at Bugle during 1906. 'Metro' 2-4-0T 459 is on a train to Newquay. The front coach is a GWR 6 wheeled clerestory. The original Cornwall Minerals Railway signal box is prominent in the background. The engine was withdrawn in May 1933. Casks loaded with china clay lie on the ground in the foreground awaiting loading into wagons.

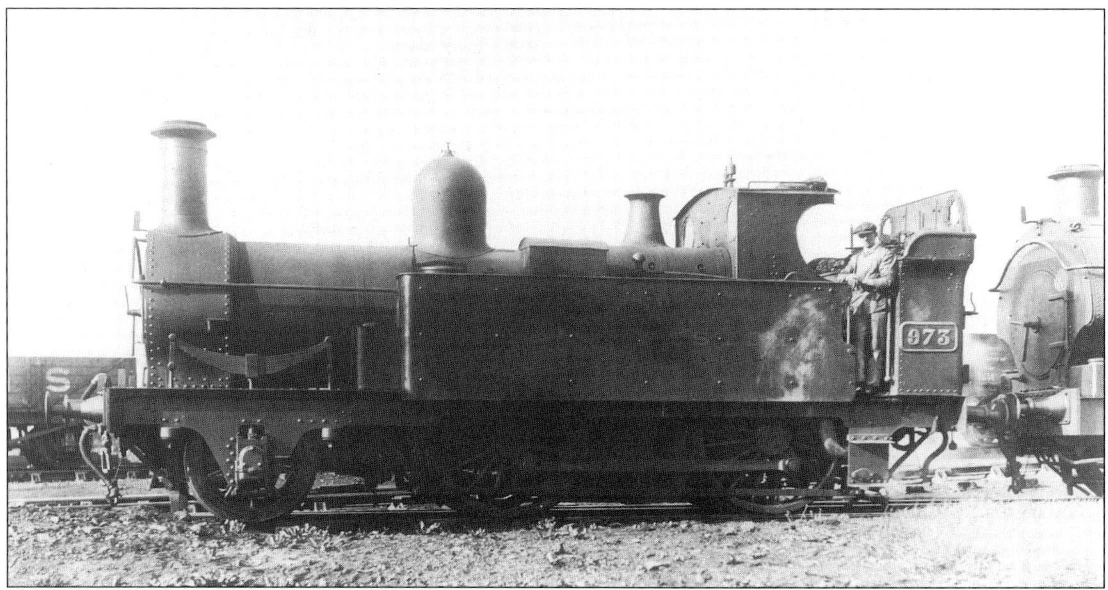

'Half-cab' 'Metro' 2-4-0T 973 is in the shed yard at Truro on an unknown date accompanied by a saddle tank. This engine was withdrawn during May 1932.

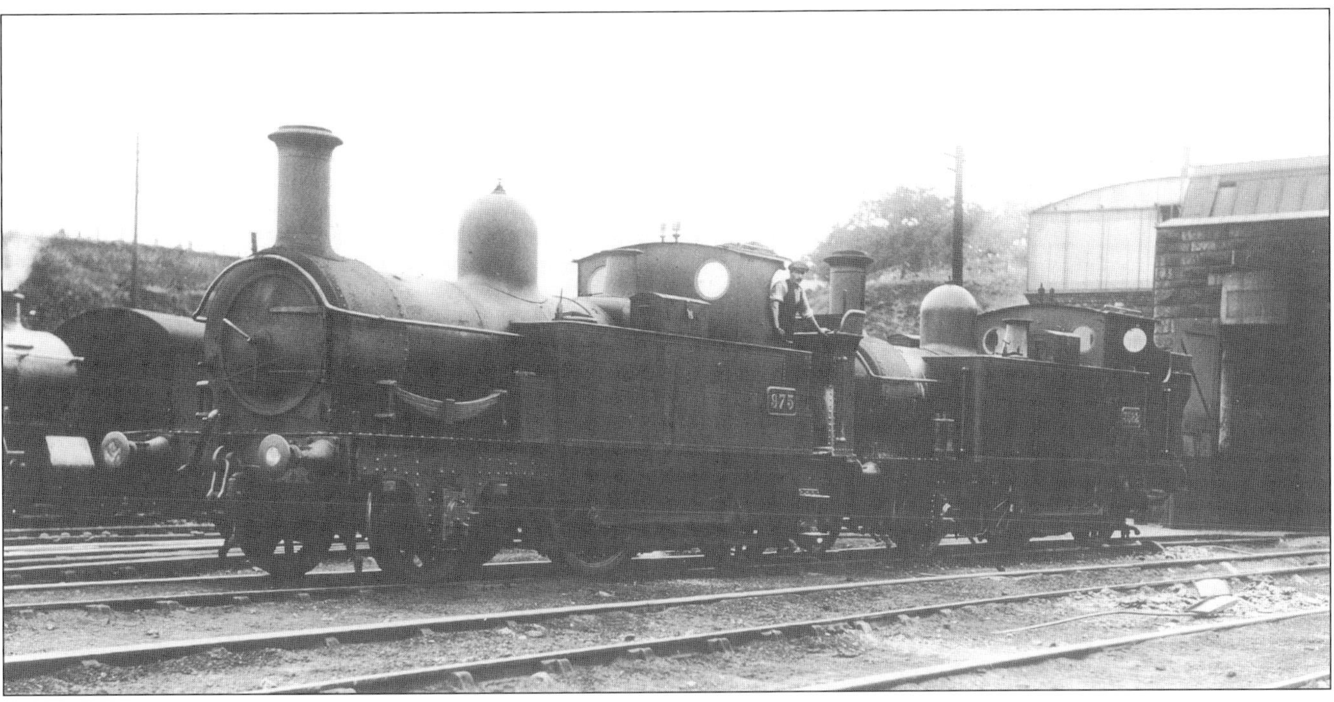

A pair of 'Metro' 2-4-0Ts stand outside Truro shed, again on an unknown date. 'Half cab' 975 is in front of 'full cab' 3582. 975 was withdrawn in April 1934 but 3582 survived until November 1949. Both engines are quite clean which suggests a date in the 1920s.

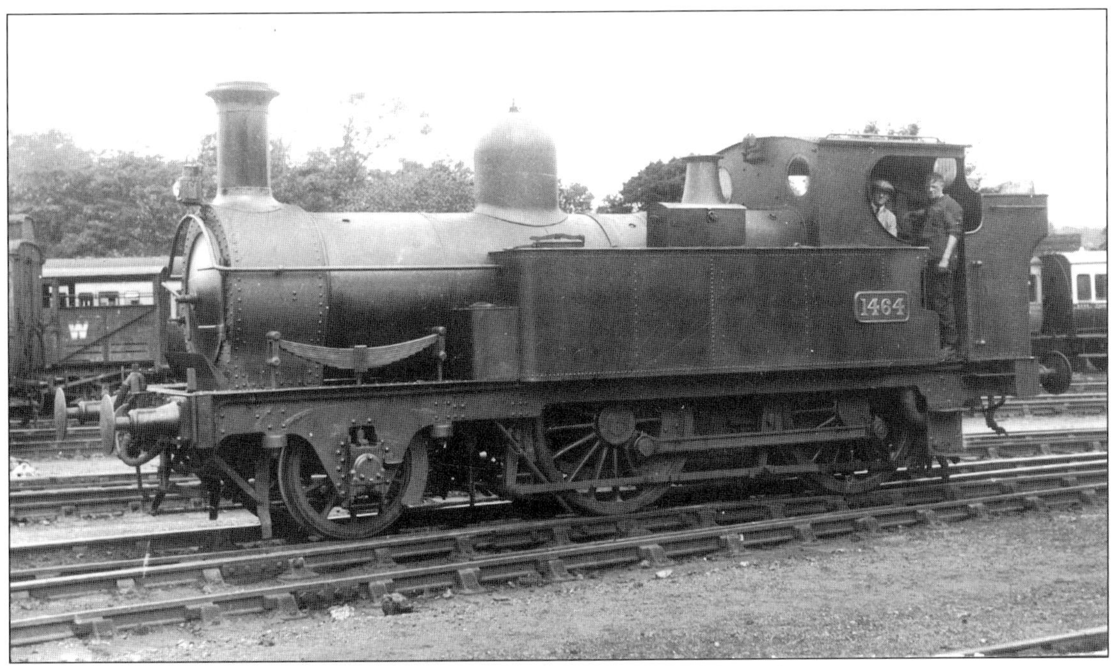

Truro was obviously a favourite haunt for 'Metro' 2-4-0Ts as 1464 has paused whilst shunting in the yard there. As this engine was shedded at Truro on 1 January 1934 and was withdrawn during January 1936, that gives a clue to the period when the photo was taken. Part of a GWR cattle wagon is visible in the yard.

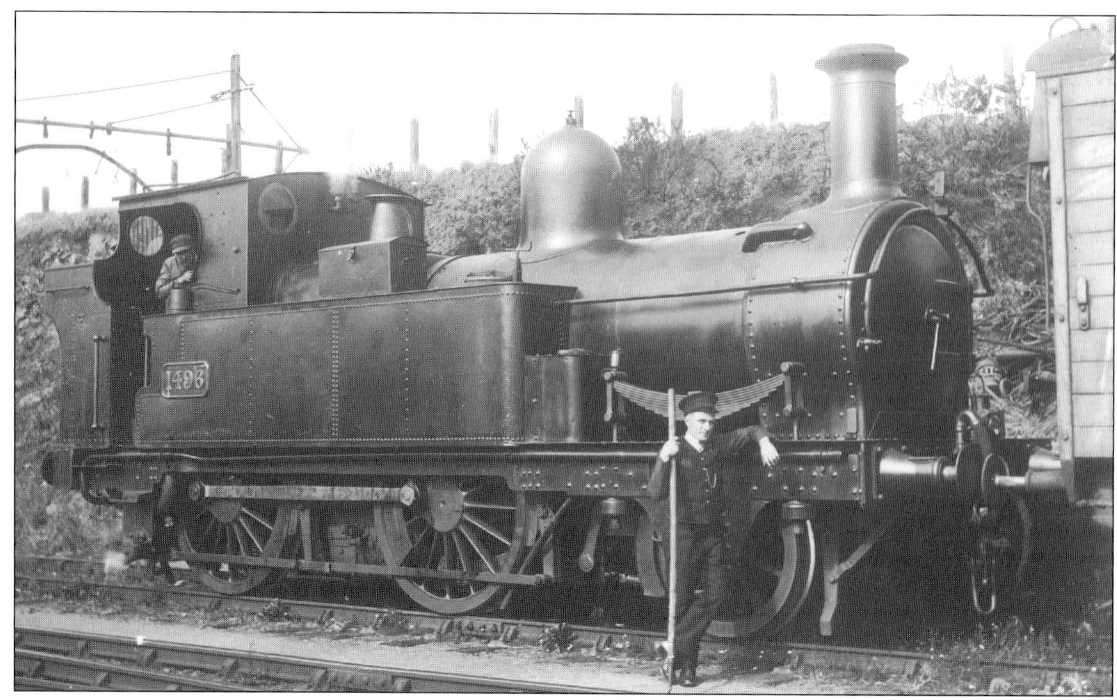

Going farther west 'Metro' 2-4-0T 1496 has paused between shunting vans on the line from the goods shed and sidings at Helston. The engine is attached to a GWR Mica meat van. The fireman peers from the cab and the shunter poses with his shunting pole for the camera alongside the very clean loco. This engine was shedded at Helston during1934 and was withdrawn from Long Rock shed in October 1935.

Now we see 1496 again but this time it is at St Erth on a passenger train for St Ives on 28 June 1924. Note the Midland Railway wagon in the yard, which contains many empty baskets to be returned to the termimus, probably to refilled with fresh fish for a distant market. The Locomotive Club of Great Britain/Ken Nunn Collection.

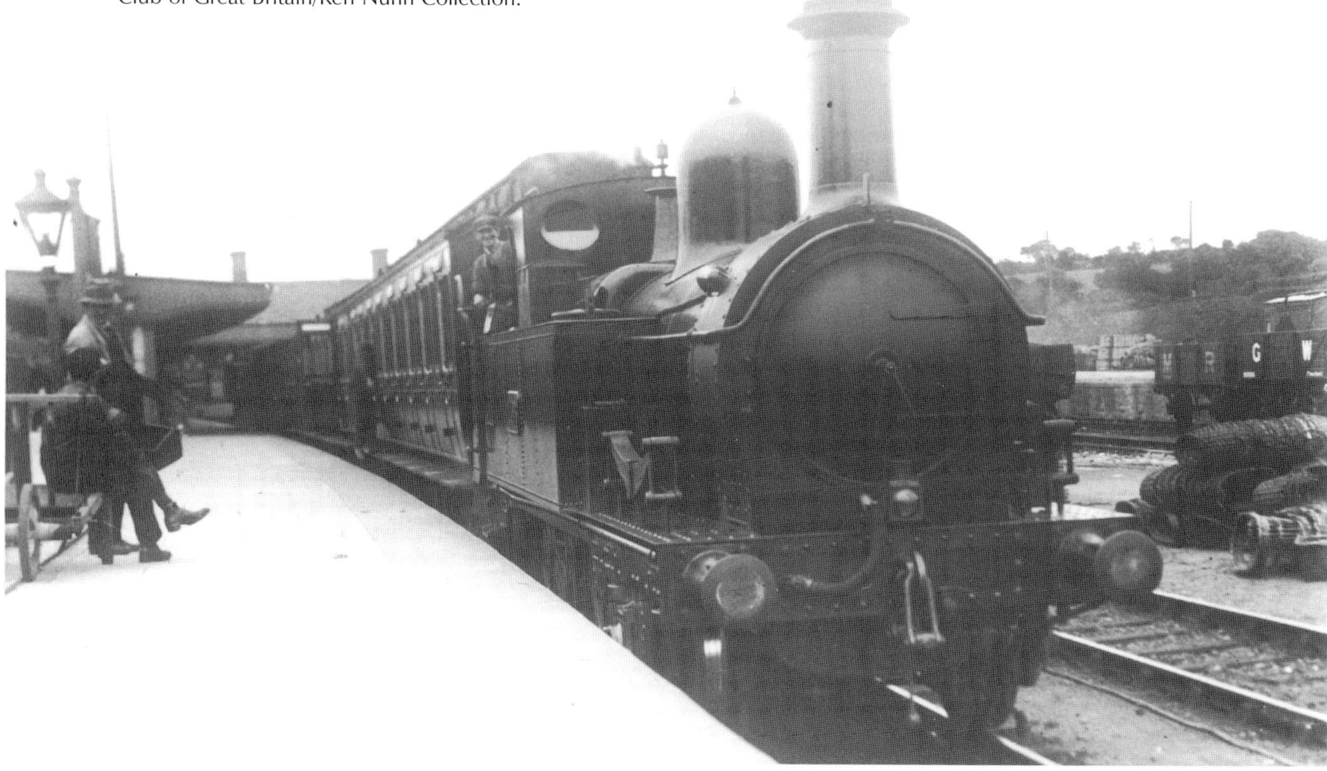

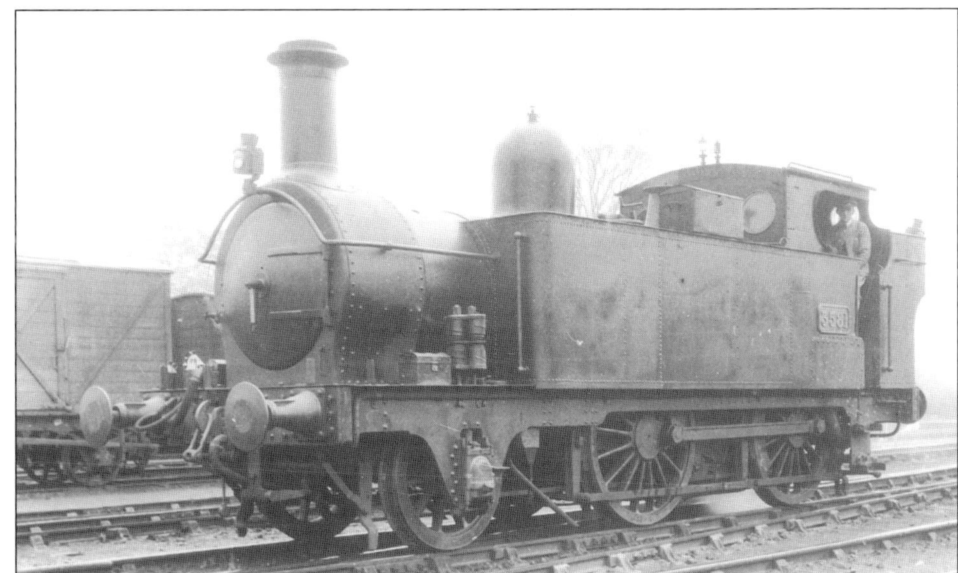

Another 'Metro' 2-4-0T, 3581 stands in the yard at Truro. It was shedded there in the late 1920s and later worked from Newton Abbot shed but ended at St Blazey for Fowey branch duties. I saw this engine at Lostwithiel several times in 1943/44 as I travelled between North Road and St Austell. It ceased work in November 1945. The van on the left in the yard is an ex North British Railway wagon.

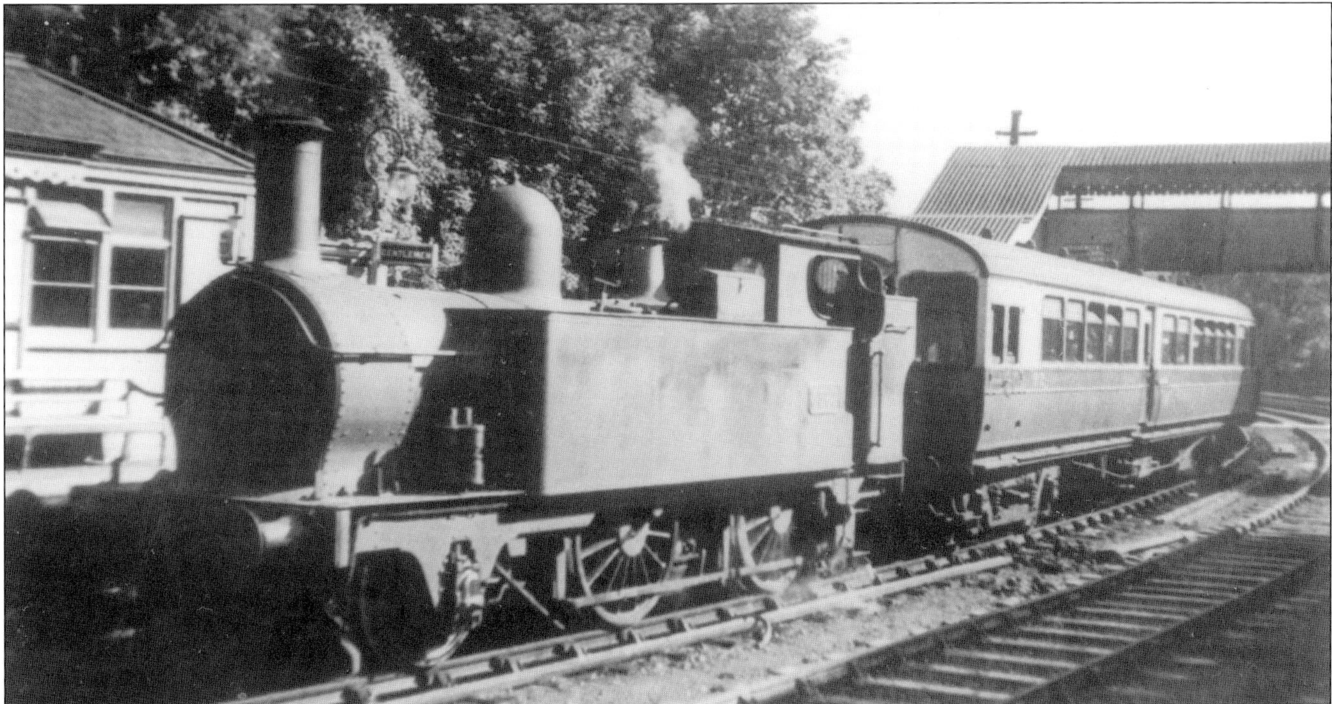

Following the withdrawal of 3581 the line from Lostwithiel to Fowey was worked by 6420 which came from Taunton. When we passed through Lostwithiel during late May 1945 we were amazed to see 3583 on the train to Fowey. This engine was shedded at Oxford at that time and the credibility of this sighting has been questioned by several eminent railway historians. However, the carriage was filled with schoolboys returning to Plymouth for the half term holiday weekend and as many of us were 'engine spotters' we filled the corridor and the cry of 'It's 3583 not old 3581' echoed all around. As we had all read the number and shouted out in surprise, that to me is proof enough of the loco's presence. 'Metro' 2-4-0T 3582 was transferred from Taunton and 6420 moved to Laira. This Metro' tank, which had been at St Blazey for periods in the 1930s, is at Fowey on a train to Lostwithiel on 11 September 1937. It was withdrawn from St Blazey during November 1949.

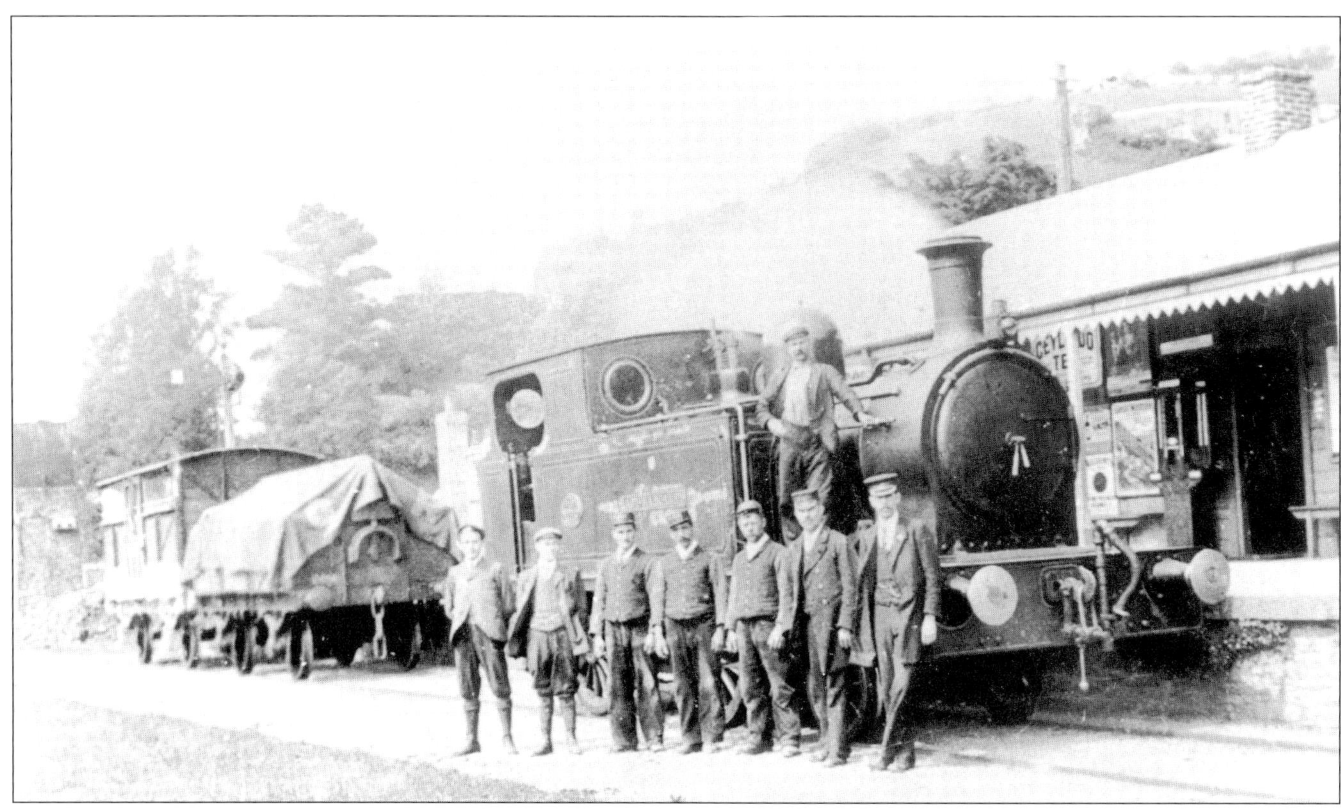

When the Liskeard & Caradon Railway 0-6-0ST 'LOOE' was found to be unsuitable for duties on that line the railway obtained a 2-4-0T. It was built by Andrew Barclay, their works no.956 in 1902, and was named 'LADY MARGARET'. It is alongside the station at Looe in the early 1900s along with most of staff who appear to be standing in rank and height, almost, from left to right. Behind the engine is a GWR open wagon with a tarpaulin bar and a GWR cattle wagon. The engine was taken over by the GWR and became 1308. It remained on the line until about 1920 from when, apart from a brief period at Exeter where it worked on the Hemyock branch, it was at Oswestry, mainly for working the Tanat Valley line. It worked until May 1948.

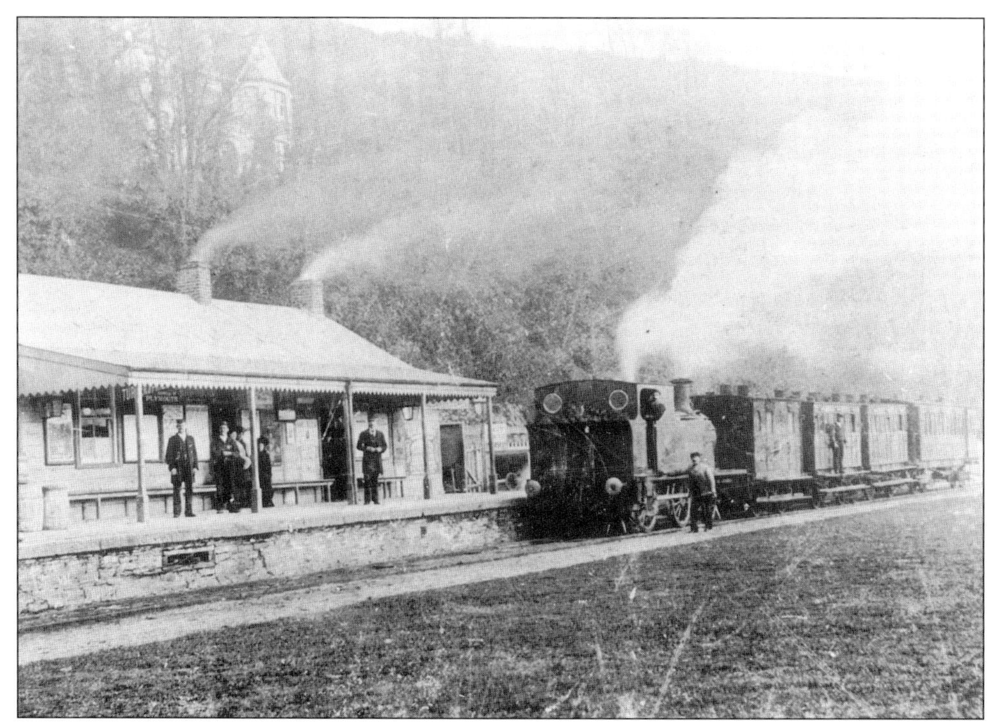

Most of the staff appear in this scene as 'LADY MARGARET' brings a train for Liskeard into Looe in the early 1900s. Having arrived at Looe from Liskeard, a passenger train had to proceed south from the station to enable the engine to 'run round' the train in the loops and sidings which adjoined the engine and carriage sheds.

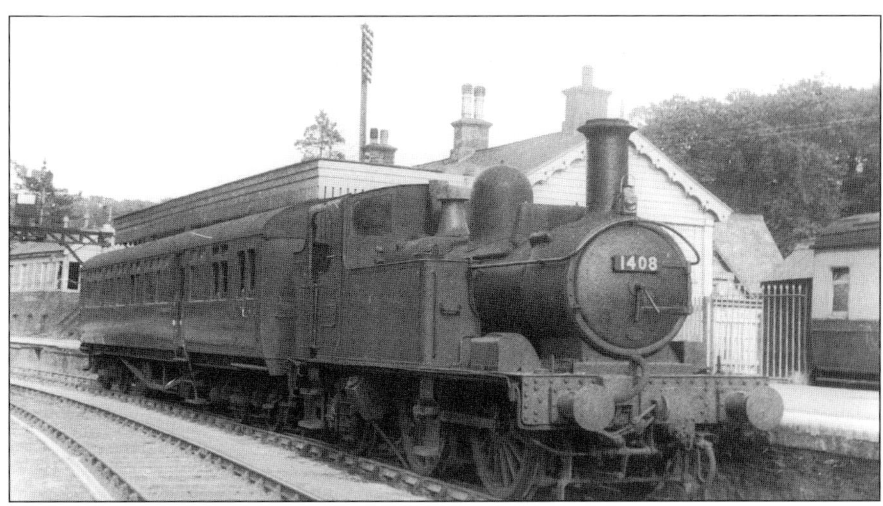

Now we look at the smaller 0-4-2Ts. With the demise of 3582, to our surprise 4800 class 0-4-2T 1419 was transferred from Goodwick (Fishguard) shed to St Blazey to work the Fowey line. Over the years when the Fowey branch engine required repairs, Laira usually sent a replacement down to St Blazey 'on loan'. This had occurred when Laira's 1408 was on the train at Fowey on 14 June 1956. This class had originally been numbered in the 48XX series as their class numbers implies. When it was decided to convert a number of engines to burn oil fuel in 1947, members of the 2800 and 2884 class 2-8-0s which were converted were renumbered in the 48XX series. Prior to this, to release that series of numbers for the 2-8-0s, the 4800s were renumbered to 1400s. From then on, many authors have referred to them as the 1400 class but I firmly believe that they should be correctly referred to as the 4800 class.   R.Cogger.

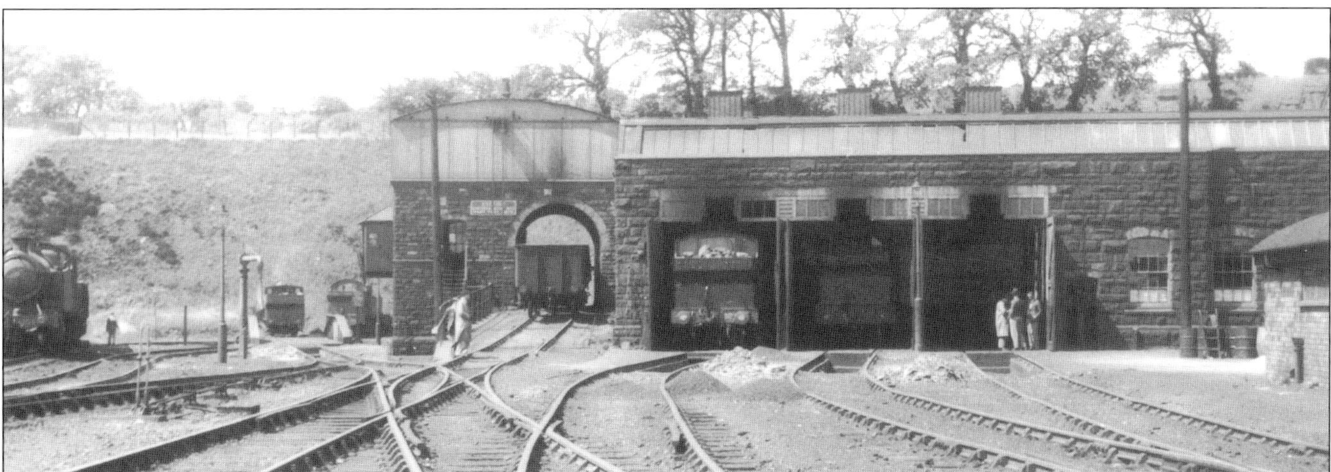

Normally a photo like this would be placed in the 'GWR shed scenes' section of my collection but as it contains a very rare record of an engine, I have this photo in the section for that class. It depicts Truro shed and is an undated view. However, to find the engine on the left there was somewhat unusual as it is 4200 class 2-8-0T 4298 from St Blazey shed. A 0-6-0PT and a 4500 class 2-6-2T are on the stub sidings beyond the turntable. These sidings could each accommodate one tank loco. The engine on the left hand line just inside the shed is the great rarity for photographic records. At first glance it appears to be a 8750 class 0-6-0PT. Luckily the GWR painted gold coloured numbers on the front and back buffer beams of their engines and this has enabled the engine to be identified as 4827. It is not generally known that a few members of the 4800 class worked in Cornwall from St Blazey and Truro sheds for short periods in the late 1930s and this is the only photographic record of them which I have been able to locate. This engine was shedded at Truro between March and September 1936 which dates the period of the photo. The engine to the right of 4827 appears to be a 4575 class 2-6-2T. An organised shed visit by a group of enthusiasts appears to taking place. Thankfully, one of them recorded this view.   Rail Archive Stephenson (Photomatic).

The great thing about visiting an engine shed was that although one mostly knew which engines may be seen, there could always be the odd surprise or two. This occurred when I was going around St Blazey shed during the evening of 7 August 1956. To my utter amazement, 4800 class 0-4-2T 1427 from Newton Abbot shed was under repair in the three road 'Factory', so I did my best to carry out a time exposure. Maurice Dart.

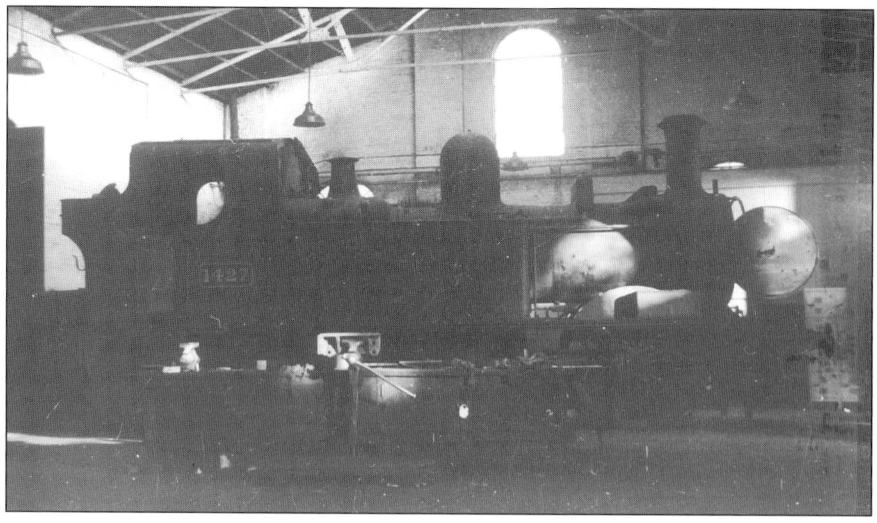

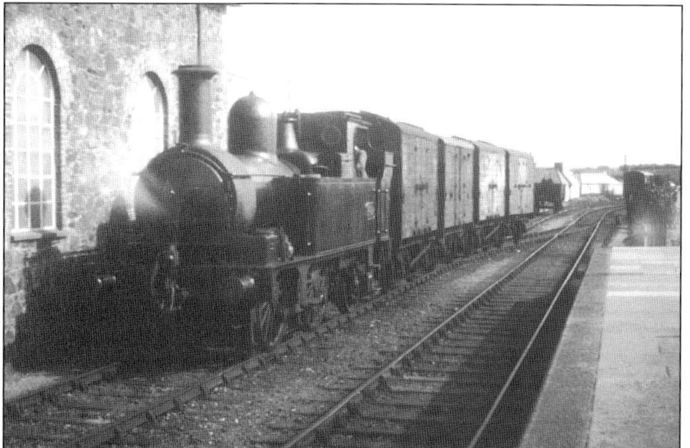

This photo of a 517 class 0-4-2T shunting four GWR Mica meat vans at Helston was taken during September 1930. On the reverse the engine is stated to be 549 but as that engine was withdrawn in August 1929 this cannot be correct. Under close examination it appears that it could possibly be 529 which, if correct, was withdrawn shortly after the photo was taken. Unfortunately, the number on the buffer beam is unreadable. It is stated that 'the engine had just come in on the afternoon mixed train and the wagon behind the engine had a defective buffer'. I.C.Allen.

This photo which probably dates from the early 1920s has a 517 class 0-4-2T which has brought a train from Gwinear Road to Helston into Praze station. As usual the photographer has attracted the attentions of the train crew, station staff and passengers. The engine appears to be 833 which was withdrawn during March 1934.

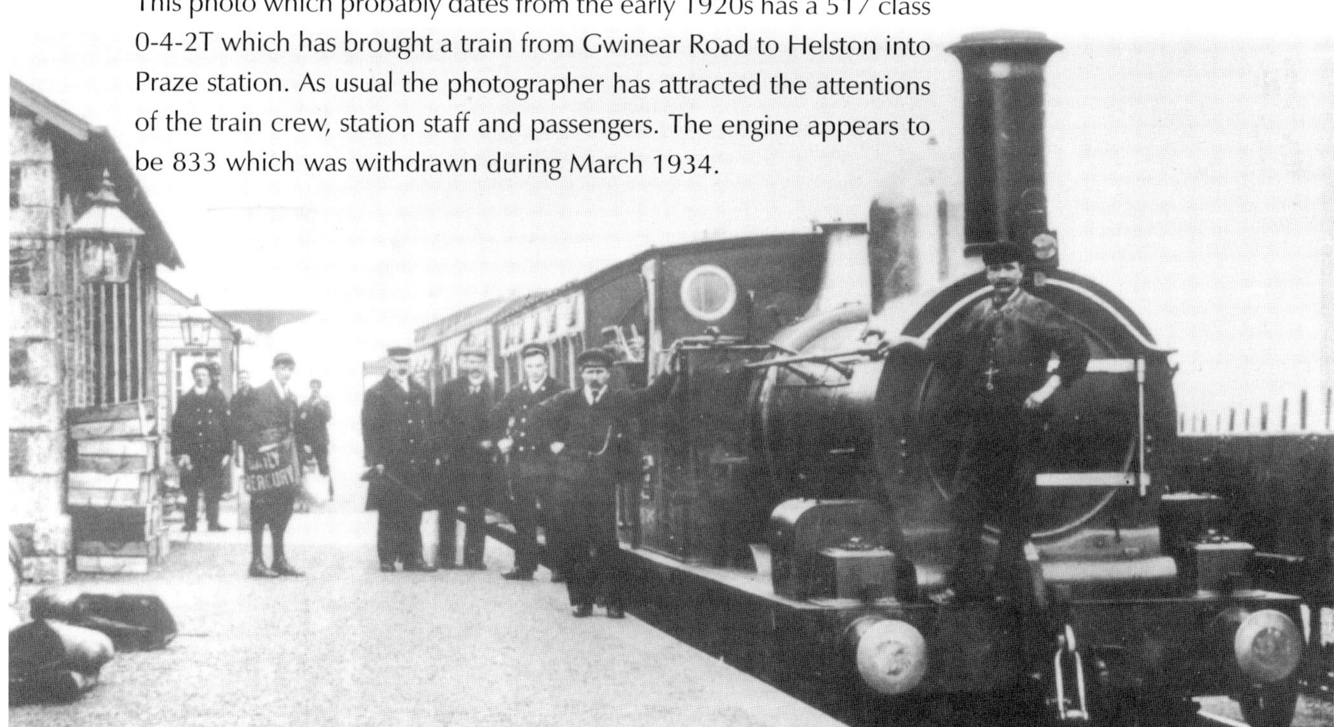

18

GWR OIL-BURNERS , BROAD GAUGE AND STEAM RAIL MOTORS

This larger section starts with a selection of the locos which were converted to burn oil in 1947 during the fuel crisis. I have been unable to locate any photos of the oil-burning 2-8-0s in Cornwall but there are 'Castles' and 'Halls'. These are followed by a few photos of Broad Gauge engines in the Duchy. Photos of these appear to be rather rare. The section ends with quite a few scarce photos of GWR steam rail motors which worked local trains on the main line and on many of the branch lines in the county.

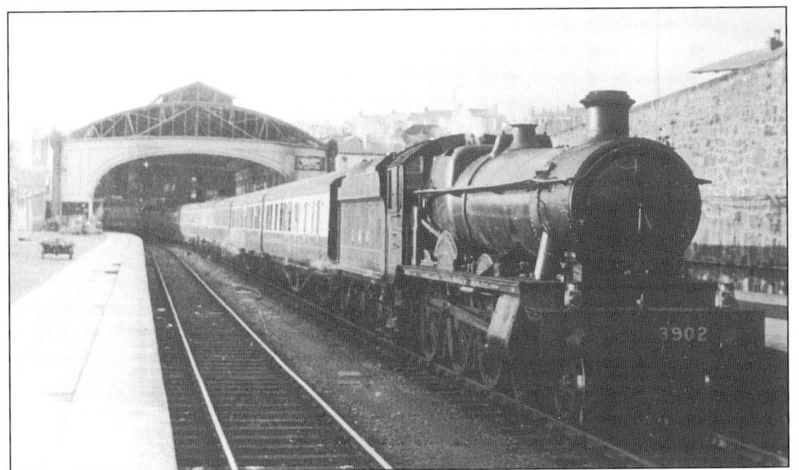

This engine was originally numbered 4948 but after conversion to burn oil fuel it was renumbered 3902. 'NORTHWICK HALL' from Laira shed waits to depart from Penzance with an express to Paddington. As it only ran as an oil-burner from May 1947 until September 1948 this photo was taken at that time. As there was no coal dust around, the green paintwork on these oil-burners was always immaculate. I saw this engine at Laira shortly after it was converted.

Whereas the 4900 series Halls were renumbered starting from 3900, those in the 5900 and 6900 series were renumbered starting from 3950. Just emerging from Higher Town tunnel west of Truro, with a Down express is, 3955 'HABERFIELD HALL' from Laira shed. This engine was originally numbered 6949 and operated as an oil-burner from May 1947 until April 1949. I also saw this newly converted at Laira shed.

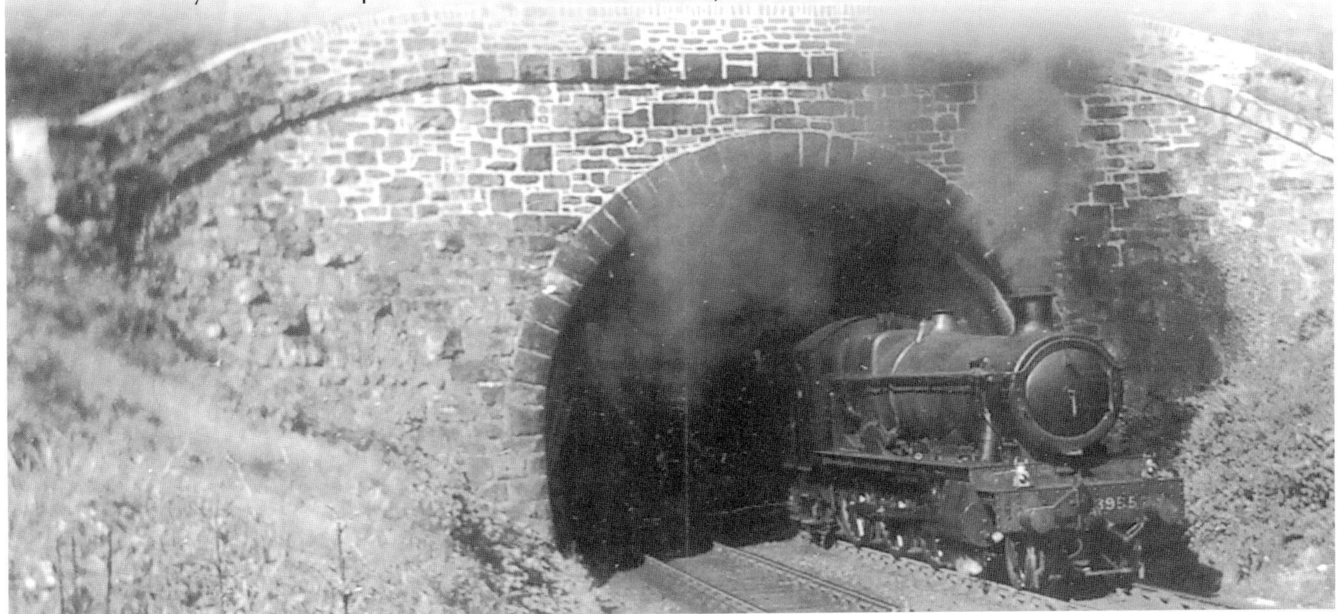

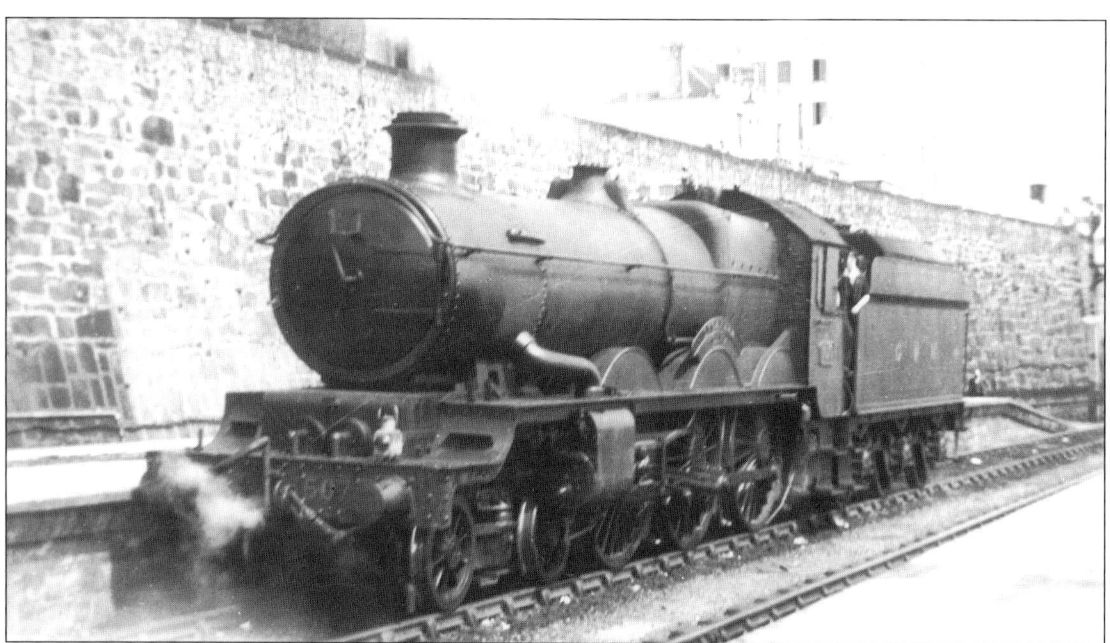

A small number of Castle class locos were converted to burn oil fuel but these retained their original numbers. Laira's 5079 'LYSANDER' is backing out of Penzance station to go to Long Rock shed for turning. It ran as an oil-burner from January 1947 until October 1948. This was the first oil-burner to arrive at Laira and was placed inside the roundhouse for a short period. I saw it soon after it arrived and I remember walking around the gleaming green engine several times just gazing at it in awe and admiration. A.G.Ellis.

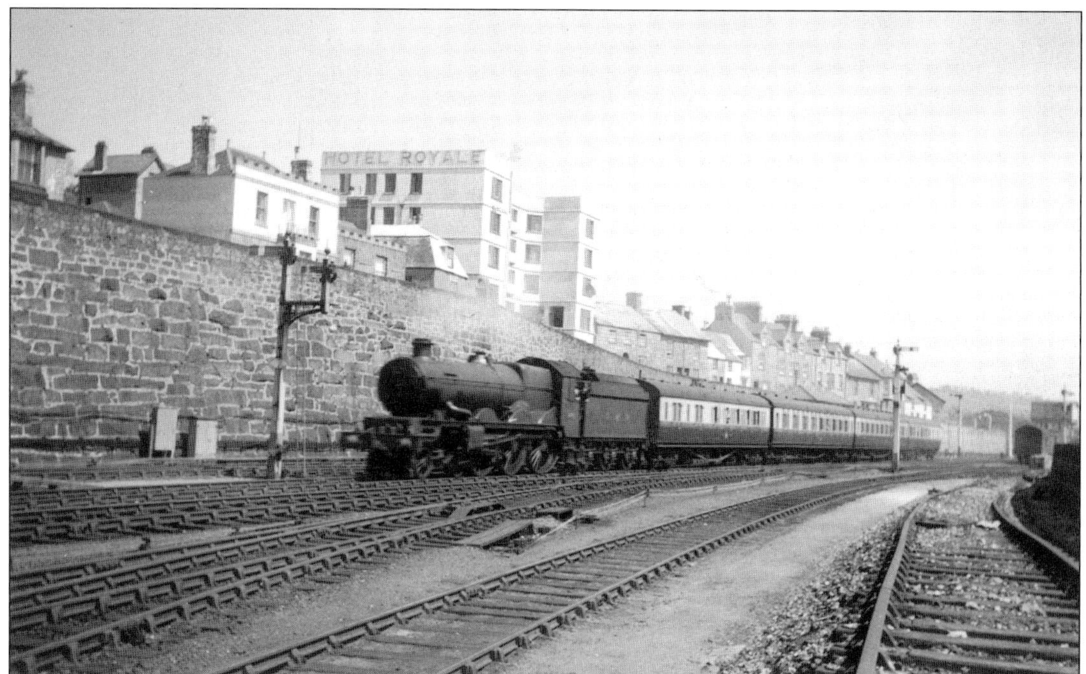

It was mainly oil-burners from Laira shed which worked to Penzance but here is 5083 'BATH ABBEY' from Bath Road shed, Bristol. It is running into the terminus on a short four coach express at 11.45am on 30 May 1948. A portion of the train had been detached at North Road. This engine operated as an oil-burner from December 1946 until November 1948. This engine had started life as 'Star' class 4063 and was taken out of service in March 1937. It was rebuilt as a 'Castle' class and re-entered service in June 1937.

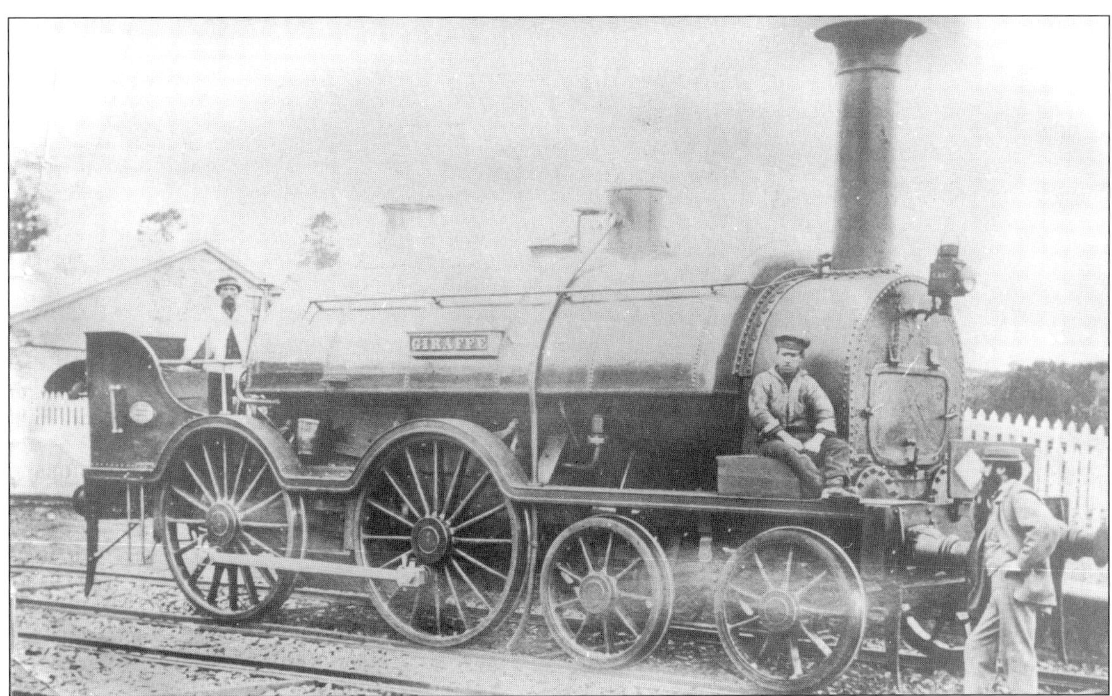

Now we turn to a small selection of Broad Gauge engines and start with South Devon Railway 'Hawk' class 4-4-0ST 'GIRAFFE'. The crew pose for the photographer together with a non-railway person. When the Cornwall Railway opened in 1859 these engines of the 'Hawk' class regularly worked passenger trains into the Duchy. This photo appears to have been taken at Par as the dual gauge Goods shed for exchanging traffic can be seen behind and to the left of the engine. The Cornwall Minerals Railway line from Bugle was Standard Gauge so facilities were provided to permit the exchange of traffic. This engine which was built in June 1859 became GWR 2112 and ran until October 1877.

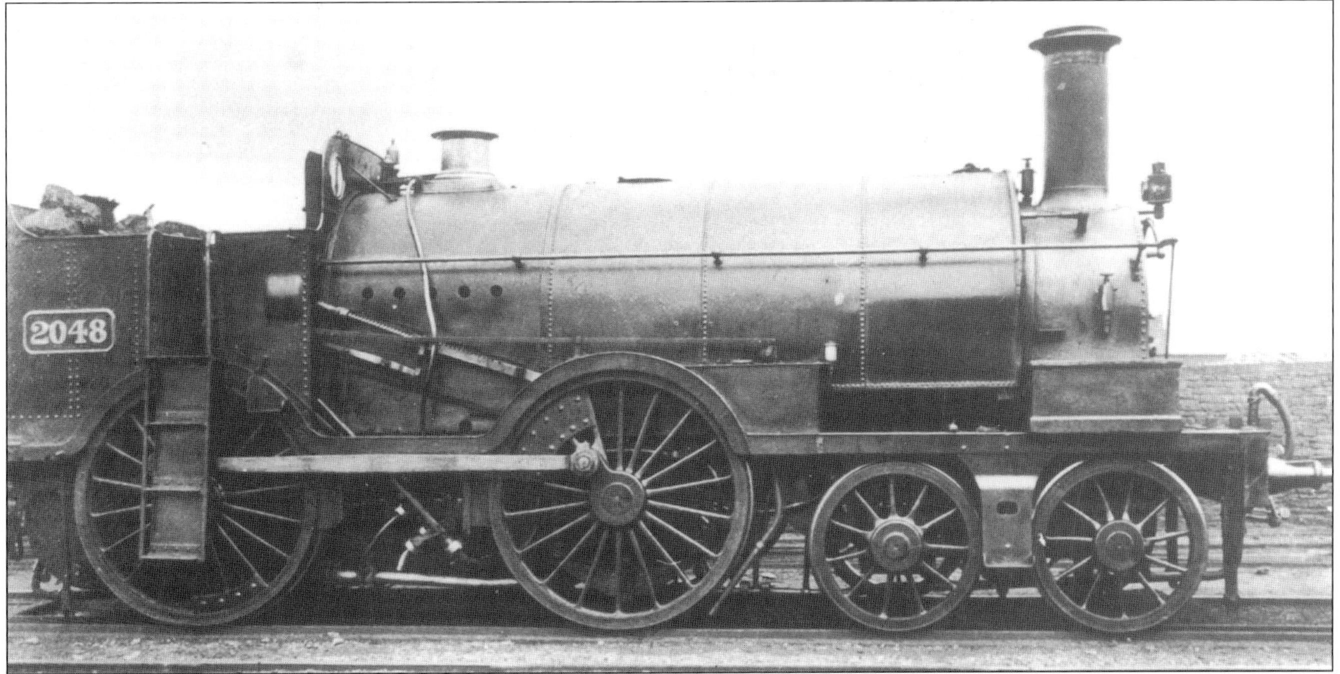

This 4-4-0ST was built in November 1872 for the Bristol & Exeter Railway and became GWR property in 1876. Numbered 2048 it is standing in the shed yard at Carn Brea. This passenger tank engine was withdrawn in May 1892 when the Broad Gauge was abolished.

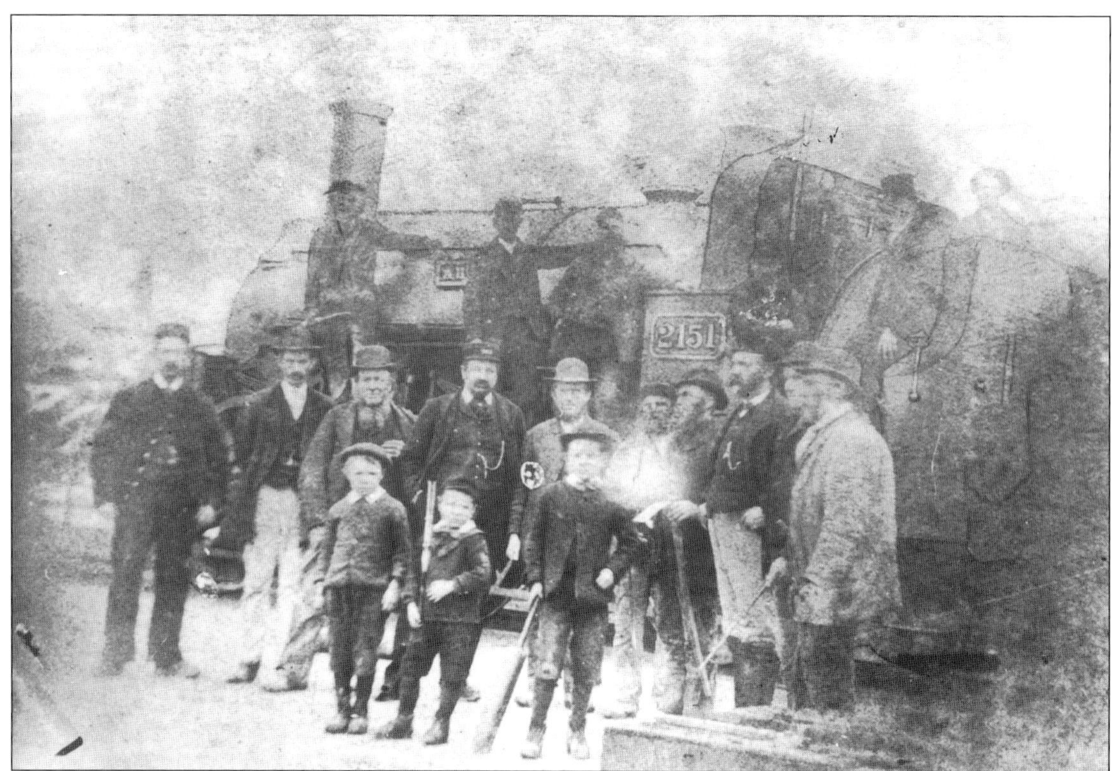

We end the Broad Gauge section with a photo which is by no means perfect but is included because of its rarity. It came from a private collection and depicts ex South Devon Railway 0-6-0ST 2151 'ARGO'. It must have been taken on either the 19 or 20 May 1892 as it is stated to be the last Broad Gauge engine at Drinnick Mill. On the left is Stationmaster Michael Harris who later moved to Burngullow. To his right is Eric Francis Lillicrap who was the grandfather of the person from whom I obtained the photo. On his right is Tom Bullen who was foreman carpenter at Drinnick clay works. Two more to the right is another of the family, Richard Lillicrap. On the far right is Ganger Hendry. A clay kiln with its stack can be seen dimly in the left background. This engine lasted from October 1863 until May 1892. The shot was taken by a photographer from St Agnes. G.Bellina.

Now we move to a selection of views of Steam Rail Motors in Cornwall and start with a shot of two of the units, one of which appears to be 35. The train has arrived at Saltash on a working from either Plympton or Millbay. This was taken before December 1922 when the unit was withdrawn for conversion to an Auto trailer.

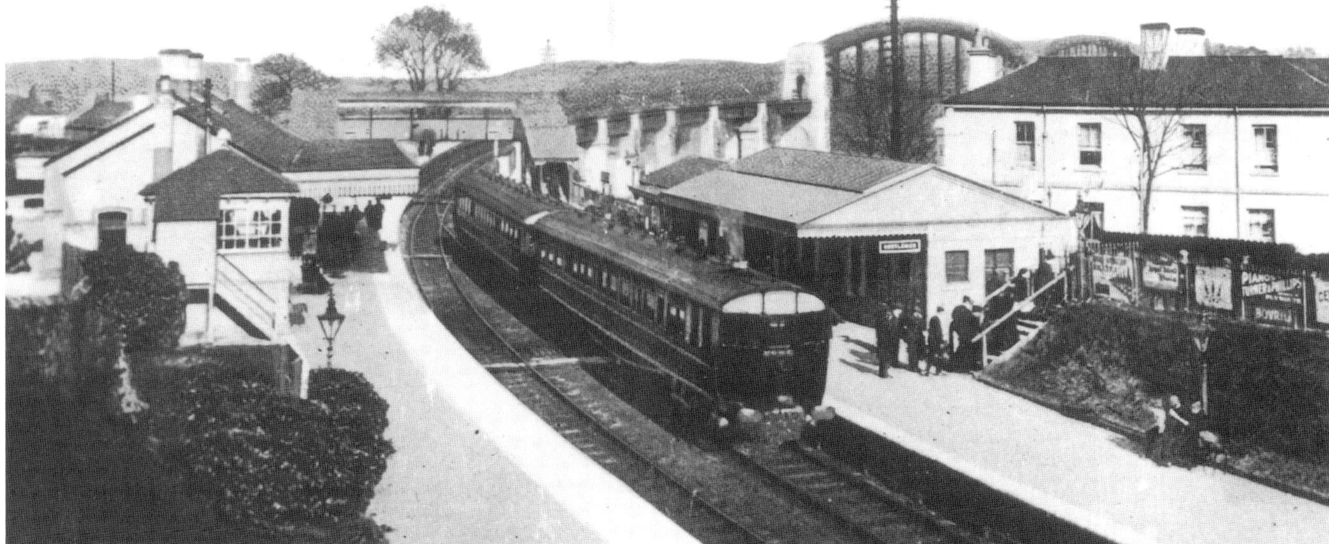

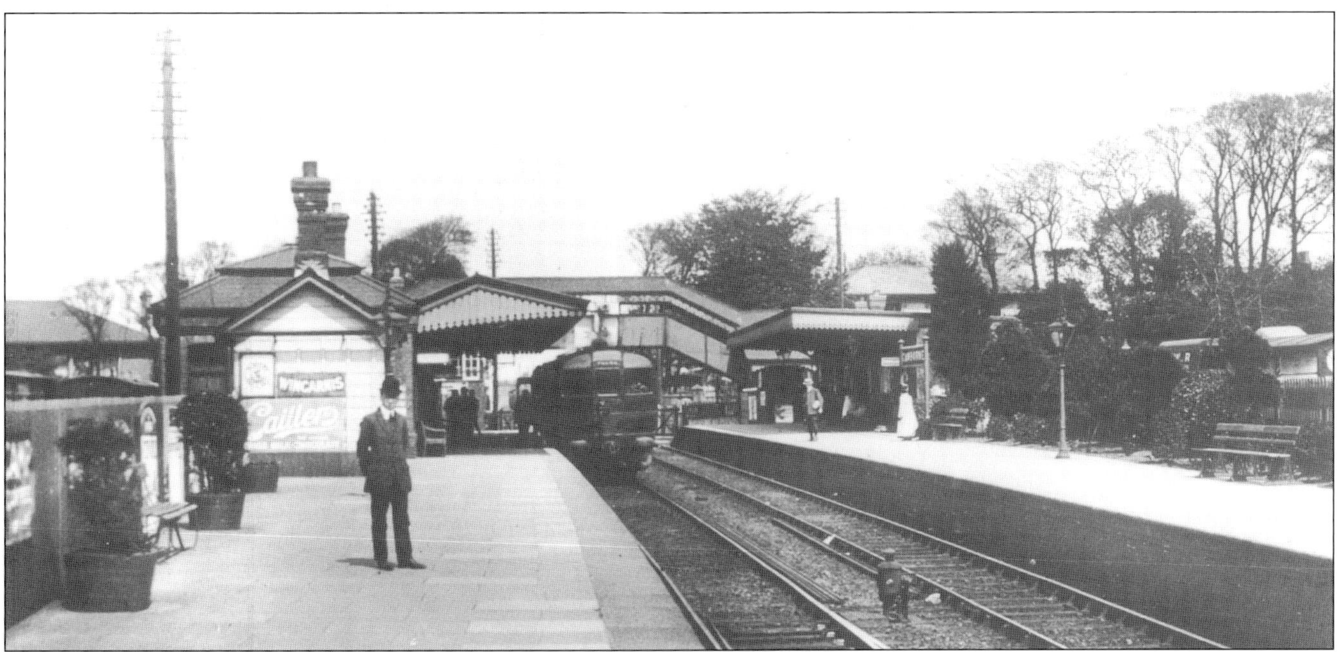

In this shot unit No.72 is stopped at Camborne with an up service probably soon after it entered service in July 1906.

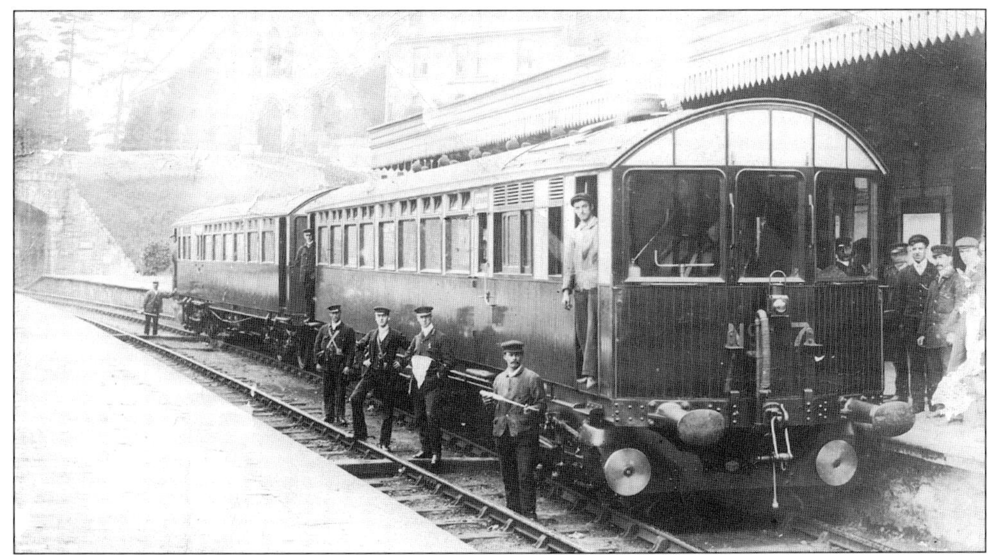

The staff are obviously proud of the presumably new pair of these units waiting at Saltash to return to Millbay. The leading unit No.7 entered service in May 1904 so the photo probably dates from then.

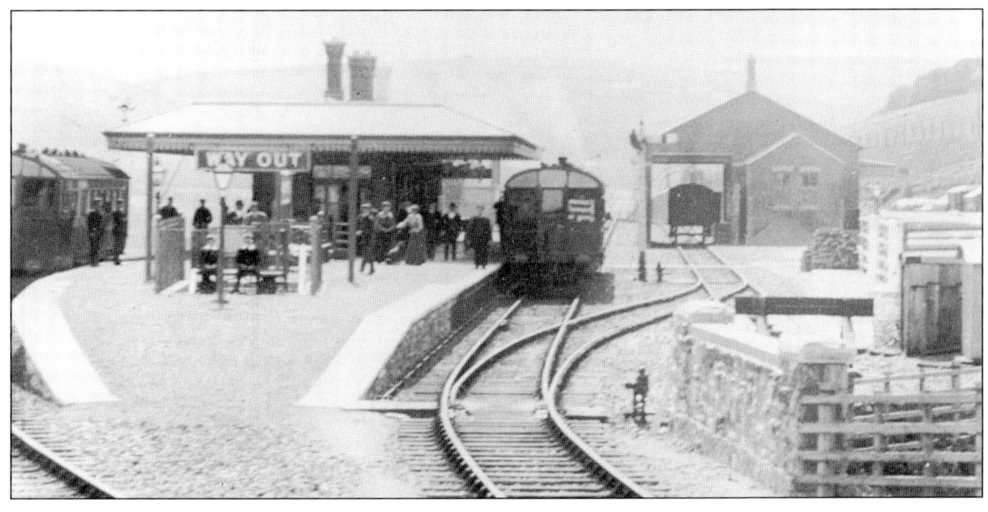

This view of Perranporth from the early 1900s contains two of the units. On the extreme left an earlier design is running in on a train to Newquay whilst a later design, from that resort to Truro, is waiting at the platform. The Goods shed is prominent.

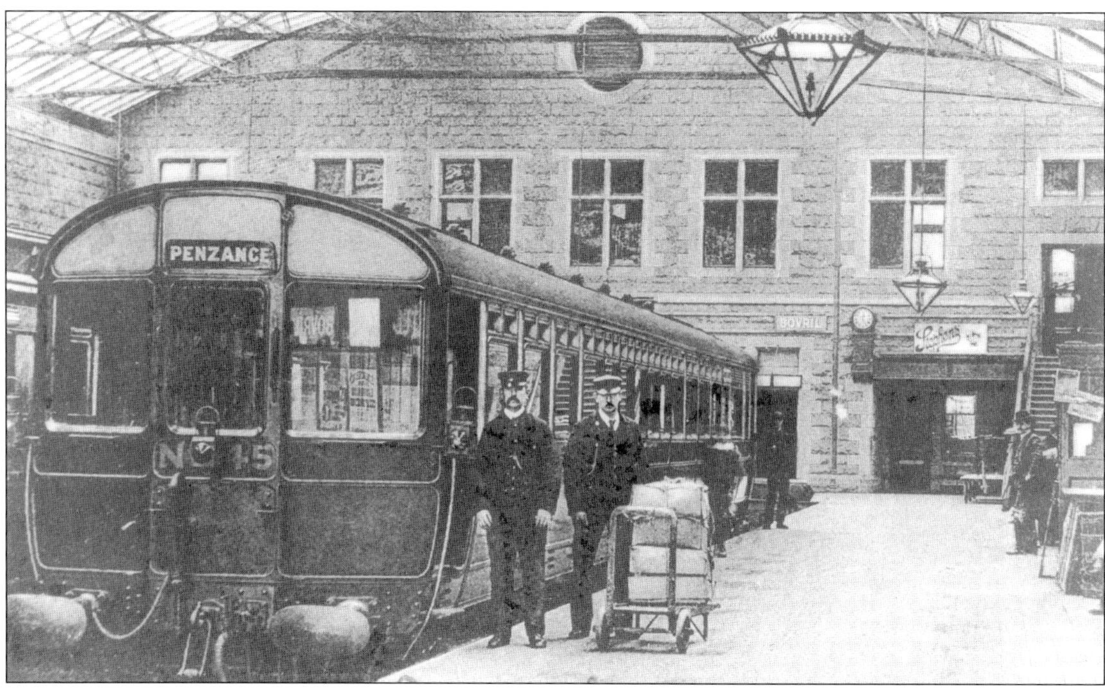

Unless it berthed in sidings, this is as far west as one of these units could have reached. No.45 is at the buffers at Penzance with some staff posing for the camera. Boxes of produce await loading into the unit at 12.25pm in the early 1900s.

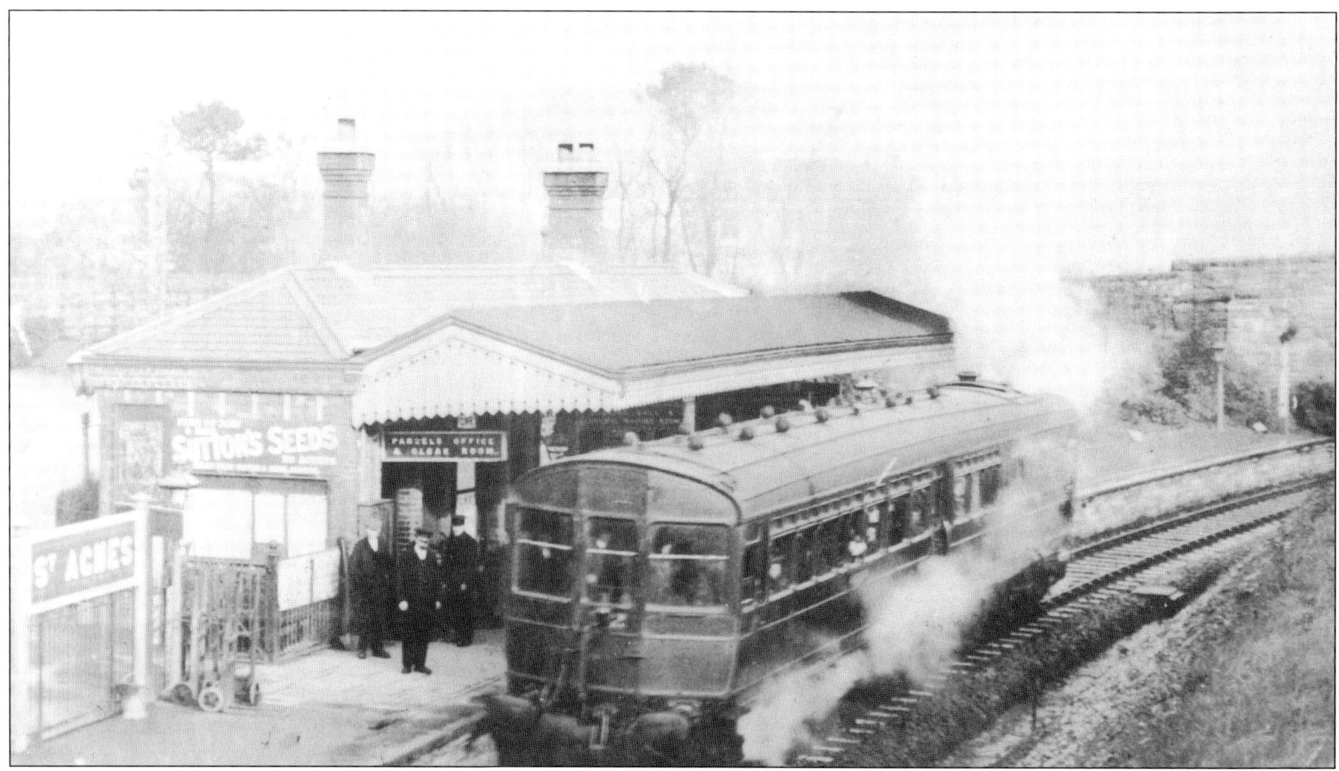

This scene from early 1920s, before 1926, has what appears to be No.92 stopped at St Agnes. As the crew are in the cab nearest to the camera the unit is heading for Truro.

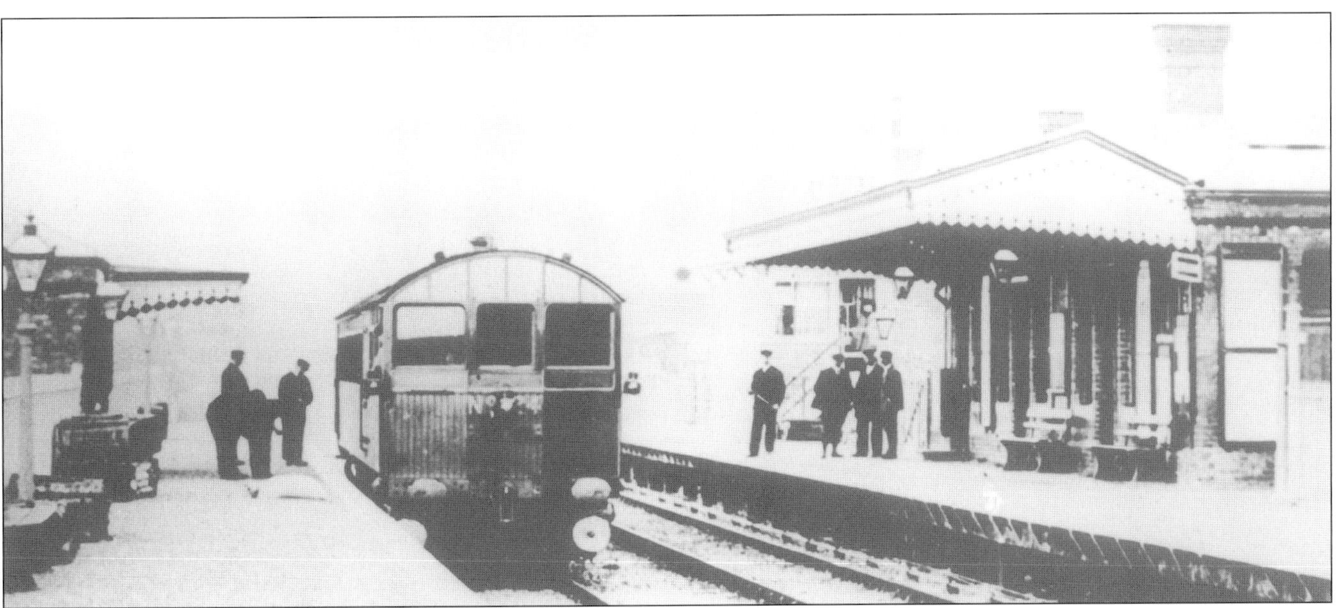

These units appear to have worked regularly on the line from Chacewater to Newquay. Staff stand around on both platforms as No.24 waits at Shepherds to proceed to Newquay.

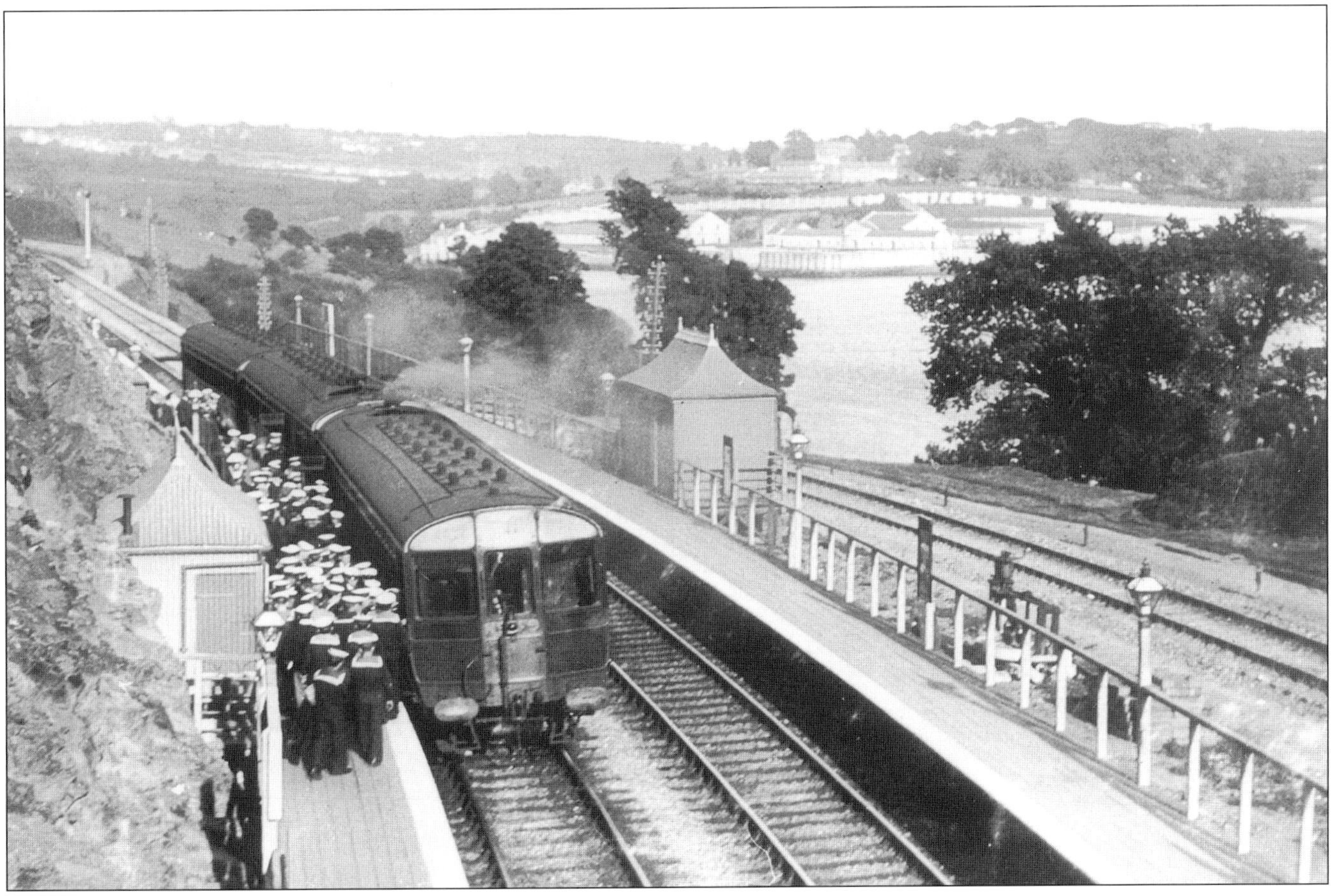

We end this section with a very interesting view of two units with a carriage in between them. It is stopped at the very rarely photographed halt at Defiance, west of Saltash, to pick up a large contingent of sailors, probably from the training establishment from which the halt took its name. They are probably bound for Devonport or Plymouth Millbay to have a Saturday night out. A remnant of the pre 1908 route can be seen behind the down platform.

19

DIESEL LOCOMOTIVES

From 1958 examples of Diesel Hydraulics started to work trains into Cornwall. As the Hydraulics were withdrawn they were replaced by Diesel Electric locos of various types. Examples of most of the types that have worked in Cornwall are depicted including some unusual modern visitors.

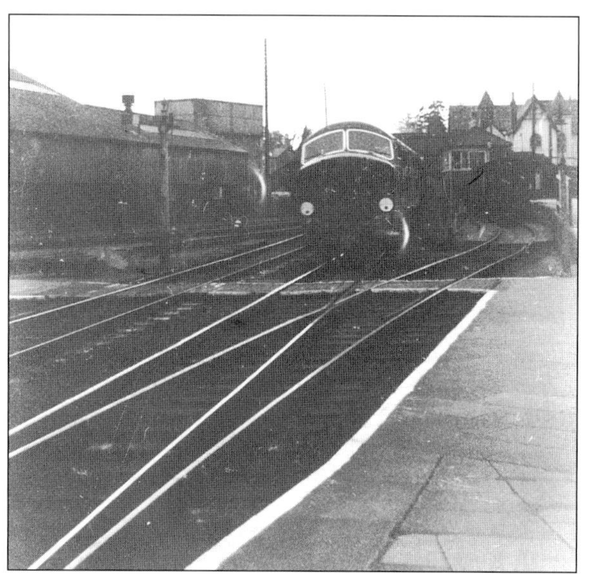

The first type of main line diesel hydraulics to appear in Cornwall were locally called the 'North British Warships'. There were only five in the class and all worked from Laira, with some latterly being sub-shedded at St Blazey. Though by no means photographically perfect this shot was taken by myself as D600 'ACTIVE' approached St Austell at 60mph with the return working of its first test run to Penzance on 21 April 1958. The time was 8.25pm so it was becoming dusky. I had not seen the Down working during the day as I had been at work. Maurice Dart.

The next type to appear was the second class of 'Warship' which we locally referred to as 'Maybachs' as the first and last batches of this group were fitted with engines of that name. One member, D830, was fitted with a Paxman engine and D833 to D865 had Man engines. At times they were used in pairs on trains between Penzance and Paddington. The Down 'Royal Duchy' is entering Liskeard on 7 September 1963 headed by D858 'VALOROUS' leading D848 'SULTAN'. Railway Correspondence & Travel Society.

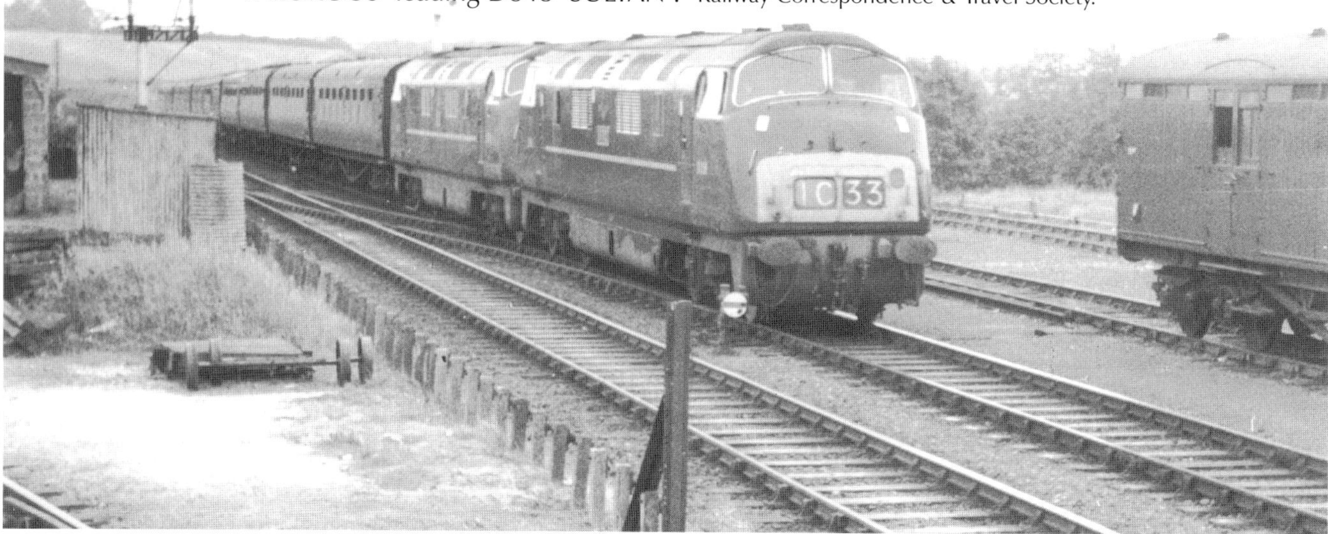

We now see a few examples of the less well liked and far less reliable D6300s. I had travelled down from Plymouth on this train from Manchester London Road. It had been taken over at North Road by D6304 leading and working in multiple with D6301. D6304 failed near Lostwithiel and D6301 struggled on to Par. It is at Par on 30 September 1959 whilst 'Hall' class 6931'ALBOROUGH HALL' was crossing over to remove the Hydraulics from the train. Maurice Dart.

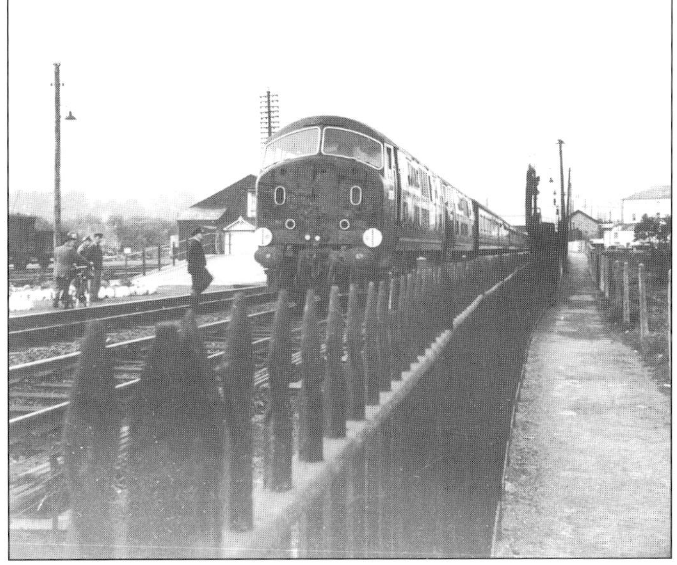

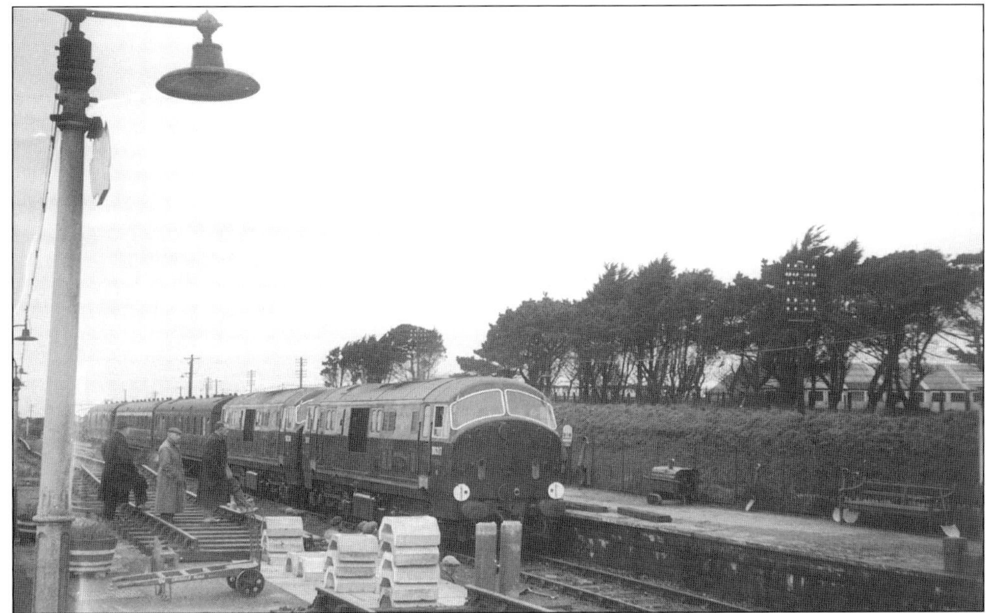

Another pair, D6317 leading D6316 pass slowly through Gwinear Road with a Sunday up train on an unknown date when the down main line was being relaid.

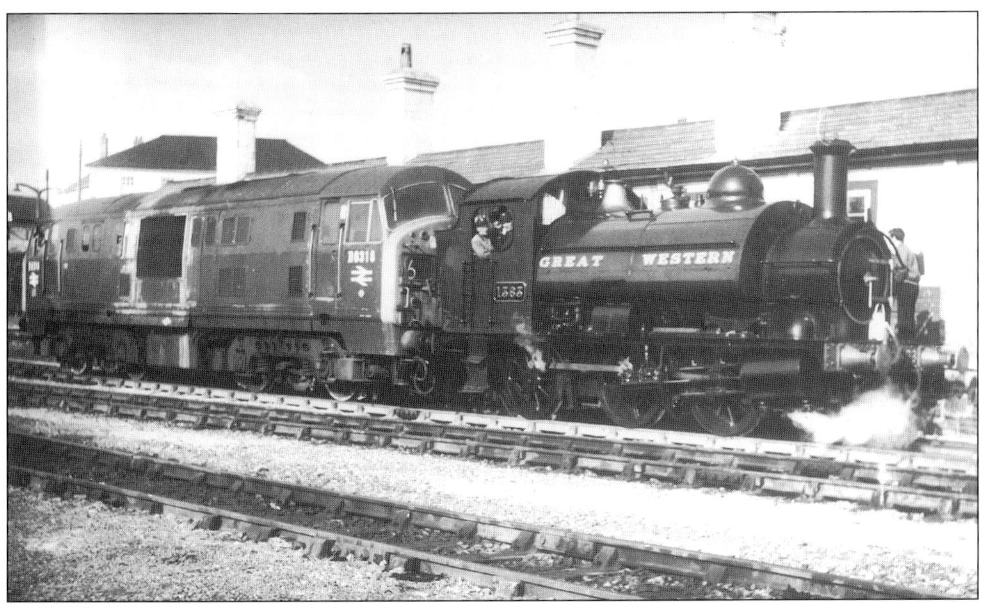

This interesting shot has D6318 leading 1361 class 0-6-0ST 1363 halted at Par on the way to return the saddle tank to the Great Western Society at Bodmin General on 1 May 1971. 1363 had participated in an 'Open Day' at St Blazey depot. Martin Orme is on the footplate of the saddle tank. The long building on the platform housed the station buffet.

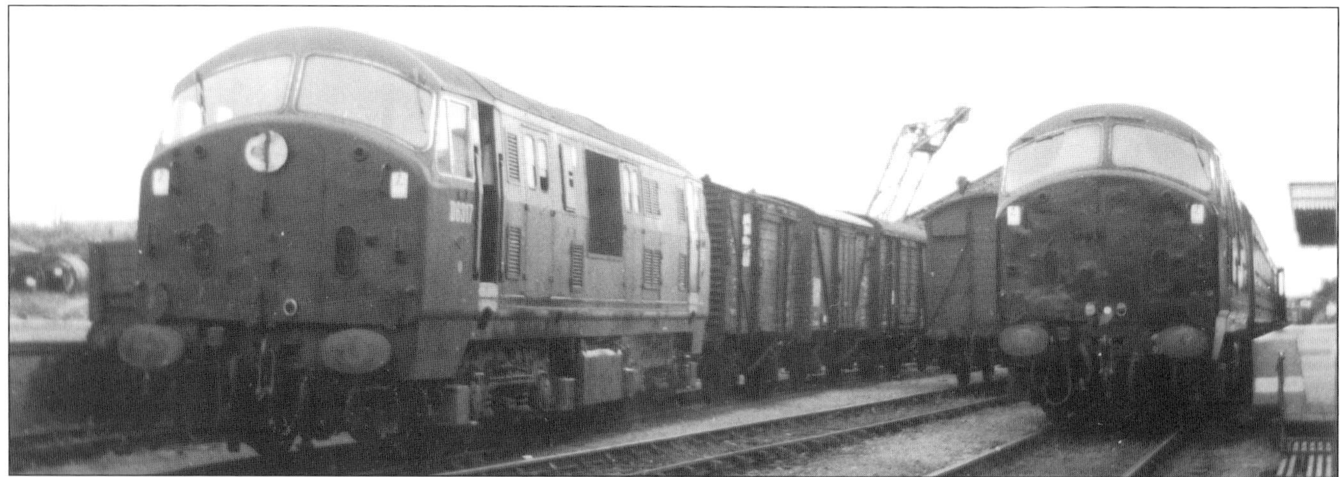

This is a busy scene at Helston on 24 July 1962. D6317 has marshalled a goods train and awaits departure later, whilst D6311 waits at the platform with a passenger train for Gwinear Road.   David Hall, Butterley Archives.

We end this batch of diesel hydraulics with a shot of one of the later 'Western' class locomotives. These were superb locos with a distinctive design. D1001 'WESTERN PATHFINDER' is ready to depart from Falmouth with a train of scrap. metal in 1967. The guard is walking back to board his van at the rear. The sole remaining platform still boasts its curved arch roof.

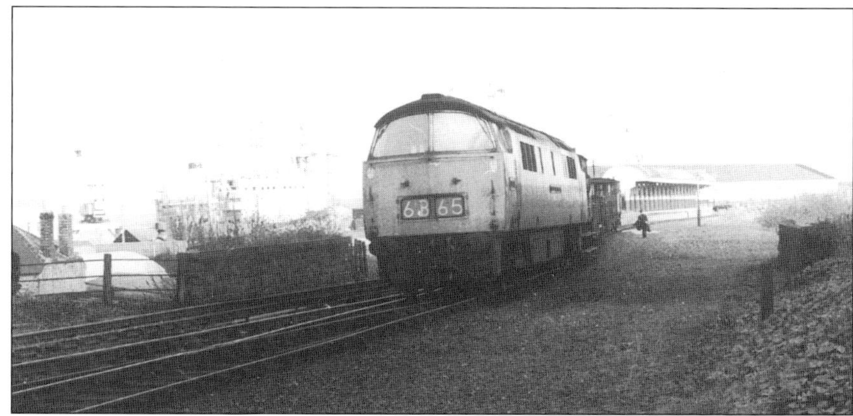

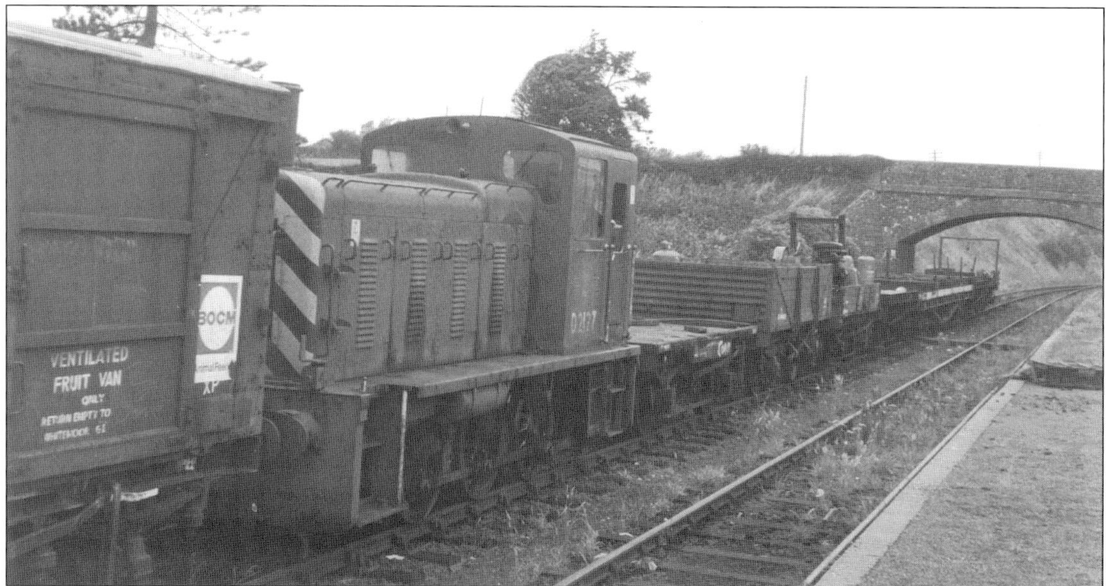

Next we see a small selection of standard BR diesel shunters in the county. Very few members of the 03 class operated in Cornwall but a couple worked from St Blazey and Wadebridge sheds for a short spell. This most unusual shot has D2127 at Tresmeer on the North Cornwall line with a 'track lifting' train in 1967. The van on the left partially in the photo is 'ventilated fruit van, and also bears emblems for carrying animal feed but was obviously being used in a different capacity in this train. This engine was transferred to St Blazey in August 1964 and moved back to Laira in May 1967.   The Transport Treasury.

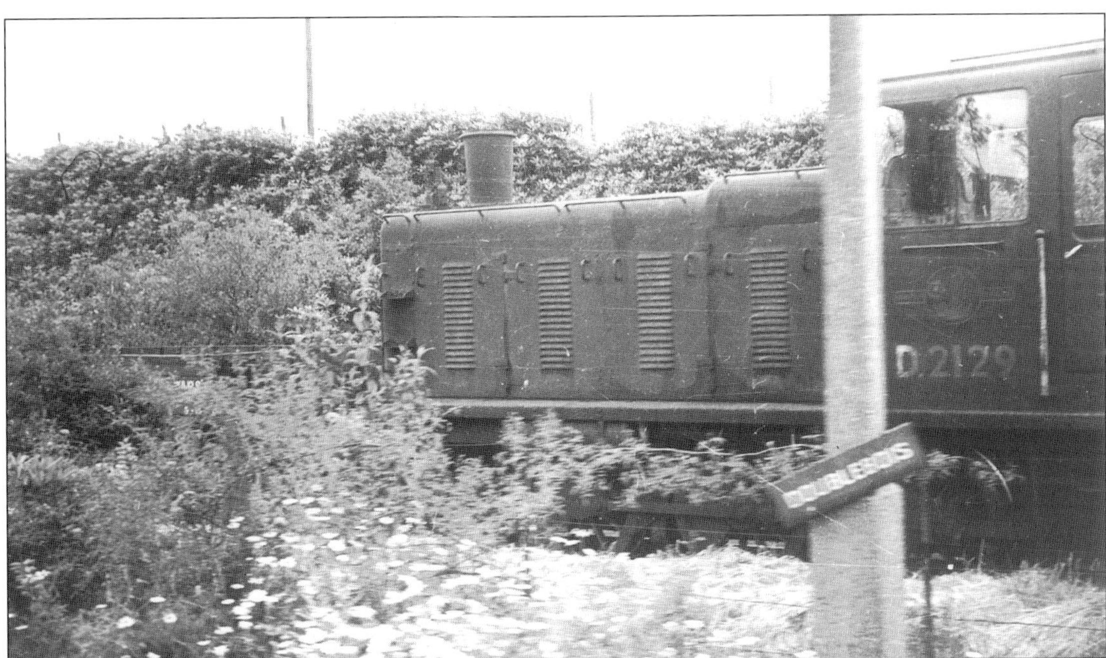

This shot of D2129 at Doublebois was taken from a passing down train. During the period that this engine was shedded at St Blazey it was out-stationed at Doublebois for a spell during July 1963 for duties in the Permanent Way yard on the Down side of the line at the east end of the station. When not in use it was left in the Down loop in this very un-photographable position. Mike Daly.

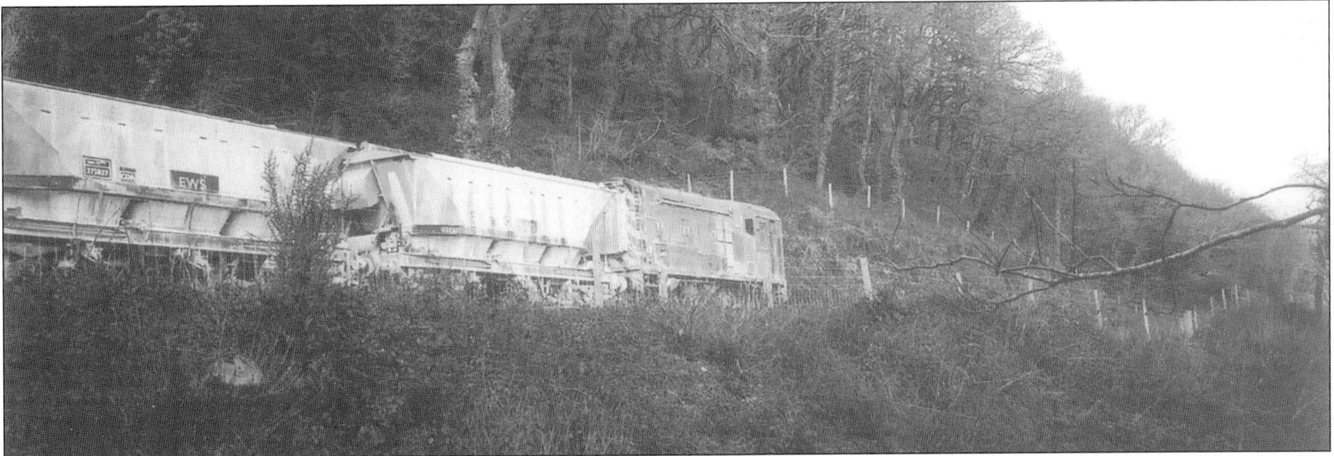

Now we move on to look at a small selection of the standard 350HP class 08 shunters in Cornwall. Quite a number of this type have operated from St Blazey over the years and English China Clays bought two representatives from BR after they had been withdrawn from service. Numerous photos have been taken of both of those at their normal places of work but this shot is a great rarity. On 10 March 2005 a train of CDA wagons loaded with china clay was descending the incline from Luxulyan to St Blazey. As the train crossed 'Clay Dry' (Prideaux) viaduct the track 'spread' and this caused caused several of the wagons to become derailed. These damaged the superstructure of the viaduct with one wagon hanging over the side towards the river. The class 66 was at the lower end of the train and eight wagons at the rear remained on the track. To assist in the recovery operation ex 08398, owned by Imerys Minerals Ltd, numbered P402D and named 'ANNABEL', was specially authorised to work over Network Rail track. It normally works at Rocks Dryers, adjacent to Goonbarrow Junction on the Par to Newquay line but on 10 March 2005 it made two trips to the scene of the derailment, returning up the bank with four loaded CDA wagons in tow. This photo, which I took from a nearby footpath, shows the engine at the top end of the rake of CDA wagons ready to take four of them back to Goonbarrow Junction. Maurice Dart.

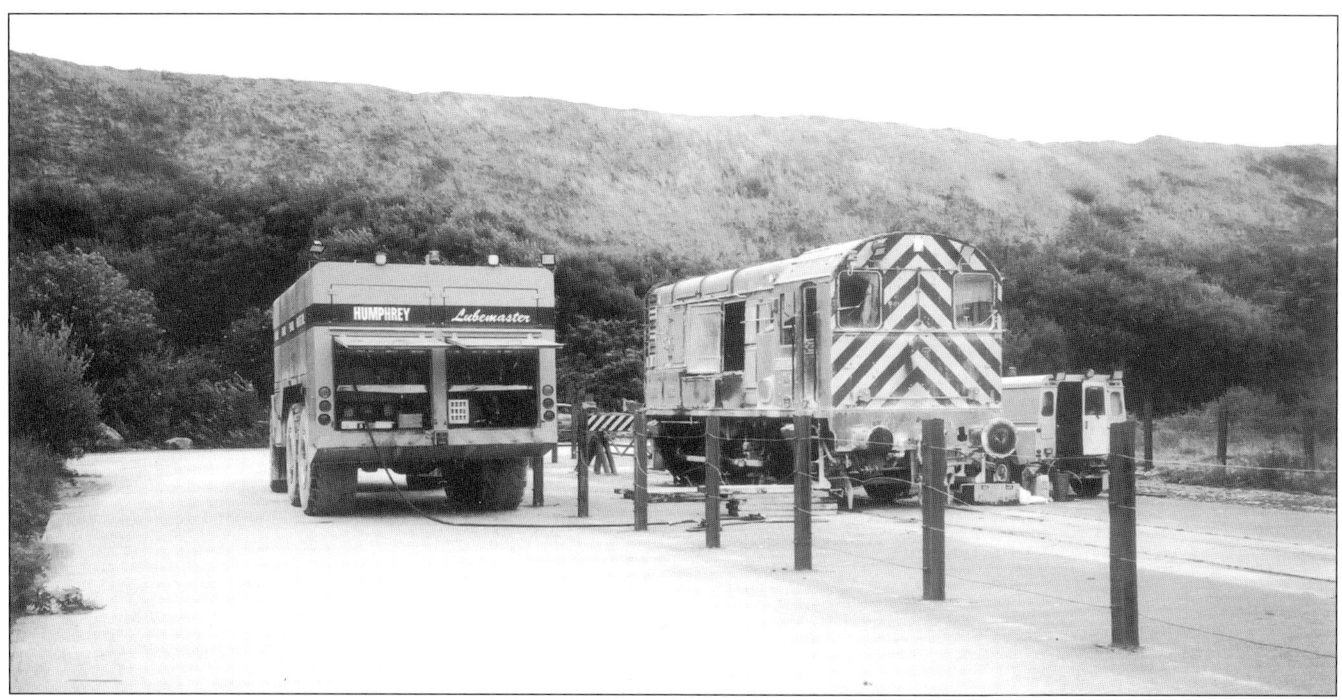

This is another look at 'ANNABEL', taken this time at the back end of the Imerys site at Rocks Dryers on 26 August 2005. An inspection pit was situated at this end on the 'inside' line to the right of the van and when not in use the engine was usually left in that area. On this date the drying plant was temporarily closed down and 'ANNABEL' was most unusually positioned on the 'outside' line where it is receiving some maintenance and being refuelled. The bank in the background is a grassed-over clay works sand tip. Maurice Dart.

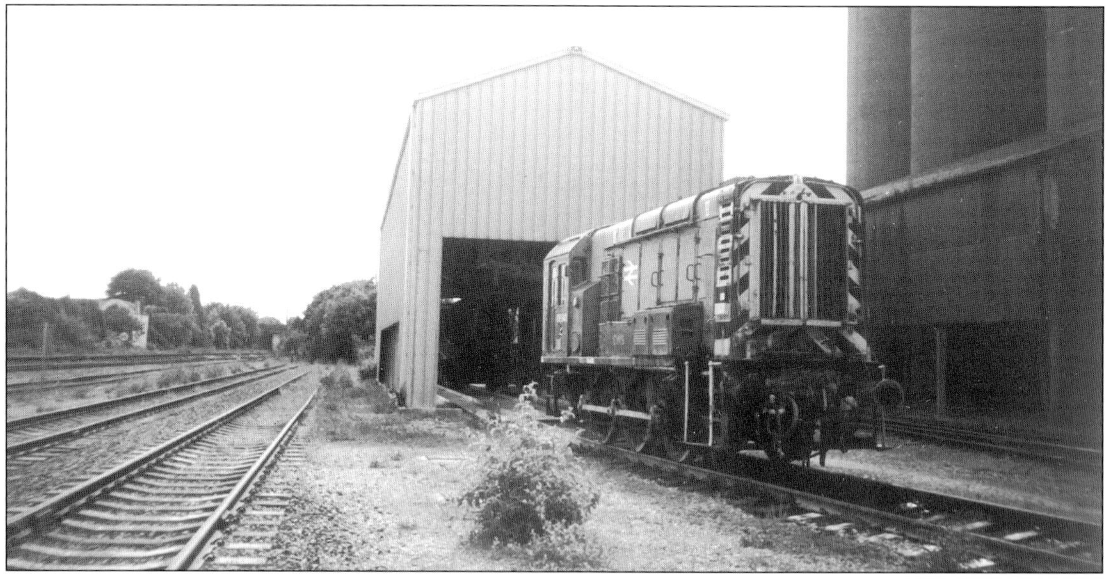

The other member of this class owned by Imerys Minerals, ex 08320 now numbered P400D and named 'SUSAN', works at Blackpool sidings, Burngullow, one mile west of St Austell. When it required some maintenance in the past, a RollsRoyce/Sentinel diesel named 'DENISE' has been 'brought down around the corner' from nearby Crugwallins siding to work at Blackpool for a short period. However in 2001, 08941 was hired from EWS St Blazey and is seen at Blackpool sidings on 10 June of that year. Having worked at Fowey docks earlier in the year, later that year Imerys hired it again, this time to work at Rocks Dryers when 'ANNABEL' was under repair. Maurice Dart.

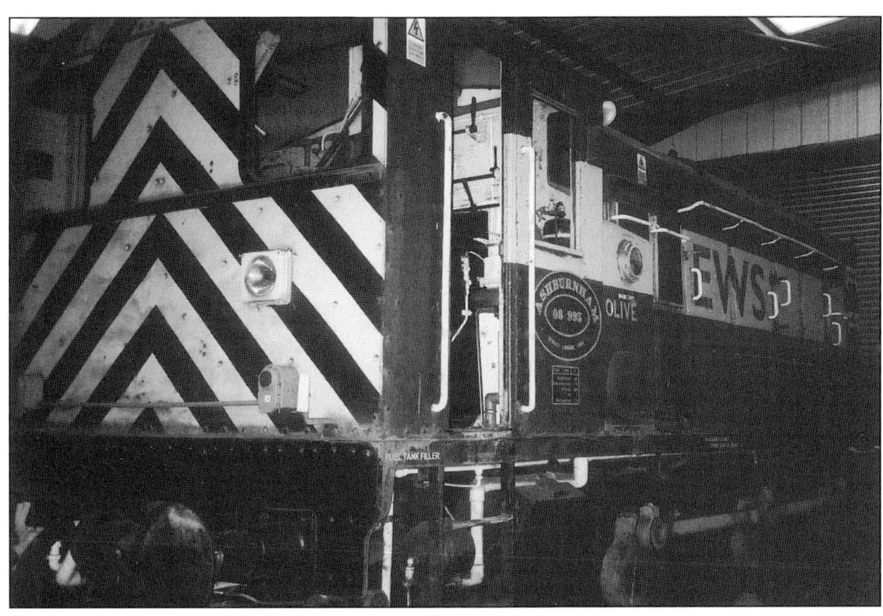

We end this section of photos of shunters with a view of 08993 inside the 'Elephant House' as the repair shop is known at St Blazey depot on 17 March 2006. Work was carried out to prepare the loco for a move to Doncaster for an overhaul. It carries a combined name and number plate with the name 'ASHBURNAM'. This dates from the period when its cab roof was 'cut down' to permit it to work over the route of the Burry Port & Gwendreath Valley Railway, from Kidwelly to Cwm Mawr. The loco also carries a painted-on name 'OLIVE'. When it arrived from Canton depot, Cardiff it was named 'CLIVE' but St Blazey subtly altered the name. This engine had previously been numbered 08592. Maurice Dart.

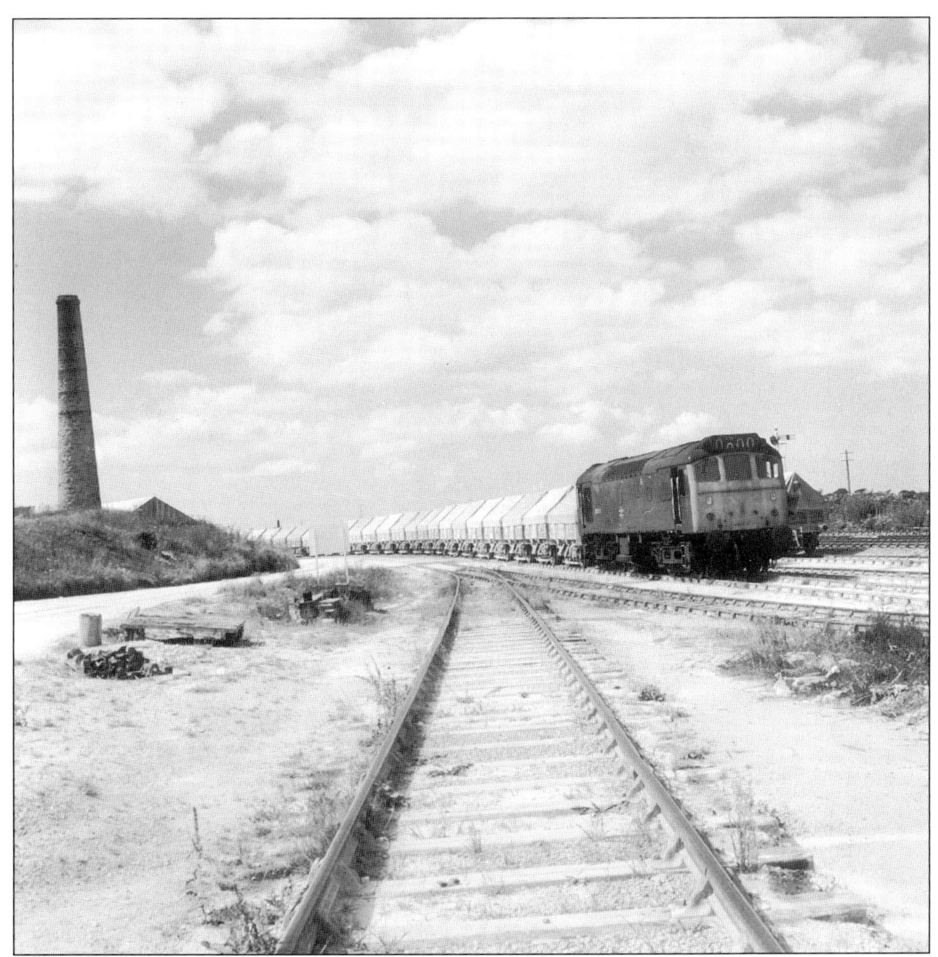

Now we look at photos of larger diesel electric locos which worked on the main lines following the withdrawal of the diesel hydraulics. This scene at Goonbarrow Junction dated 5 August 1976 has class 25 25216 bringing a train of loaded 'Clay Hoods' out of Wheal Henry siding for Fowey. The wagons had been loaded at Rocks Dryers which are behind the camera. Class 25s worked trains over the mineral branch lines following the withdrawal of the 'Warship' and 'Western' diesels and at times could be found working passenger trains on the main line. Maurice Dart.

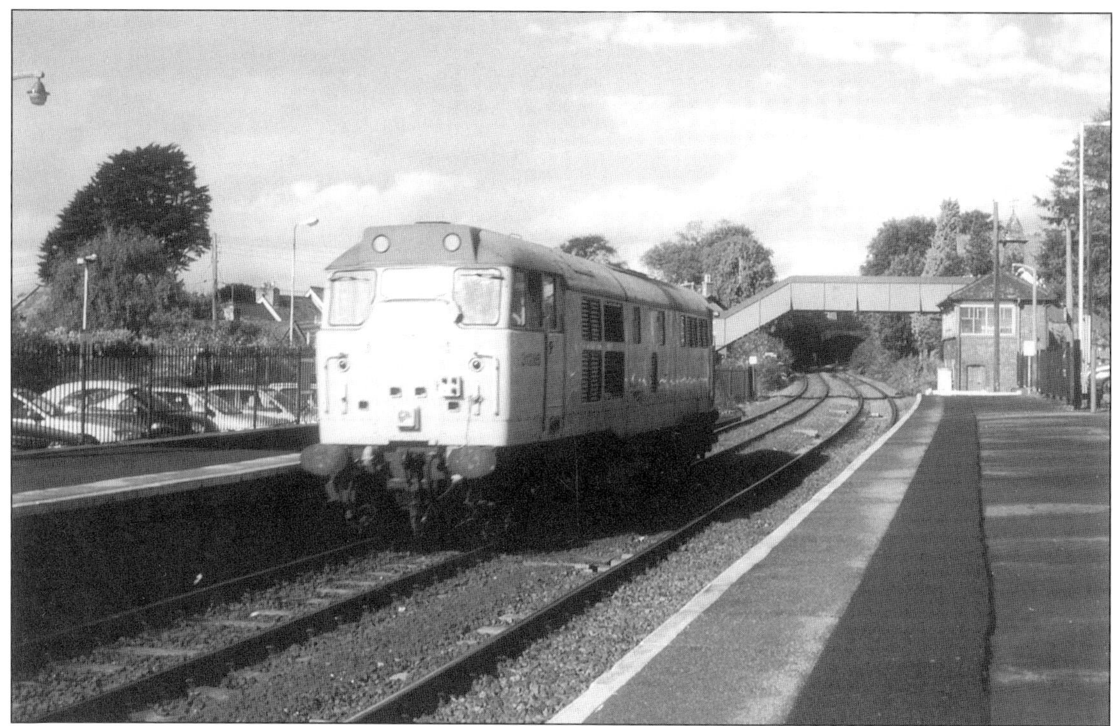

Class 31s had rarely appeared in Cornwall until recently when they commenced working 'Route Learning' specials. 31285 passes down through St Austell on one of those runs to Penzance for FM Rail at 09.50 on 20 September 2005. The long closed signal box is on the right. The footbridge originally spanned some tracks at St Blazey to provide access to the station platforms. Maurice Dart.

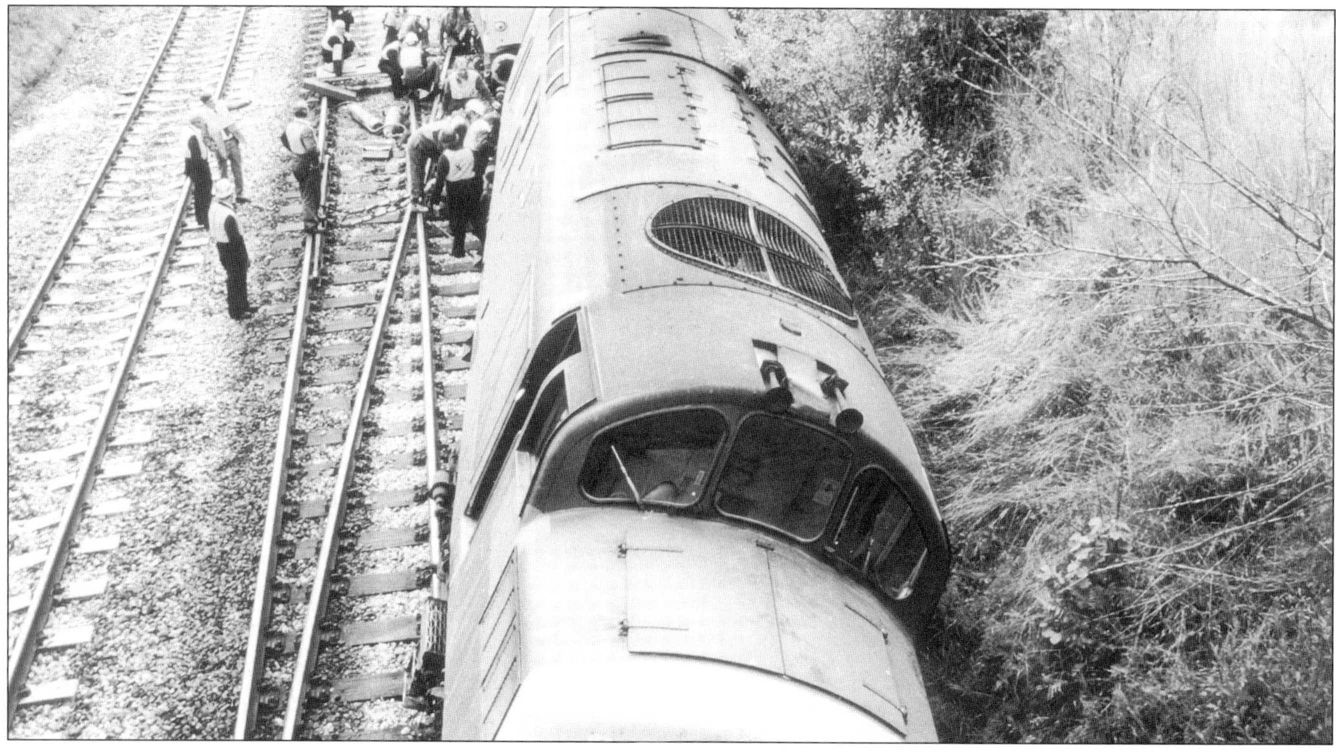

Class 37s replaced the class 25s on work over the mineral lines. On 7 September 1984 a pair of these, 37207 'WILLIAM COOKWORTHY' and 37307 were routed into the up loop east of Lostwithiel. For some reason the train ran past a signal set at Danger and 37307 became derailed at the exit points. It occurred in a very awkward spot to record photographically! Maurice Dart.

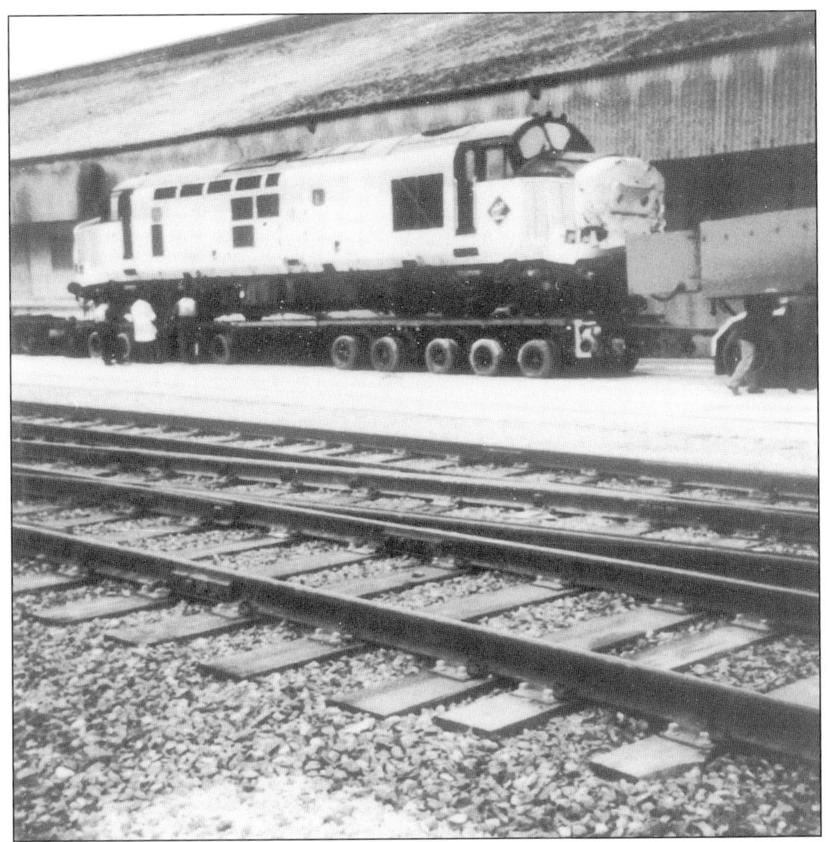

On 3 December 1993 37411 was shunting empty china clay wagons at Blackpool sidings, Burngullow and to facilitate a movement proceeded a short distance beyond the 'Limit of shunt' sign. At the same time a heavy loaded china clay train of air-braked wagons hauled by 37669 came down the branch line from Parkandillack. The driver applied the brakes in good time but it was raining very hard and the weight of the train caused the engine to slide down the 1 in 50 gradient. As it rounded the curve it collided with 37411 just below the over-line bridge. Whilst an enquiry into the cause of the accident took place the two locos remained at Blackpool sidings. Here we see 37411 ready to leave Blackpool for repair on a low-loader on 6 March 1994. Graham Griggs.

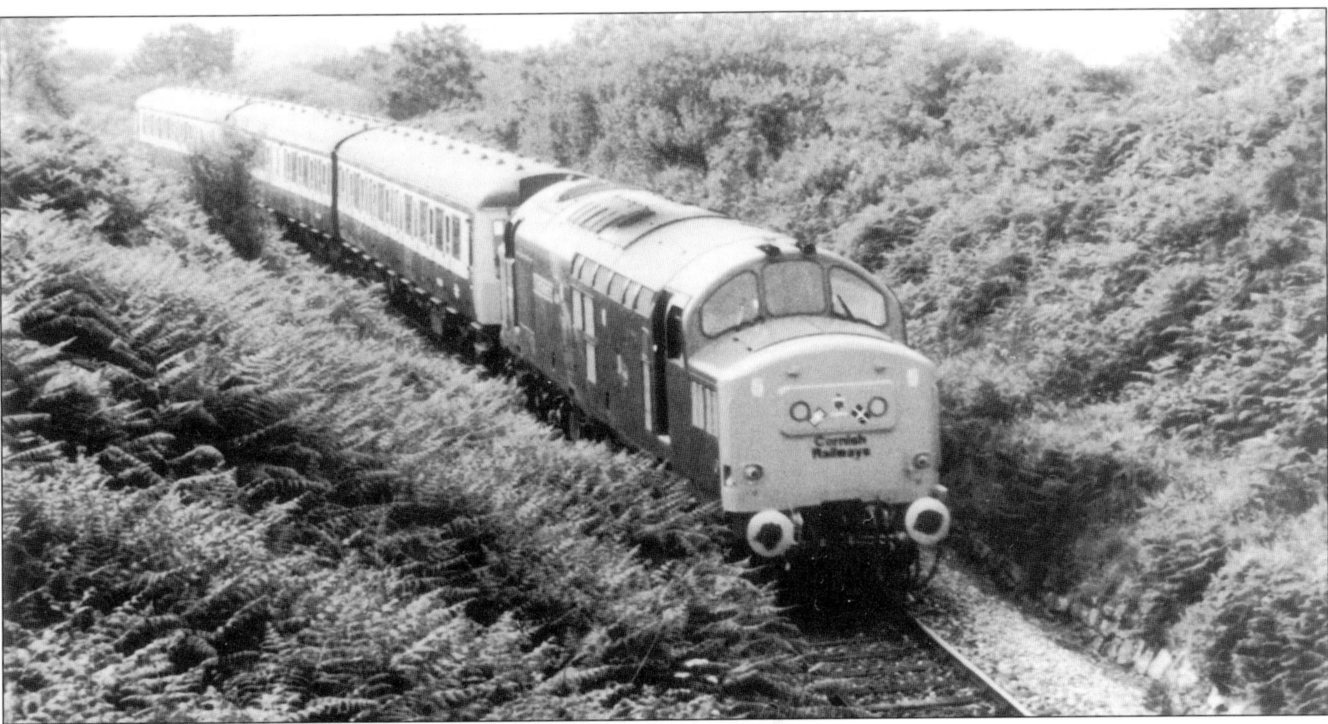

Diesel Multiple Units used on main line stopping trains and for branch line services failed at times especially when working on the steeply graded line between Par and Newquay. In July 1984 a three car DMU failed and was rescued by 37207 'WILLIAM COOKWORHTY'. It is seen passing Criggon, between Roche and Bugle, returning from Newquay. The loco is carrying the emblems and inscription of short lived but very successful 'Cornish Railways'. These were painted on to the loco by then local artist and railway guard, Vic Millington. This engine is awaiting return to traffic on the Plym Valley Railway, Charlie Saundercock.

Following the withdrawal of 'Warship' and 'Western' class Hydraulics, Class 47 locos became commonplace in the county. Latterly they were used on Postal trains (TPOs) and some of these stabled overnight and at weekends at St Blazey. Late afternoon on 10 April 2003, empty TPO stock bound for Plymouth comes around the curve from St Blazey to Par hauled by 47782. Maurice Dart.

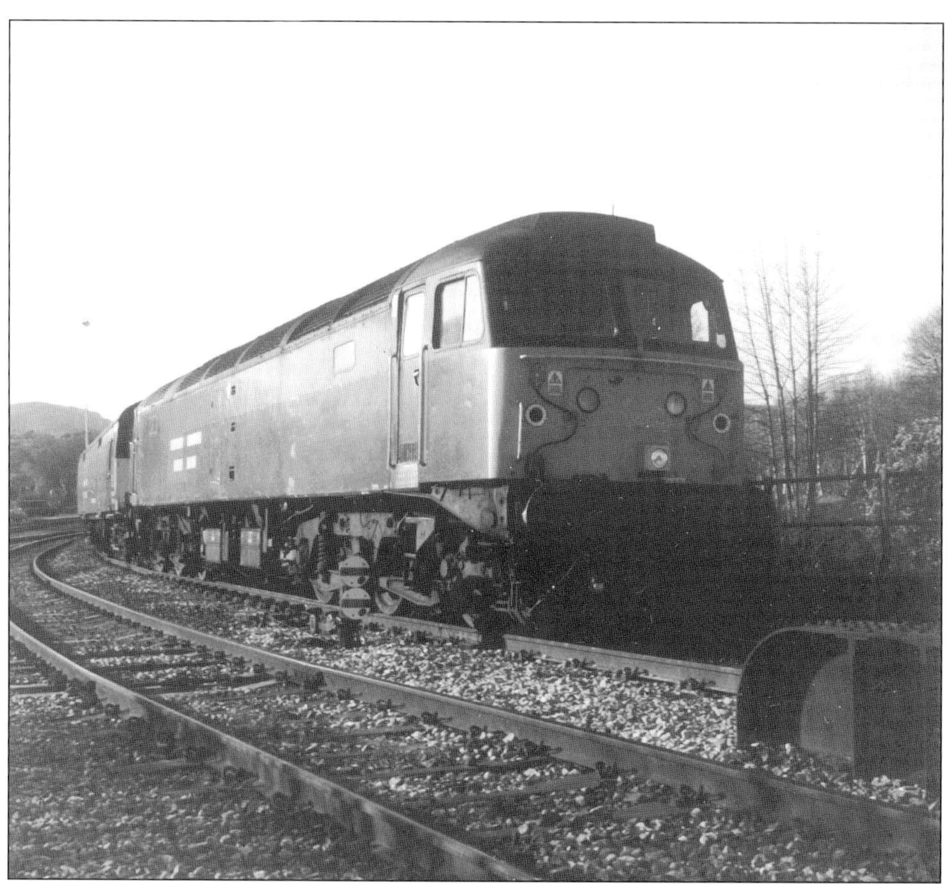

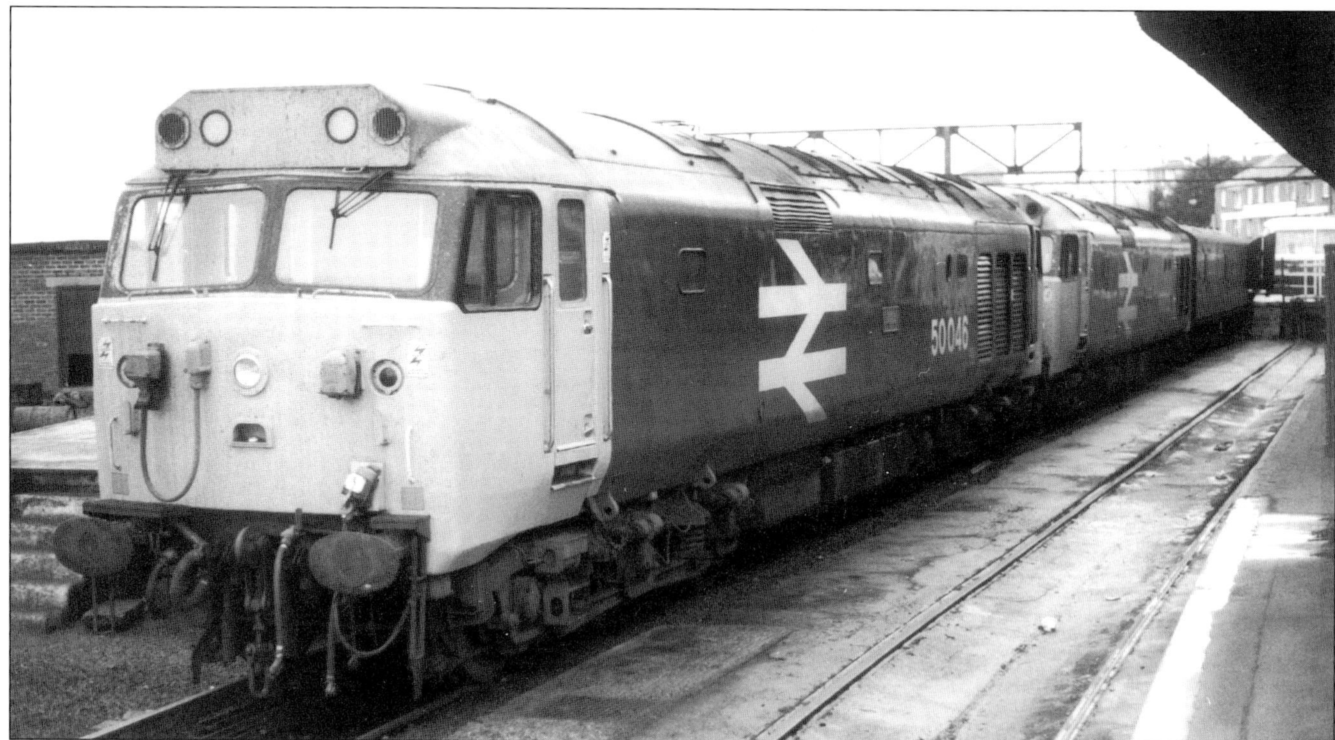

Following the withdrawal of 'Western' class locos, class 50s were transferred from the London Midland Region to the Western Region and worked the main express services. For a while a 'Stabling Point' at Penzance station was used to berth locos between duties. This is where 50046 'AJAX' and 50005 'COLLINGWOOD' are seen on a damp murky 12 July 1984.

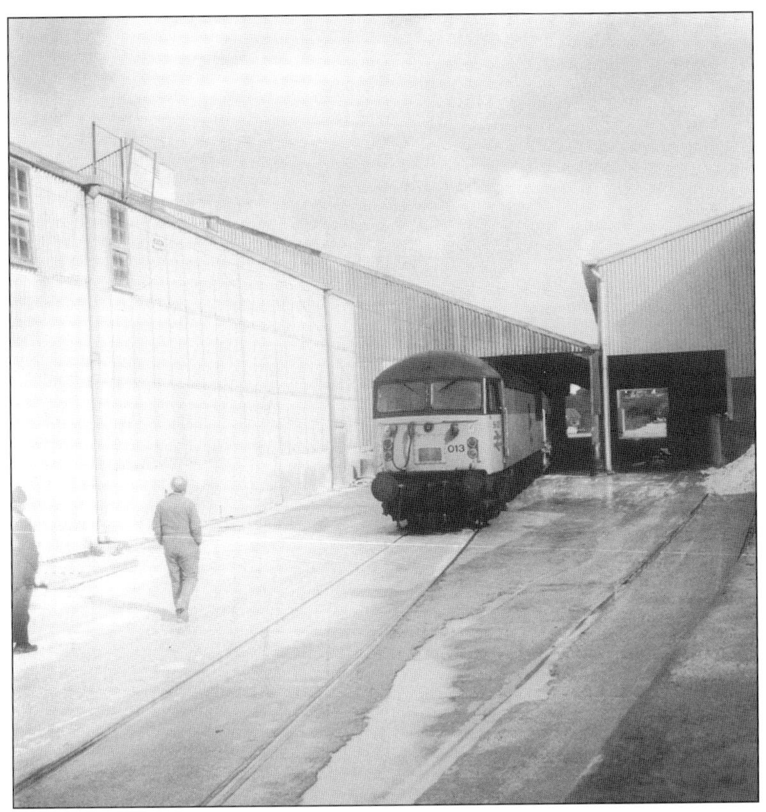

Class 56s have visited the county infrequently but trials were arranged for 27 February 1990 to assess the suitability of the class to work clay trains on the mineral lines. The locos journey down was eventful as 47815 which was working the 'Down Sleeper' failed near Lostwithiel. The class 56 propelled the stricken train to Lostwithiel where it ran around, went on in front of 47815 and hauled the train to Penzance. Following that incident it returned to St Blazey for fuel and proceeded to work the trials. It was a day of incessant heavy rain and most enthusiasts attempting to record it became well and truly 'soaked to the skin'. Luckily whilst 56013 was under the loading area at Trelavour siding, near Parkandillack, the sun broke through for about five minutes and I obtained this shot of the rare visitor as clearances were being checked. One could almost have 'paddled' in the siding on the right following the deluge, which commenced again before the loco reached Drinnick Mill on its return run. Maurice Dart.

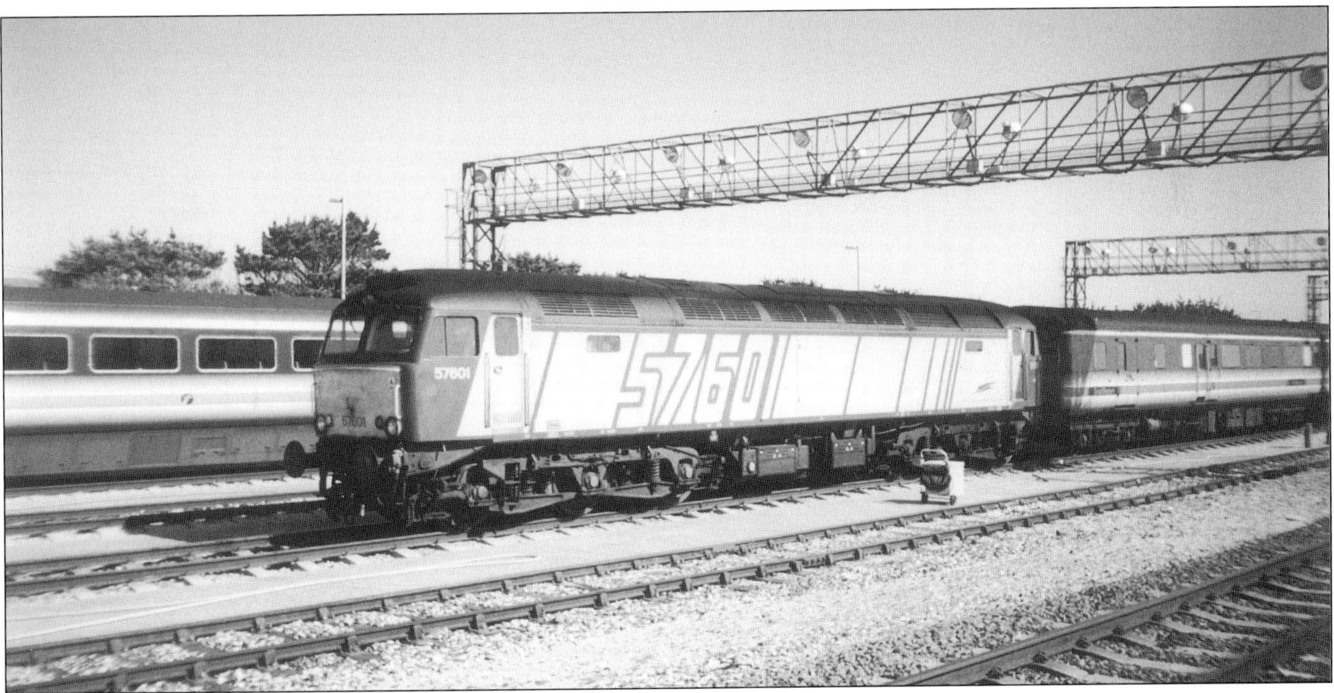

47825 was rebuilt at the Brush works with a more modern engine and motors and was used to work the 'Sleeper' and other trains. It was painted in 'Porterbrook' purple and grey livery and numbered 57601.It is in Long Rock stabling sidings near Ponsondane depot, east of Penzance on 7 April 2002. This loco had previously been numbered 57401 but never ran with that number. Prior to that it had carried 47825, 47590, 47165 and D1759. Maurice Dart.

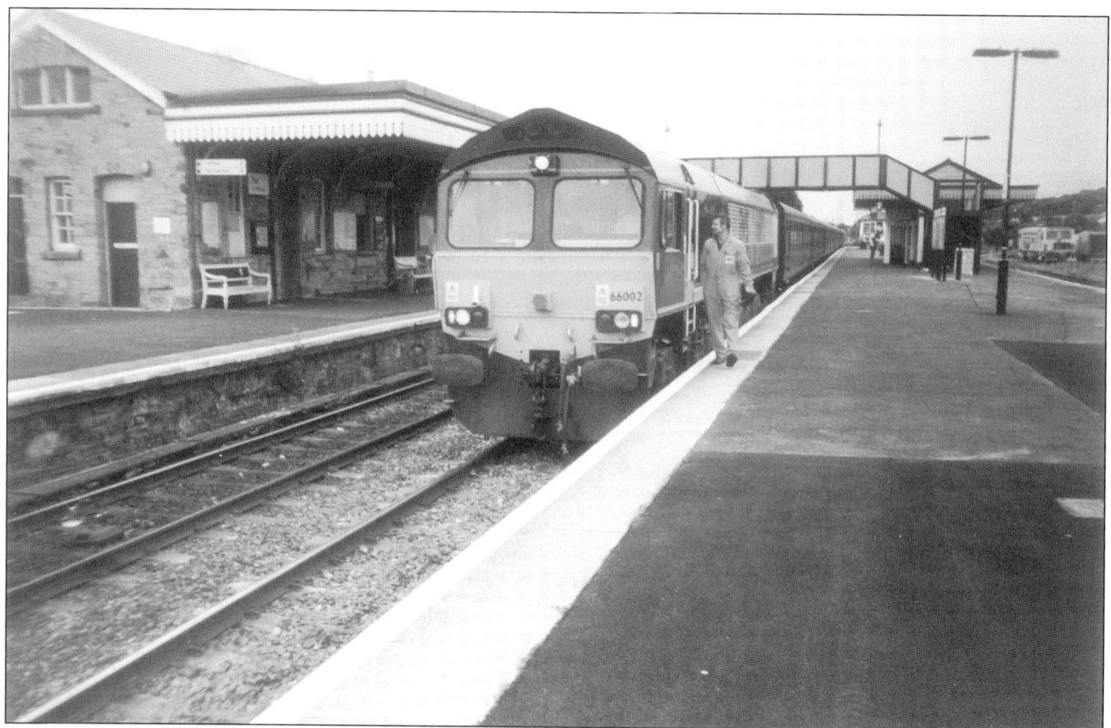

The Canadian built class 66s were designed as heavy freight locos but were used to work numerous special trains operated to Devon and Cornwall to bring visitors to witness the Total Eclipse of the Sun on 11 August 1999. Empty stock of one train, for servicing at St Blazey, has arrived at Par from Penzance hauled by 66002. Maurice Dart.

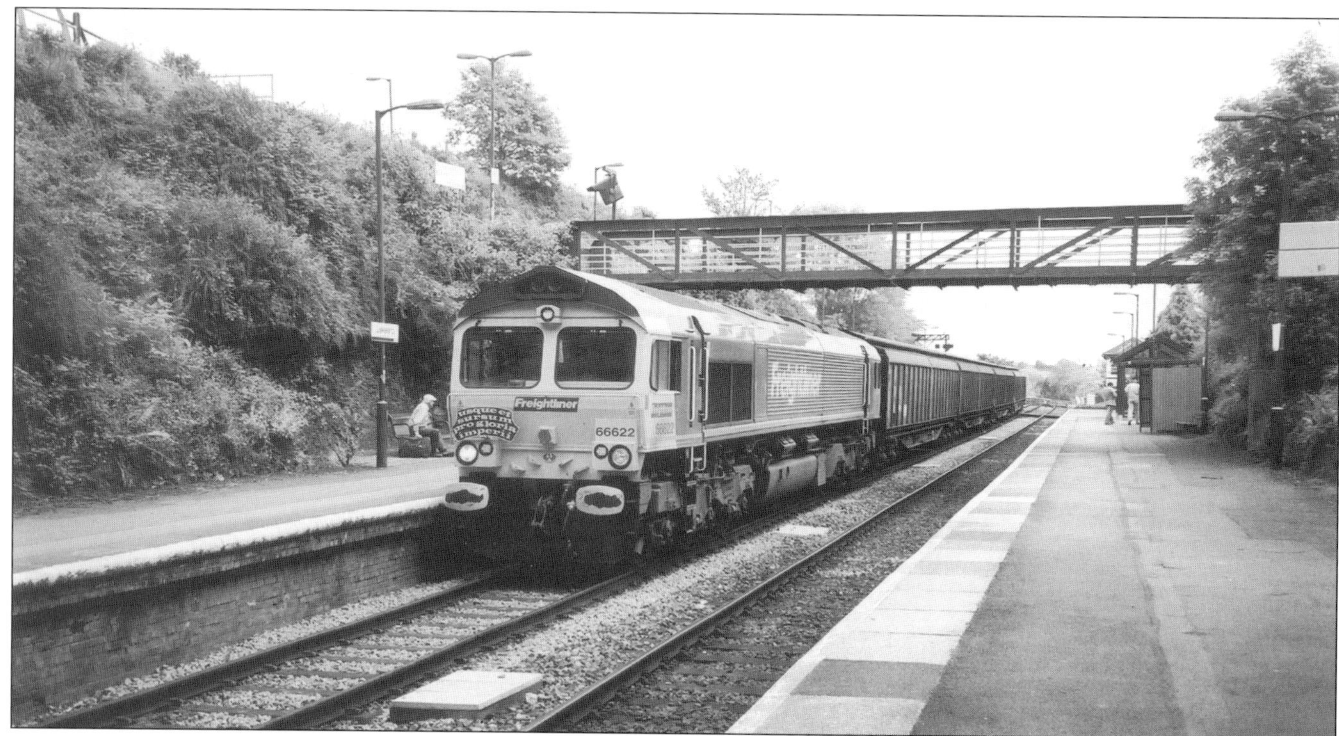

Freightliner took over the working of cement traffic from Hope, Derbyshire to Moorswater, near Liskeard from EWS. When returning with empty wagons the train has to run down through Liskeard on the up line. On 9 June 2005 the train is carrying out this movement being hauled by 66622. The train is carrying a headboard which bears the Latin inscription 'Usque et sursum pro gloria imperii!' Maurice Dart.

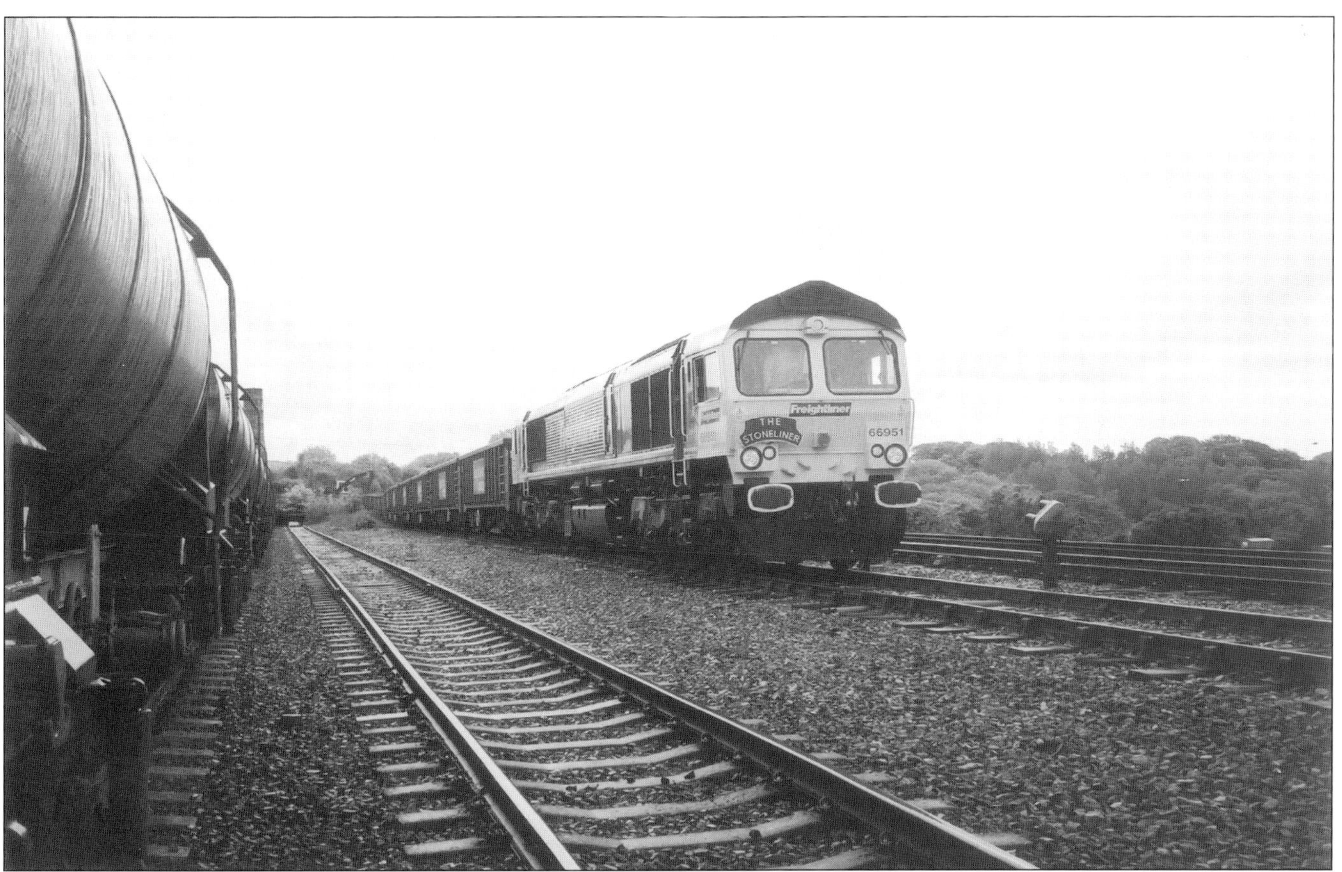

Following on from the main batch of class 66s for Freightliner, two further locos with 'green' exhausts were delivered from Canada. Unexpectedly, one of them worked a stone train to Methrose siding, Blackpool. I recorded it there as unloading was in progress on 3 June 2005. The loco is carrying a 'Stoneliner' headboard.

Another rare visitor came to Methrose to load aggregate destined for Bow, east London, on 14 April 2006. Freightliner had hired two locos from Direct Rail Services of Carlisle and one of them, 66407, is positioning wagons as they are being loaded at Methrose.   Maurice Dart.

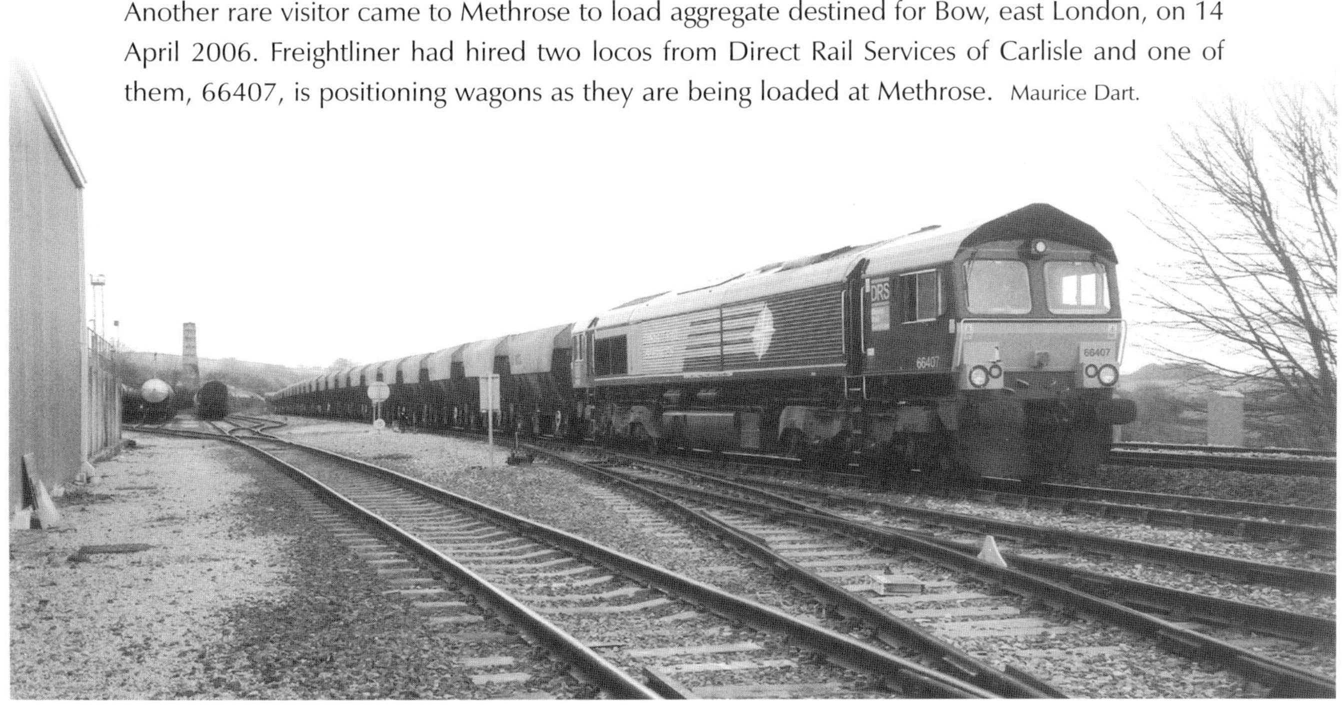

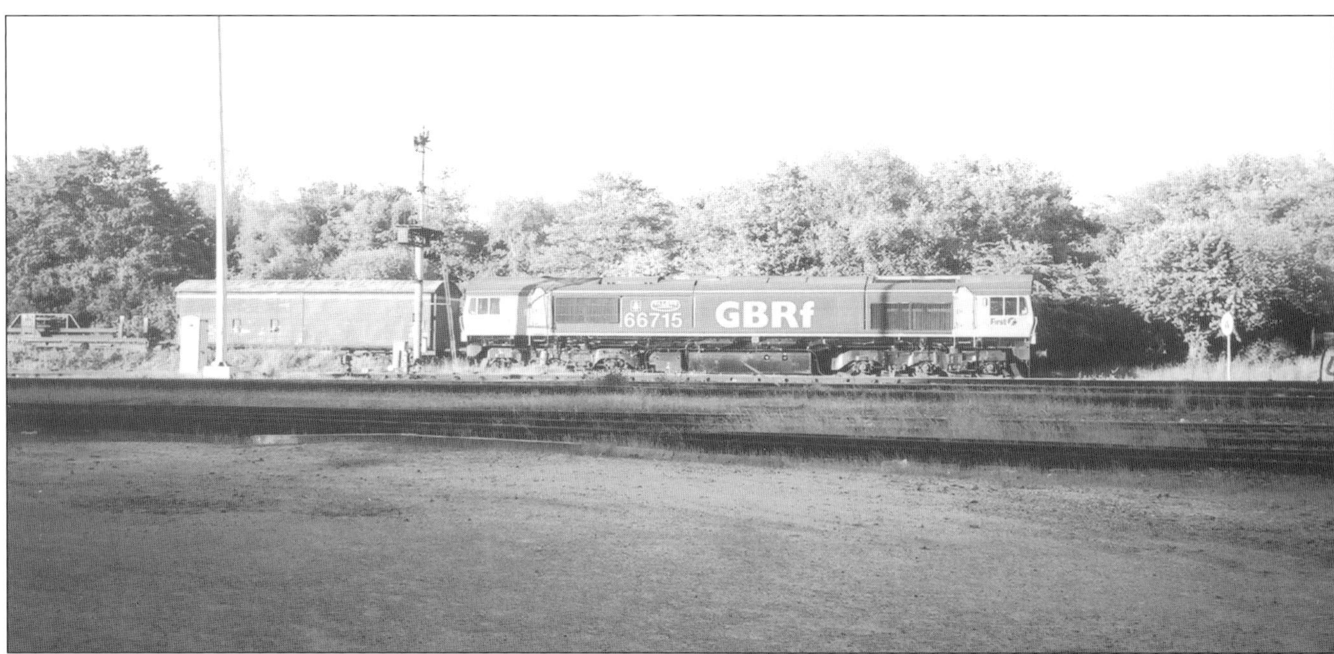

When track renewal was being undertaken at Penzance in June 2006, more unusual locos arrived in the county. The train was worked by two locos from GB Railfreight with one at each end. During the day the train returned to and stabled at St Blazey, where 66715 is seen on 8 June 2006. Maurice Dart.

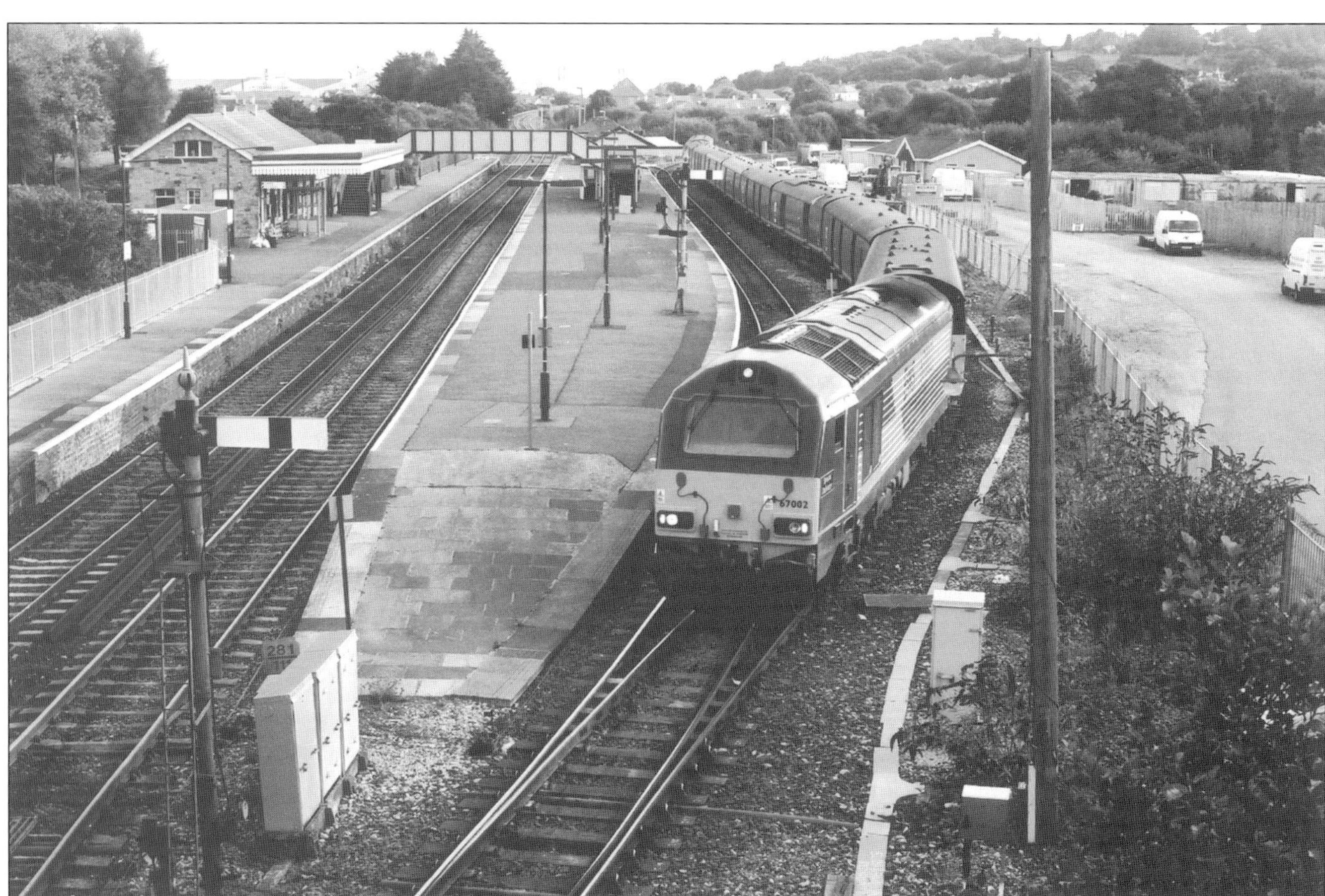

The last type of diesel loco in this section is the class 67 which replaced the class 47s on TPO trains until the cessation of the services. 67002 'SPECIAL DELIVERY' moves a long train of TPO stock out of Par for Plymouth, early evening on 25 September 2003. Maurice Dart.

20

BODMIN ROAD TO PADSTOW

Whereas most of the sections of my collection are arranged in order of size of locomotives, as I am actively involved with the Bodmin & Wenford Railway I keep all photos taken in this area quite separate from the main collection to enable easy access and reference to them to be available. Therefore, this section follows the route from Bodmin Road, now Bodmin Parkway, to Padstow. So locomotive types in this section are completely mixed up in contrast to the remainder of my collection. I have not included any photos of the preservation era as those could constitute a separate volume on their own.

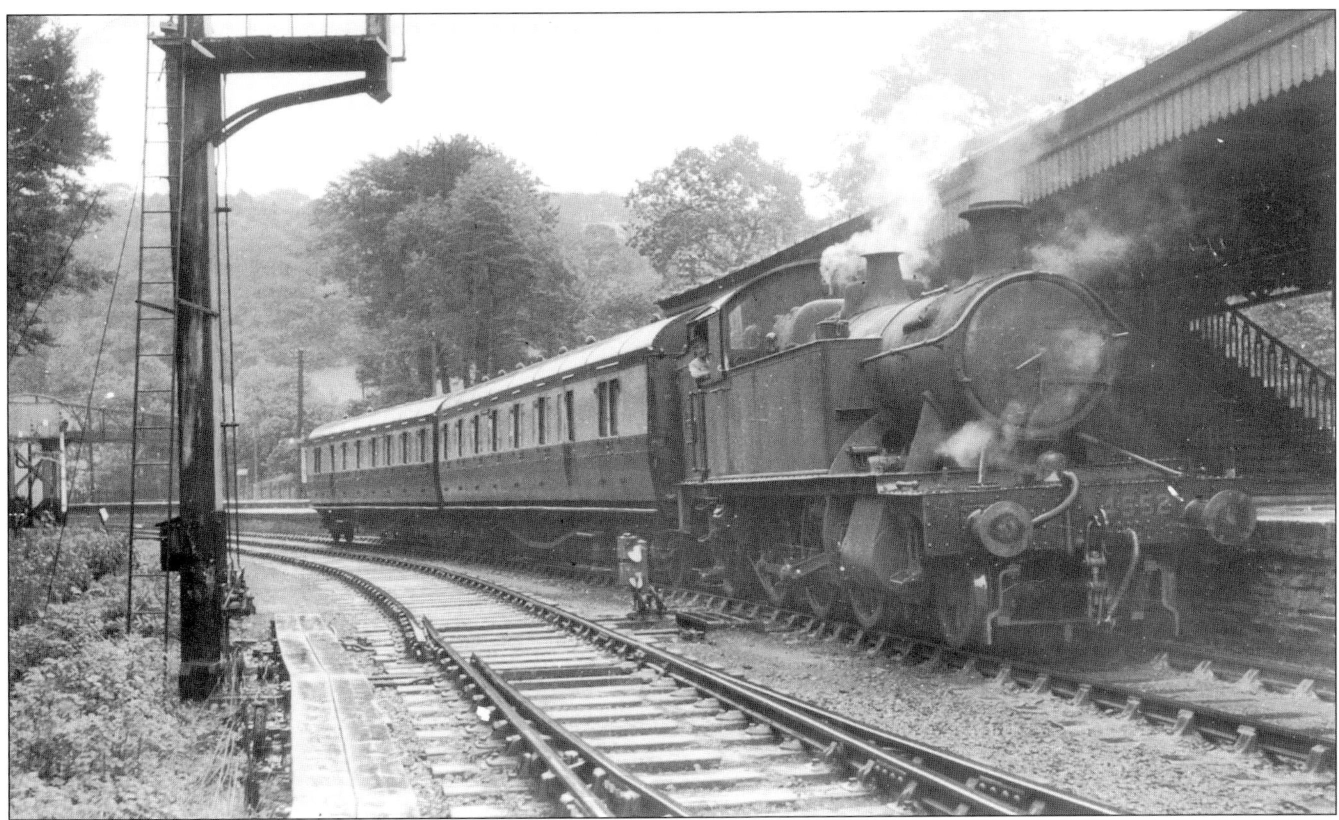

We commence our journey to Padstow having alighted from a main line train at Bodmin Road. We have crossed the footbridge to reach the branch platform and find 4500 class 2-6-2T 4552 from St Blazey shed but sub-shedded at Bodmin with a two coach GWR 'B' set waiting to depart to Bodmin. This view dates from 1946/47. W.A..Camwell.

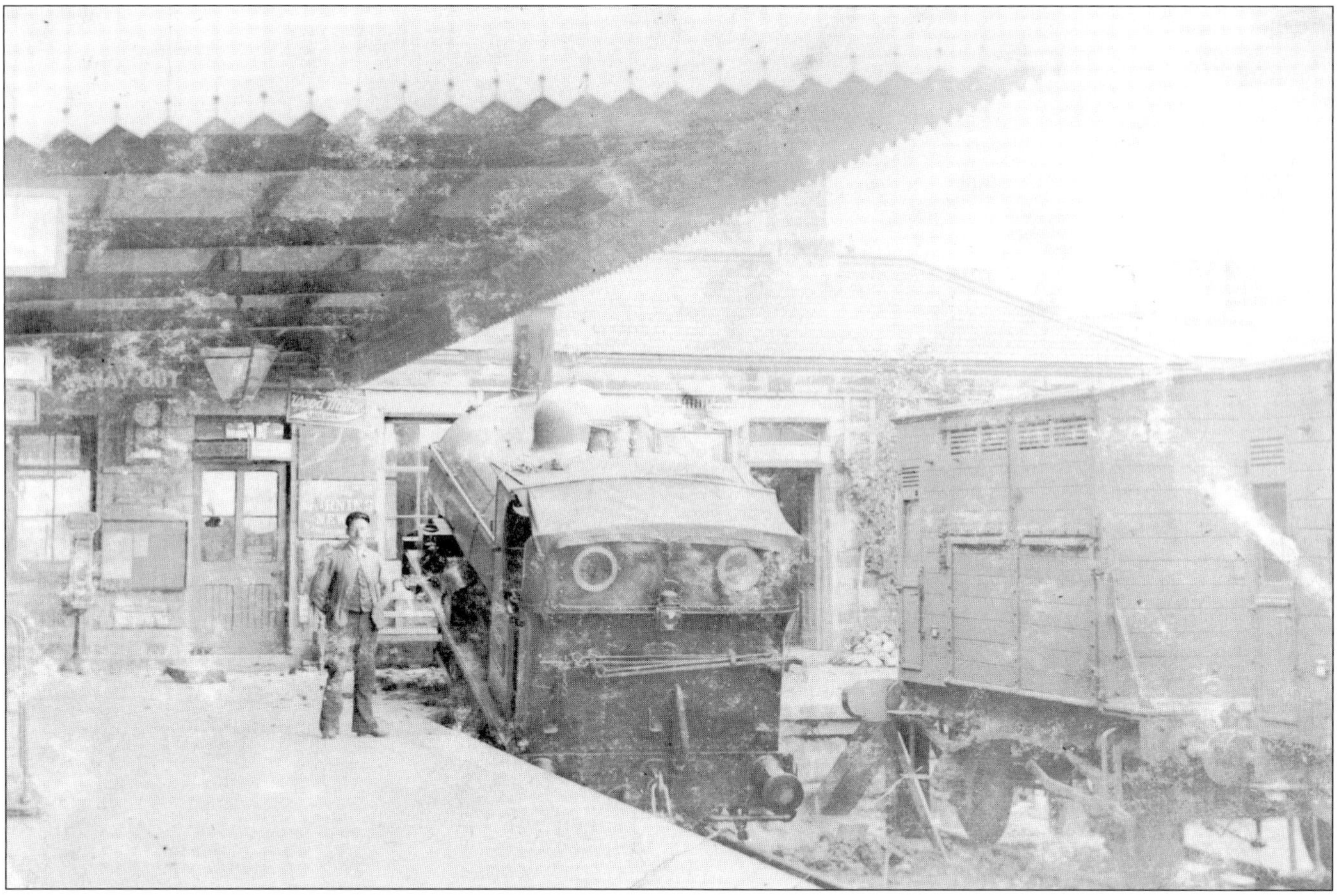

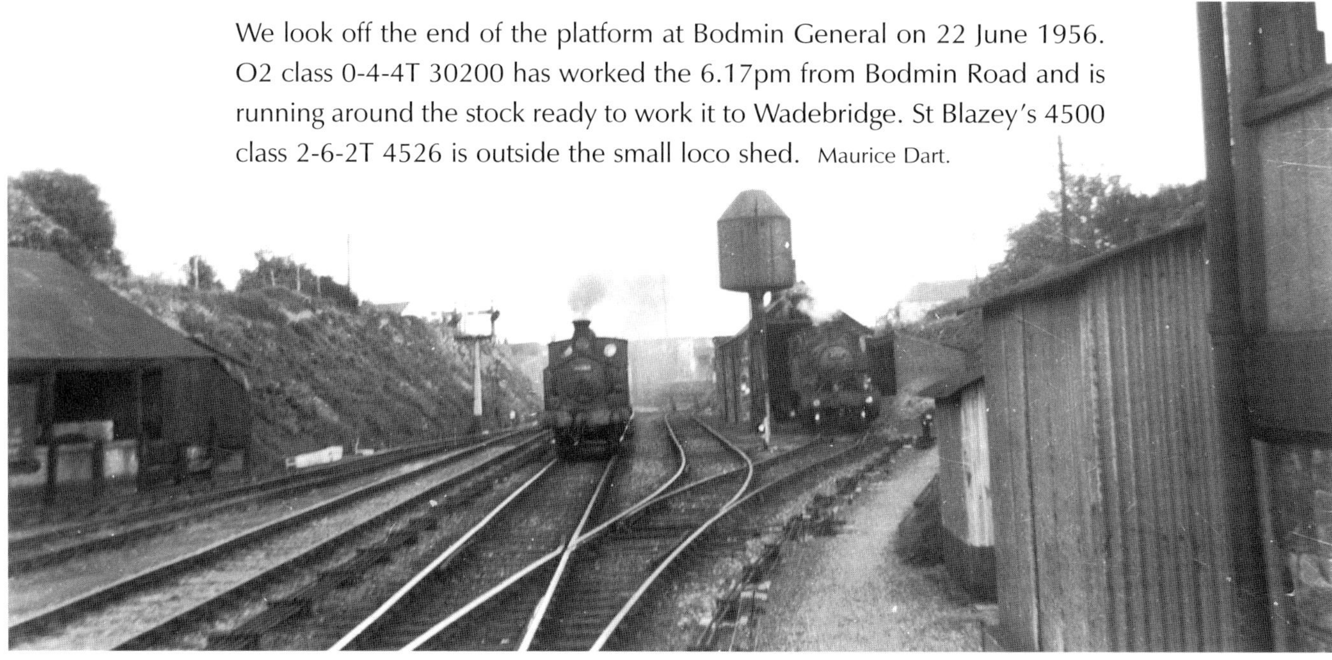

In August 1910 a slight 'mishap' occurred at Bodmin GWR; the GWR never had 'accidents'! Approaching from Bodmin Road there is a downgrade from 'the Quarry' and also from the station points when approaching from Boscarne Junction. 850 class 0-6-0ST1905 ran away down the incline, hit the buffers and tried to climb on to the platform, where it is depicted in this shot. Perhaps the loco was attempting to obey the 'WAY OUT' sign or the crew wished to use the Nestles chocolate machine! Two GWR Horse Boxes are on the right. The station is little changed from this scene.

We look off the end of the platform at Bodmin General on 22 June 1956. O2 class 0-4-4T 30200 has worked the 6.17pm from Bodmin Road and is running around the stock ready to work it to Wadebridge. St Blazey's 4500 class 2-6-2T 4526 is outside the small loco shed. Maurice Dart.

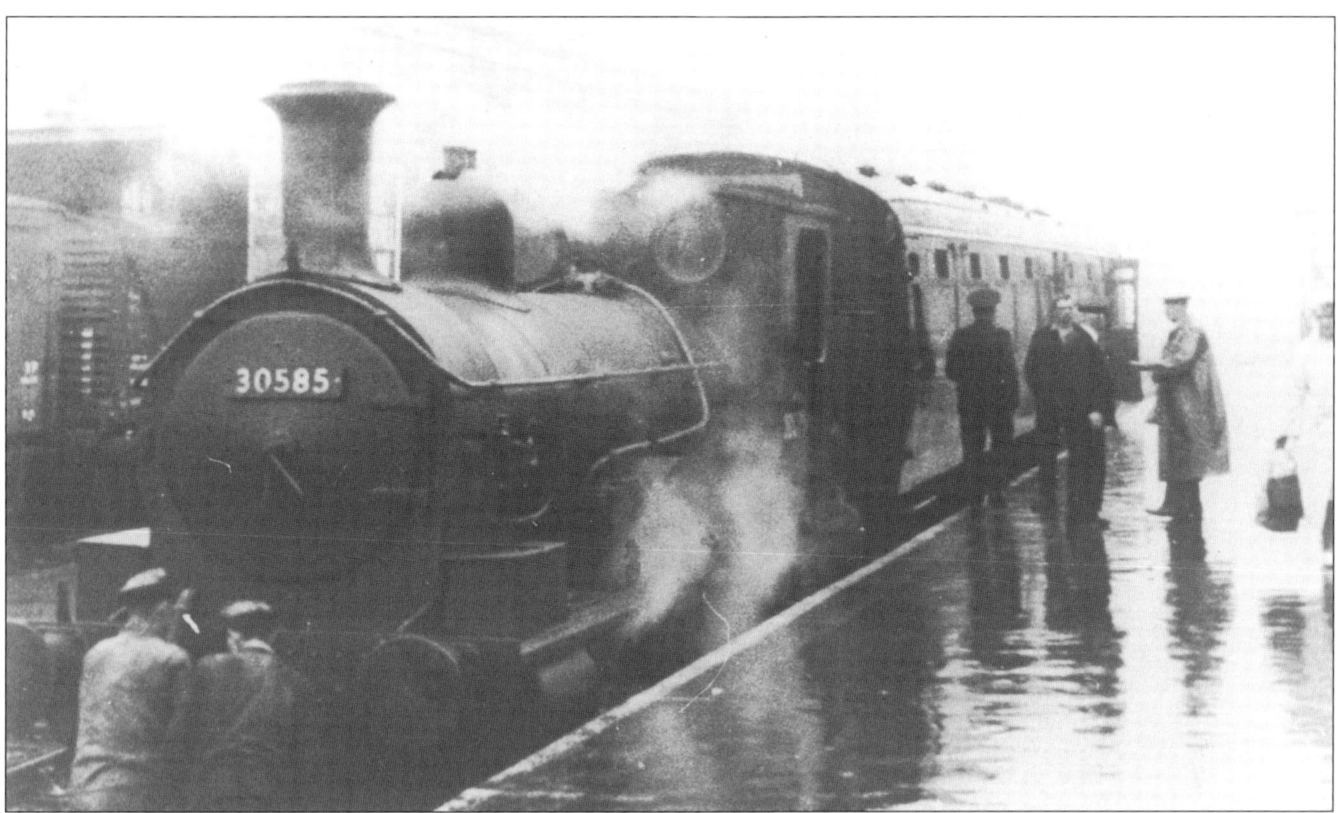

The Beattie Well 2-4-0WTs did not normally visit Bodmin General, especially not on passenger trains. On 13 July 1962 (look at the rain - it is summer) a pair of D6300 diesels failed (surprise, surprise!). So 30585 was used to work a special 'School' train from Wadebridge to Bodmin General where it is seen after arrival. This is probably the last occasion that a Beattie Well tank worked a revenue passenger train, although a charter special touring branch lines west of London was worked by one of the class. Charles Whetmath Collection.

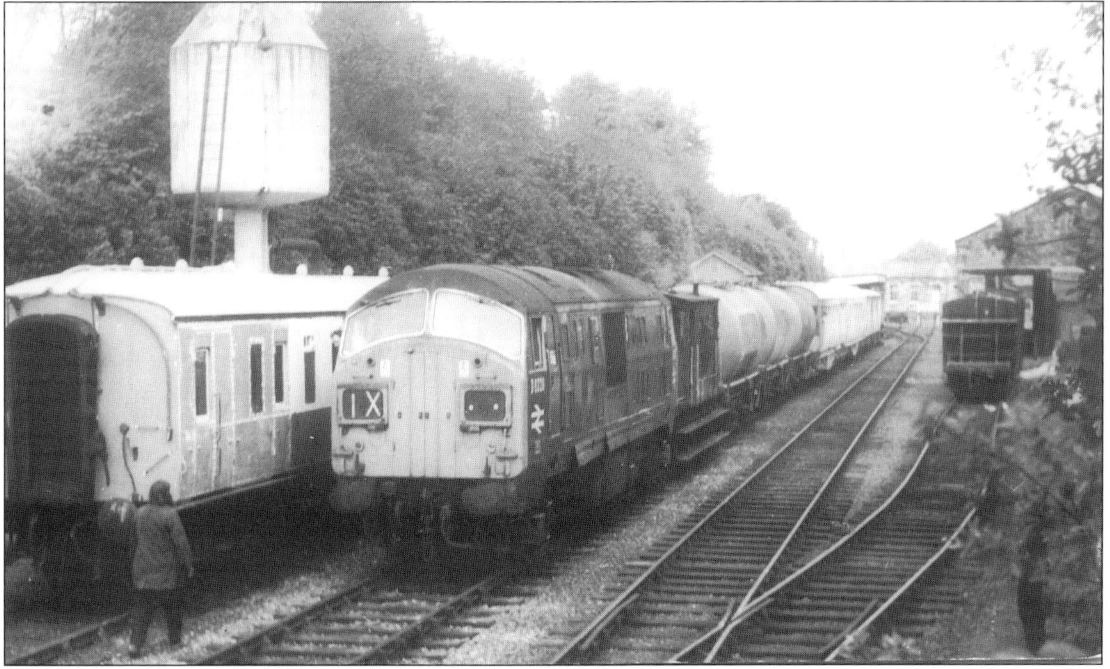

The 'Weed Killing' train visited the branch on 16 May 1971 when it is seen at Bodmin General waiting to depart in charge of D6326. Presflo wagons are in front of the Goods shed and a Hawksworth coach is visible. This was being restored on site by the Great Western Society.

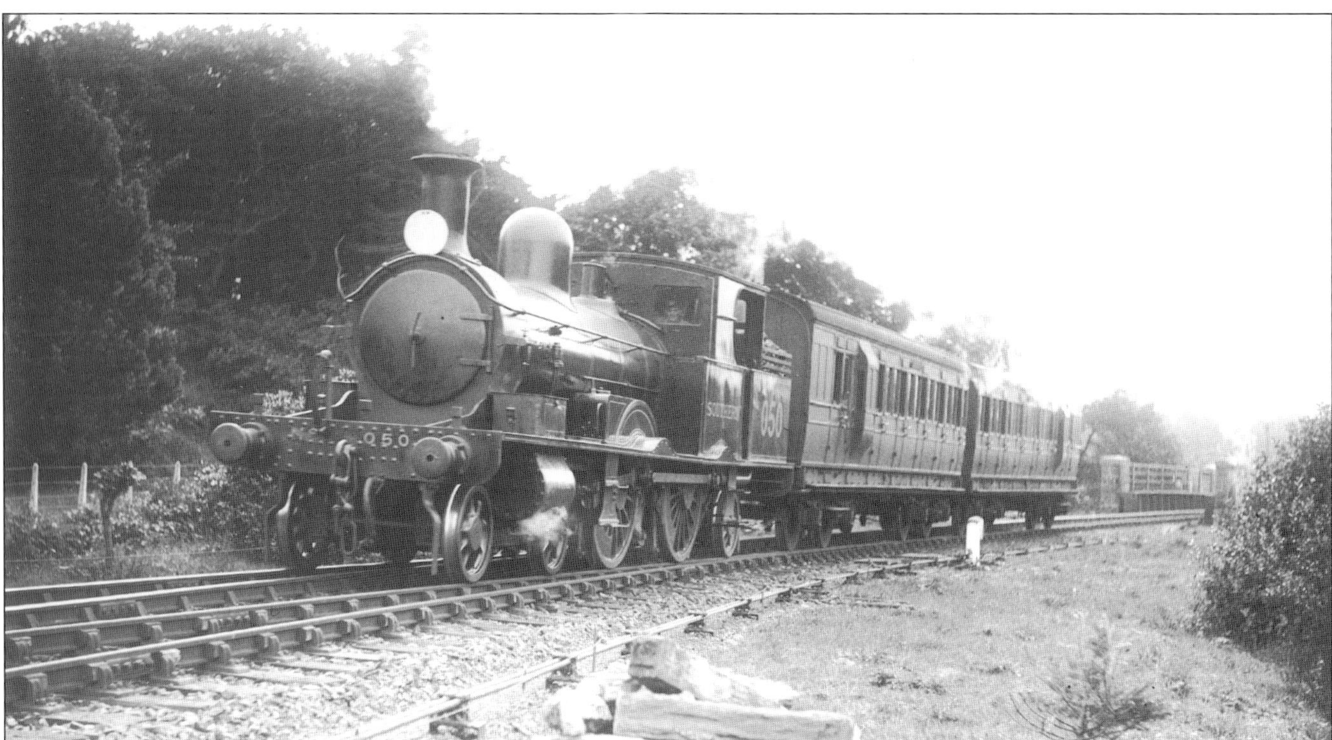

We move down the line to Boscarne Junction and reverse and run back up the ex Bodmin & Wadebridge Railway route to Dunmere Junction. 0415 class 4-4-2T 050 heads a train from Padstow to Bodmin on 8 August 1925. These engines were called 'Radial Tanks' and this engine worked regularly from Wadebridge shed. It was withdrawn in December 1927. Stephenson Locomotive Society.

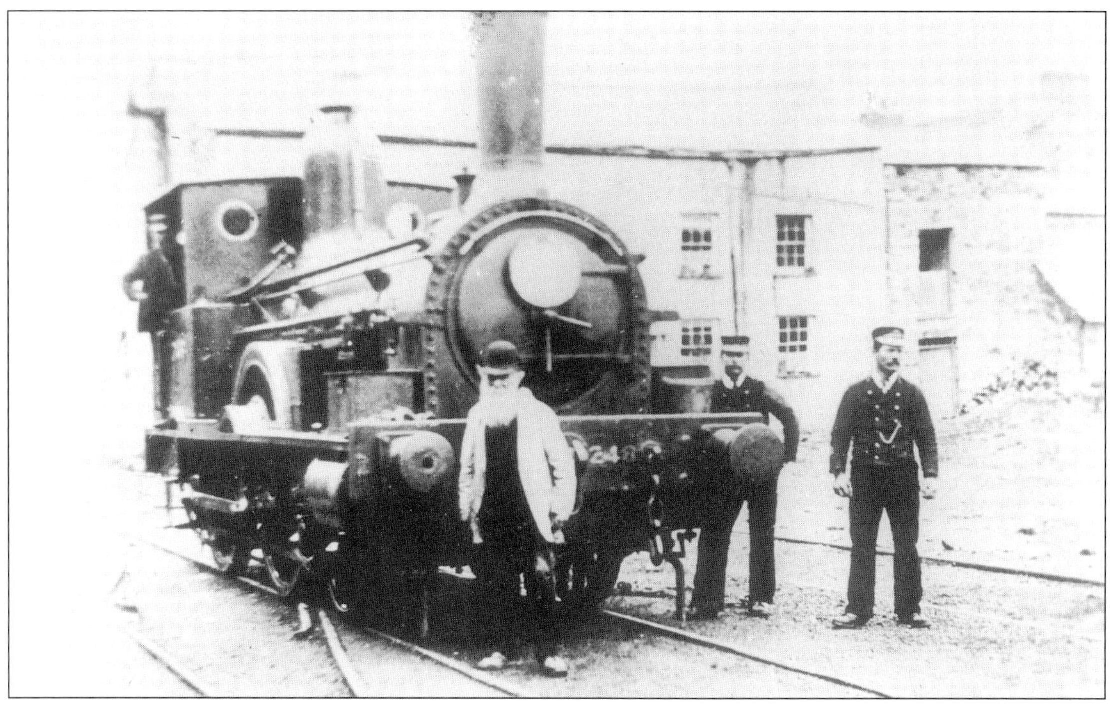

This a shot of Beattie Well tank 248 which came to Wadebridge early in LSWR days but did not remain there. It is at Bodmin Wharf which was later replaced by the Bodmin station. Prominent in front of the loco, with his white beard, is Sam Worth. He was 'Wharfinger' at Bodmin Wharf and joined the Bodmin & Wadebrigde Railway when it opened in 1834. Bodmin Town Museum.

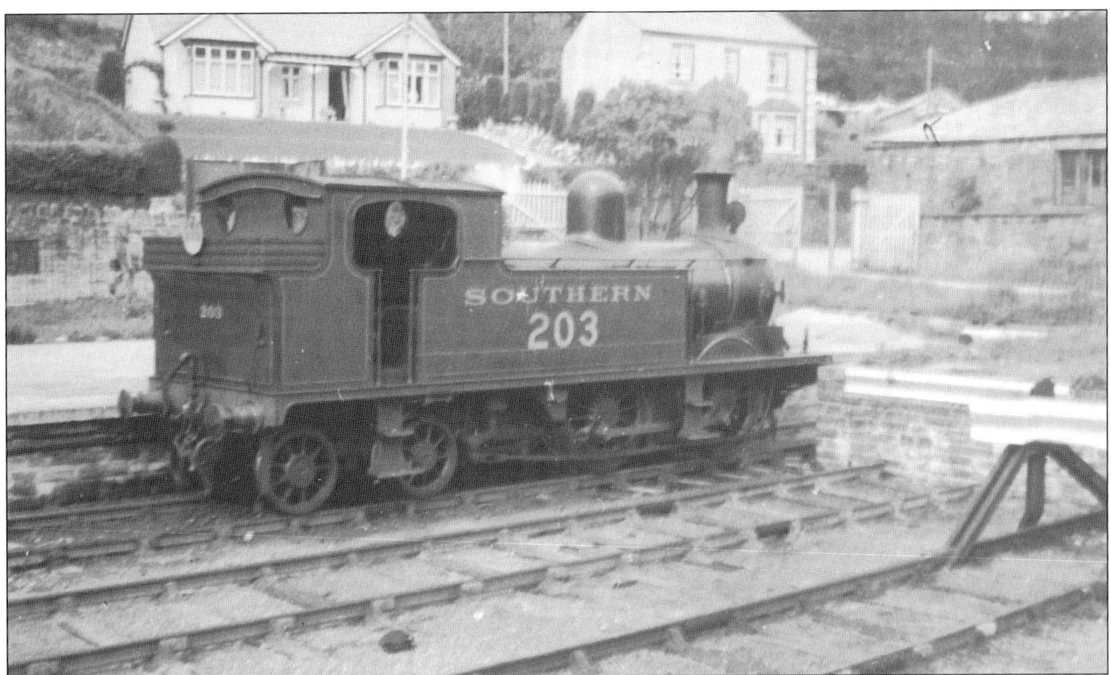

Both of the stations at Bodmin were termini. O2 class 0-4-4T 203 is at the buffers at Bodmin SR waiting to run around its train in 1939. This class of engine worked the branch to Bodmin following the withdrawal of the 'Radial Tanks'. A.G.Ellis.

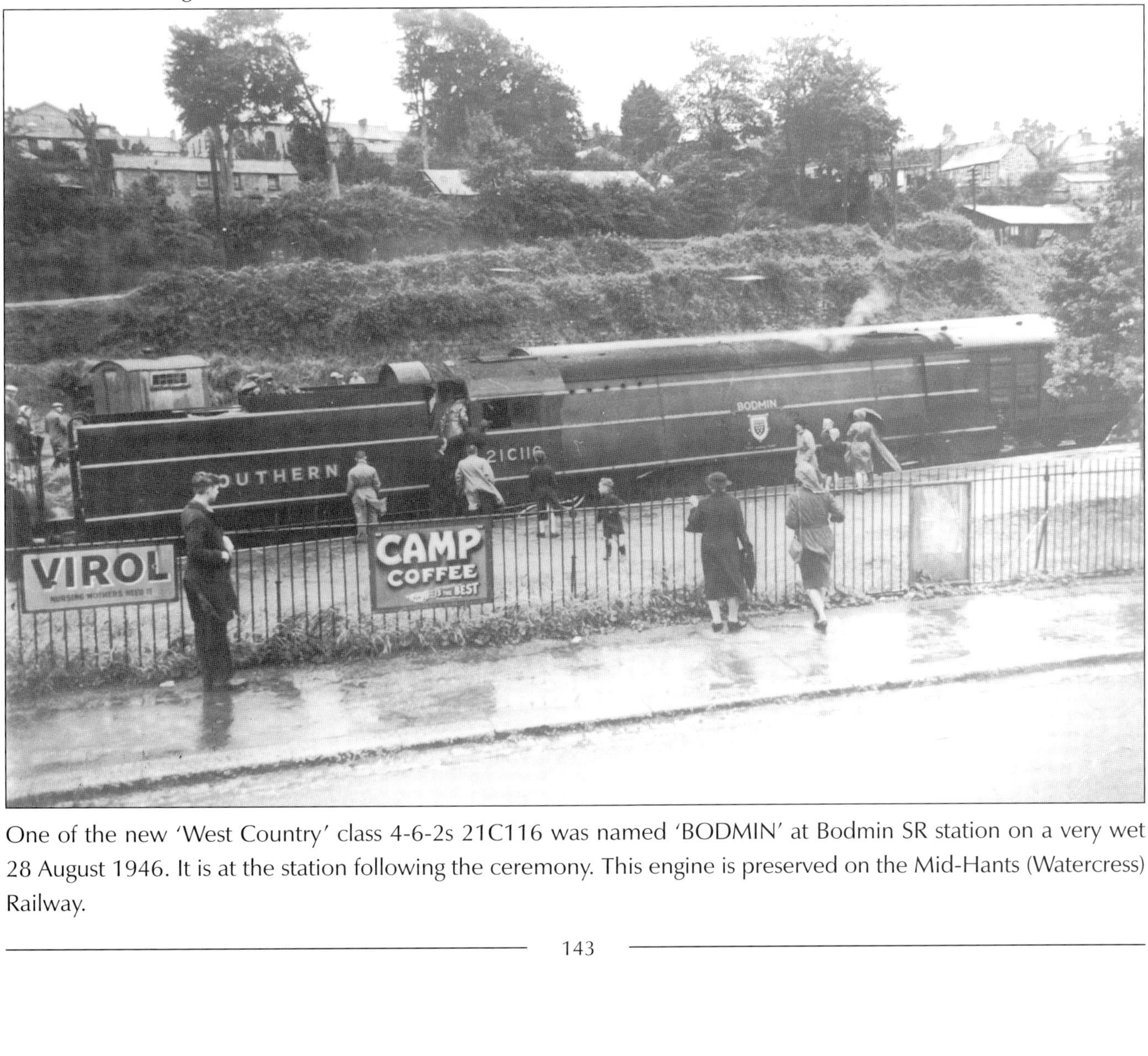

One of the new 'West Country' class 4-6-2s 21C116 was named 'BODMIN' at Bodmin SR station on a very wet 28 August 1946. It is at the station following the ceremony. This engine is preserved on the Mid-Hants (Watercress) Railway.

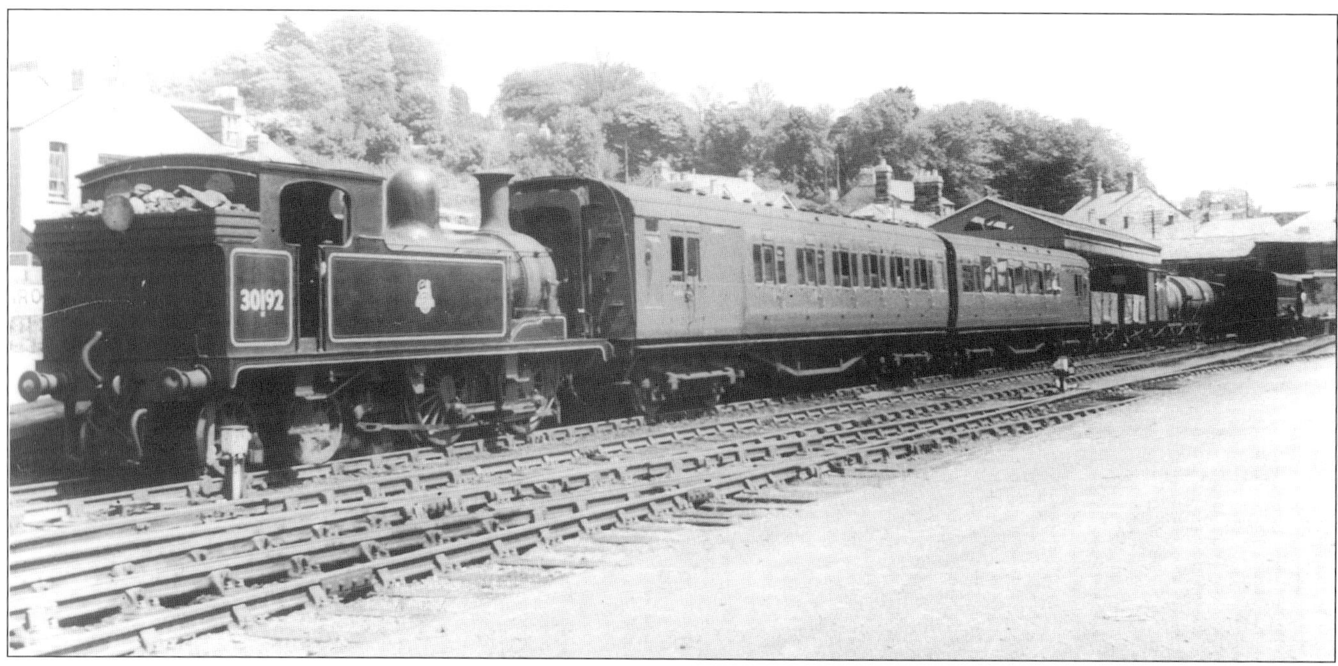

A mixed train, containing a Maunsell set is ready to depart from Bodmin North for Padstow on 22 May 1952. The loco is O2 class 0-4-4T 30192. R.K.Blencowe collection.

Following the withdrawal of the Beattie Well tanks, services on the Wenford Bridge branch were worked by three ex GWR 1366 class 0-6-0PTs. They did not usually stray from that work apart from working as 'Station Pilot' at Wadebridge. However, on 24 July 1964, 1369 unusually worked a goods train to Bodmin North where it seen arriving. The train consists of a Shell/BP tank wagon, a pair of BR standard 12 ton vans and a LMS Brake van. J.H.Aston.

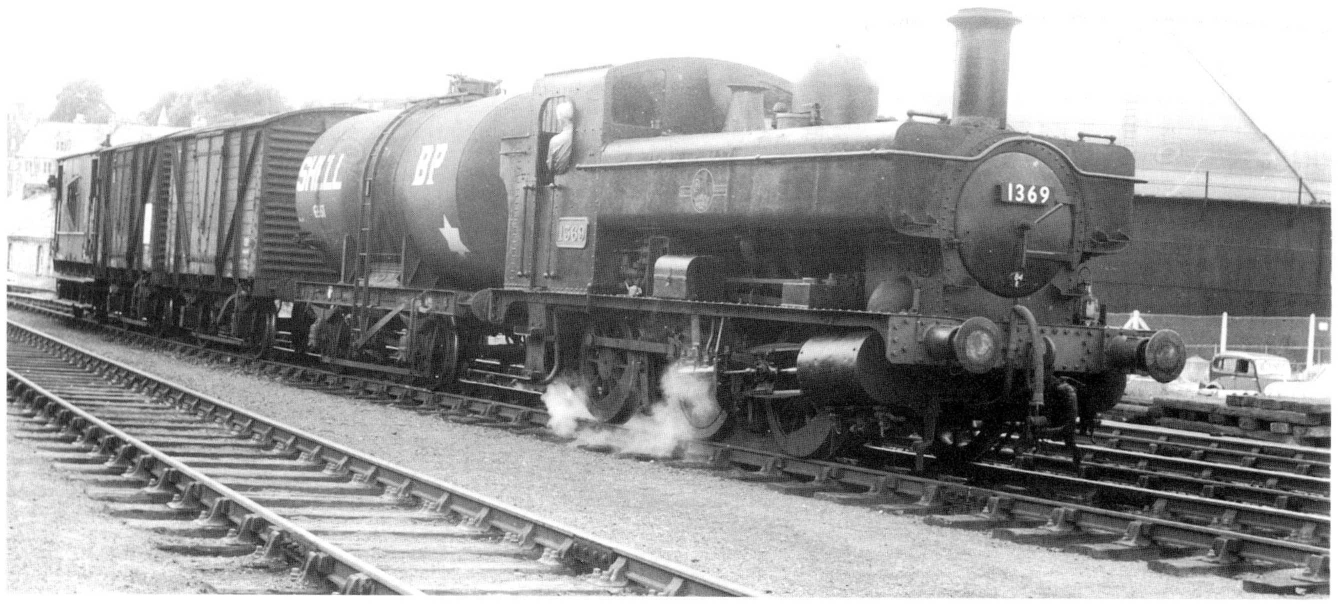

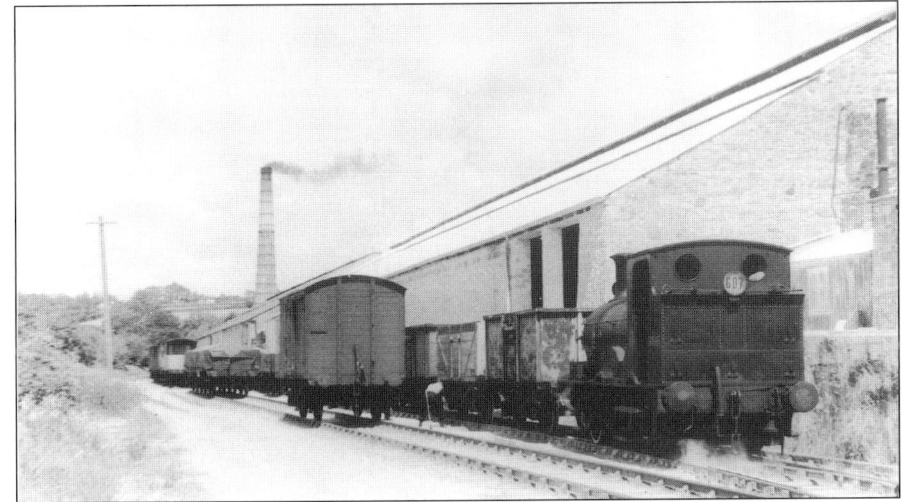

So many photos of trains on the Wenford Bridge branch and of the Beattie Well tanks have appeared in books that I have only included a couple on that line. Beattie Well 2-4-0WT 30585 shunts coal wagons at ECLP Wenford kilns during the 1950s. On the left there is an LNER van. G.Powell.

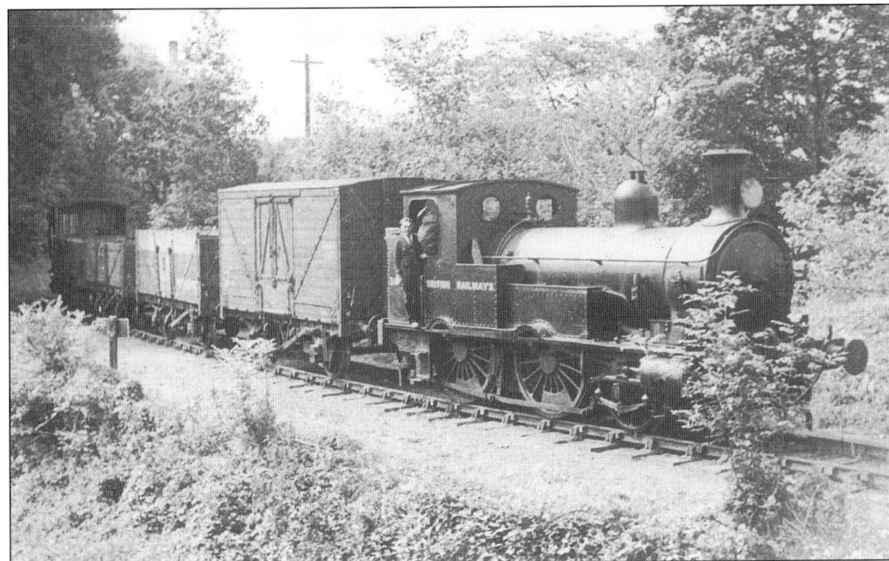

Of the three Beattie Well tanks at Wadebridge shed, 30586 was not normally used on the Wenford branch. This was because the tank water filling inlet was positioned slightly higher than on the other two locos and presented a problem when using the famous supply locally known as 'The Spring'. It did make a trip on the line in August 1948 and was photographed between Wenford china clay sidings and Wenford Bridge. An LNWR van is behind the engine. Locomotive & General Railway Photographs.

Photographed passing Guineaport, soon after departure from Wadebridge with the 9.47am train to Bodmin Road, in March 1926, is 2021 class 0-6-0PT 2127. The engine is fitted with a domeless boiler

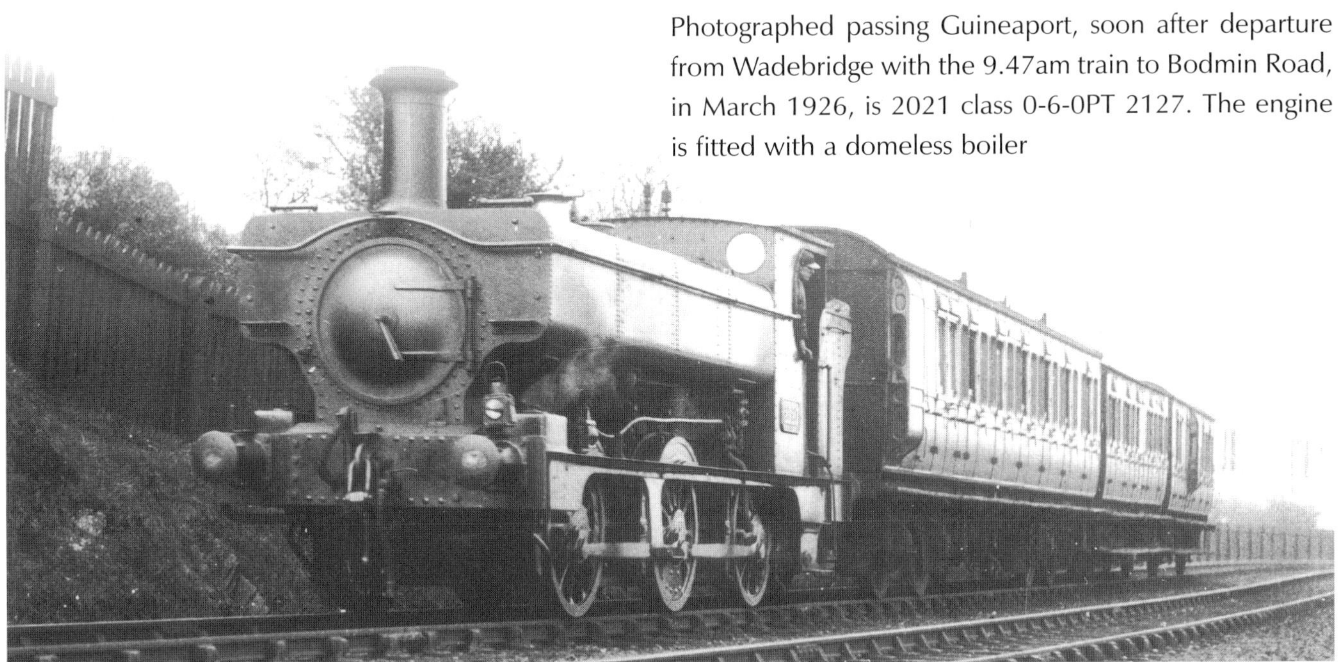

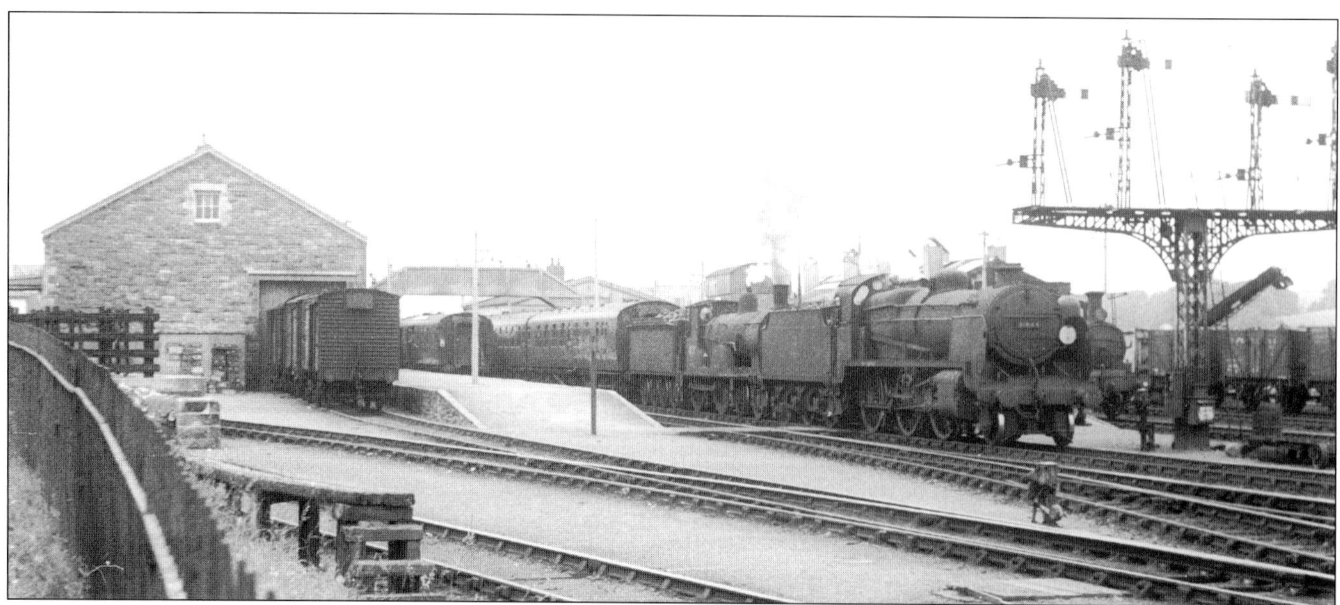

Next we look at some scenes taken at Wadebridge station. A double headed train for Exeter Central awaits departure on 5 July 1952. N class 2-6-0 31844 is pilot to T9 class 4-4-0 30711. Both engines were from Exmouth Junction shed. Beattie Well tank 30587 is visible to the right of the leading engine. The signal gantry is prominent and the rear of a train to Padstow can be seen at the Down platform. The goods shed stands on the left and the footbridge, constructed of Exmouth Junction concrete, links the platforms. T.C.Cole.

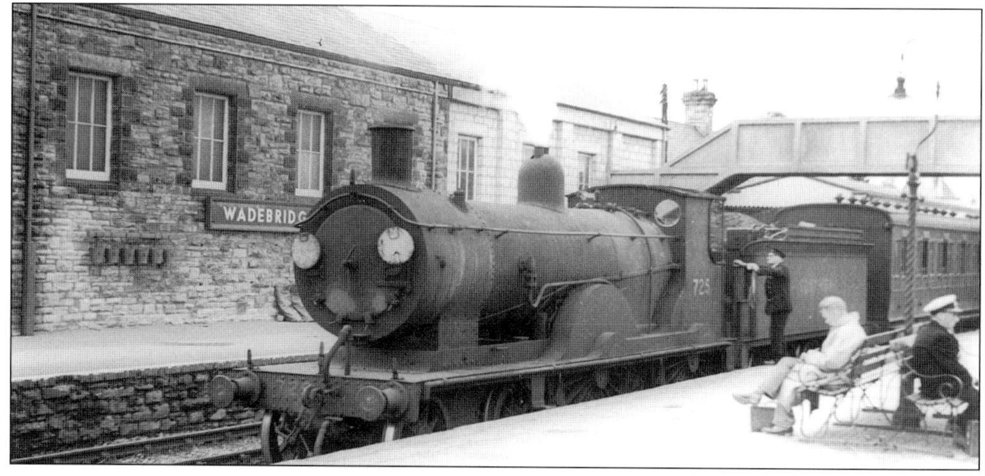

Passengers await a train as Exmouth Junction T9 class 4-4-0 725 waits at the head of a departure for Okehampton on 9 August 1948. This engine was transferred to Salisbury shortly after this date. R.Cogger.

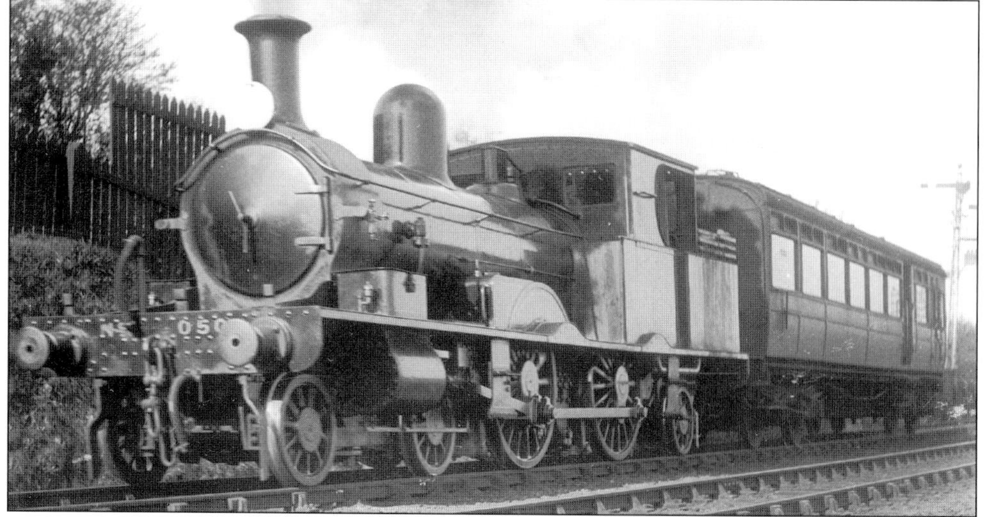

We go back to the early 1920s as 0415 class 4-4-2T 050 departs past Guineaport with a train from Wadebridge to Bodmin SR. The engine is in immaculate external condition. Stephenson Locomotive Society.

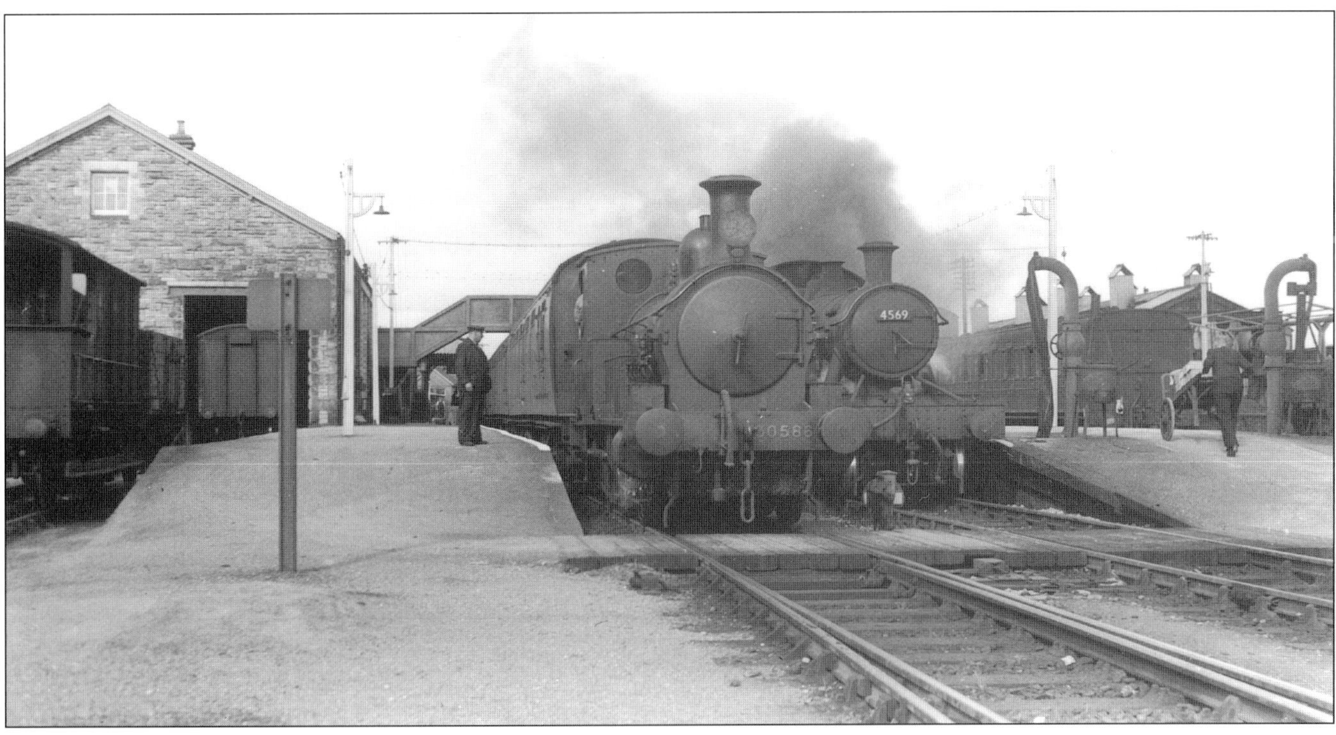

A busy scene at Wadebridge on 4 October 1949 has Beattie Well 30586 coupling up to detach carriages from a train which has arrived from Okehampton. To its right, 4500 class 2-6-2T 4569 awaits departure with the 11.48am from Padstow to Bodmin Road. A GWR Toad brake van is on the left. T.J.Edgington.

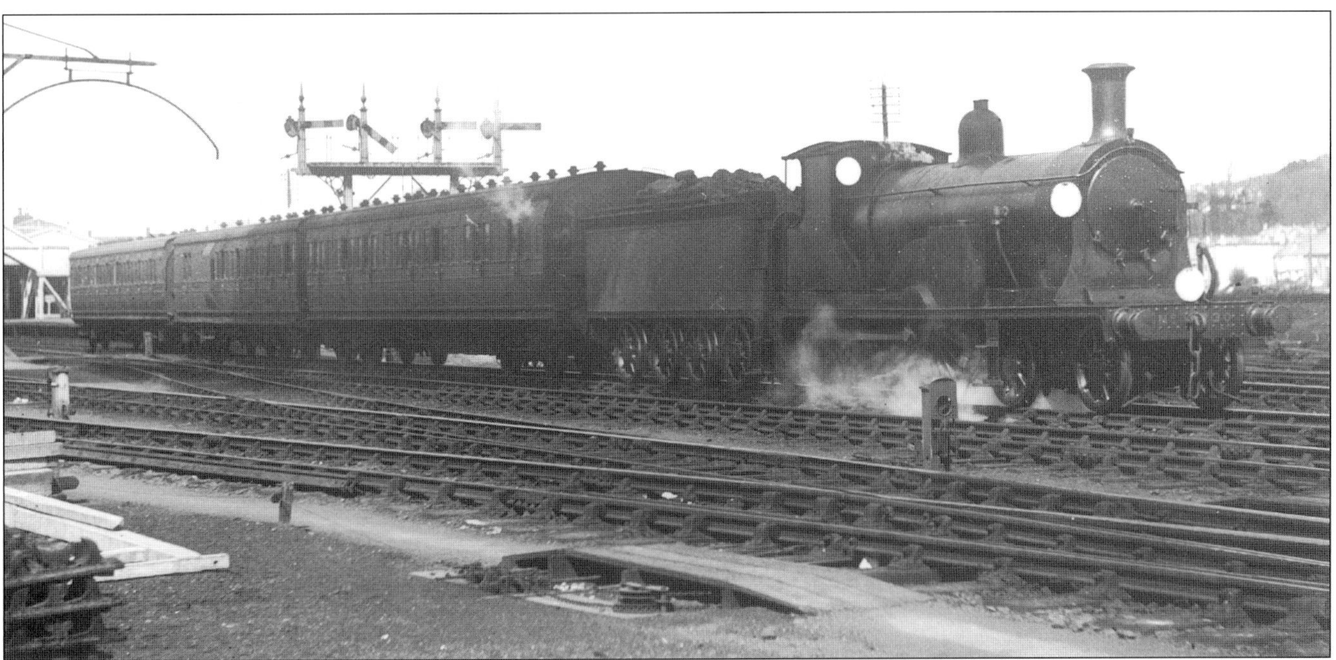

On a date between 1924 and 1926, T9 class 4-4-0 730 pulls out of Wadebridge with a train to Okehampton. Stephenson Locomotive Society.

It was unusual to find an engine at Wadebridge in a dirty condition. However on 25 July 1933 the number on O2 class 0-4-4T 216 can only just be read whilst the 'Southern' inscription above it is barely readable. The engine is at the main arrival platform, probably after its carriages have been removed by the station pilot. This engine may have been 'on loan' from Exmouth Junction. A.G.Ellis.

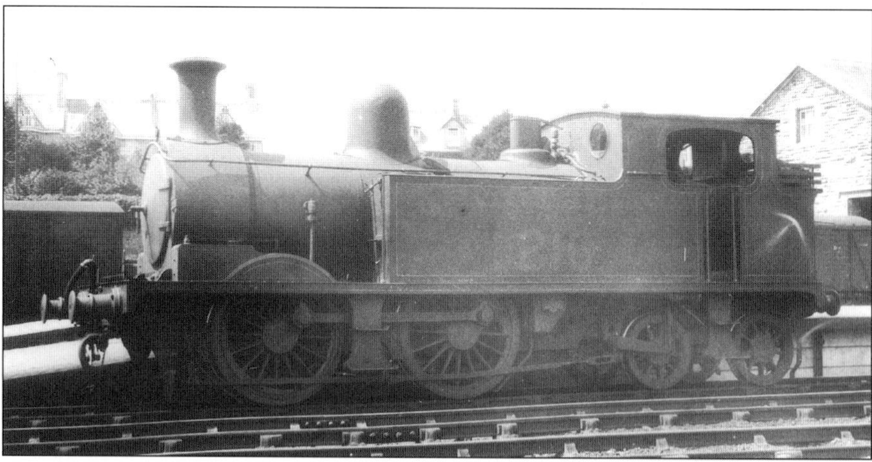

Another O2 class 0-4-4T E 182 waits at Wadebridge with some vans on 6 August 1928. Judging by its condition this was a Wadebridge engine at the time. Locomotive Club of Great Britain/Ken Nunn collection.

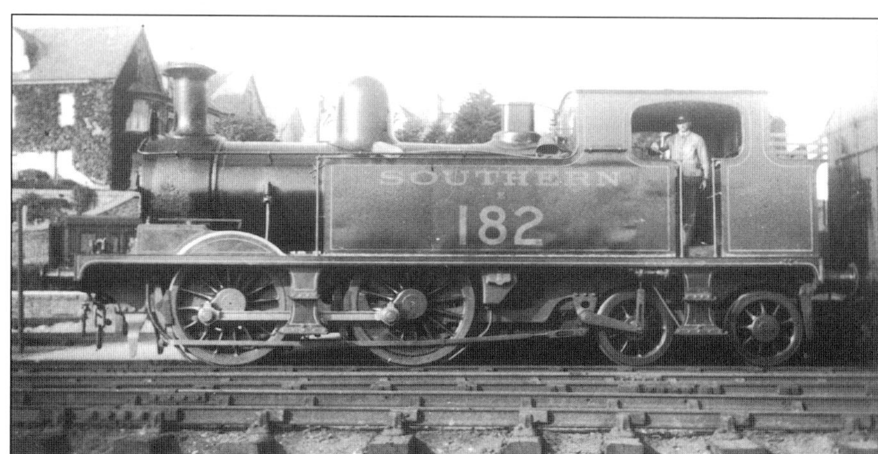

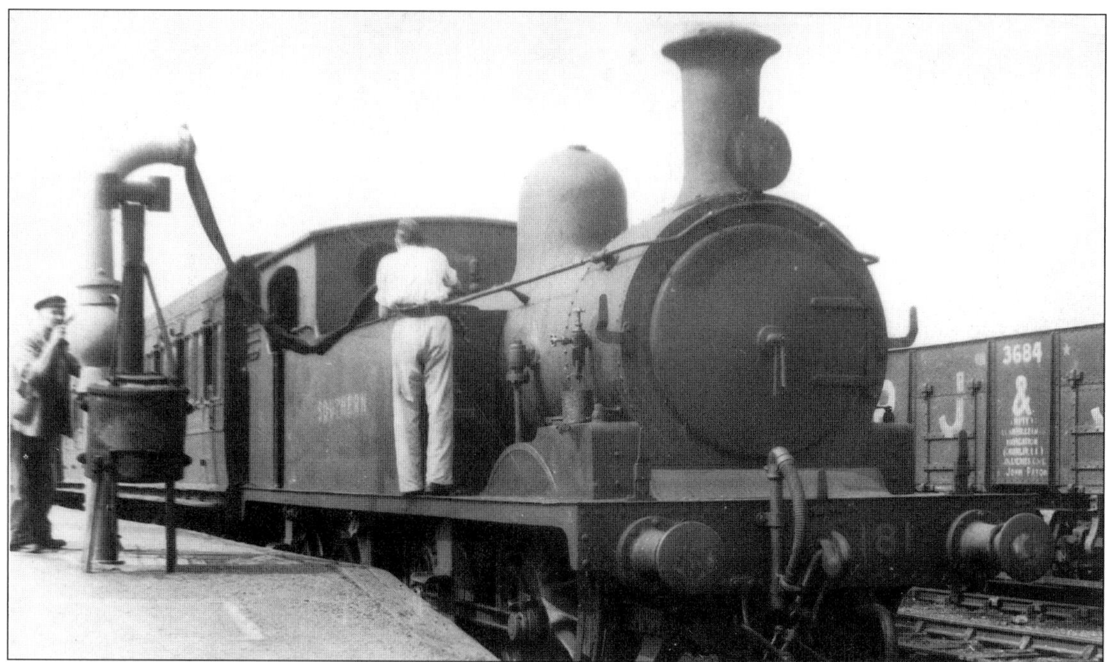

During and immediately following the Second World War, the standard of cleanliness of engines everywhere deteriorated. This is apparent in this shot of O2 class 181 at Wadebridge around 1947. It is taking water prior to working a train to Bodmin SR. In April 1949 this engine was transferred to the Isle of Wight. It was renumbered to W35 and named 'FRESHWATER'. Visible on the right is a 21 ton mineral wagon that was built under the auspices of the GWR.

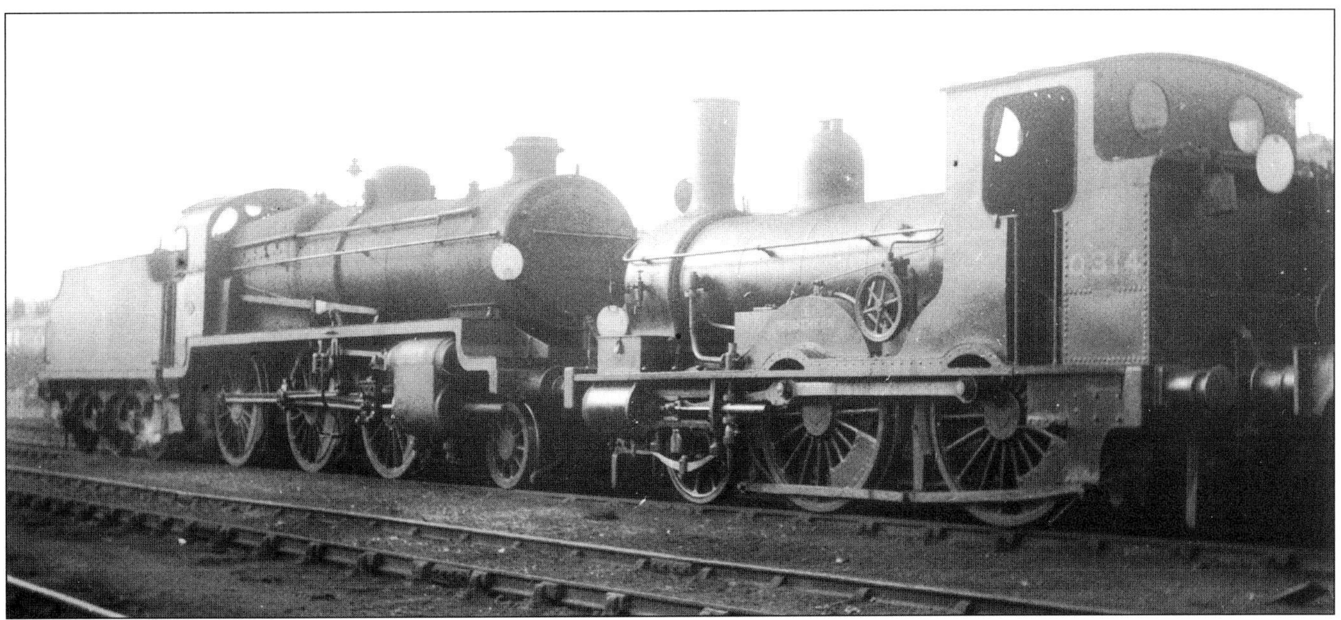

Having looked at Wadebridge station, a selection of scenes taken around the two road engine shed follows. A line up of engines outside the front of shed on 6 August 1928 includes N class 2-6-0 A 850 and Beattie Well E 0314. The 'A' prefix on the N class indicated that Ashford works was responsible for its maintenance. This was taken before smoke deflector plates were fitted to the loco which became 1850. The N class locos were nicknamed 'Woolworths'. Locomotive Club of Great Britain/Ken Nunn collection.

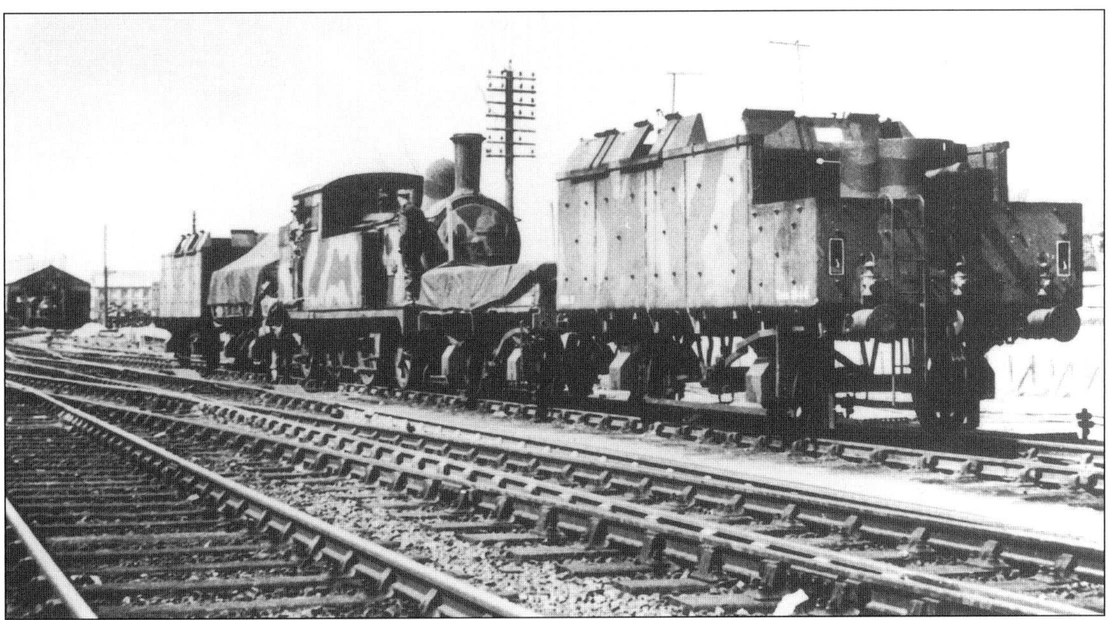

During the Second World War when the threat of invasion by German forces was considered a probability, a series of 'Armoured trains' were constructed. They were composed of various armoured wagons and vans and ex Great Eastern Railway 2-4-2Ts provided the motive power. One train was sent to Wadebridge to patrol lines in the area. Later it was replaced by another similar train. The trains were identified by a large white letter painted on the bunker of the engine except for some 'spare' locos which were unlettered. The engine on train 'A' train at Wadebridge developed problems and was replaced by one of the 'spare' locos. As no letter is visible on the loco in this shot it can be said with reasonable accuracy that this is Train 'A' with F4 class 2-4-2T 7177 and it was taken between July and August 1941. In the background outside the shed are two O2 class 0-4-4Ts and a T9 class 4-4-0. North Woolwich Station Museum.

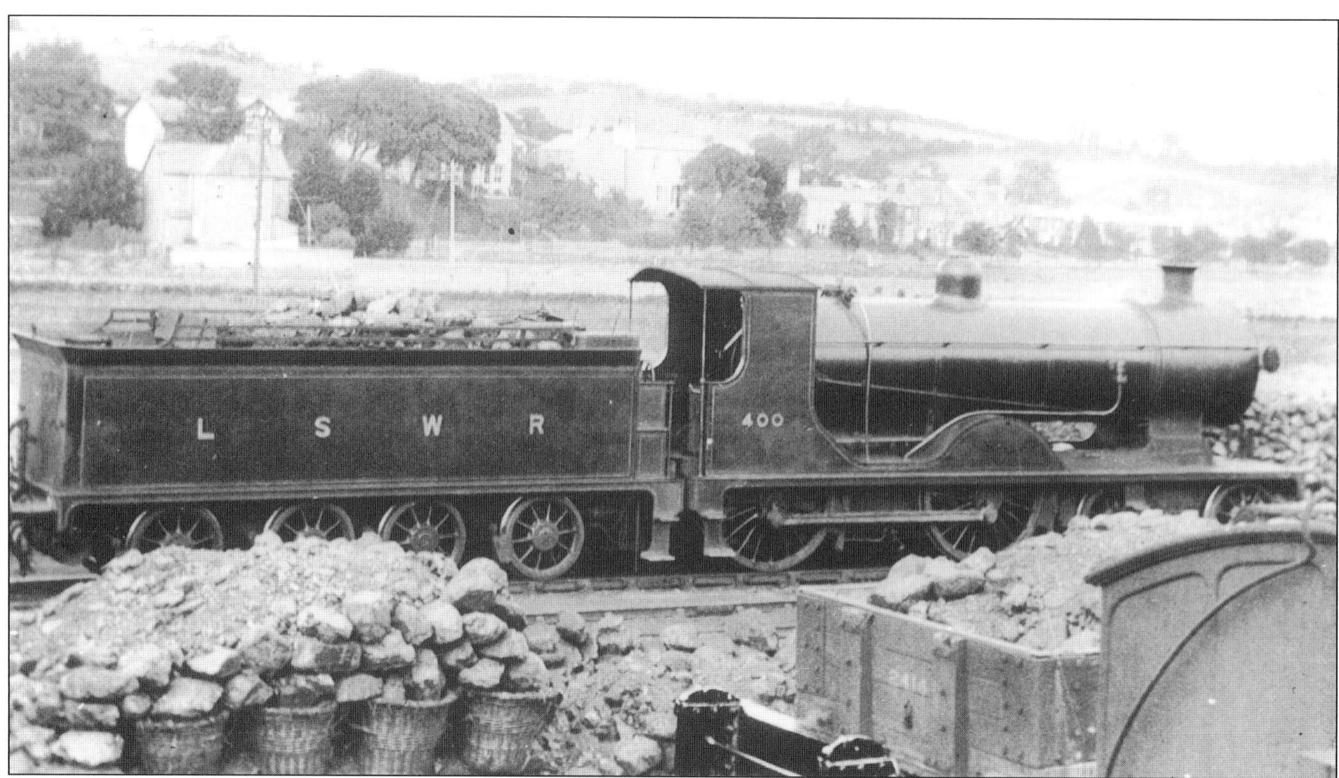

Standing at the back end of the engine shed on 10 August 1922 is S11 class 4-4-0 400. These locos worked passenger services on the North Cornwall line. The tender is lettered LSWR.

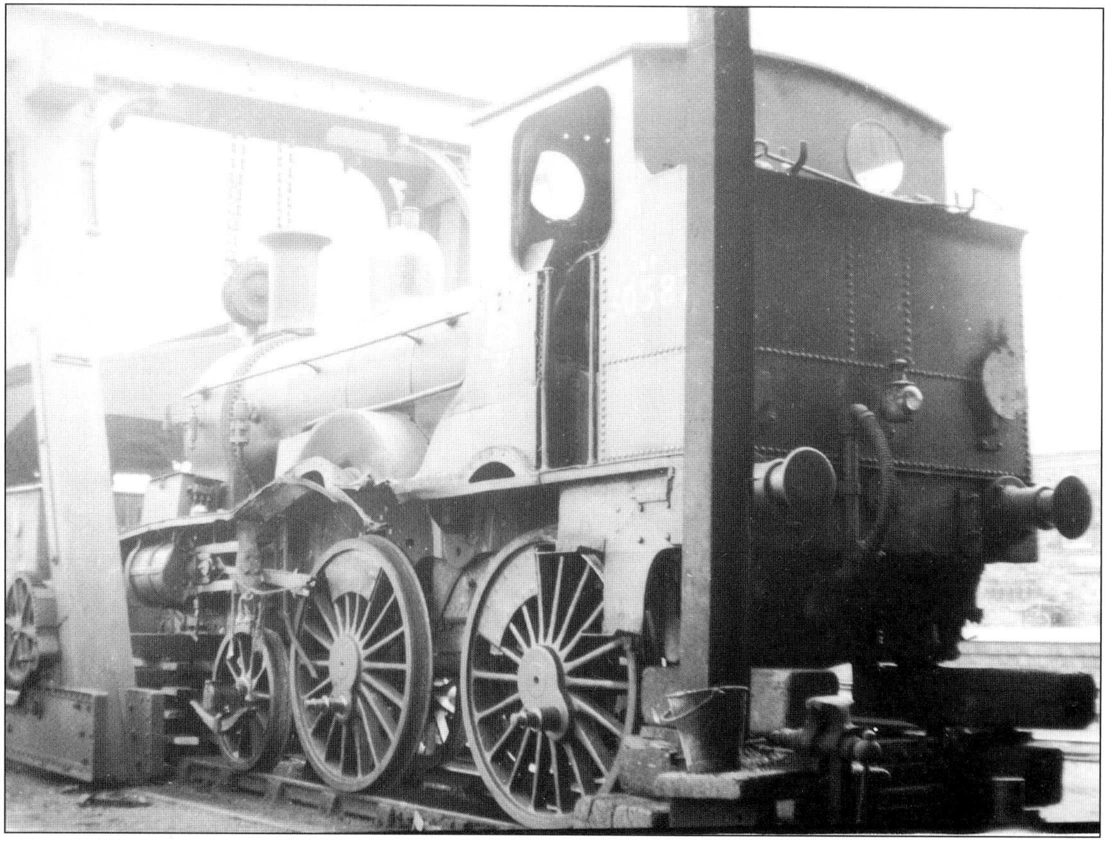

The three Beattie Well tanks suffered accidents at times. During August 1957 30587 was under the hoist, under repair at Wadebridge shed having sustained damage to its frame. This engine is preserved and is based on the Bodmin & Wenford Railway. Terry Nicholls.

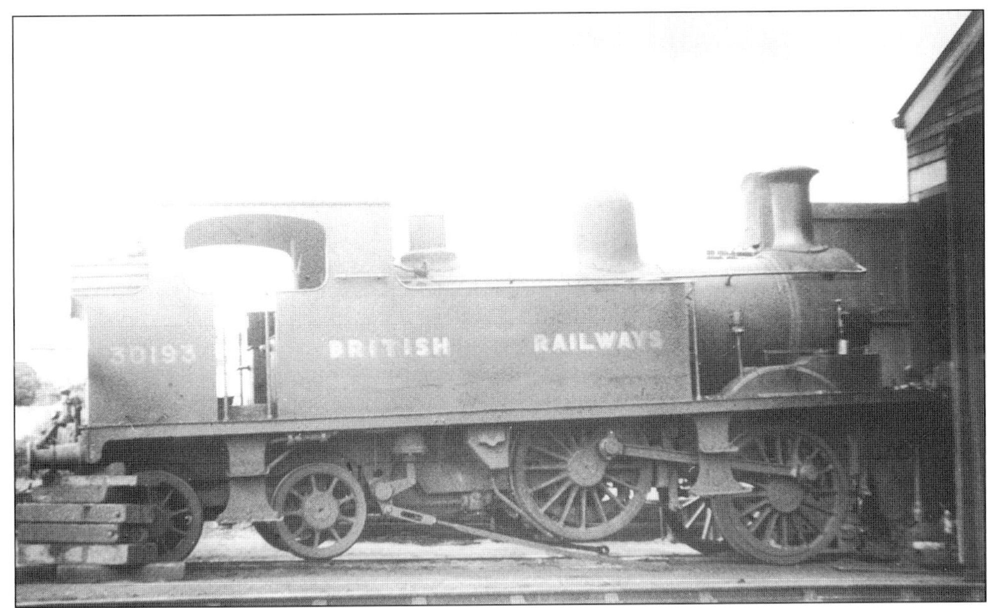

Another loco was under repair at Wadebridge shed during 1948/49. O2 class 0-4-4T 30193 is raised up on jacks outside the rear of the shed.

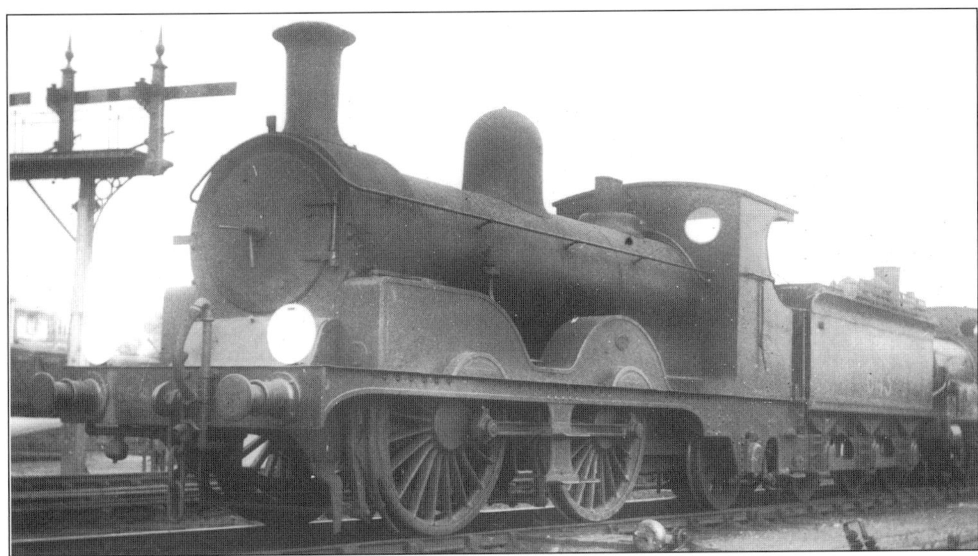

Regular power on the line was provided by Adams A12 'Jubilee' class 0-4-2s. On 6 August 1928 one of those, E 643, is outside the shed in front of Beattie Well 3329. Locomotive Club of Great Britain/ Ken Nunn collection.

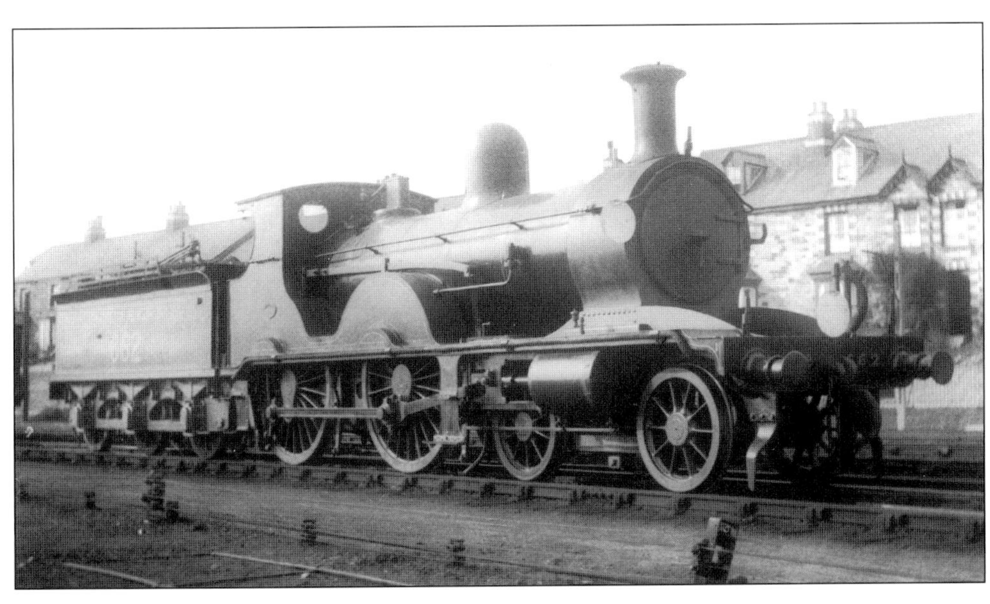

Also on 6 August 1928 the shed yard contained an earlier 4-4-0 in the shape of X6 class E 662. This engine ran until March 1933. Locomotive Club of Great Britain/ Ken Nunn collection.

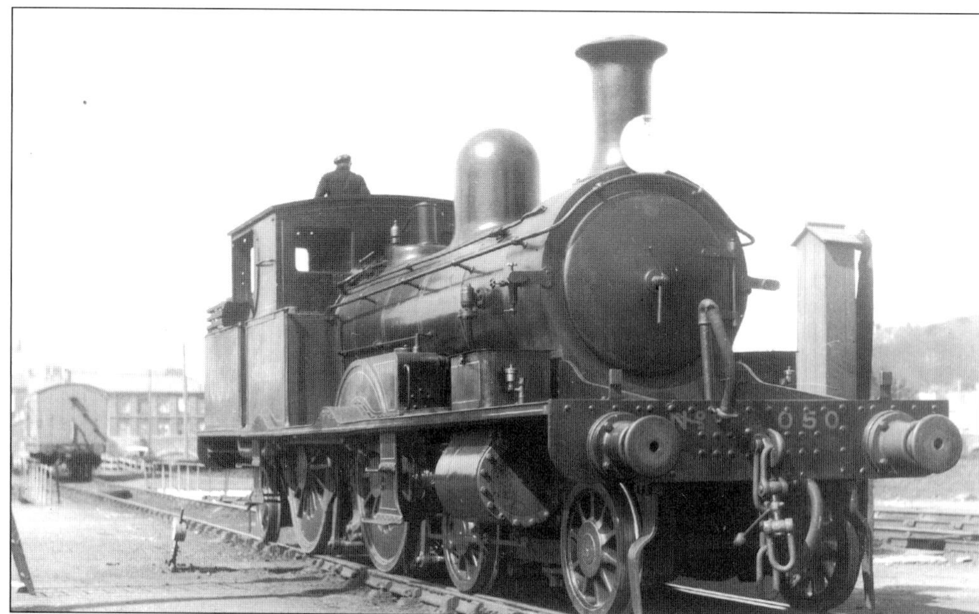

Here is a third shot of 'Radial Tank' 0415 class E 050. It is near the turntable in the shed yard in the 1920s. The loco is fitted with a Drummond chimney.

Stephenson Locomotive Society.

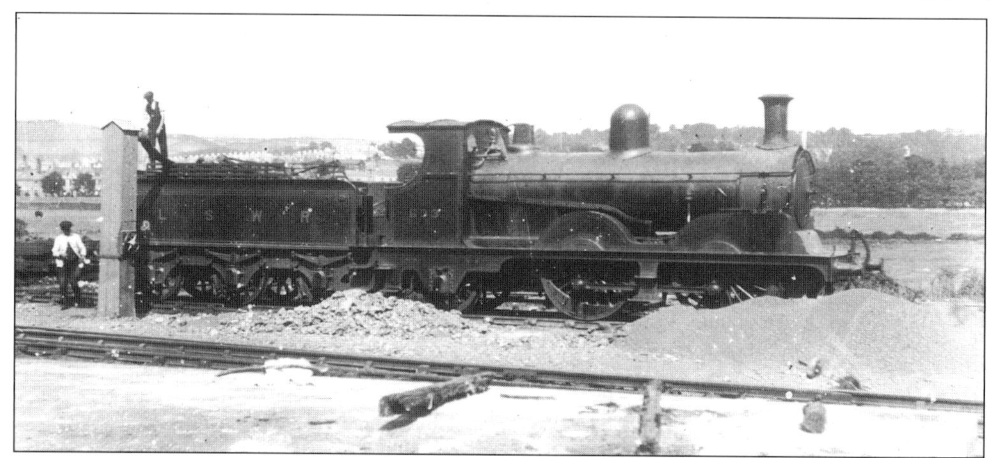

Another Adams A12 class 'Jubilee' 0-4-2 is standing near the turntable in the shed yard on an unknown date but probably in the early 1920s, as the tender is lettered LSWR. This engine, 533, was withdrawn from service during October 1929. A.G.Ellis.

Another O2 class 0-4-4T, E 198 is in the yard at the rear of the shed on 21 September 1936. This engine was transferred to the Isle of Wight in April 1949. It was renumbered W36 and was named 'CARISBROOKE'.
R.G.Jarvis/Midland Railway Trust.

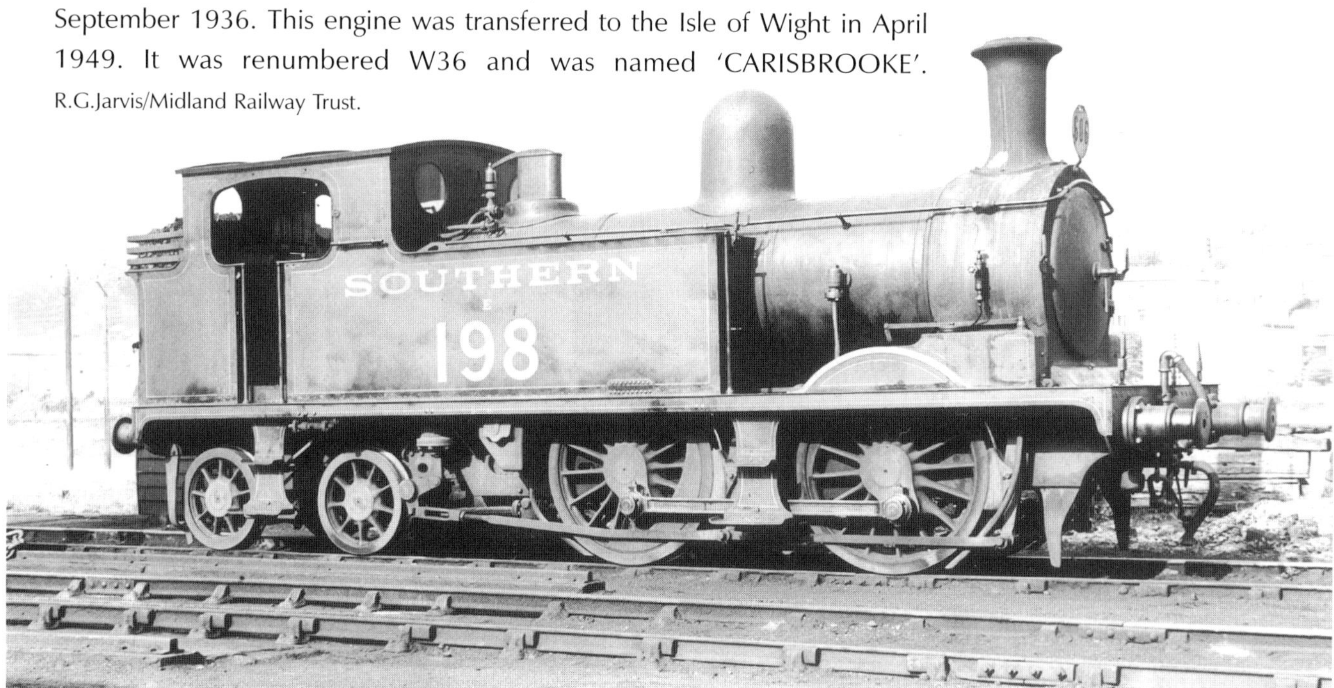

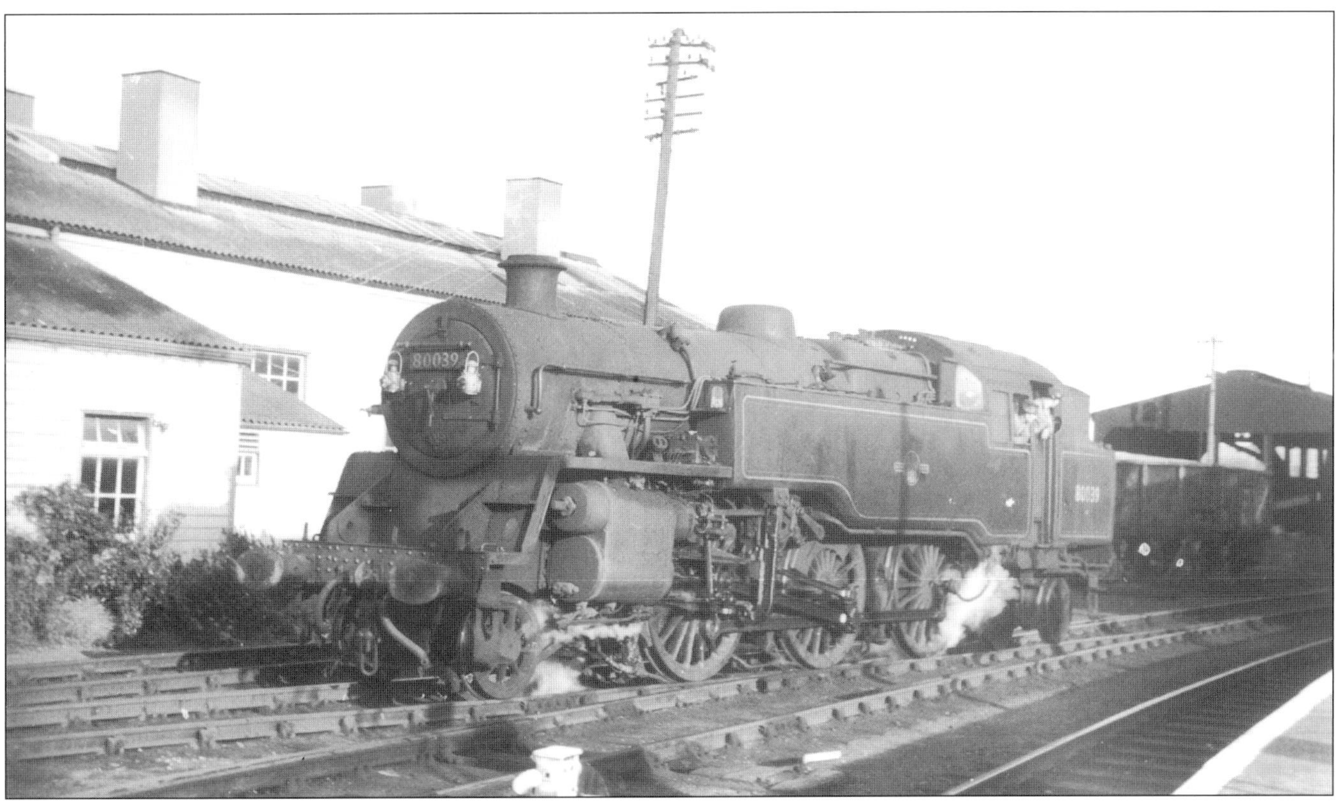

The last shot at the shed features BR Standard Class 4 2-6-4T 80039 from Exmouth Junction shed as it moves past the shed in 1964. This engine was sub-shedded at Okehampton. Rex Conway collection.

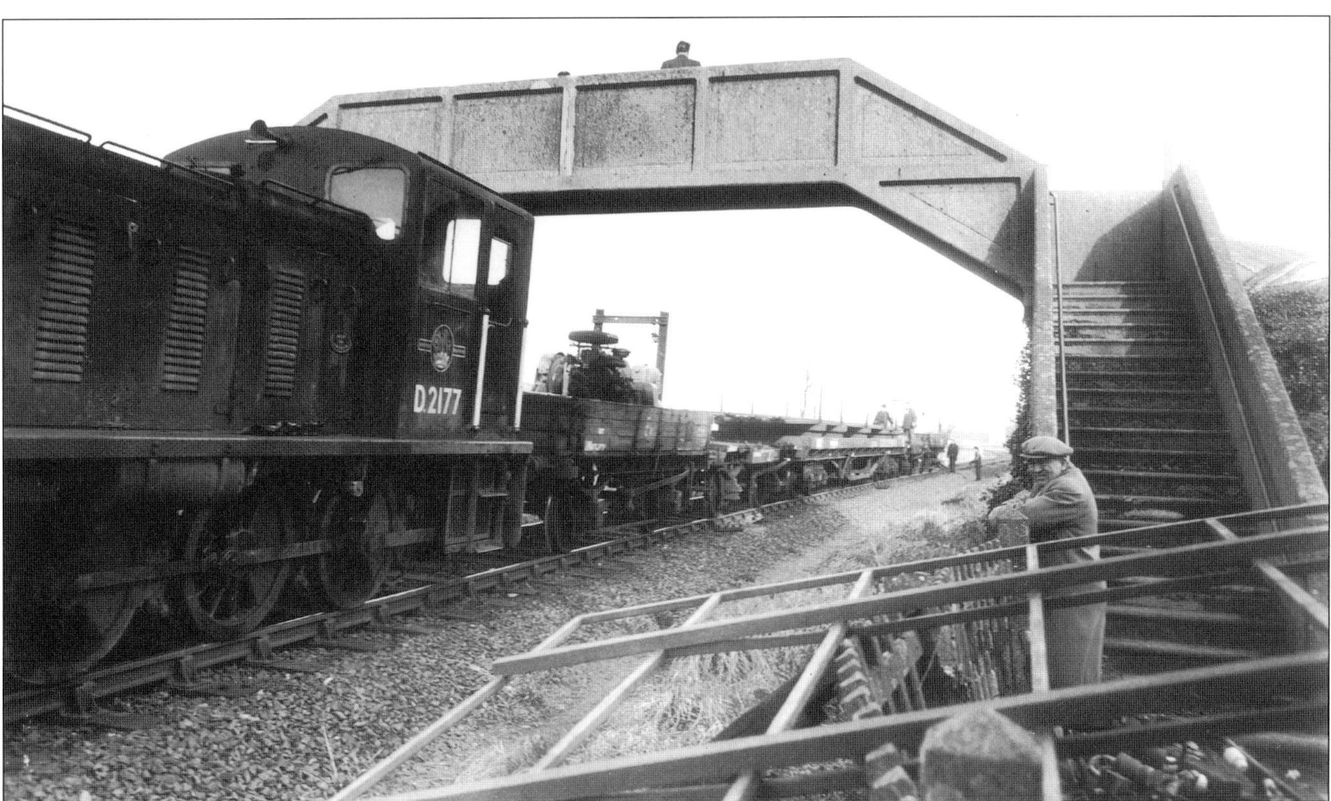

Here is shot of a track lifting train near Padstow on 1 March 1968. The vehicle next to the engine is a LMS 3 plank wagon. The train is being worked by O3 class diesel shunter D2177 which was allocated to Laira depot. Cornish Studies Library.

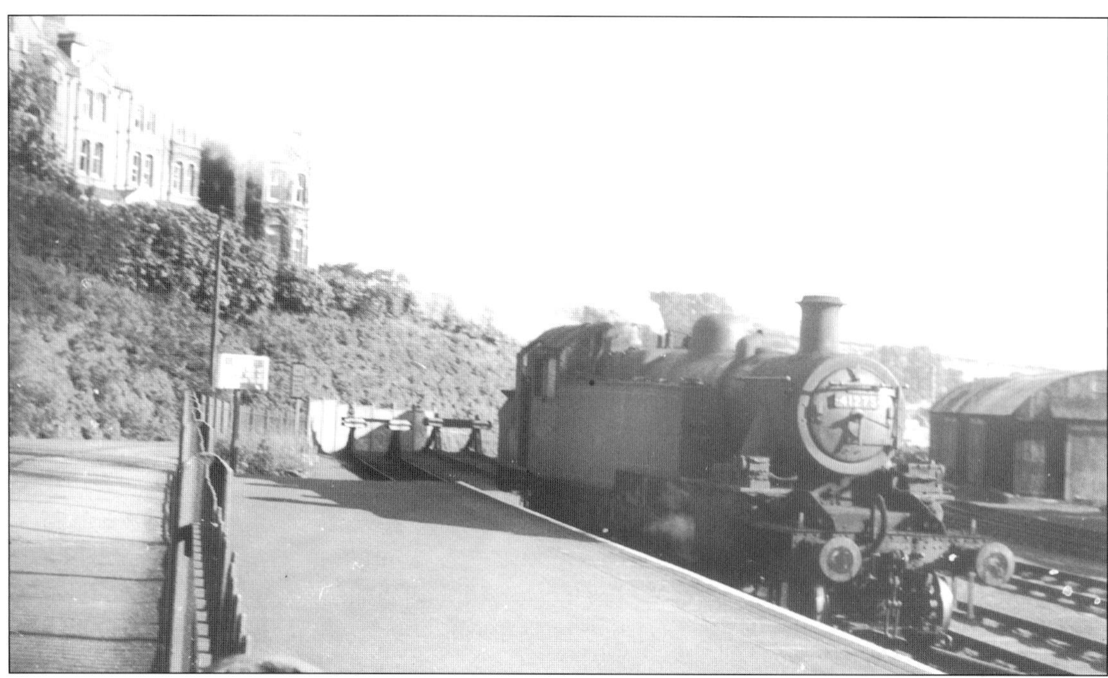

Ivatt type 2 2-6-2T 41275 from Wadebridge shed has arrived at Padstow in 1963/64 and has uncoupled from its train prior to running around the stock. Rex Conway collection.

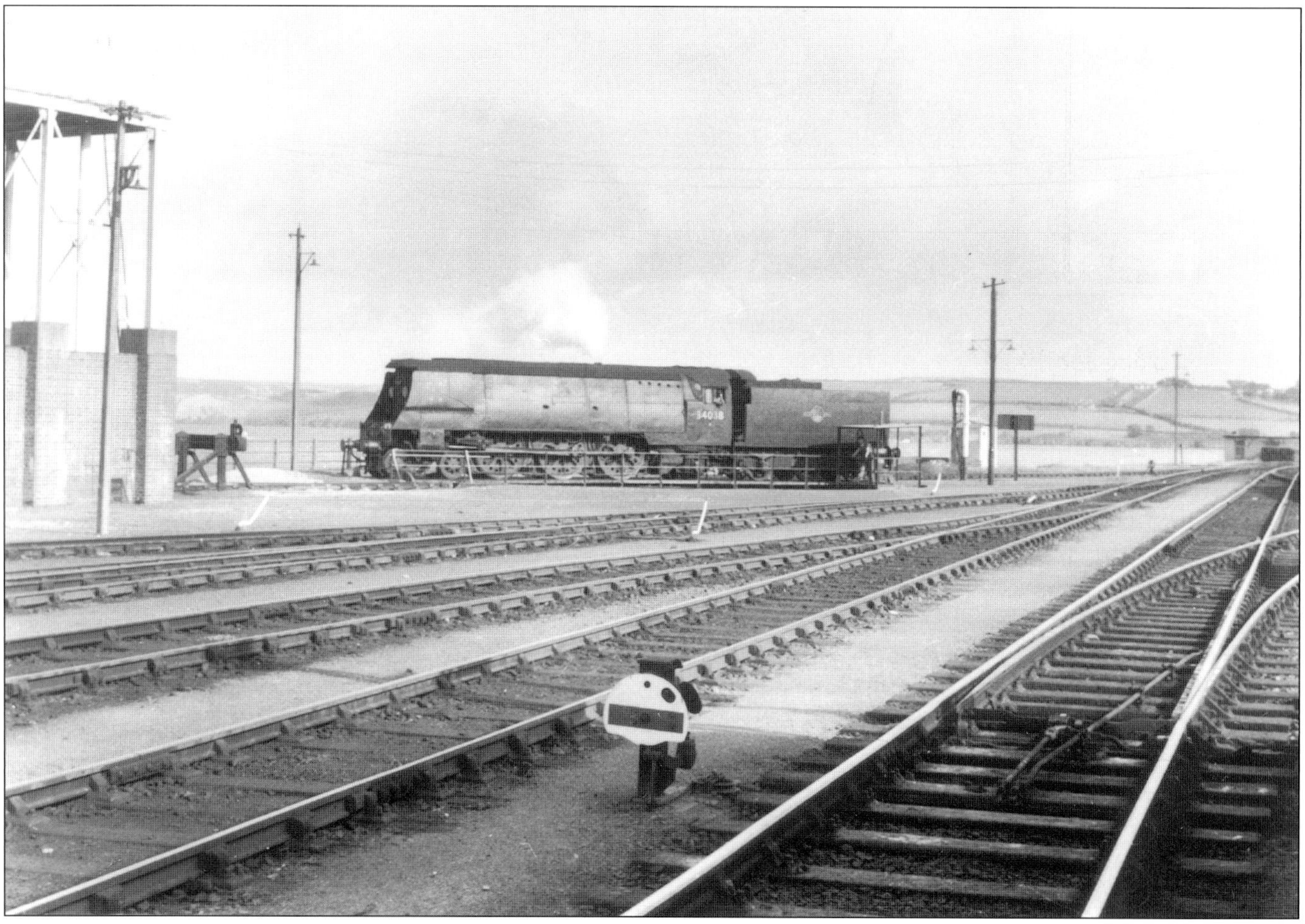

The turntable at Wadebridge shed was not long enough to accommodate the Bulleid Light Pacifics. These locos had to use the turntable at Padstow where West Country class 4-6-2 34038 'LYNTON' is seen in the 1950s.

INDUSTRIAL LOCOMOTIVES

We end this selection of photos of various locomotives in Cornwall with a few of the many which operated on industrial lines in the county. Numerous lines laid to a variety of gauges served industrial locations throughout the county. So I have selected some of the more obscure of them for this last section.

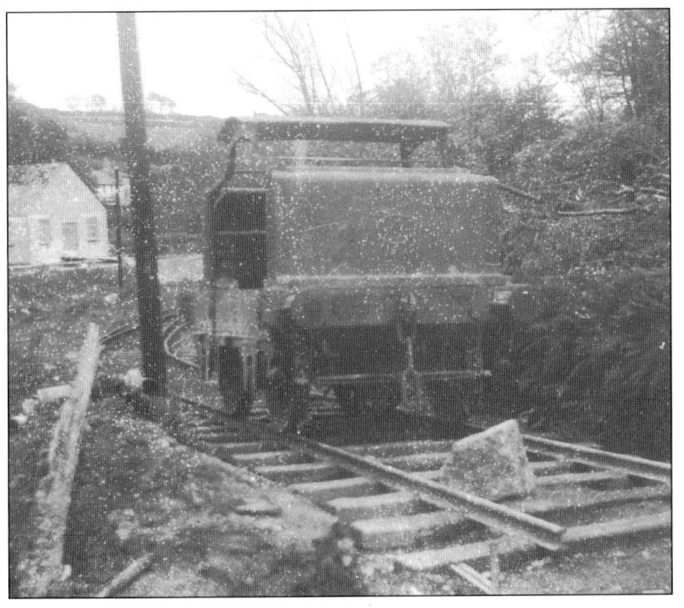

A standard gauge line ran from Pontsmill along the floor of the lower section of the Luxulyan Valley. Initially it served granite quarries but later the relaid line served Trevanney or Central Cornwall china clay kiln. Two four wheeled petrol locos built by Motor Rail worked the line from 1919 but in 1922 one of these ran away down the gradient and crashed, after which it was returned to its makers. The other was works no. 2032 and was built in 1920. It was converted from a petrol to a diesel engine in 1948 and survived until the system became disused in 1965. The loco is seen at Pontsmill on 4 November 1956 standing on a short siding which has obviously been truncated. In case the driver should accidentally move the loco up the gradient, a small block of granite has been placed between the rails to stop any movement. Mike Daly.

This odd looking locomotive was fitted with a 'steam engine lookalike' funnel, which probably carried the exhaust fumes away! It was built by Ruston & Proctor in 1916 and was a paraffin burner. Its works number has recently been correctly identified as 51168 and it was built for a gauge of 1000mm. It was purchased from the Cotton Powder Co. Ltd, in Kent during 1921by English China Clays and taken to their Blackpool China Clay works, Trewoon, north west of St.Austell. The intention was to use it to haul trucks loaded with 'overburden' from two clay pits which connected by a short tunnel to a tip. Rails were never laid and the loco gradually rusted away alongside the fitters' shop at the works where it is seen on 24 November 1956. Luckily it has been saved and after periods at several locations it is undergoing restoration. I have to admit that when I first saw this engine I was at a complete loss as to quite what type it was! Maurice Dart

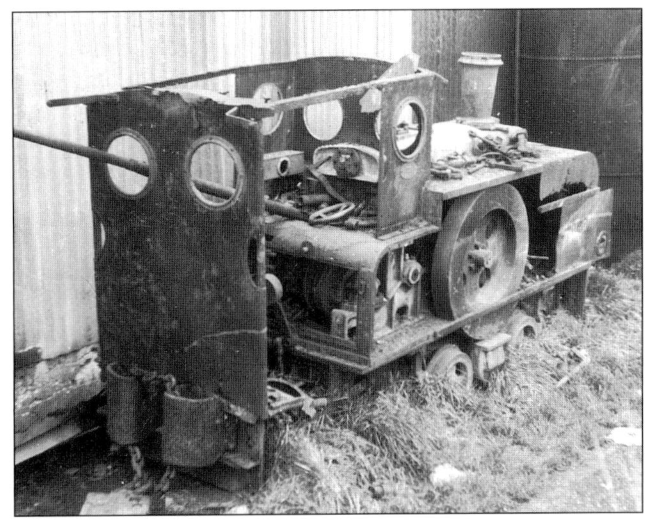

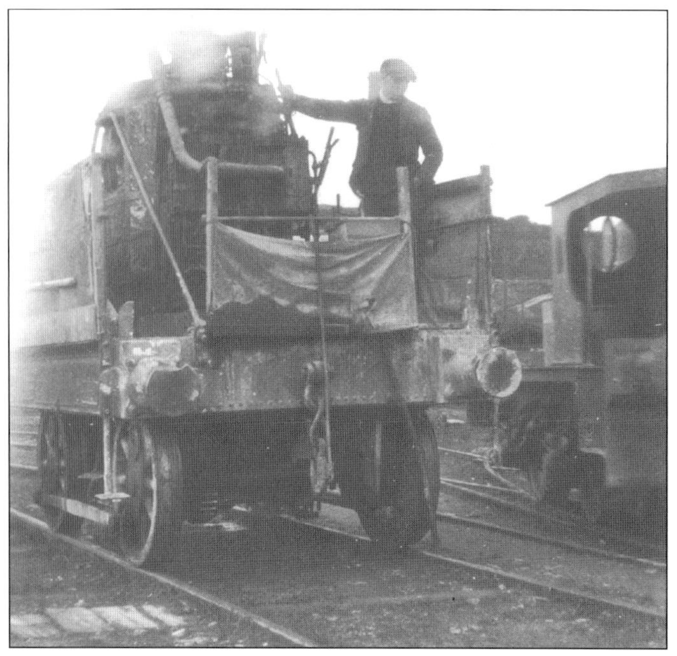

A system of standard gauge lines served the harbour at the china clay port of Par. Although somewhat 'fogged' this rare photo is included because it depicts two of the more unusual locos that worked on the lines there. On the left is an 0-4-0 vertical boiler tank loco called 'PUNCH'. This had started out as a 0-4-0ST built by Manning Wardle works no.713 which was built in 1879. An 0-4-0 vertical boilered loco was built by Sara & Burgess of Penryn in 1912. This was the fourth loco built by that firm and had worked at Par Harbour. When it was scrapped in 1936 saddle tank 'PUNCH' was rebuilt using the vertical boiler from the original loco and worked until 1944. I was lucky to see this unusual engine from a passing train around 1944 when it lay out of use behind the small engine shed at the harbour. The loco shunting on the right, 'TOBY', was works no.6520, built by Sentinel in 1927 and was scrapped during January 1961.

Now we move to a photo taken on 14 September 2003 in sidings that serve the Blackpool storage and transit site of Imerys Minerals. RollsRoyce//Sentinel no.10029 built in 1960 usually works at Crugwallins siding, a short distance along the branch line to Drinnick. It had come here for some attention. It carries the number P403D and is named 'DENISE'. Maurice Dart.

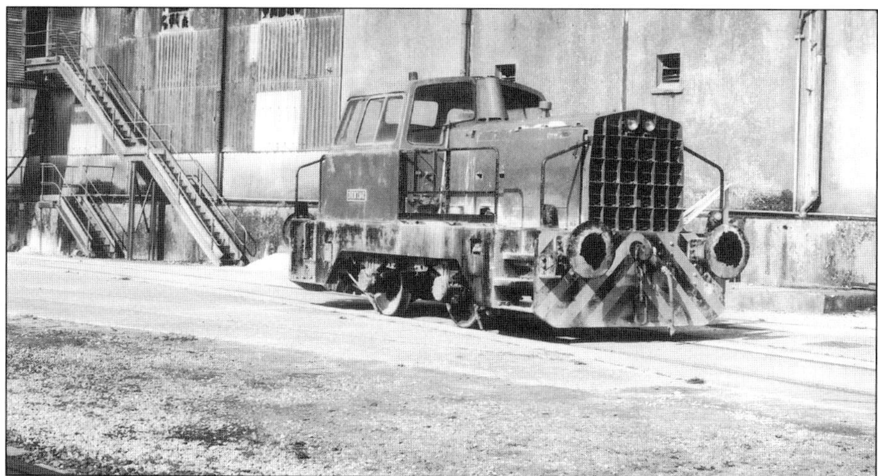

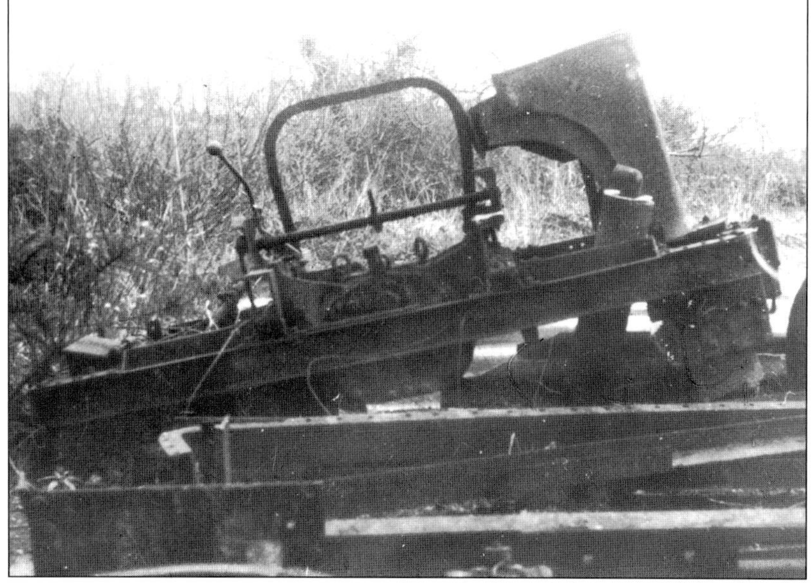

This is the remains of a 4w petrol loco at Tor Quarry, Burraton Coombe, near Saltash on 13 January 1957. The only clue to its identity was a plate inscribed Dixon-Abbot who built Motor Rail locos under licence. A 2ft gauge line linked the quarry via the crushing plant to Forder Quay. Originally owned by Jefford & Sons, it was acquired by English Clays Lovering & Pochin in 1948. This and three similar locos at the site were all scrapped during March 1960. Maurice Dart.

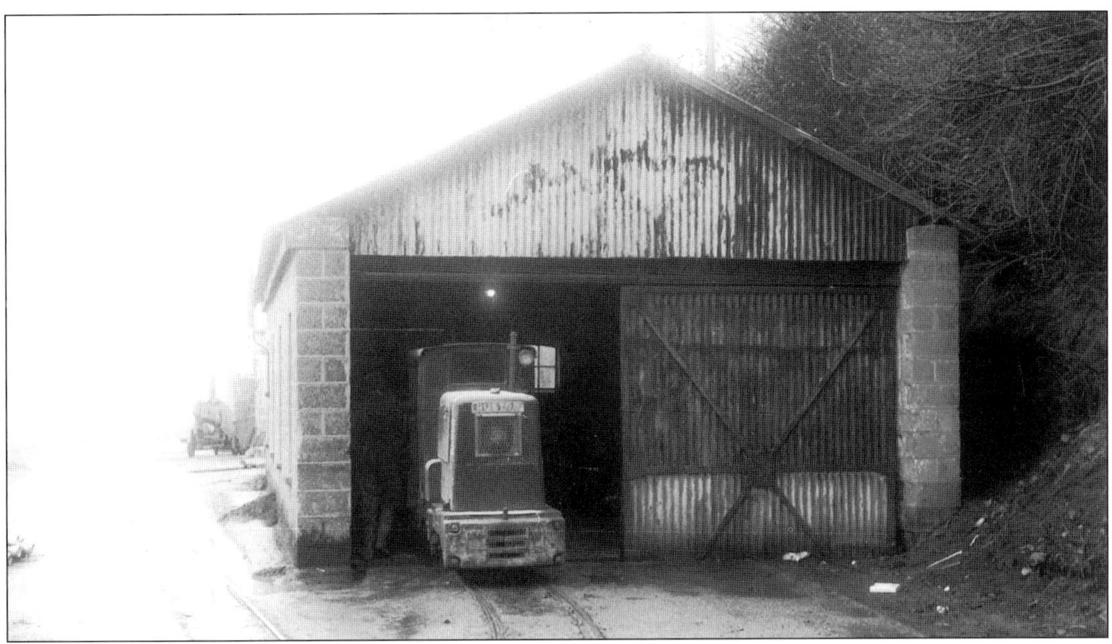

Now we move west of Penzance to Penlee quarry, Newlyn, where 2ft gauge lines connected the crushers/graders to a loading jetty on the west side of the harbour. Ruston & Hornsby 4wDE works no. 375315 built in 1954 stands in the entrance to the loco shed on 13 March 1965. It was named 'J.W. JENKIN'. The railway system was taken out of use on 31 July 1972 and this engine was sold during 1975. Roger Hateley.

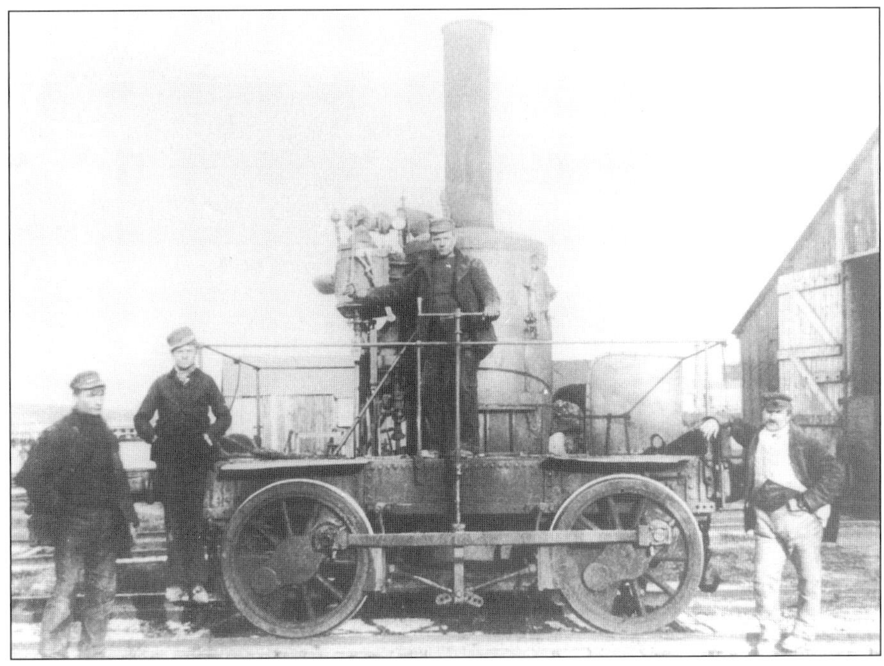

Falmouth docks possessed an internal railway system which dated from soon after the docks were incorporated during 1859. Originally the lines were laid to the GWR Broad Gauge of 7ft ¼in. which were worked by four vertical boilered locos built by Sara & Burgess. As the loco in this pre 1892 photo does not carry a name or number, it is most likely no.4 which was always devoid of either.

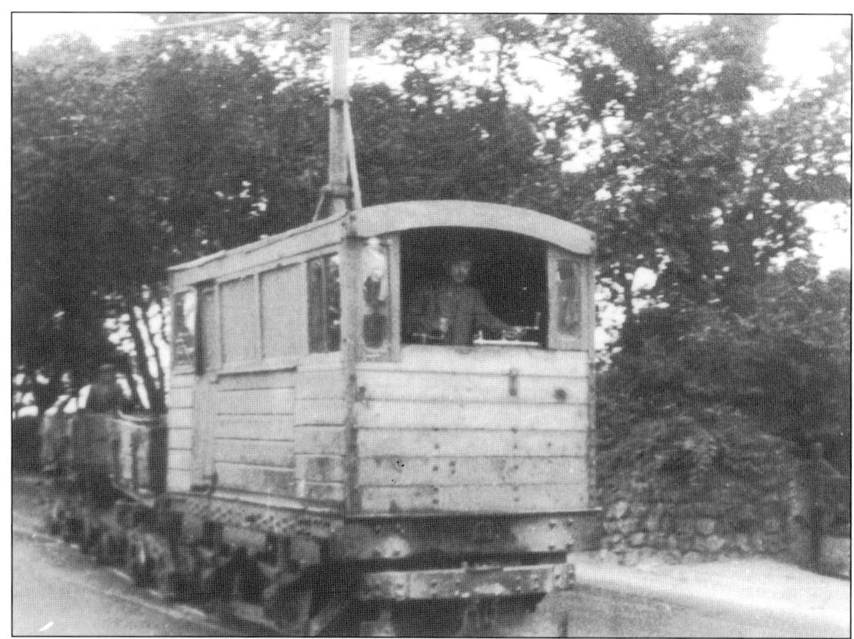

Cornwall possessed a 3ft 6in gauge overhead wire electric street tramway. The Camborne & Redruth Tramway operated a passenger and parcels service between the towns. There were also three mineral branches off the line which served tin and copper mines. To work these branch lines the company purchased two electric locos. At first these had open sides and ends but they were rebuilt to afford some protection to the crews from the elements. Built by BTH in 1903 they lasted until 1934. This photo shows rebuilt No.2 in the loop at East Pool Road, Trevenson, on a train from Tolvaddon Stamps on an unknown date but probably in the early 1930s.   Cornish Studies Library.

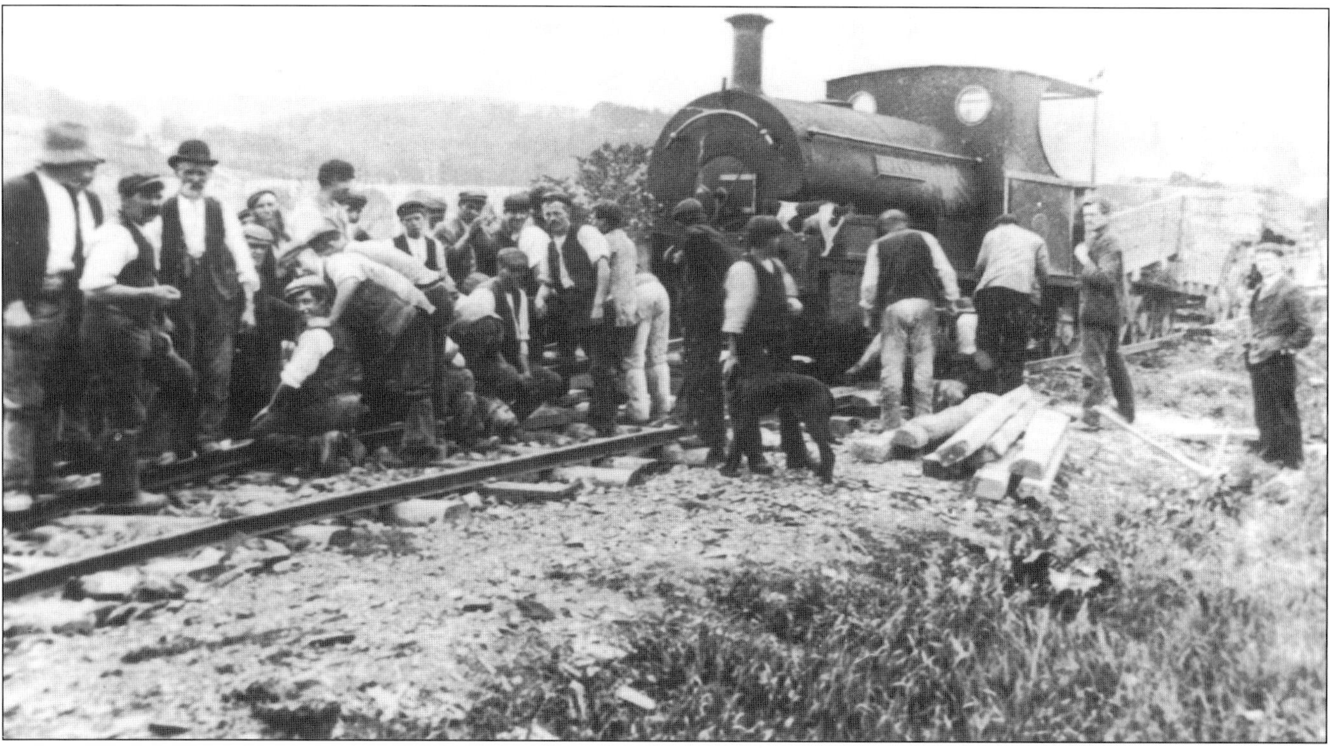

J.C.Lang, of Thomas Lang & Son at Liskeard, gained the contract to convert the 3ft 6in gauge East Cornwall Mineral Railway to Standard gauge and to construct the extension to Beer (later Bere) Alston. Three locos were used and one of these named 'BLANCHE' is in this photo. A gang are at work laying track at Calstock in 1907. The engine was built by Peckett in1893 and was works no.505.

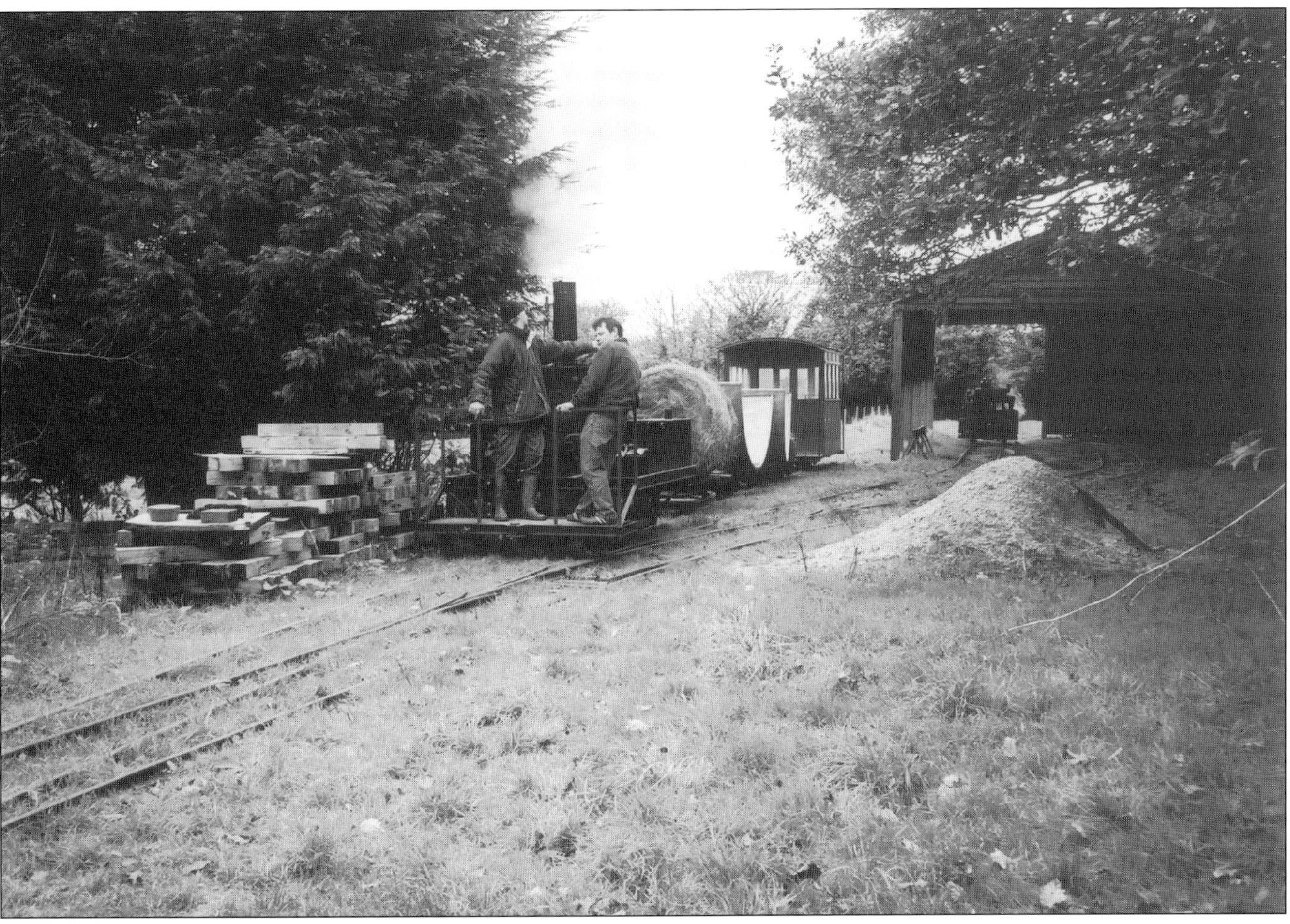

To complete this survey of motive power in Cornwall we see a real oddity. It is a 0-4-0 vertical boilered loco that was built in 2005 to work on a 1ft 11½ in gauge line at Tevaylour Farm near Truro. It is seen working a train carrying farm equipment and bales of produce on 16 November 2005. The engine is Roanoke no.0507. A 4w diesel loco Motor Rail no.8886 from 1944 is inside the small shed. This is a private location and the author's visit was by invitation. Maurice Dart.

INDEX TO LOCATIONS